An Introduction to Homeopathic Medicine in Primary Care

Sidney E. Skinner, MSN, FNP, RN, C
Family Nurse Practitioner
San Francisco, California

AN ASPEN PUBLICATION®
Aspen Publishers, Inc.
Gaithersburg, Maryland
2001

The author has made every effort to ensure the accuracy of the information herein. However, appropriate information sources should be consulted, especially for new or unfamiliar procedures. It is the responsibility of every practitioner to evaluate the appropriateness of a particular opinion in the context of actual clinical situations and with due consideration to new developments. The author, editors, and the publisher cannot be held responsible for any typographical or other errors found in this book.

Library of Congress Cataloging-in-Publication Data

Skinner, Sidney.
An introduction to homeopathic medicine in primary care / Sidney E. Skinner.
p. cm.
Includes bibliographical references and index.
ISBN 0-8342-1676-0 (alk. paper)
1. Homeopathy. 2. Primary care (Medicine) I. Title.
RX72 .S556 2000
615.5'32–dc21
00-040159

Orders: (800) 638-8437
Customer Service: (800) 234-1660

About Aspen Publishers • For more than 40 years, Aspen has been a leading professional publisher in a variety of disciplines. Aspen's vast information resources are available in both print and electronic formats. We are committed to providing the highest quality information available in the most appropriate format for our customers. Visit Aspen's Internet site for more information resources, directories, articles, and a searchable version of Aspen's full catalog, including the most recent publications: **www.aspenpublishers.com**
Aspen Publishers, Inc. • The hallmark of quality in publishing
Member of the worldwide Wolters Kluwer group.

Editorial Services: Timothy Sniffin
Library of Congress Catalog Card Number: 00-040159
ISBN: 0-8342-1676-0

Printed in the United States of America

1 2 3 4 5

CONTENTS

FOREWORD

The time is ripe for this well-crafted book by Sidney Skinner. Homeopathic medicine is on an upswing as a result of studies suggesting that it may be effective in the treatment of some common disorders and that, unlike pharmaceuticals in the orthodox materia medica, it is completely harmless when practiced as an adjunctive to biomedical treatment. With this book the physician, nurse practitioner, or physician's assistant who is engaged in family practice can learn how to integrate an alternative therapy in the form of homeopathic medicines considered useful for many common complaints. To that end, I believe many will find *An Introduction to Homeopathic Medicine in Primary Care* a valued introductory text and reference book.

Homeopathy enjoys considerable popularity as a major alternative to mainstream medicine, particularly in England, France, Germany, and India. In the United Kingdom homeopathy has remained more accepted than in most other nations. For several generations the kings and queens of England have retained homeopaths as family physicians. Margery Blackie, physician to Her Majesty, published a widely read book in 1976 that advocated homeopathic medicines. Homeopathic medicine is offered by the National Health Service, and the Royal London Homeopathic Hospital is served by physicians trained in both regular and homeopathic medicine.

Perhaps for these reasons, the *British Medical Journal* published in 1991 a review of clinical research on the efficacy of homeopathic medicine, which Skinner discusses in Chapter 1. With that publication, homeopathy turned a corner. The authors, who were not themselves homeopaths, were amazed to find so much supportive evidence for homeopathic treatments. While their enthusiasm was dampened by the poor quality of many of the studies, they noted that others suggested possible effectiveness in cases of arthritis, migraine headaches, allergies, influenza, respiratory infections, injuries, and childbirth (Kleijnen, Knipschild, & ter Reit, 1991). A more recent review was conducted by a team of high profile medical investigators (Linde et al., 1997). The investigators made a provisional conclusion that homeopathic medicines appear to be effective, beyond merely serving as placebos.

No one knows how medicines—which are diluted beyond the point at which (according to physical laws of probability) not a single molecule of the original substance would remain—could be more curative than placebo. Because of the plausibility issue, caution is advised. Yet, there are studies that suggest that these medicines are effective when controlled for the placebo effect (see also Bellavite & Signorini, 1995).

As Skinner points out, precisely because the most potent homeopathic medicines are chemically neutral, they cause no harm. One takes no risk, then, in prescribing them as additional to whatever standard biomedical care one may offer. Readers will be tempted to consider homeopathy as part of integrated practice. In spite of the fact that orthodox medical practitioners are firmly wedded to the principles of evidence-based medicine, they appear to be quite eager these days to find ways to integrate conventional medicine with alternative where there is reason to believe that it may be beneficial and will cause no harm.

What is not usually noted, however, is that there are basically two ways that integration can take place. One way is to establish practice settings or referral networks that permit medical practitioners to collaborate with alternative clinicians—medical doctors with homeopathic physicians, for example. The other is for medical practitioners to identify alternative therapies they can master in order to improve their own effectiveness in the practice of biomedicine. Skinner has opted for the latter approach to integration, and it raises a question about fairness.

Is it fair, indeed ethical, for mainstream health care providers to adopt the therapies of alternative clinicians and in the process to continue to leave alternative providers still on the fringes and all the poorer to the extent that some of their patients will subsequently obtain alternative care from mainstream providers?

Skinner demonstrates sensitivity to this issue. The instructions for adding homeopathic medicines to family practice include clear reminders that the recommendations apply only to common acute disorders and not to complex and/or chronic ones. Those who need a homeopathic specialist will not be tempted away, and those who receive homeopathic medicines based on this approach will likely be patients whose conditions would not usually lead them to homeopathic clinicians for care.

In fact, the most unequivocal benefit of this approach is that it provides a way for the practitioner to meet patient demands in a better way than usual. As clearly explained in the text, patients often insist on leaving the medical office with a prescription. Providers feel impelled to prescribe antibiotics and other medicines when they are not clearly indicated and may even be harmful. For these patients, a homeopathic prescription provides a substitute for prescribing a powerful but inappropriate drug. It can lead to higher patient satisfaction and still perpetuate a scientifically based practice. For this reason alone, I would recommend this book as a reasonable way to move into the arena of integrated medicine.

Robert Anderson, PhD, MD
Mills College
Oakland, California

PREFACE

An Introduction to Homeopathic Medicine in Primary Care is the first guide to homeopathy expressly for North American doctors, nurse practitioners, and physician assistants. This book is designed to help primary care clinicians bring homeopathic medicines into routine use. It is intended to teach those who are completely new to homeopathy how to treat common, acute illnesses with homeopathic medicines; the discussions are restricted to conditions well within most health care providers' comfort levels.

I am a family nurse practitioner who has practiced as a homeopathic specialist in urban, rural, and suburban settings for over 17 years. My goal is to make this a user-friendly and applicable guide for those who want to broaden their knowledge base as healers, while focusing on the actual conditions and problems faced by primary care clinicians in developed countries today.

As the new century dawns, people are seeking health care from alternative and complementary therapies in ever-increasing numbers. In 1990 38% of adult Americans reported having used at least one unconventional therapy in the previous year. By 1997 the number had increased to 42.1%. The probability that users of these therapies had consulted an alternative medicine practitioner increased from 36.3–46.3%. The number of visits to alternative medicine providers consistently exceeds the number of visits to all U.S. primary care physicians; a conservative estimate of the costs to consumers in 1997 was $21.2 billion, much of it paid by the patient out of pocket (Eisenberg et al., 1993, 1998). These visits included those to doctors of chiropractic, massage therapists, weight loss centers, spiritual or energy healers, naturopathic doctors, traditional Chinese medicine practitioners, herbalists, nutritional counselors, hypnotists, and homeo-pathic clinicians.

Many hospitals are in the process of opening holistic health care clinics. Acupuncture, massage therapy, chiropractic, botanical medi-cines, and nutritional interventions are in the vanguard of therapies beginning to be integrated into standard medical settings. Main-stream medicine is beginning to assimilate the alternative medical services that patients demand. The greatest demand is for healing modalities that can be utilized cost-effectively and swiftly without generating a need for longer patient visits. Therapeutic touch, which can be applied discreetly and rapidly, has already been integrated (sometimes covertly) into many nurses' repertoires over the past two decades.

Not much research has been conducted regarding the attitudes of nurses and physician assistants toward alternative medicine, but it is clear that physicians' attitudes are divided on the subject. The bal-ance, however, is being subtly shifted in favor of an open-minded approach to complementary and alternative medicine (CAM) thera-pies as the older generation of doctors retires. An analysis of 25 surveys of physicians in 82–95 practices describing their beliefs about the ability of CAM to prevent and treat a variety of health-related problems showed that a significant minority refer to CAM practitio-ners (Astin, Marie, Pellatier, Hansen, & Haskell, 1998; Ernst & Pittler, 1998). Across surveys, physicians referred to acupuncturists the most often (43%); chiropractors were next (40%); and massage therapists followed (21%). Of those physicians surveyed, 26% believed there was some value in homeopathy, 13% in botanical medicines, and 51% in acupuncture (Astin et al., 1998).

A survey of faculty associates at Hennepin County Medical Center in Minneapolis, Minnesota, showed that most physicians predicted that integration of CAM in that public hospital would result in positive treatment, professional, and social outcomes (Boucher & Lenz, 1998). This sample from the Midwest showed high rates of referrals to alternative practitioners, and most faculty surveyed agreed that physicians should be knowledgeable about the most popular alternative therapies.

There appears to be a communication gap between doctors and patients about CAM. Of 860 Michigan pediatricians surveyed, 83% believed some of their patients use CAM therapies (Sikand & Laken, 1998). But more than half of these pediatricians (55.1%) believed that less than 10% of their patients were using them—an extreme under-estimate, according to recent surveys of health care consumers (Eisenberg et al., 1993, 1998; Elder, Gillcrist, & Minz, 1997). In fact, 55% of those same pediatricians being surveyed said they themselves would use CAM therapies. In addition, 50% would refer to at least some CAM therapies such as biofeedback, self-help groups, relaxation techniques, hypnosis, and acupuncture or acupressure. Indeed, 54% expressed an interest in courses on CAM therapies (Sikand & Laken, 1998). This desire to learn more about CAM therapies is reflected in the course content at U.S. medical schools. Course content about CAM therapies is found in at least 123 U.S. medical schools; most of these courses are freestanding electives (Wetzel, Eisenberg, & Kaptchuk, 1998).

Primary care providers in conventional settings are finding two seemingly polar stressors in their relationship with their patients. On the one hand, there is a group of people who are disappointed to leave the office without a prescription in hand even when the illness is unlikely to benefit from conventional drugs. On the other hand, in most practices, there is a growing group of patients who are reticent to fill a prescription because of past experiences with poor results and adverse reactions, or a philosophical belief that something more natural and holistic would be better (Jonas, 1997). An even larger group of patients may already be using alternative therapies in addition to treatments that have been prescribed by their primary care clinicians, often without the knowledge of those clinicians (Elder, Gillcrist, & Minz, 1997).

Those clinicians who find value in CAM therapies can refer patients out for these services. This book, however, is based on *integrative medicine*. This term is being used by Dr. Andrew Weil and others for bringing both conventional and alternative therapies under the primary care roof. The first postdoctoral fellowship in integrative medicine has begun at the University of Arizona Medical School. Clinicians are learning new skills. An integrative primary care clinician might offer garlic for cardiovascular fitness, homeopathic *Belladonna* for otitis media, meditation instruction for stress, education about acupressure points for the patient with dysmenorrhea, and antibiotics for pneumonia. Or a physician lacking these integrative skills may bring nurse practitioners and physician assistants into the practice (or health maintenance organization) who already possess them. I believe that the integration of homeopathic medicines into a conventional family or pediatric practice will provide swifter and more comfortable healing from acute illness and prevent serious sequelae. The implications for building a strong client base are obvious.

Homeopathy is not for everyone. Those who have little interest in the relationship between emotional and physical health will not be drawn to homeopathy for anything other than first aid prescribing. At this stage of its development, one is required to have at least a tolerance—if not a fascination with—a good mystery.

While various models have been described by scientists to explain how homeopathy works, at this point it is a mystery. If it were not for a significant body of research that shows that it does indeed work and a multitude of satisfied patients, homeopathy would be relegated to a footnote in the history of medicine.

This book is divided into four parts. Part I contains a succinct summary of background information about homeopathic medicine needed in order to begin to use it in primary care, including a brief introduction to the research and other modern literature. Attention is paid to data gathering, recordkeeping, and the legal and regulatory ramifications of beginning to use these medicines. There is also a description of the homeopathic pharmaceutical manufacturing process. A streamlined approach to finding the right medicine, appropriate potency, and treatment schedule is presented. Finally, the safety and cost-effectiveness of homeopathic treatment are discussed. Part II presents the main features of 15 homeopathic medicines that would be a valuable addition to integrative primary care practice, with the key symptoms emphasized. Part III covers prescribing differentials for patients with specific diagnoses. Part IV is for the reader who wishes to pursue homeopathy further. It delves into the history of homeopathic medicine and some conceptual frameworks (historical and contemporary) that have been proposed for how it might work. Finally, there is information for those who want to continue their professional development in homeopathy, including clinical, professional, and research roles. Appendixes are provided with helpful reference material, including an invaluable guide to the makeup of official homeopathic medicines.

I hope you will be as gratified as I have been with the effectiveness of homeopathic medicines, and that you will find them as indispensible in your practice as I do.

ACKNOWLEDGMENTS

After many years in practice as a homeopathic specialist, I have accepted that I have no special insights into homeopathy or healing and will, therefore, never make a unique contribution to the field. Fortunately, a reference book is not expected to be a highly original work. This book is an update and compilation of the work of hundreds of homeopathic researchers, clinicians, and study participants over the past 200 years. Most helpful were the twentieth-century *Materia Medica of Homeopathic Medicines* of Dr. S.R. Phatak of Bombay (1977) and *The Twelve Tissue Remedies of Schussler* by W. Boericke and W.A. Dewey of San Francisco (1914). Dr. Jouanny of France made significant contributions to this field in 1984, as did Dr. G.R. Royal of Iowa in 1923. Writing this book has made me appreciate their efforts, and I have borrowed ideas and clinical differentials at times. To readers trained in conventional medicine, for whom therapeutic texts are out of date after 5 years, it may seem laughable that homeopathic clinicians use old texts alongside the new. Homeopathic treatments do not change each year, and medicines rarely become obsolete. Language changes, however, as does what homeopathic clinicians are called upon to treat.

I am grateful to Drs. David Taylor Reilly and Bob Leckridge, who have demonstrated that it is possible to teach practical primary care homeopathic medicine to the broader health care community through their highly popular continuing medical education class in Scotland.

Lucy Vaughters, PA-C; Kathleen Grandison, MD; William Shevin, MD; Read Weaver, ND; and Jacquelyn Wilson, MD, were all kind enough to read chapters and offer suggestions. Janet Zand, OMD, provided material about chemical dependency treatment and homeopathy. Michael Quinn, RPh, of Hahnemann Laboratories provided the information about the homeopathic pharmaceutical manufacturing process and access to the pharmacological literature. Dr. Clark Baker and Jay Bornemann of the Homeopathic Pharmacopoeia of the United States provided the list of current official homeopathic medicines and current spellings for consistency in nomenclature. The editorial staff at Aspen helped me to meet my goal to be much more rigorous and precise in print than I am in life, and provided the encouragement I needed to finish the job. I have my editors Mary Anne Langdon and Timothy Sniffin to thank for that.

On a personal note, I could not have written this book without the love and support of Deb Janes; Elizabeth Faith Chiment; my parents, Phoebe and George Skinner; Lama Tharchin Rinpoche; and my friends at Last Chance Gompa. Gerald Janes suggested I write a book, and here it is.

How To Use This Book Effectively

In a busy family or pediatric practice, the clinician may have several texts that are used as protocols or reminders of the standard medical treatment for particular diseases, or for convenient diagnostic differentials. Therefore, one might be inclined to turn to Part III and use this book in that way. Unfortunately, that approach will lead to some unnecessary therapeutic failures.

Standard medical protocols assume the reader has studied the basic principles of pharmacology. Likewise, to be used effectively, homeopathic protocols require the user to have some basic knowledge. For that reason, the clinician should study Parts I and II of the book first. Chapter 1 prepares the clinician to gather appropriate data from the patient, homeopathically assess the situation, and develop an appropriate treatment plan. Part II contains pertinent information about the 15 most frequently encountered homeopathic medicines in primary care. These medicines can become as indispensable to practice as the 15 most prescribed conventional medicines (e.g., antibiotics, antihistamines, and anti-inflamatories). One can "heal two birds with one mineral" (or plant) by learning about these medicines first because the group of medicines profiled will be used in a variety of conditions.

The word *prescribe* is used in this book for lack of a better one even though most medicines are technically nonprescription items.

One possible approach to study would be to learn about one essential homeopathic medicine, prescribe that medicine only when one sees a patient whose symptom set clearly matches it, then expand to the next remedy, and so on. If the essential features of 15 medicines could gradually be learned in this way, at least several of the patients seen each day by the primary care nurse practitioner, physician assistant, or physician could be treated with homeopathy.

Part III presents clinical prescribing differentials that can be used as a reference when the symptom set of a familiar medicine is not present in the patient. Through the process of repeatedly returning to Part III, the clinician's familiarity with homeopathy would expand to include a working knowledge of the next group of more than 100 medicines, which are adequate to handle the majority of the routine acute illnesses seen in primary care practice.

PART I

The Fundamentals

Part I covers the basics of homeopathic medicine, which will serve as an orientation to a system of healing that may be unfamiliar. The research base of this system of medicine, an introduction to homeopathic pharmacy, and the process of arriving at a homeopathic medicine for acute illnesses will all be addressed. The implications of introducing homeopathic medicines into an integrative primary care practice, including patient safety as well as legal and professional issues, will be reviewed.

CHAPTER 1

An Introduction to Homeopathic Medicine

INTRODUCTION

The homeopathic medical profession in North America at the opening of the twenty-first century could boast of great accomplishments, or mourn supreme failures. On the one hand, computer technology and the Herculean efforts of teachers and researchers have rapidly accelerated the clinical effectiveness of the upper echelon of experts in homeopathy. There are many homeopathy patients who report cures of chronic diseases that had been completely unresponsive to mainstream therapies. On the other hand, the majority of Americans, including health care professionals, have had no personal experience with the use of even a single homeopathic medicine. In 1997, for example, only 16.5% of the Americans surveyed who use any alternative medical therapies reported that they had been to a practitioner for homeopathy in the prior 12 months (Eisenberg et al., 1998). Even this may be an inflated number because many people have misconceptions about homeopathy and confuse it with botanical medicine or holistic healing in general. Yet, the interest in homeopathy is rapidly expanding, as evidenced by greatly accelerated sales of over-the-counter homeopathic medicines; these sales have been growing at 20–25% per annum since 1990 (Ullman, 1999).

One might say that homeopathy at its most sublime is practiced by a person with a good background in the sciences, clinical diagnosis, and physical exam skills common to all health professionals, as well as at least 10 years of in-depth study in classical homeopathy, including extensive clinical supervision. This is the role of the homeopathic specialist, who is not a specialist in the current sense of the word,

3

which means a health practitioner who sees only patients with an ailment of one body part or physiological system. Instead, he or she is a holistic health care provider, often a family practitioner, who undergoes extensive continuing education to refine the accuracy of his or her homeopathic prescribing.

A sick person who wishes to consult with one of the few hundred clinicians in the United States and Canada with this level of expertise will need to pay for a 1–2-hour initial office visit. This comprehensive initial office visit is required for the homeopathic specialist to accurately prescribe for a chronically ill person. The visit and/or the provider may not qualify for insurance reimbursement. The patient may also have to travel much farther than he or she would travel to see a local doctor, given the scarcity of homeopathic specialists. Thus, the sublime becomes the unattainable for everyday people.

There is something more subtle that has been an obstacle to the expansion of homeopathic medicine as well. Homeopathic medicine on the specialist level operates according to a different conceptual framework than that of the prevailing medical culture, which may be difficult for people entirely new to holistic forms of medicine to understand. Clinicians interested in an overview of the theory of health and disease that was developed 200 years ago at the founding of homeopathy may read the overview in Chapter 29, History and Conceptual Framework of Homeopathic Medicine, but it is the thesis of this book that belief in, or even knowledge of, the elaborated theory is not important to the practice of basic homeopathy for the sick visit.

Homeopathy is a specific system of medical practice that is based on the principle that "like cures like." The pattern of physical symptoms as well as alterations in cognitive and emotional functioning of a patient are evaluated holistically by a clinician. The complete symptom set is then matched with the complete symptom set of a group of healthy subjects who have all taken a medicine as participants in an experimental trial. The medicine that is most parallel to the person's state of illness is then prescribed as an ultradilute aqueous solution, or as sugar pellets medicated with such a solution.

Integrative primary care providers can begin to use homeopathic medicines safely and effectively in a manner that is affordable and comprehensible to patients, without making it a lifetime study. While the treatment of chronic illness should be left to the homeopathic specialist, the treatment of many acute diseases of mild to moderate intensity can be incrementally mastered by studying this book and beginning to actively prescribe.

HOMEOPATHIC MEDICAL RESEARCH

The field of homeopathic medical research is rapidly changing, from decades of underfunded studies by a tiny disenfranchised group of researchers into an era in which some funding is available and mainstream American medical journals promise equal consideration of homeopathic monographs for publication. *The Journal of the American Medical Association* (JAMA) recently did an about-face from having virtually no interest in publishing manuscripts about complementary and alternative (CAM) therapies to soliciting them for inclusion in a special issue on the topic (November 11, 1998). This change in policy can be attributed to *JAMA* physician readers' identifying alternative medicine as the 7th (of 73) most important topics for publication in *JAMA* (Fontanarosa & Lundberg, 1997).

The most recent and thorough review of all existent homeopathic research was published in the *Lancet* in 1997 (Linde et al., 1997). It identified 186 homeopathic double-blind and/or placebo-controlled trials from an exhaustive review of the literature. Of those, 119 studies met their inclusion criteria; 89 had adequate data for meta-analysis. The authors concluded, "The results of our meta-analysis are not compatible with the hypothesis that the clinical effects of homeopathy are completely due to placebo. However, we found insufficient evidence from these studies that homeopathy is clearly efficacious for any single clinical condition." The combined odds ratio for the 89 studies entered into the main meta-analysis was 2•45 (95% CI 2•05, 2•93) in favor of homeopathy. The odds ratio for the 26 good-quality studies was 1•66 (1•33, 2•08), and when corrected for publication bias was 1•78 (1•03, 3•10). Translated into common parlance this means that it is extremely unlikely that the effectiveness homeopathy has shown in the research published so far is from good luck, or the tendency of researchers not to publish negative findings.

A previous meta-analysis of 25 years of clinical studies in homeopathic medicine was published in 1991 (Kleijnen, Knipschild, & ter Riet, 1991) in the *British Medical Journal*. That meta-analysis covered 107 controlled trials, of which 81 showed that homeopathic medicines were effective, 24 showed they were ineffective, and 2 were inconclusive. The authors, medical school faculty who did not themselves practice homeopathy, stated that they were surprised at the number of successful trials.

The internal validity of most studies has been mediocre, and they have been conducted without funding, mostly by homeopathic physicians in their own practices. Both meta-analyses showed that the better the studies were designed and performed, the more effective homeopathic treatment was shown to be compared with placebo.

Abstracts of relevant studies to each clinical topic have been provided in Part III of this book. The following are some of the most interesting and credible findings selected from that body of research.

Influenza—There have been four published randomized, placebo-controlled studies on homeopathic treatment of influenza with *Oscillococcinum*, a proprietary product of Boiron Laboratories in France (Ferley & Zmirou, 1989; Papp, Schuback, Beck, Burkard, Siergfried, & Belch, 1998 [report of two studies]). *Oscillococcinum* (the trade name for *Anasbarbariac hepatis cordis extractum*) was consistently found to be significantly more effective than placebo in shortening the duration, lowering the fever, and reducing the severity of symptoms of influenza. Refer to Chapter 25, Infectious Disease, for a discussion of the homeopathic treatment of influenza.

Childbirth—A double-blind placebo-controlled study was conducted in which women in the ninth month of pregnancy were given twice a day a complex medicine containing the following remedies: *Arnica montana, Caulophyllum thalictroides, Cimicifuga racemosa, Gelsemium sempervirens*, and *Pulsatilla* (Dorfman, Lasserre, & Tetau, 1987). The women given the homeopathic medicines experienced a 40% shorter labor than those given a placebo, and had 75% fewer complications in labor. One of the ingredients in that medicine, *Caulophyllum thalictroides*, was administered to women in the active phase of labor in a single-blind, placebo-controlled study (Eid, Felisi, & Sideri, 1993). The length of labor for those women given the homeopathic medicine was 38% shorter than for women in the placebo group. Researchers later completed a double-blind trial and corroborated these findings (Eid, Felisi, & Sideri, 1994). British veterinary researchers conducted trials showing that *Caulophyllum* could lower the rate of stillbirths in pigs (Day, 1984). Another researcher had a highly positive result in shortening labor in human subjects enrolled in a double-blind placebo-controlled trial of *Caulophyllum* (Coudert, 1981). Refer to Chapter 27, Gynecology and Primary Care for Pregnancy and Childbirth, for a discussion of the homeopathic care in pregnancy and labor.

Otitis Media—Friese, Kruse, and Moeller (1997) conducted a prospective study that compared conventional and homeopathic treatment of acute childhood otitis media in five German otolaryngological practices. Roughly 95% of the children in the homeopathic group were cured of their ear infections by homeopathy alone. The conventionally treated group had to be treated longer and was more likely to have recurrences. Refer to Chapter 20, Ear, Nose, and Throat, for a discussion of the homeopathic treatment of otitis media.

Allergy—A study of the efficacy of the homeopathic medicine *Galphimea glauca* for pollen allergy has shown a significant benefit over placebo. This finding has been replicated 11 times (Wiesenauer & Ludtke, 1996). Drs. Reilly and Taylor and colleagues (1985, 1986, & 1994) of the University Department of Medicine, Glasgow Royal Infirmary in Scotland have had three studies published so far in collaboration with other authors on the treatment of allergies with homeopathic medicines made from the allergen. Symptoms were significantly less intense in the homeopathically treated groups. Chapter 20 contains a thorough discussion of homeopathic treatments for allergy that primary care providers can integrate into practice.

Vertigo—A double-blind study of patients with vertigo showed therapeutic equivalence between a complex homeopathic medicine for vertigo and betahistamine in terms of frequency, duration, and intensity during a 6-week trial period (Weiser, Strosser, & Klein, 1998). A second descriptive study evaluated the effectiveness of a complex homeopathic medicine in treatment of patients with vertigo. The majority of subjects in this group had improvement of their symptoms (Morawiec-Bajda, Lukomski, & Latkowski, 1993). More information is available on vertigo treatment in Chapter 20.

Childhood Diarrhea—Finally, in 1994 Jacobs, Jiminez, Gloyd, Gale, and Crothers had a study published in *Pediatrics* regarding the treatment of childhood diarrhea with homeopathic medicines. This randomized, placebo-controlled, double-blind study done in Nicaragua showed a statistically significant decrease in duration of diarrhea in the treatment group. The study is unusual in that medicine was individualized to the child's complete symptom set in the classical homeopathic manner.

Chronic Illness—Chronic or recurring illness is what brings most people to homeopathy. Case studies of cured cases of chronic illness abound in the homeopathic literature and as case presentations, often with video and laboratory confirmation, at homeopathic conferences. Yet, thus far there has been a limited number of clinical studies conducted on the effectiveness of homeopathy in chronic diseases or for disease prevention. Studies on the long-term treatment of chronic disease are expensive and labor-intensive, and only recently have funds been available for alternative medicine research.

A randomized, double-blind, placebo-controlled clinical trial ($n =$ 50) of homeopathic treatment of chronic effects of mild traumatic brain injury was funded by the National Institutes of Health, conducted at Spaulding Rehabilitation Hospital in the Boston area, and published in the *Journal of Head Trauma Rehabilitation* (Chapman et al., 1999). Patients had significant improvement of their functioning, and some were able to return to work after years of disability. Homeopathic treatment was the only significant or near-significant predictor of improvement in the functional subtests ($p = .009, p = .058, p = .027$). There was no significant difference in the control and treatment groups on the cognitive/linguistic instruments after 4 months of treatment (see Chapter 17, Injuries and Emergencies).

A small study on rheumatic disease showed a positive effect of homeopathy over placebo in terms of decreased subjective pain, articular index, stiffness, and increased grip strength (Gibson, Gibson, MacNeill, & Watson, 1980). The comparison was between an anti-inflammatory plus placebo, and an anti-inflammatory plus homeopathy. Another placebo-controlled, double-blind study (Andrade, Ferraz, Atra, Castro, & Silva, 1991) of the homeopathic treatment of rheumatoid arthritis had only a mildly positive result. Two studies of a homeopathic complex for rheumatoid arthritis also showed a slightly positive effect (Kohler, 1991; Wiesenauer & Gaus, 1991). None of these studies used the same protocol.

Nollevaux (1994) showed a small positive effect on preventing upper respiratory infection using *Mucococcinum* in an unpublished controlled study of 200 subjects (Linde et al., 1997). Several other studies in the prevention of upper respiratory infection and influenza found certain homeopathic medicines and complexes to be ineffective (Davies, 1971; de Lange de Klerk, Blommers, Kuik, Bezemer, & Feenstra, 1994; Ferley, Zmirou, D'Adhemar, & Balducci, 1987; Heilmann, 1992).

A study was done on premenstrual syndrome (PMS) using a homeopathic medicine (Folliculinum) routinely prescribed for PMS; it had positive results (Lepaisant, 1994). Another smaller study found placebo more effective than classically prescribed homeopathy in the treatment of PMS (Chapman, Angelica, Spitalny, & Strauss, 1994).

A small pilot study on aphasia (Master, 1987) had a very positive result for the individualized homeopathic treatment of this condition compared with placebo. The single medicine *Blatta orientalis*, 6C prescribed routinely was not effective for the treatment of asthma (Frietas, Goldenstein, & Sanna, 1995), and a certain complex of homeopathic medicines was ineffective for chronic sinusitis (Weiser & Clasen, 1994).

THE FUNDAMENTALS

Homeopathic therapeutics are conducted based on the principle that the best therapy for any given patient is a the single medicine whose adverse effects most closely mimic the symptoms of the illness (Hahnemann, 1982). Data is compiled from the medicine's trial on healthy volunteers, a study akin to what the American health care system terms a Phase I Clinical Trial (when a new drug is tested to see its effects on healthy volunteers). Symptoms of the diseases or syndromes that the homeopathic medicine is prescribed for are contained within this list. For example, the plant *Belladonna* (commonly known as deadly nightshade) contains the active alkaloid atropine. Atropinergic effects include dilated pupils, red face, throbbing headache, and fever. In homeopathic medicine, *Belladonna* is used to treat a fever or throbbing headache accompanied by dilated pupils and red face.

Historically, like contemporary clinical trials, homeopathic research administered substantial doses of the material to subjects with the hope that the experiment would be discontinued before serious toxic pathology could occur. In recent times, substances are prepared for the trial by a homeopathic pharmacist through the standardized homeopathic manufacturing process. This methodology eliminates toxicity and allows the subtle effects of the medicine to be noted.

Several protocols have been developed for the design of experiments to ascertain the effects of new medicines. The future use of the drug is entirely reliant on these experiments, called *provings* after the German homeopathic nomenclature developed by the physician who founded homeopathy 200 years ago. Healthy volunteers take the medicine until symptoms occur, then stop taking the medicine, and carefully log the times and characteristics of all the changes they observe in themselves until the symptoms have entirely disappeared. This data is meticulously reviewed with the subject and often augmented by frequent interviews of the subject by the researcher or an assistant (Sherr, 1994). Because mental and emotional effects of the substance can be of importance in prescribing, these are carefully recorded as well. Even the subject's dreams may have importance in prescribing for chronic diseases (Sankaran, 1991). A placebo-control group is being included in some contemporary proving methodologies.

Trials of this nature on healthy volunteers do not illuminate the organ damage or neoplasms that a homeopath might treat with certain substances since the homeopathic medicines do not cause them. Symptoms in the initial trial may hint at that substance's use in the treatment of significant pathology. For example, burning pains in the epigastrium when fasting might signify that a medicine could be effective in the treatment of gastric or duodenal ulcers. Additional information is collected by the investigator from the toxicology literature from accidental poisonings with the undiluted substance from which the medicine was derived.

HOMEOPATHIC PHARMACY

Homeopathic medicines have been made from plants, minerals, metals, diseased tissues, exudates, animals, and synthetic chemicals. Each medicine is designated by a unique Latin name. A guide to the common names for each official homeopathic medicine is provided in Appendix A.

There are three systems of manufacture; the most common system yields what is called the *centessimal potency*, which is prepared as follows. If the original substance is soluble in water or alcohol, it is extracted in 9 parts diluent to 1 part substance. Then that solution is diluted again with 99 parts distilled water. This resulting solution is vigorously pounded by striking the vial against a rubber mat or book at least 10 times, a process called *succussion*. This is the first centessimal potency, which is denoted by the number 1 and the letter C (or CH in Europe). The 2C potency is prepared by diluting the 1C 99 to 1 with distilled water again, and succussing again. The process repeats itself serially, and each time the numeric value of the solution increases by one. A 1,000th centessimal potency is called a 1M, a 100,000th potency is called a CM.

Nonsoluble substances are made identically from the 5C level and beyond. But they are originally powdered, mixed with 99 parts lactose, and ground in a ball mill for 8 hours, or by hand for 1 hour to create a 1C. One part of this dilution is then mixed with 99 parts lactose again to create a 2C, and the 3C is created by repeating this process. Then 1 g of the 3C is added to a flask and filled with distilled water to 100 ml. This solution is succussed to form the 4C. A single drop of the 4C is added to a vial containing 5 ml of 95% ethanol and succussed to produce the 5C.

The process of manufacture is referred to as *potentization*, another term from the original German nomenclature that has been grandfathered into contemporary use out of respect for tradition. This term has an important connotation; the higher potencies are regarded as more effective than the lower potencies. There are two other systems of manufacture. The first are decimal potencies, produced as above except diluted in a ratio of 9 to 1, instead of 99 to 1, and signified by the letter X (e.g., a 30X potency), or by the letter K in Europe. The second is a less common system that involves dilutions of 50,000 to 1. These potencies are called LMs, Q potencies, or 50th millesimals.

Homeopathic medicines can be administered as drops of the aqueous solution of the desired potency (with alcohol added to prevent spoilage), but are more commonly dispensed in the form of medicated pellets. Sucrose or combined lactose/sucrose pellets are moistened by the manufacturing pharmacy with drops of the desired potency. In the United States, by agreement with the Food and Drug Administration (FDA), homeopathic medicines are not available off the shelf for consumers in potencies of 200C and above.

Homeopathic medicines are regulated as drugs by the FDA. Like conventional pharmaceuticals, homeopathic medicines sold over the counter must have common indications for self-limited, acute illnesses printed on the label. This leads to confusion for consumers who often get the impression that because a label reads that a specific medicine can treat, for example, headaches, that it should work for their headaches. In actuality, there are many medicines that might be used for an individual with a headache (or any other condition), and a prescription must be individualized to that person's symptoms. Likewise, a specific homeopathic medicine may be useful for dozens of conditions if it is indicated by a the holistic symptom set of the person. A patient may feel that a drug was mistakenly prescribed by a clinician for his or her condition when that condition is not listed on the label.

The critique of homeopathy is that these medicines are nothing but placebos, given their extreme dilutions (Stapleton, 1997; Wadman, 1997). Therefore, skeptics argue that to sell or prescribe these medicines is fraud at best, and potentially negligent of serious medical conditions at worst. Critics argue that there is a prohomeopathy publication bias. They cannot accept that the balance of clinical research on homeopathy shows a positive effect for homeopathy over placebo. Although the charge by its very nature cannot be proven, these critics such as the National Council Against Health Fraud (1994) assume that substantial numbers of homeopathic studies (generally undertaken by homeopathic physicians) must have been withheld for publication when they had negative outcomes, thus tipping the balance in favor of homeopathy.

The homeopathic profession argues that the lack of scientific explanation of how homeopathy works should not prevent us from utilizing it, especially since it has been empirically demonstrated to work. *Chemical hormesis*, a phenomenon that has been repeatedly documented by biologists for the better part of a century, appears to confirm the positive effect of ultradilute aqueous solutions. Beneficial effect, such as growth stimulation or healing, can be observed from extremely low exposures to a given chemical, which would have adverse effects at high exposures, and is called hormesis. A comprehensive effort was recently undertaken in the field of environmental toxicology to identify articles describing this phenomenon (Calabrese & Baldwin, 1998). Nearly 4,000 potentially relevant articles were reviewed, and chemical hormesis was judged to have occurred in approximately 350 of the studies. "Chemical hormesis was observed in a wide range of taxonomic groups and involved agents representing highly diverse chemical classes, many of potential environmental relevance. Numerous biological end points were assessed; growth responses were the most prevalent, followed by metabolic effects, longevity, reproductive responses, and survival." The authors concluded that the study suggests that chemical hormesis is a "reproducible and relatively common biological phenomenon."

PROPER HANDLING OF HOMEOPATHIC MEDICINES

The activity of a homeopathic medicine cannot be determined by examining the pellets. Based on convention derived from clinical experience, a homeopathic medicine is believed to be rendered inert by exposure to great heat, strong odors, direct sunlight, and X-rays (for example at the airport). Boiron Laboratories has conducted experiments showing the dielectric constant of a homeopathic solution is different from that of a plain solution. This difference in dielectric constant is destroyed if the homeopathic solution is heated to 120°C for 20 minutes.

Therefore, homeopathic medicines should not be heated to great temperatures, or stored or administered in a clinic treatment room, botanical medicine storage room, or a patient's home medicine cabinet containing such volatile substances as camphor, perfume, moth balls, or herbs (Jouanny, 1980).

In-House Stock

If a pharmacy or health food store that carries homeopathic medicines is not readily available for patients, an in-house stock of medicines should be maintained. Appendix E is a list of manufacturing pharmacies that sell to clinics and medical offices, or offer a stock of medicines on a contractual basis. Homeopathic medicines are generally quite inexpensive. Despite the expiration date that manufacturers are required to put on their products, there is no evidence that homeopathic medicines become ineffective over time when stored and handled correctly.

There are many homeopathic medicines that could be used in an integrative medicine practice. The author has chosen to highlight the following 15 medicines, which should be available for patient use: (1) *Arnica montana*, 30C, 200C; (2) *Arsenicum album*, 30C; (3) *Belladonna*, 30C, 200C; (4) *Bryonia alba*, 30C; (5) *Chamomilla*, 30C; (6) *Ferrum phosphoricum*, 30C, 200C; (7) *Gelsemium sempervirens*, 30C; (8) *Hepar sulphuris calcareum*, 30C; (9) *Ignatia amara*, 30C; (10) *Mercurius vivus*, 30C; (11) *Nux vomica*, 30C; (12) *Phosphorus*, 30C; (13) *Pulsatilla*, 30C; (14) *Rhus toxicodendron*, 30C; and (15) *Sulphur*, 30C.

PRESCRIBING FOR ACUTE ILLNESS OR INJURIES

Data Gathering

Patient data gathering includes supplemental questions for the patient interview (because the patient's subjective experience of the illness is more significant in making a homeopathic prescription than a conventional one), and a careful physical exam.

The Patient Interview

Good diagnostic reasoning demands thorough data gathering from the patient or parent, which begins with relaxed attentive listening. The clinician should take care to ask open-ended questions because precise subjective data are much more important for a homeopathic prescription than they are in standard medicine. Introducing more pauses in the consultation for the patient to reflect—to whatever degree possible, given time constraints—will elicit the most accurate answers. It cannot be emphasized enough that the chronic symptoms and neuroses of the patient should be clearly distinguished from symptoms that have arisen at the same time as the presenting acute illness. At this level of prescribing, the focus is on health alterations of recent onset.

What follows is a description of an ideal homeopathic patient interview. Things will rarely proceed in order during a real interview. Actually, the apparent disorder of the patient's agenda can provide clues to the medicine that is indicated, either by revealing the patient's current emotional state or level of cognitive focus, or by revealing physical symptoms that can be a guide to the homeopathic prescription, even though these symptoms appear unrelated.

The clinician should initially ask the patient the reason for the visit. After he or she has finished spontaneously describing the illness, the clinician should ask more questions about the *local* symptoms. Local symptoms are symptoms of the part of the body that is the seat of the chief complaint. Details about the symptoms can be filled in with such questions as:

- What color is the mucus?
- Can you describe the discomfort?
- Where exactly is it (e.g., left side, right side, radiating, or moving somewhere else)?
- What makes it better or worse?
- What color is the stool, urine, or menstrual blood?
- Is the bleeding clotted or unclotted?

Next the patient should be asked whether anything unusual happened prior to the onset of symptoms (e.g., emotional upset, becoming chilled, or exposure to a disease vector).

Next the clinician should ask questions about any *general* symptoms the patient might have. General symptoms are symptoms of the whole person such as sensitivity to coldness or warmth, being aggravated or alleviated by being indoors or out or by moving or being still—specific sensations that occur at more than one place in the body, or feeling generally worse at a certain time of the day. Some homeopathic literature also subsumes food cravings, food aversion, thirst, and the time and qualities of fever or chill under general symptoms. Consequently, lines of inquiry that should be pursued include:

- striking changes in thirst (four to six glasses a day of liquids is average for people in temperate climates)
- specific food and drink desires and aversions
- factors that make the person feel generally better or worse (besides drugs)
- the time of day the symptoms are noted

The care provider should also conduct a quick review of systems while noting any concurrent symptoms (even when the latter do not fit the clinician's concept of what could be related to this illness).

Finally, the clinician should inquire about changes in mood. If the patient seems concerned with the clinician's motivation for asking, the provider can say, "Some people find that a change in mood comes along with an illness like this. I'm curious if you've been feeling any different from usual emotionally."

When pressed for time, the homeopathic portion of the patient interview can be limited to five crucial questions that can elicit the subjective information necessary to make a prescription. Is there a change in subjective temperature (e.g., does the patient feel overheated or chilly)? Is there a change in thirst from the usual? Is there a change in the patient's mood or concentration? What factors alleviate or aggravate the main symptom? What makes the person feel better or worse in general?

Objective Symptoms

The usual focused physical exam and diagnostic workup should be conducted, and a medical diagnosis made. Any unusual features of the patient's affect and behavior in the office should also be noted. Discoloration of the integument, tongue, and mucous membranes should be noted. The clinician should be alert to the color, texture, and odor of discharges and blood.

Recordkeeping

Some may find it helpful at first to use a data collection form, such as Exhibit 1–1, during the patient interview because it provides reminders about lines of inquiry that are unfamiliar.

It is valuable to record striking symptomatology in the patient's own words. Symptoms that are volunteered and strongly stated may be underlined. Unfortunately, in this litigious age there are legal

Exhibit 1-1 Data Collection Form

Patient Name:

Date:

Chief Complaint:

Local Symptoms:

Aggravated by: Alleviated by: Quality of discomfort:
                                                Burning, aching, sore,
                                                needle-like, formicating,
                                                pressing, bursting, pulsating,
                                                shooting, knife-like,
                                                stinging, radiating
                                                Extending to:

General Symptoms:

Aggravated by: Alleviated by: Sensitive to ambient: heat
                                                cold
                                                Thirst: 1 2 3 4 5 6 7 8 9 10
                                                glasses/day

                                                Prefer drinks: ice-cold cold
                                                tepid warm

Foods:

Desire for: Aversion to:

_____   _____

_____   _____

_____   _____

Concurrent Symptoms:

Cognitive:

Emotional:

Physical:

Probable Etiology:

ramifications to recording too much in the way of emotional data. If this document is kept in the patient's record, it might provide fuel for legal arguments that, for example, a worker's compensation claim is really a preexisting psychological disorder. Since most offices have space constraints, some clinicians may want to shred such documents after they are done with them, and maintain the customary brief notes.

In the long term, the patient's symptoms may be charted in standard medical format. A linear narrative format is marginally more suitable to homeopathic recordkeeping than a review-of-systems approach, but it may not be acceptable to the health care facility, or to the board reviewing the physician's charts for certification purposes.

Case Analysis

Common Symptoms

Symptoms peculiar to the individual are very important in homeopathic prescribing because the homeopathic treatment is all about strengthening the host, not killing the vector of the disease. Conversely, the common symptoms of a medical condition are of very little assistance in the quest to select the correct homeopathic medicine from the dozens that may have been successfully used to treat a specific disease. For example, a cough is a usual feature of bronchitis, and a runny nose is a ubiquitous part of upper respiratory infection. However, information about agents and conditions that excite or alleviate that common condition can be crucial in decision making. Likewise, if a common symptom has some striking characteristic it becomes important in homeopathic reasoning (e.g., a cough stimulated from a tickle in the throat pit when inhaling cold air, or a green nasal discharge so viscid that it can be stretched out in strings). Laboratory work is of little value in selecting between homeopathic medicines.

General Symptoms

The symptoms of the person's physicality as a whole, if present, are more important than a localized symptom. For example, a fever that spikes from 3:00 to 5:00 p.m. is a more significant symptom to the homeopath than a nondescript sore throat would be. An increased sensitivity to ambient cold since the start of an illness is more important prescribing information than the patient's hemorrhoids itching, the chief complaint.

Concurrent Symptoms

These are the symptoms that a conventional medical clinician may disregard because they do not fit with her or his understanding of the disease process. For instance, the person has a stabbing headache concurrent with hemorrhoids, which is her or his chief complaint, or there is constipation concurrent with an acne outbreak. These can be helpful in distinguishing among the medicines that might be prescribed.

Distinct mental and emotional changes since the person has been ill can be the most helpful of all in prescribing the correct medicine. For example, irritability, forgetfulness, anxiety, weepiness, or a desire or aversion for sympathy can often lead one right to the correct prescription.

Local Symptoms

In conventional medicine, the least attention is paid to the local symptoms. In homeopathy, the local symptoms are only of great importance when they are distinctive, striking, peculiar, or if there are no general or concurrent symptoms present.

The Treatment Plan

Selecting the Medicine

The challenge that faces the clinician accustomed to practicing in the predominant medical paradigm is to utilize two dissimilar forms of diagnostic reasoning simultaneously while attending to the patient. A medical diagnosis must be made, but a second diagnosis—the homeopathic medicine most suitable to the holistic state of the patient—must be made concurrently.

The clinician should make his or her medical diagnosis first, then rank the symptoms according to the above criteria. In summary, notable concurrent mental and emotional changes are the most significant, and changes in the general physical state of the person rank second. The distinctive concurrent physical symptoms rank third, the specific local symptoms (and what aggravates and alleviates them) rank fourth, and the common symptoms of the illness are of trifling import.

There are two ways one could arrive at a medicine for a patient using this book as a reference. One is by recognizing the characteristic pattern of symptoms of one of the common medicines after having studied it in Part II. This is a quick and legitimate way to begin to prescribe on the spot in a busy practice. The second is to do a case analysis as presented above and find if any of the medicines profiled in the medicine differentials in Part III match the distilled and prioritized essence of the case in question. See Exhibit 1–2 for sample cases for examples.

No one patient will have all the symptoms produced in a medicine's proving. The absence of a symptom in a patient does not itself constitute a symptom. Thus, if the patient is emotionally normal during the illness, this would not contradict a prescription of *Arsenicum album*, which has anxiety as part of its symptom set, because normal is not a symptom. On the other hand, a distinctive sense of apathy in the patient would contradict a prescription of *Arsenicum album* because apathy is a symptom that excludes anxiety.

Likewise, there will always be symptoms in a patient that are not represented in the profile. The purpose of case analysis is to be sure that the most important symptoms (according to homeopathic criteria) are known to be a feature of the medicine prescribed. If a medicine cannot be found that covers these priority symptoms, no homeopathic medicine should be prescribed. This introductory guide cannot cover every medicine that might be needed.

Classical homeopathic treatment is to give one homeopathic medicine at a time. *Complex homeopathic medicines* are composed of several medicines—usually in low potencies—mixed together and used routinely for specific diseases. Some of these formulas are marketed by pharmaceutical houses primarily to the public; others are primarily marketed to clinicians. Classically trained clinicians sometimes frown on the use of these medicines, but the clinical research thus far shows a rough overall equivalence in efficacy between the two approaches to acute prescribing (Linde et al., 1997).

Isopathic medicines are medicines made from the same substance that caused the illness and prepared in homeopathic potency, such as pollen or house dust for allergies, or *Candida albicans* for vaginitis. The studies using isopathic medicines are few in number, but thus far have been shown to be more effective than any other approach to prescribing (Linde et al., 1997).

Exhibit 1–2 Sample Cases

Case 1

A 41-year-old woman presents with knee pain following falling onto her knee during a bicycle accident 3 days ago. The knee felt very sore for the first 2 days. In the past 24 hours, she has experienced intense sharp shooting pains in the knee during weight bearing. Radiographs reveal a possible chip of the anterior tibial tuberosity. She says she feels okay otherwise.

Analysis

There are only local symptoms in this case. The one distinctive symptom is the quality of the pains (shooting), and that the pains followed an injury. There are several medicines that should be considered. See Chapter 17, Injuries and Emergencies, for information on care for injuries.

Ruta graveolens is a medicine used for contusion-like injuries of the periosteum. *Symphytum officinale* is used for persistent pain from fractures or periosteum injuries. *Arnica montana* is used for soft tissue injuries and hematomas. *Hypericum perforatum* is for shooting pains from nerve injury. The latter is indicated because the most current and distinctive symptom is shooting pains from injury. The shooting pains will subside after a prescription of *Hypericum*, but soreness will remain. *Ruta* could then be given, which should help speed healing. If *Ruta* is not effective, *Symphytum* can be used.

Case 2

An 11-year-old girl presents with an occipital headache that began 7 days ago. The pain is nondescript and does not radiate. It occurs most often before mealtime. Her thirst has increased, and she has been drinking eight glasses of ice-cold water a day. She has been craving steak this week, and to a lesser degree, licorice and ice cream. She appears very attentive and precocious when asked questions, then stares off into space when not being addressed.

Analysis

How can these symptoms be divided into the homeopathic categories? The general symptoms include increased thirst for ice-cold drinks, desire for steak, and possible impairment of blood sugar regulation. The concurrent symptom is cognitive: poor concentration, feeling "spaced out." There are only common symptoms in the local symptom category.

This is a case in which the local symptoms are of no significance in determining the medicine. One needs to prescribe based on the general

continues

Exhibit 1–2 continued

and cognitive symptoms. *Phosphorus* is not among the most common medicines for headache; therefore, it is not in the headache differential in Part III. *Phosphorus* is one of the 15 prominent homeopathic medicines in Part II and has all the general symptoms and a notable state of poor concentration. Two general symptoms, desire for cooked meat and licorice, are not known features of *Phosphorus*.

Case 3

An 8-year-old boy presents with throbbing pain in the left ear. The pain started last night at bedtime, and he was up intermittently during the night crying. He has a temperature of 101°F, and his cheeks are brilliant red. In the office, he is quiet, and the parents answer questions for him. He has no thirst and no appetite. On exam the left tympanic membrane is red and bulging with effusion; the right tympanic membrane is within normal limits.

Analysis

Here is a case in which all of the general symptoms and most of the local symptoms clearly correspond to the medicine *Belladonna*. However, one local symptom, the fact that the otitis media is on the left side, does not fit. *Belladonna* is known to be associated with right-sided or bilateral ear infections. *Belladonna* should still be prescribed because a variation in one local symptom does not outweigh the rest of the symptoms of the case. *Belladonna* has a profile in Part II and is also featured in the section on otitis media in Chapter 20, Ear, Nose, and Throat.

Case 4

A 65-year-old woman who is the patient of another provider you are on call for telephones you at 11:30 p.m. She states that your colleague diagnosed her with shingles 2 weeks ago. It began with a rash, which is now drying up. She has been given routine care for herpes zoster and sounds angry that she has not yet obtained relief from the pain. The right side of her back burns terribly, and she has been tossing and turning in agony before calling you, unable to sleep. She noted that she has also had diarrhea this week, which burns her rectum and anus. She hints that she is afraid she received the wrong diagnosis, and that she really may have a life-threatening disease.

Analysis

This case demonstrates several key points. First, colleagues who cover for each other should be asked whether they are open to homeopathic

continues

Exhibit 1–2 continued

prescriptions for their patients. Also, this case demonstrates the useful-
ness of patients' owning their own homeopathic remedy kits so that the
medicines are available after hours.

It is important to recognize that burning is a general symptom.
Anxiety about health and irritability are the most important symptoms
in the case because they are clear emotional concurrent symptoms. The
appropriate medicine can be determined from knowing something of
its key symptoms found in Chapter 3, *Arsenicum album*, or by using the
herpes zoster prescribing differential.

Case 5

A 7-year-old girl presents at 2 p.m. with vomiting of unknown
etiology that began at 4 a.m. She has vomited five times, and the nausea
is not relieved after the emesis. The child is afebrile, and the physical
exam is within normal limits, including a soft, nontender abdomen
and uncoated tongue. The child has no appetite, and her thirst is
normal for her. Everyone in her family has eaten the same foods, and
no one else has become ill. Yesterday was a typical day for her.

Analysis

At first, there appear to be no general or concurrent symptoms in this
case, but the tongue is coated in most people who have been vomiting;
therefore, a clean tongue is a symptom. Repeated vomiting with no
other symptoms, except a clean tongue, is best addressed with *Ipecacuanha*. This medicine is addressed in the gastritis section in Chapter
23, Gastrointestinal System.

Posology

Once a medicine has been chosen, the posology needs to be
determined (i.e., the potency to prescribe, frequency of administration, and duration). A moderate and readily available potency is 30C;
hence for simplicity's sake, it will be the recommended potency for
most purposes in this book. Certain inflammatory conditions and
injuries are reputed to respond better to higher potencies; these are
specified under the appropriate topic in Part III. Higher potencies are
generally prescribed for more intense illnesses and injuries, and lower
for milder illnesses. The commonly accepted definition of high potency in the United States is 200C, 1M, 10M, and higher. Low potency
is defined as 6C, 9C, 12C, and 15C; 30C is a medium potency. By

convention, the potencies named above are those most commonly sold in North America.

In France and some other locations in Europe and South America, a 30C is defined as a high potency, and by convention, potencies such as 4C, 7C, and so on, are more available in their pharmacies. Potencies above 30C are not prescribed as often. The reluctance to prescribe higher potencies reflects a desire to make homeopathy more credible to conventional pharmaceutical thinking by avoiding potencies that are inconceivably dilute.

Prescribing is determined based on the state of the person and the intensity of the illness, not on the nature of the base substance from which the homeopathic medicine was made. A routine prescription for an acute viral or bacterial infection or inflammation of mild to moderate intensity would be for the patient to self-administer several pellets of a 30C potency of the indicated medicine at 3-hr intervals for up to three doses. Definite improvement should be noted by that time. If there is none, another medicine can be prescribed in the same way. If the medicine demonstrates a therapeutic effect, then it should be taken three times a day until symptoms are completely resolved. Sophisticated self-observant patients can be instructed instead to self-administer a dose each time subtle relapse is noted. The clinician learns about the action duration of medicines for different conditions by listening to patients' feedback about how frequently they need to repeat medicines.

Initial improvement in the patient's general condition is commonly noted by increased comfort and relaxation. The patient may describe feeling better in general, or may be observed to go to sleep, become quieter or less restless, or complain less of discomfort. Objective findings such as elevated temperature, pulse, and respiratory rate may or may not yet be improved after the third dose of the correct medicine. A correct prescription may cause a fever to increase before it reduces, accompanied with increased comfort and rest. In a similar way, there may be one more episode of emesis or diarrhea before acute gastroenteritis subsides.

In patients whose primary symptoms are a state of weakness, pallor, and apathy, improvement in general condition will be determined by increased alertness, strength, and activity.

For more intense illnesses, the medicine can be prescribed as often as every 15 min if the clinician is certain of the prescription. The repetition of dose for injuries is a bit more variable, and will be spelled out in the protocols in Chapter 17, Injuries and Emergencies.

Administration of Medicine

While there is no standard dose in the homeopathic literature, three to five pellets is typical. The general consensus in the field is that there is no difference in efficacy between one pellet and many. Most patients need to be given an exact number, however, because of their past experience with dose in conventional pharmacology. The pellets are dissolved in the mouth, sublingually or on top of the tongue. The medicine should be administered when the mouth is free of strong tastes (e.g., food, toothpaste, and cough drops). It is ideal not to touch the medicine while administering it, but this may not be possible for very small children. The nurse, parent, or patient can toss the medicine into the open mouth from the cap without touching the cap to the tongue.

Follow-Up

If there is no improvement in the patient's general condition after the third dose, the medicine was not similar enough to the patient's illness to have a therapeutic effect. The patient should self-administer no more doses. Another remedy can be selected and given without delay based on the original patient interview, which may be amended if the patient calls to report symptom changes. The procedure for evaluating the second prescription is the same as for the first. Conventional treatment (or another complementary therapy) should be offered at any point that the patient or clinician is unhappy with homeopathic treatment, or if there are concerns about patient safety.

On occasion, an illness or injury may require one medicine early in the illness. Meanwhile, the initial group of symptoms on which that prescription was based subside, and new symptoms arise, which require a different prescription. For example, a medicine to prevent bruising and swelling may be needed initially for a sprain, and then a medicine for lingering stiffness may be indicated some days later.

DRUG INTERACTIONS, ADVERSE REACTIONS, AND CONTRAINDICATIONS TO HOMEOPATHIC TREATMENT

There have been no reports of adverse drug interactions with conventional medications, botanical medicines, or nutritional supplements noted in the homeopathic literature. One homeopathic dentist has made anecdotal reports that numbing agents work less effectively when the homeopathic remedy *Hypericum perforatum* had been taken by the patient. The effectiveness of homeopathic treatment is difficult to evaluate when palliative therapies, such as nonsteroidal, anti-inflammatory drugs, acetaminophen, and aspirin, are administered concurrently.

Some conventional medications can interfere with homeopathic treatment of chronic diseases (see Part IV). Consultation with the patient's homeopathic specialist would then be advisable before other medications are prescribed. Likewise, coffee (not caffeine), camphor-containing skin products, naphthalene, electric blankets, high-speed dental drilling, marijuana, and aromatic herbs like mint and eucalyptus are often cited by homeopathic educators as interfering with the long-term homeopathic healing process in some patients. They may not interfere with homeopathic treatment of the self-limited acute illnesses addressed in this book, but ideally they should be discontinued, if possible, during treatment.

Skeptics believe homeopathic medicines cause no adverse reactions because they are inert sugar pills, and it is generally true that homeopathic medicines do not. However, patients should beware of taking more than three doses of a medicine for an acute illness unless it is clearly effective. Homeopathic clinicians and researchers have not reported adverse symptoms from a 30C potency of any homeopathic medicine prescribed according to the protocols in this book. However, the administration of an inappropriate medicine may produce proving symptoms in sensitive patients, especially if it is repeated frequently more than three times (Sherr, 1994). These temporary symptoms will mimic the functional symptoms produced by an overdose of the medicine's source material. Consequently, the suggested treatment plans in Part III call for evaluation of the effectiveness of the medicine after three doses. If symptoms appear that are not part of the illness for which the patient is being treated, no more doses of that medicine should be given. The proving symptoms will then gradually abate and resolve.

It is generally best for new homeopathic prescribers to avoid treating medically fragile patients, such as those with multiple sclerosis or severe asthma held in check by oral steroidal drugs. Also, it is best not to prescribe for people with severe eczema who use steroid creams. These cases should be referred to clinicians with a higher level of expertise, because homeopathic treatment may trigger suppressed symptoms.

PATIENT EDUCATION

Often there is not enough time after a consultation for patient education about homeopathy. Two sample patient handouts that are helpful in this regard are included in Appendix D. The first is a brief overview of homeopathic medicine; the second gives patient instructions about how to take the medicine. There is room on the patient instruction form for the clinician to circle the recommended treatment plan and write in the name of the medicine. If pressed for time, the clinician can delegate to office staff the task of reviewing the information with the patient before sending the handout home with the patient.

For patients who want more information, there are many books on the market that clearly explain in layman's terms homeopathy and the relevant scientific research in depth (e.g., Ullman, 1996). Many medical offices sell these texts at the front desk because of patient demand. In addition, self-care enthusiasts may want to learn how to take care of themselves and their family for minor, self-limited, acute illness with a home remedy kit.

Most important for patient safety, the homeopathic clinician must tell the patient not to discontinue his or her other medications unless instructed to do so by the prescribing clinician. Specifically, there have been several rumors of deaths resulting from abrupt discontinuation of asthma inhalers, presumably because the patients thought they would be instantly cured of chronic asthma by homeopathic medicine. Clinicians must document that these instructions have been given to their patients.

THE REGULATORY FRAMEWORK AND LEGAL IMPLICATIONS OF INTEGRATIVE PRACTICE

The regulation of homeopathic medicines as drugs in the United States has proved a mixed blessing for the homeopathic profession. On the one hand, it has made homeopathic medicines less vulnerable to the vicissitudes of the FDA that botanical medicines and food supplements have endured. On the other hand, regulation means that anyone who prescribes homeopathic medicines for a fee could be considered to be practicing medicine—a major obstacle for homeopathic professionals who are not licensed to prescribe conventional drugs. A few homeopathic medicines are prescription-only. Certain prescription homeopathic medicines are indicated exclusively for serious medical conditions or chronic disease because they do not have over-the-counter indications. Others are extremely low potency (not ultradilute) medicines made from potentially toxic substances (e.g., a 4X potency would be a 10^{-4} dilution).

The result of this legal framework is that the only legal requirement to prescribe homeopathic medicines in the United States is the clinician's ability to prescribe conventional pharmaceuticals. In certain states, doctors of chiropractic, naturopathic doctors, and licensed acupuncturists have circumvented this restriction by including the right to prescribe homeopathic medicines in their state practice acts. Homeopaths who are not medical providers are actively working to establish a legal framework under which they can openly practice.

It is extremely rare for MDs and DOs to encounter licensure issues relating to prescribing homeopathic medicines. However, the state medical licensing board in North Carolina distinguished itself by suspending the license of a medical doctor (George Guess) who was a homeopathic specialist, solely on the basis of his use of homeopathic medicines (393 SE.2d 833, 327 N.C. 46, Guess, In re. [N.C. 1990]). The people of North Carolina responded by passing legislation that protects doctors from this kind of action (N.C. Gen. Stat. § 90–14 [1999]).

The other main legal issue is liability. The malpractice risks for integrative clinicians as compared to their conventional colleagues have not been investigated. A recent legal review of the issues involved in referring to alternative medicine specialists reviewed the claims that have been filed against the insurers of such providers in 1996 (Studdert et al., 1998). For doctors of chiropractic, there were 2.2 claims for 100 policy holders. For massage therapists, there were 0.1 claims per 100 policy holders. In comparison, for medical doctors in conventional practice, there were 9.0 per 100 policy holders. This article about liability concluded that physicians who currently refer to practitioners of alternative medicine should not be overly concerned about the malpractice liability implications of their conduct, unless the referral itself was negligent or the physician knows the practitioner is incompetent. The liability issues for doctors who themselves include homeopathy in their own practices have not yet been studied.

Legal issues for clinicians who want to make homeopathy a major part of their professional life are discussed in Chapter 30, Taking It Further.

PROFESSIONAL ISSUES IN THE WORKPLACE

Managed Care and Hospital-Based Care

Only a small number of clinicians are using homeopathic medicines in a managed-care environment (Ullman, 1999). The main obstacles to licensed health care providers seeking to introduce homeopathic treatment of acute illness and injury in their managed-care practices are fourfold. The first is that administrators may require board certification in homeopathy, which is available for each group of medical professions, but is an involved process more suitable for clinicians who want to specialize in homeopathy (see Chapter 30 for more information). The second is that questions may arise about the efficacy of homeopathic treatment. These can be addressed to some degree by the body of homeopathic research, but many conditions have not been studied. The third is concern about cost-effectiveness. Fortunately, there are several large and small studies from France, England, and Scotland that show the care provided by homeopathic physicians to be substantially more cost-effective than that provided by conventional physicians (Ullman, 1999). More large studies are currently underway. The final obstacle is opposition from physician colleagues. In the 1990s, some medical groups within preferred provider organizations mounted organized opposition to overt reimbursement for homeopathic services by physicians and midlevel providers in health plans. Senior physicians on hospital staffs have thrown up roadblocks to the inclusion of homeopathy in outpatient clinic services, especially when this inclusion meant incorporation of homeopathic medicines into the formulary. Yet at the same time, a survey of primary care physicians who were members of the American Medical Association showed 49% wanted training in homeopathy (Berman et al., 1995).

Communication among Colleagues

"Coming out of the closet" about one's interest in homeopathic medicine and complementary therapies to both patients and colleagues is essential to the inclusion of these therapies in a mainstream setting. This forthrightness will allow patients to have the kind of care they want, and also to feel free to talk to their providers about the therapies they are already using. A good-natured and humble approach that focuses on patient welfare works best, but tenacity will probably be required. Those who work in a hospital setting will need to initiate the process of including homeopathic medicines in the formulary, which can be a highly charged process. Nurse practitioners, physician assistants, and nurse midwives in institutional settings will need to negotiate protocols or standardized procedures with those entities. Implications for quality assurance will need to be negotiated in advance.

Integrative clinicians are breaking new ground in the health care system. As with any pioneering effort, there are both personal rewards and challenges to being part of a historical process. Support is available for these efforts from colleagues in the homeopathic professional organizations (Chapter 30).

PART II

Fifteen Essential Homeopathic Medicines

In the chapters that follow, the main features of 15 homeopathic medicines that would be a valuable addition to integrative primary care practice are presented. These medicines will be mentioned again and again in the prescribing differentials for specific illnesses and injuries presented in Part III. If some effort is put into memorizing the key symptoms that are highlighted in each of the following chapters, the clinician will be able to recognize when that medicine is indicated, no matter what condition the patient presents with.

These profiles are intended to extract from the vast homeopathic literature only what is relevant to the reader. Consequently, most material about historical uses of medicines for epidemic disease and about conditions requiring expert homeopathic care (and a comprehensive office visit) are omitted. To learn more, the interested reader should purchase some of the dozens of reference texts in print called *Materia Medica* (e.g., Morrison, 1993; Vermeulen, 1997) that select from the proving and, to a lesser extent, the clinical literature of homeopathic medicine what are believed by the authors to be the most characteristic symptoms of the drug. These books are essential to the ongoing study of homeopathy. However, it is easy for a novice to be overwhelmed by the amount of information in such texts and to form an erroneous impression that any clinical use of homeopathy must take years to master.

In each chapter that follows, there are lists of factors that aggravate the patient's condition, and those that alleviate it. These aggravating and alleviating factors are termed *modalities* in homeopathy and are considered to be extremely important in selecting an appropriate medicine for a patient. Modalities are determined by proving trials, where healthy people are given a substance to see what adverse reactions it causes. These reactions are then used as a guide to prescribing.

The second section in each chapter is a brief comparison of the medicine with others with which it might be confused. The reader is given information about how to distinguish between the two or referred to other places in the text.

It is important to remember that homeopathy is an evidence-based system of medicine. The primary criterion for prescribing a homeopathic medicine for a patient with a certain set of symptoms is not a body of folklore, or even the clinical experience of homeopathic physicians. The fundamental criterion of appropriate prescribing in homeopathic medicine is the proving (or trial) of the medicine on healthy volunteers. The trials of all the widely used medicines presented here were conducted in the nineteenth century. The symptoms of the subjects in the trials were recorded in the common language of that era. Relevant verbatum material from subjects in that trial (Allen, 1875) are provided in display at the end of each chapter. Homeopathic providers are concerned with subtleties of speech. For example, a subject in the trial of *Chamomilla* engaged in "pitious moaning," while a subject in the *Pulsatilla* experiment simply "wept" (Allen, 1875). If "crying" were substituted in both instances because they sound old fashioned, an important nuance would be lost. Weeping is softer and sweeter than crying or piteous moaning, and evokes sympathy in others rather than irritation. An unpoetic scientific approach of matching the bare bones data from the trial to the symptoms in the patient cannot communicate the *art* of homeopathic prescribing.

The symptoms in the clinical trial are arranged under anatomical headings, roughly head to toe: Cognition, Emotions, and Affect; General; Appearance; Head and Neck; Eyes; Ears; Nose; Face; Mouth, Parotid Gland, and Pharynx; Larynx; Lymphatic System; Abdomen; Gastrointestinal System; Rectum; Heart and Lungs; Respiratory System; Genitourinary System; Female Reproductive Tract, Male Reproductive Tract; Back; Extremities; Skin; Perspiration; Sleep; and Dreams. No chapter contains all headings, because each medicine has its primary effect on certain parts of the body, and no significant effect on other parts. The heading General refers to symptoms of the whole person. Under this heading fall fevers, chills, any sensation that occurs in multiple regions of the body (e.g., burning pains), and any sensation experienced in a general way by the patient, about which he or she might say "I feel _____."

All the distinctive dreams that subjects experienced during the trial are also included. Recently, there has been renewed interest in these dreams, in the more psychologically and philosophically oriented segment of the homeopathic profession. They are included for the readers' interest, again a nod to the more symbolic side of homeopathic medicine. Those who are so inclined can look for correspondences with the physical and emotional symptoms of the awake patient, which are quite marked in some cases.

CHAPTER 2

Arnica montana

Scientific Name: *Arnica montana*
Scientific Family Name: Compositae
Common Name: Leopard's Bane

OVERVIEW

Arnica montana is a beautiful mountain daisy. It is found in acidic soils and mountain pastures. Its stems terminate in single composite flowers with bright yellow ray florets on a conspicuous green calyx. *Arnica montana* is used in botanical medicine primarily in external preparations and compresses for bruises. *Arnica* was in the U.S. pharmacopeia from the 1800s to 1960 for this purpose.

Arnica montana's uses in primary care homeopathy are primarily related to trauma. It is the first medicine that should be given after a concussion, especially with epidural and subdural hematomas. Some of the many varieties of cephalalgia that emerged in the nineteenth-century clinical trial are in the display below. It is the most common medicine for contusions and hematomas of any part of the body, especially of the nose, extremities, breasts, or male genitalia. It is also the first medicine that should be given for ankle or wrist sprain/strain.

Many have assumed that *Arnica montana* could have wider uses in trauma and postsurgical care, but the research has not supported this assumption (Ernst & Pittler, 1998). *Arnica*, 30X had a large clinical trial for muscle soreness following long-distance running (Vickers, Fisher, Smith, Wylie, & Rees, 1998) and was shown to be ineffective. A trial of *Arnica montana* was also performed to see if it would significantly decrease bleeding time or impact various blood coagulation tests on healthy volunteers in the period immediately following its administration (Baillargeon, Drouin, Desjardins, Leroux, & Audet, 1993). It had no effect.

Likewise, several studies have been done on *Arnica* as a postsurgical medicine. *Arnica* was shown *not* to relieve pain and prevent complications from dental extraction (Kaziro, 1984; Lokken, Straumsheim, Tveiten, Skelbred, & Borchgrevink, 1995), or to prevent complications after oral surgery (Kennedy, 1971). It was one ingredient in a complex medicine that showed some benefit for postsurgical ileus (Aulagnier, 1985).

Arnica montana has, however, shown strongly positive results in its traditional use in treatment of hematomas in two studies of only fair quality. These studies showed the 5C potency had a significant effect over placebo in relieving pain in this condition. One is, unfortunately, an unpublished thesis (Bourgois, 1984) on 29 subjects, using a pain score as the evaluative outcome criteria. The study was ranked by independent reviewers on two internal validity scales, and given a 40 (Jadad scale) and 36 (more elaborate internal validity scale) on a scale of 100 (Linde et al., 1997). The second study on 39 subjects is only available in a French journal (Dorfman, Amodeo, Ricciotti, Tétau, & Véroux, 1991) and received a Jadad score of 20 and a second internal validity score of 43 when reviewed independently (Linde et al., 1997).

The emotional state is familiar to anyone who has cared for injured people. The patient is afraid of being touched or even approached. In some cases of shock, the patient may claim to be uninjured so that medical personnel will not approach, expressing anger at those who try. The patient may be dazed from shock, or unconscious from concussion.

If when in bed, the person complains that the bed is too hard, *Arnica montana* is indicated. This sensation is common in the pushing stage of labor, as well as after injuries.

Arnica montana is given for angina with needle-like, jolting, or squeezing pain, especially when it extends to the elbow of the right arm. In pregnancy, *Arnica* is given routinely at the end of labor when the woman is sore. It is also given after miscarriage from a blow, shock, or overexertion when the bleeding is painless and the blood is red and coagulated with clots. Further details are given in Chapter 27, Gynecology and Primary Care for Pregnancy and Childbirth.

In dermatology, *Arnica* is a main medicine for small furuncles in groups, as well as acne that is symmetrical.

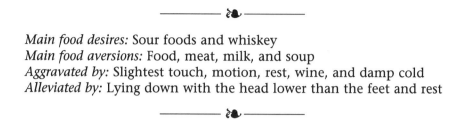

Main food desires: Sour foods and whiskey
Main food aversions: Food, meat, milk, and soup
Aggravated by: Slightest touch, motion, rest, wine, and damp cold
Alleviated by: Lying down with the head lower than the feet and rest

COMPARISONS

- *Bellis perennis*—Sore bruised feeling in muscles and joints; also sprains and lameness; specific to soreness of older people after physical labor, such as gardening; and contusions of the pelvic muscles and organs (see Chapter 17, Injuries and Emergencies)
- *Hypericum perforatum*—Injuries to areas rich in nerves, such as fingers and toes, coccyx, spine, and neck; pains that shoot proximally along the nerve (see Chapter 17)
- *Ruta graveolens*—Sprained ankles, follows *Arnica montana* when nondescript pain and stiffness remain (see Chapter 17)
- *Cimicifuga racemosa*—After auto accident; specific to acceleration-deceleration cervical injuries (whiplash) (see Chapter 17)

KEY SYMPTOMS OF *ARNICA MONTANA*

- Contusions, especially of the nose, extremities, breast, or male genitalia
- Shock
- Concussion
- First medicine to be given in ankle or wrist sprain/strain
- Fear of being touched and being approached
- Head hot and body cold

Typical Symptoms

The following contains symptoms reported in the nineteenth-century trial or in accidental poisonings (Allen, 1875), annotated with related modern medical diagnoses.

Recorded Symptoms	Modern Diagnoses
Cognition, Emotions, and Affect	
Hopelessness	Postconcussion syndrome (with
Violent attacks of anxiety about the	irritability and poor concentration)
present and future	Postconcussion amnesia
Frightfulness, horror of instant death	Shock
Peevish, contradictory, quarrelsome,	
sullen, or morose	
Indifference to everything	
She does not speak a word	
Want of memory; he forgets the word he	
is speaking	
General	
Sensation of being bruised over the	Labor
whole body	Influenza
Shivering over the whole body and the	
head, at the same time heat in the	
head and redness and heat in the	
face, accompanied by coolness of the	
hands and a feeling as of the hips,	
the back, and the anterior surface of	
the arms being bruised	
Head	
Heaviness and confusion of the head	Concussion
Violent headache on waking in the	
morning, which reached such a point	
at 8 a.m. that while walking in the	
open air, he almost fell from	
dizziness; disappeared at 10 a.m.	
Burning in the brain, the remainder of	
the body being cool, or at least not	
hot	
Pressing headache as if the head were	
being distended from within outwards	

continues

continued

Recorded Symptoms	Modern Diagnoses
Pain as if a knife were drawn through the head transversely from the left side; this is immediately followed by internal coldness of the head, which causes the hair to stand on end	
Pressing pain in the forehead, which increases near the warm stove as if the brain were rolled up in a lump	
Headache, pressing, over the eyes, extending toward the temples, with a sensation as if the integuments of the forehead were spasmodically contracted	
Headache as if a nail had been thrust into the temple	
Great heat in the head with cold body	

Nose

The nose pains him from above downwards as if he had a violent fall upon it	Nasal contusion or fracture

Gastrointestinal System

Eructations bitter like bad eggs	Diarrhea
Distention of the abdomen with frequent passing of wind	Flatulence
	Eructations following injury
Offensive flatus	
Diarrhea resembling brown yeast	
Involuntary stool at night when asleep	

Heart

Pain in the region of the heart as if it were squeezed together, or as if it got a shock	Soreness of the heart after overexertion
Stitches in the cardiac region	Angina
Pulse feeble, hurried, irregular	Tachycardia
Pulse 100, feeble, fluttering	

Back

The small of the back painful as if it had been beaten	Back injuries such as from automobile accident, bicycle accident, or falling
Pain in the right scapula, toward the back as after a violent fall or blow	

continues

continued

Recorded Symptoms	Modern Diagnoses
Extremities	
Pain in all the limbs as if they had been bruised	Contusions of the extremities and the joints of the extremities
Paralytic pain in all the joints during motion as if the joints were bruised	Sprains and strains of the ankles and wrist
The arms feel weary as if he had been bruised from blows	
Pain in the balls of both thumbs as if they had been knocked against something hard	
Pain in the thighs when walking as from a blow or contusion	
Pain as after a violent blow over the calf of the right leg accompanied by lassitude of the legs	
Pain as from a strain in the tarsal joint	
Pain as from a sprain in the wrist	
Dreams	
He dreamed of men being flayed; this appeared frightful to him.	
Dreams about frightful objects, of lightning having struck, graves, etc.	

CHAPTER 3

Arsenicum album

Scientific Name: *Arsenic trioxide*
Common Name: White Arsenic

OVERVIEW

The toxicology of arsenic trioxide is well-known. Arsenic irritates or ulcerates all mucous membranes, gastrointestinal tract, respiratory tract, and urogenital tract. It damages the kidneys, liver, and adrenal glands. It damages the nervous system, causing progressive paralysis with cramping. High doses cause convulsions and coma (Jouanny, 1984).

These indications hold true in homeopathic prescribing. In the hands of homeopathic specialists, *Arsenicum album* reputedly cures or palliates the serious diseases that mimic arsenic poisoning. It is the data from the nineteenth-century trial, however, which brought out many functional symptoms that show the usual indications for this medicine in contemporary primary care.

The proving symptoms, as selectively reported in the display, paint the portrait of a restless, anxious, and critical patient, who is weak and chilly and complains of burning pains. He or she wants to have company and is more anxious when alone. The patient has a fear of dying from the illness, which may or may not be verbalized. Since the symptoms are aggravated from 11 p.m. to 3 a.m., *Arsenicum album* should always be considered when a patient calls at these late hours, especially when the anxiety over the illness exceeds its actual threat. The patient is worried about loved ones. The patient displays restless anxiety with fear of being alone. The patient may experience anxious hyperventilation, such as from panic attacks or anxiety disorder, and great fear and anxiety from lung diseases, such as asthma.

One strange emotional symptom that has been observed concurrently with a physical illness treated with *Arsenicum album* is anxiety about untidiness of the environment. The patient can become distressed if anything is out of place. There may be general irritability and criticalness of others, and the patient may give exacting instructions to others about how his or her living space should be arranged.

The patient is chilly. The pains tend to be burning in quality, and these are alleviated by warm applications. He or she desires small sips of liquid often, preferably warm drinks like tea. The patient may carry a bottle of water to the clinic and sip on it while in the waiting room or consultation room. Complaints are more often right-sided.

This is a common medicine for pharyngitis, which is distinctly alleviated by warm drinks. Pains are burning and constricting.

This is a very frequently indicated medicine for severe diarrhea (with the usual caveat that the general symptoms must fit). This may be an exhausting and frequent bacterial, viral, or parasitic diarrhea, or a functional diarrhea from eating fruit or other watery foods. Diarrheic stool may be of any description, including bloody. *Arsenicum album* and *Veratrum album* are the two most commonly prescribed medicines for simultaneous diarrhea and vomiting, and resulting hypovolemia and hypokalemia. There is often burning in the abdomen and/or rectum accompanying the diarrhea. Not every patient who needs *Arsenicum album* will have soft stool, however. The stool may be normal or even hard and small.

The patient may have an aversion to sweets, butter, fats, and meat, as well as a desire for sour things, brandy, coffee, and milk. Gastralgia may follow the smallest intake of food or drink. It is one of the medicines for gastric and duodenal ulcers with burning pains as well as esophagitis, reflux, and pyrosis, when the general symptoms and characteristic affect are present.

Acute asthma that is aggravated at night, with audible whistling and wheezing, accompanied by the above emotional state will be helped by *Arsenicum album*. In the long term, it is "constitutional" treatment by a homeopathic specialist that will most benefit the patient with asthma, however. *Arsenicum album* is indicated for dyspnea that prevents the patient from lying down and which is aggravated by inhaled allergens (especially those of midsummer), laughing, ascending stairs, and turning in bed, and alleviated by drinking coffee. *Arsenicum* is also indicated for asthma during an upper respiratory infection, and bronchitis with a cough that alternates dry (at night) and loose. The cough is aggravated by drinking and alleviated by sitting up. The expectoration may be almost any color: green yellow, brown, bloody, transparent, white, purulent, and/or frothy. There may be burning or coldness in the chest. Pleurisy may be present with darting pain through the upper third of the right lung.

Arsenicum album is a fairly common medicine for influenza and colds. These illnesses are accompanied with restlessness, anxiety, desire for company, and external chilliness with burning pains internally. The patient has cravings for sips of warm drinks and may have a high fever, with cold perspiration and shaking chills. *Arsenicum album* is indicated for heart palpitations, accompanied with anxiety, which are aggravated at night (especially 3 a.m.), in a supine position, and when ascending stairs.

Arsenicum album is one of the main medicines for burning skin lesions, or lesions that both burn and itch, such as may be present in herpes zoster, skin ulcers, herpes simplex, or eczema.

While the conditions most commonly associated with *Arsenicum album* in primary care are usually gastrointestinal and respiratory, on occasion *Arsenicum album* will be needed for the following:

- Bacterial vaginosis with profuse acrid, yellowish, and thick vaginal discharge aggravated by standing or passing flatus
- Urinary tract infection with sore or burning pain on beginning to urinate
- Sciatica alleviated by walking and hot applications
- Cramps in the calves
- Swelling of the feet
- Herpes zoster
- Restless anxiety in the final stages of the dying process

Main food desires: Olives, olive oil, warm drinks (during chills), warm food, bread (especially rye), coffee, acid fruit, meat, milk, refreshing things, and wine

Main food aversions: Any kind of food, high-fat foods, meat, sausage, and sweets

Aggravated by: At night (11 p.m. to 3 a.m.), cold drinks, cold food, cold air, wet weather, eating vegetables, watery fruits, drinking liquids, infectious disease, bad food or water, inhaled allergens, lying on affected part, and exertion

Alleviated by: Warm compresses, warm food and drinks, warm covers and clothing, motion, walking around, lying down with head elevated, sitting erect, company, perspiration, open air, and from raising the head on pillows or elevating the bed.

COMPARISONS

- *Nux vomica*—Upper respiratory tract infection with watery nasal discharge, exacting mood, and chilliness (see Chapter 20, Ear, Nose, and Throat)
- *Phosphorus*—Influenza and bronchitis with anxiety, desire for company, increased thirst, and burning pains (see Chapter 21, Lower Respiratory System, and Chapter 25, Infectious Disease)
- *Veratrum album*—Severe gastroenteritis with chilliness (see Chapter 23, Gastrointestinal System)

KEY SYMPTOMS OF *ARSENICUM ALBUM*

- Anxious and exacting
- Fear of death and being alone
- Chilly
- Burning pains
- Restless
- Increased thirst for sips of liquids

Typical Symptoms

The following contains symptoms reported in the nineteenth-century trial or in accidental poisonings (Allen, 1875), annotated with related modern medical diagnoses.

Recorded Symptoms	Modern Diagnoses
Cognition, Emotions, and Affect	
The anxiety and restlessness are indescribable	Anxiety
	Anguish of dying people
He has so much fear that he jumps out of his bed	Hypochondriasis
Anxiety in the evening on lying down at 3 a.m.; he felt hot now as if he would vomit	
Anguish and despair driving her from one place to another for relief	
Excessive anguish with oppression of the chest and difficult breathing	
He despairs and weeps, and imagines that no one can help him, that he must die; he is cold and chilly, and afterward generally weak	
With great anguish, he turns and tosses to and fro in his bed. "Kill me," he cried "or relieve my pains"	
Dread of death coming on suddenly when left alone	
The slightest cause was sufficient to put her into anger and rage, which especially occurred when one spoke of her complete recovery, which she considered wholly impossible	
She is vexed about every trifle, and constantly talks about other people's faults	
General	
Excessive thirst	Influenza
Very great restlessness	Sepsis
Weakness and prostration	
Burning pains, especially in the inner organs, skin, and ulcers	
Shuddering while walking in the open air	
Fever at 2 a.m.	
Burning heat internally	
Heat with anxiety after midnight	
Cold clammy sweat	

continues

continued

Recorded Symptoms	Modern Diagnoses
Appearance	
Face covered with cold sweat	Cachexia
Face expressive of genuine mental agony	Fluid volume deficit
	Malnutrition
Deathly color of the face	Hepatitis
Pale yellow, cachectic look	Anxiety
Sunken face	Alcoholism
	Terminal illness
Eyes	
Corrosive tears, making the cheeks and eyelids sore	Allergies
	Upper respiratory infection
Nose	
Watery excoriating discharge from the nostrils	Upper respiratory infection
	Allergic rhinitis
Smarting and burning in the nostrils that disappeared in the open air	
Mouth and Pharynx	
Dry and brown-colored tongue	Aphthae
Feeling of dryness in the mouth, with violent thirst; he drinks a little at a time	Glossitis
	Pharyngitis
	Increased thirst
Burning in the mouth along the pharynx and in the pit of the stomach	
Gastrointestinal System and Rectum	
Loathing of food	Gastritis
Nausea	Gastroenteritis (food poisoning, "travelers' diarrhea," and dysentery)
Vomiting violently and incessantly, and excited by any substance taken into the stomach; even water is immediately vomited every time. Vomiting brings no relief	
	Colitis
	Gastric and duodenal ulcers
	Hemorrhoids
Vomiting with apprehensions of death	
Anxiety in the pit of the stomach	
Burning in the stomach	
Rectum	
Tenesmus as in dysentery, constant burning, with pain and pressure in the rectum and anus and violent tearing cutting pains in the intestines	Esophagitis
Burning at the anus after stool like fire	
The evacuations excoriated the area around the anus	
Black acrid putrid stools	
Purging with extreme coldness of the extremities	

continues

continued

Recorded Symptoms	Modern Diagnoses
Heart and Lungs	
Frequent oppressive shortness of breath in every position of the body, causing anxiety	Asthma
	Bronchitis
	Anxiety disorder
Oppression, want of breath and nocturnal asthma makes him spring up at midnight	Heart palpitations
	Arrhythmia
Oppression of the chest when walking fast	
Irregular heart palpitations, but so violent at night that he imagines he hears it; accompanied by anguish	
Palpitation of the heart and tremendous weakness after stool; he has to lie down	
Heart palpitations, arrhythmia, weak irregular pulse	
Extremities	
Uneasiness in the lower limbs, he cannot lie still in the night, and had to change the position of his feet all the time or to walk about to get relief	Restlessness in bed
	Insomnia
Skin	
Eruption around the mouth, burning and painful	Herpes zoster
	Skin ulcers
Itching, which is increased with scratching	Herpes simplex
	Eczema
Burning ulcer on the skin, covered with a gray crust and surrounded with an inflamed border	
Burning itching of the body	
Dreams	
Dreams frightful, anxious, full of danger	
Full of care, sorrow, and fear	
Thunderstorms	
Fire	
Black water	
Darkness	
Death	

CHAPTER 4

Belladonna

Scientific Name: *Atropa belladonna*
Scientific Family Name: Solanaceae
Common Names: Deadly Nightshade, Dwale, and Fair Lady

OVERVIEW

Atropa belladonna is native to Eurasia, where it grows in woods and wastelands. Deadly nightshade has naturalized in the eastern United States. It has bell-shaped purplish-brown flowers in the early summer, which are followed by glossy black berries in the late summer. Its active alkaloids are anticholinergic: atropine, scopolamine, and hyoscyamine. These are extracted from the leaves and root for conventional medicines. These alkaloids are used in conventional medicine in combination with other drugs for allergies (Atrohist), irritable bowel syndrome and duodenal ulcer (Donnatal and Spacol), diarrhea (Lomotil), and relief and treatment of urinary tract infections (Urised). Atropine sulfate is used alone to create mydriasis and cycloplegia of long duration for opthalmic exams and procedures (Isopto Atropin). The homeopathic indications are opposite of those for its conventional use. Dryness of the mucous membranes, constipation, urinary retention, and illnesses accompanied by flushed face and dilated pupils are a few of the conditions *Belladonna* is used to treat in homeopathic medicine.

Historically, *Belladonna* juice is said to have been used by the prostitutes of Italy as eye drops to make their pupils dilate, eyes sparkle, and cheeks flush, thereby making them more attractive to their customers. Hence, its name . . . beautiful woman. In mythology, Atropos was one of the three Fates of Greek mythology—the one who cut the thread of life. The deadly effects of even the smallest amount of the plant or its berries taken orally is certainly well-known. The devil is said to tend this plant, which has taken many curious children to an untimely death.

Belladonna is used in primary care homeopathy primarily when the classic symptoms of inflammation are present: pain, heat, erythema, and swelling. When pain is present in a *Belladonna* case, it is usually intense, and it typically has a pulsating quality. Illnesses requiring *Belladonna* usually arise rapidly. A red fire engine is a useful mnemonic device for *Belladonna*—red, fast, and with a pulsating light on top. This state may be localized, for example a cut that is becoming infected (throbbing, hot, and turning red), or generalized, for example a child with a high fever (102°F and above) that has begun suddenly and generated a *red face*, throbbing headache, dilated pupils, delirium, and so on.

Decreased thirst is nearly always present in acute illnesses requiring *Belladonna*, unlike illnesses needing *Ferrum phosphoricum*, which is also useful for the first stages of inflammation, but when the patient is thirsty instead of thirstless. Lemons are said to be craved by the patient who requires *Belladonna*, but this is rarely seen in practice.

The patient is aggravated from being jiggled and jarred. It is said that when homeopathic hospitals were common in the United States, the homeopathic physicians who did in-patient rounds would sometimes "accidentally" jiggle the bed as they approached to examine the patient. The *Belladonna* patients would cry out because this aggravated the pain.

Belladonna is homeopathy's most famous medicine for febrile illnesses. It is the most common medicine for febrile conditions of childhood, and for scarlet fever with typical rash and red papillae (strawberry tongue). There may be delirium with the fever, including frightful hallucinations that invoke the fight or flight response. The patient may try to run or hide from the hallucinations, strike, bite, or kick. There may be febrile convulsions. In a routine fever, the patient may simply appear to lack concentration and have a glazed-over look with glistening eyes.

Because the toxicity of the plant is such that it produces a state that resembles mania, rage, or even psychosis, it has a place in the homeopathic treatment of psychiatric conditions.

Belladonna is also used to treat headaches when there is a throbbing quality to the pain, but especially when the symptoms are right-sided.

The head feels congested with blood. *Belladonna* is one of the top medicines for both migraine and cluster headaches and is indicated when there is head pain with a red face, aggravated by light, noise, and being jarred. The patient may bore his or her head into the pillow from the pain. There may also be unusual sensitivity of the scalp.

Belladonna is one of the top medicines prescribed for otitis media, most often in the right ear. Children wake up in the middle of the night screaming from pain. The tympanic membrane is infected and bulging. The external ear is painful as well. Throbbing is a useful distinguishing characteristic, but unfortunately many of the patients who have earaches treatable with *Belladonna* are too young to describe the quality of the pain. In this case, the medicine is prescribed on general symptoms and appearance of the patient.

Belladonna is indicated in conjunctivitis when the conjunctiva is injected and feels dry; the eyelids are swollen and red as well. This medicine should be thought of when pupils are dilated in any illness.

Belladonna is prescribed for pharyngitis and tonsillitis, with deep erythema. Historically, it was one of the medicines for mumps, a condition rarely seen since the MMR (mumps, measles, and rubella) vaccine has come into widespread use.

When the gums are sore and inflamed during the eruption of deciduous dentition (teething), *Belladonna* is prescribed for fever and discomfort.

Belladonna was historically used in appendicitis, reputedly sometimes eliminating the need for surgery. In an integrative practice, *Belladonna* can be given to reduce pain, if indicated, while the hospitalized patient awaits surgery (Gibson, 1981; Shepard, 1982). The indications are severe pain in the ileocecal region and pain aggravated by the slightest touch (e.g., by clothing), being jarred, moving the bed, and turning the body. The patient prefers to lie on his or her back. (Patients requiring *Bryonia alba* prefer to lie on the abdomen.) Patients may also vomit from intestinal paralysis.

In men's health, *Belladonna* was historically useful in the treatment of epididymitis and orchitis; antibiotics would be prescribed today. It is still useful in prostatitis when inflammation with pain on being jiggled remains after treatment with an antibiotic.

In women's health, it is a leading medicine for mastitis and hemorrhagic complaints. The patient wants to cradle the breast when taking a step so that it will not be jarred. In midwifery, it is used for delayed labor when the cervix does not dilate after the membranes rupture, despite the normal contractions (see Chapter 27, Gynecology and

Primary Care for Pregnancy and Childbirth). It is also useful for retained placenta and miscarriage when the general symptoms of *Belladonna* are present. When it is indicated for uterine hemorrhage, the blood feels hot, and a gush of bright red blood often follows the painful expulsion of a large dark clot. *Belladonna* is used for dysmenorrhea when there is labor-like, or sharp, knife-like, throbbing pain, with profuse hot menstrual blood. The pain is aggravated by being jarred or from motion.

Belladonna is indicated for acute arthritis, with red hot swollen joints as well as for red, swollen, throbbing, tender, and bleeding hemorrhoids. The patient has the sensation of the hemorrhoids or anus being forced downward.

Rarely does a day pass in a pediatric or family practice where *Belladonna* would not be useful.

Main food desires: Lemons and lemonade, beer, and cold drinks
Main food aversions: Coffee, drinks, sour foods, warm food, water, meat, and milk
Aggravated by: Lying down, light, noise, draft, touch, jarring, and getting the head wet or cold (Note: The person's symptoms or the person as a whole were observed to be worse in the afternoon, especially around 3 p.m.)
Alleviated by: Semierect posture

COMPARISONS

- *Ferrum phosphoricum*—Inflammation or fever with red face, high fever, quick onset, but unlike *Belladonna* thirst is usually increased (see Chapter 25, Infectious Disease)
- *Aconitum napellus*—Inflammation or fever with sudden onset, may have red face, but accompanied by thirst and fear (see Chapter 25)
- *Bryonia alba*—With headache is sensitive to light and jarring (but more gradual onset), increased thirst, and aversion to company (see Chapter 26, Brain and Nervous System)
- *Sanguinaria canadensis*—Right-sided headache (consult sections on migraine and tension headache in Chapter 26)

KEY SYMPTOMS OF *BELLADONNA*

- Sudden onset
- Redness
- High fever
- Dilated pupils
- Thirstless
- Pulsation

Typical Symptoms

The following are symptoms reported in the nineteenth-century trial or in accidental poisonings (Allen, 1875), annotated with related modern medical diagnoses.

Recorded Symptoms	Modern Diagnoses
Cognition, Emotions, and Affect	
Rage and violent fury	Mania
She attempted to bite and strike her attendants, broke into fits of laughter and gnashed her teeth	Psychosis
Inclination to tear everything about them to pieces; she tears her night dress and bed clothes	Febrile delirium
She pulls at the hair of bystanders	
Had to be held lest she should attack someone; when held, spat continually at those around her	
Fury with burning heat of the body and open staring and immovable eyes	
When put to bed, he sprang out again in delirium, talked constantly, laughed out loud, and exhibited complete loss of consciousness; did not know his own parents	
General	
Great intolerance of light and noise	Fever (especially sudden and high)
Delirium and heat	Inflammatory processes
Full frequent pulse	Viral and bacterial illness
Temperature of the head very much increased, of the rest of the body diminished	Menopausal flushes
	Hypertensive crisis
	Influenza with high fever
Appearance	
Head hot, glowing redness in the face	The appearance of patients in rage, mania, delirium, sunstroke, and febrile illness
Look wild and staring	
Pupils dilated, arteries of the neck and head visibly pulsating	
The eyes are projecting and sparkling	
Head	
Rush of blood to the head; pulsation of the cerebral arteries, and throbbing of the interior of the head	Migraine
	Cluster headache

continues

continued

Recorded Symptoms	Modern Diagnoses
Very intense headache, aggravated by noise, motion, when moving the eyes, shocks, contact, the least exertion, and in the open air	
Afraid to cough on account of the increase of pain it causes	
Pressure in the head	
Violent throbbing in the brain; the throbbing ends in the surface in painful shootings	
Jerking headache which becomes extremely violent on walking quickly or on going rapidly upstairs . . . at every step there is a jolt downwards, as if a weight were on the occiput	
At every step it felt as if the brain rose and fell in the forehead; the pain was ameliorated from pressing strongly on the part	
Stabbing as from a knife	
The head externally is so sensitive, the least contact, even the pressure of the hair, gives her pain	
Eyes	
Burning heat in the eyes	Conjunctivitis
Pupils dilated	Dilated pupils
Purulent discharge from the eyes	
Staring projected glassy appearance	
Ears	
Pressing tearing behind the right ear	Otitis media
Sensation of heat with drumming in the ears, burning in the ears with deafness	
Tearing in the internal and external ear in a downward direction	
Acute thrusts in the internal ear with pinching like earache	
Pulsation in the ears	
Mouth, Parotid Gland, and Pharynx	
The mucous membrane from the posterior third of the palate as far down as could be seen was of a deep crimson color, and the tonsils were very much enlarged	Pharyngitis Tonsillitis
Burning heat, great dryness, and roughness in the throat	
Shootings in the parotid gland	

continues

continued

Recorded Symptoms	Modern Diagnoses
Abdomen	
Tumefaction* of the abdomen, which was very tender to touch	Appendicits
Heat in the abdomen as from a hot iron	
Genitourinary System	
Retention of the urine, which only passes drop by drop	Urinary retention
Female Reproductive Tract	
Badly smelling hemorrhage from the uterus	Menorrhagia
	Uterine hemorrhages
Burning pressure uneasiness and weight in the uterus, burning in the ovaries	Dysmenorrhea
Menses too soon and very profuse of thick decomposed dark red blood	
At every step violent shootings in the genital region	
Skin	
Redness, like scarlatina of the entire surface of the body, especially the face	Dry skin
	Pustular acne
	Scarlatina
Pustules break out on the cheek and nose, which rapidly fill with pus, become covered with a crust	Viral exanthem
	Boils
Increased perspiration, or skin dry and burning	
Sleep	
He starts as if in a fright when he is just falling asleep	
The child tosses about, kicks and quarrels in its sleep	
Dreams	
Household affairs, peaceful	
Occupied with a great number of people; she wished to get away, but could not	
Performing gymnastic exercises, walking, running, riding in a carriage	
Anxious and frightful dreams	
Danger from fire	
Battles, fires, being pursued by giants	
Murderers and street robbers	
Miserable phantoms	

*Tumefaction is a nineteenth-century word that means swelling.

CHAPTER 5

Bryonia alba

Scientific Name: *Bryonia alba*
Scientific Family Name: Cucurbitaceae
Common Names: Black-Berried White Bryony, European White
  Bryony

OVERVIEW

Bryonia alba is a vine-like plant native to the woods and hedges of
Europe that bears flowers followed by black berries. It is remarkable in
its versatility; it is useful in treating the ailments of many body
systems. The characteristic emotional state is an irritability frequently
likened to a hibernating bear. The patient wants to be alone with his
or her suffering. Even children want to be left alone and not carried.
Any sympathy or attention from others is growlingly rejected. There
is a seriousness and an unhealthy focus on work; even in febrile
delirium and dreams patients mutter about work. Contradiction is
intolerable to them. *Bryonia* is primarily useful in illnesses that come
on slowly, over a period of days, accompanied with dryness of all
mucous membranes. The symptoms tend to appear on the right side
of the body, except for the headaches, which are usually left-sided
(Morrison, 1993).

Bryonia alba comes to mind in any condition where intense pain is
the predominant symptom. The qualities of the pains are tearing,
bursting, splitting, heavy, or needle-like. The most notable characteristic of the pains are that they are aggravated by motion. Unlike *Rhus
toxicodendron*, continued motion does not improve the pain. In some
ways it is like a homeopathic anti-inflammatory, and reportedly much

more effective than nonsteroidal anti-inflammatories when the symptoms as a whole match. Unlike nonsteroidal anti-inflammatory drugs (NSAIDs), *Bryonia alba* can reputedly help the body effectively fight bacterial or viral infection. There are numerous cases in the homeopathic literature and in the clinical experience of homeopathic specialists of *Bryonia* successfully treating such serious infectious diseases as pneumonia.

Headache, both tension and migraine, is one condition in which *Bryonia* is irreplaceable (Chapter 26, Brain and Nervous System). Patients isolate themselves in their rooms while they endure the pains, lying absolutely still. The room is darkened because even the motion of the irises in accommodating to light is painful. A glass of water sits by the bed, is ignored for hours, and then is gulped down in its entirety. Pressing on the head improves the pain. Stooping aggravates the pain.

Bryonia is one of the great medicines for influenza in cases where aching pains are present. The aching is aggravated by motion, and accompanied by severe headache, white-coated tongue, and great thirst at long intervals.

This medicine can treat bronchitis characterized by a dry, hard, and painful cough. The patient braces the chest and coughs shallowly to reduce the pain. The cough exacerbates or causes a headache. Sometimes, the patient is forced to sit up to cough. The cough is aggravated by eating and drinking, taking a deep breath, or coming into a warm room. Sputum is rusty, blood-streaked, or tough. Bronchitis can be accompanied by pleurisy with needle-like pains in the chest or right scapular region, or by costochondritis aggravated by deep breathing and coughing, alleviated by pressure and lying on the painful area of the chest or back. The lungs produce a dry friction sound.

Bryonia is also useful in mastitis, especially when the nipples are inflamed. The breast is hot, hard, painful, and sensitive to motion. Like when *Belladonna* is indicated, the woman supports her breast to prevent the pain associated with jarring and motion. The breasts feel *heavy and hard*, and the pains are sharp.

Gastritis that is aggravated by the least motion and alleviated by lying still can be treated with *Bryonia alba*. Other symptoms include nausea and vomiting from drinking or eating that is sometimes alleviated by warm drinks; constipation with dryness of the rectum; and dry hard stool, which is accompanied by a grumpy affect.

Bryonia alba was the most common medicine used historically to treat appendicitis (see Chapter 4, *Belladonna*), and may still be used on the way to the hospital or before surgery. The patient lies on the painful right side. The pain is aggravated by any motion and deep inspiration. Pressure may alleviate the pain, but there is rebound tenderness. Cold compresses lessen the discomfort. This medicine is also prescribed for hepatitis with jaundice. Like all the pains where *Bryonia* is indicated, it is alleviated by lying on the right (painful) side. Hepatitis is also accompanied with significant nausea.

Bryonia alba can treat back and neck pain such as painful stiffness; needle-like, aching or tearing pains in the lumbar region aggravated by walking, turning, and stooping; sciatica alleviated by lying quietly, especially on the painful side; bursitis; arthritis; fibromyalgia; tendonitis; rib fracture; and joint dislocation. All pains are aggravated by motion and sometimes are alleviated by letting the limbs hang down, or from pressure or cold compresses. Joints are red, swollen, and hot. There may be a pins-and-needles sensation in the soles of the feet, thereby preventing walking.

Main food desires: Cold drinks, warm drinks, beer, coffee, meat, warm milk, oysters, sour food, sweets, and wine

Main food aversions: Coffee, high-fat foods, all food, meat, and milk

Aggravated by: Slightest motion, touch, rising in the morning, stooping, coughing, exertion, deep breathing, hot stuffy rooms, hot weather, drinking while hot, eating, bread, flatulent foods, vegetables, and acidic foods (Note: subject appeared worse around 9 p.m.)

Alleviated by: Pressure, lying on painful part, bandaging, cool open air, quiet, cloudiness, damp days, drawing knees up, hot compresses to inflamed part, sitting up, and perspiration

COMPARISONS

- *Belladonna*—Inflammatory conditions, such as mastitis, when the patient does not want to move the painful part; in the case of *Belladonna*, this is to prevent it from being jarred
- *Eupatorium perfoliatum*—Influenza with severe aching pain that is aggravated by motion (see Chapter 25, Infectious Disease)
- *Nux vomica*—Irritable, wants to lie down in a darkened room, and constipated (see Chapter 12, *Nux vomica*)

KEY SYMPTOMS OF *BRYONIA ALBA*

- Irritable with desire to be alone
- Inflammatory pain and general symptoms that are aggravated by motion
- Symptoms that are aggravated by heat
- Dryness
- Needle-like, tearing pains
- Right-sided complaints

Typical Symptoms

The following are symptoms reported in the nineteenth-century trial or in accidental poisonings (Allen, 1875), annotated with related modern medical diagnoses.

Recorded Symptoms	Modern Diagnoses
Cognition, Emotions, and Affect	
Irrational talking of his business, prattling about business to be attended to	Overly focused on work or business
	Irritability
Imagines she cannot accomplish her work	Desire to be alone
Overbusy, works far too much	
Very ill humor, troubled with needless anxiety	
Morose, everything puts him out of humor	
Irritable, contradiction easily provokes anger	
Will not have his wife and children around him, wishes to be alone	
General	
On rising from bed, he was attacked by faintness	Orthostatic hypotension
Thirst excessive for much cold water, a great deal at once	Increased thirst
Head and Neck	
Headache commences in the morning on first opening the eyes or after rising	Tension headaches
Pain as if everything would press out of the forehead, when stooping	
Pain above the left eye followed by dull pressive pain in the occipital protuberances, whence it spread over the whole body and continued more or less severe the whole day; on quick motion and after eating the pain became so severe it seemed like a distinct pulsation within the head	
Pressive pain in occiput with drawing down the neck	
Ears	
Vertigo as soon as he rises from his chair	Labyrinthitis
	Acute exacerbation of Ménière's disease

continues

continued

Recorded Symptoms	Modern Diagnoses
In the morning on rising from bed, dizzy and whirling, as if the head were turning in circle	

Mouth
Very white coated tongue, thickly
Dryness in the mouth

Gastrointestinal System

Recorded Symptoms	Modern Diagnoses
Pressure in the stomach after eating; a feeling as if a stone were lying in it, which makes him fretful	Indigestion
Epigastric region sensitive to touch	Flatulence
Passage of offensive flatus	Constipation
Obstinate constipation, dry parched stool, with effort	

Lungs

Recorded Symptoms	Modern Diagnoses
Dry cough, hacking from the upper part of trachea	Bronchitis
Expectoration of thick gelatinous mucus	Pleurisy
Constriction of the chest; she felt the need of breathing deeply; when attempted, there was a pain in the chest as if something could not be fully distended	Costochondritis
Stitch in upper chest or (left side on inspiring—worse during motion) in the sternum on coughing; he was obliged to hold his chest with his hand	

Extremities

Recorded Symptoms	Modern Diagnoses
Weariness and heaviness in all of the limbs	Exacerbation of arthritis
Tensive painful stiffness of the knees	
Hot swelling of the feet	

Dreams
During the slumbering was continually busy with what he had read the evening previous, or household affairs, or anxiety about business
Dreams of dispute and vexation
That he tried to toss someone out of the window
Taking part in battles
Sleep talking about desire to go home, somnambulism

CHAPTER 6

Chamomilla

Scientific Name: *Matricaria chamomilla*
Scientific Family Name: Compositae
Common Name: German Chamomile

OVERVIEW

German chamomile is a small herb, frequently found in cornfields, which bears small white and yellow flowers. It is used herbally to calm flatulence, earaches, neuralgia, and dyspepsia as well as the entire person. It has no serious toxicity. It is used in botanical medicine, as it is in homeopathy, to calm people, especially children. But a large dose of *Chamomile* will have the converse effect on sensitive people, as evidenced by the symptoms elicited in its original trial (see display).

The word *peevish* used by the nineteeneth-century *Chamomilla* homeopathic trial participants means discontented, irritable, fretful, cross, contrary, or ill-tempered. The *Chamomilla* patient is all of these. This medicine is most commonly used in a variety of children's illnesses, secondarily in women's health, and rarely in men. *Chamomilla* is the preeminent medicine for screaming and whining children who must be carried around. They begin to cry again as soon as they are set down. Nothing else seems to console them. They are extremely restless. They ask for things that are rejected as soon as they are offered. Patients exhibit hypersensitivity to pain.

Chamomilla is a remarkable medicine for otitis media or otalgia when the above emotional state is present. The patient is frantic from the pain. There is a sensation as though the ear is obstructed. The child creates misery for the entire medical office, household, or airplane with shrieking uncooperativeness. Homeopathic *Chamomilla* often calms the child and is reputed to send him or her off to sleep within a few minutes. Clinicians report that it reliably cures the infection after the child is calm (Bruning & Weinstein, 1996).

It is the most important medicine for teething pains. Medical science currently rejects the traditional belief that the eruption of new teeth can stimulate colds, fevers, and otitis media. Nonetheless, there can certainly appear to be a connection between teething and other inflammatory conditions in clinical practice. These ailments will all respond to *Chamomilla* if the effect and general physical symptoms are present.

Chamomilla is also prescribed for colic when the characteristic *Chamomilla*-related whining and irritability is present. *Chamomilla* can cause/cure innumerable kinds of abdominal pain, the most characteristic being gas pains that extend to the chest and are sticking, dull, cramping, gripping, and knife-like pains. Expelling flatus does not relieve, or can even aggravate, the discomfort. Urination may aggravate the pains. Strong emotions, especially anger, can bring on colic. Warm compresses alleviate it. The most common time for colic is at sunrise, but discomfort may occur at other *regular* intervals. The area around the umbilicus may be especially uncomfortable.

Chamomilla may be indicated for a fever of unknown origin in a child with one cheek red and the other pale. The child is restless, thirsty, and irritable. It is also known to stem epistaxis when the general symptoms of the medicine are present.

In the adult gastrointestinal system, *Chamomilla* is useful for painful diarrhea with green stool that appears like spinach or chopped grass. There may be painful flatulence from emotions (compare with *Colocynthis, Magnesia phosphorica* in Chapter 23, Gastrointestinal System). The pain is alleviated by a heating pad or hot water bottle.

Chamomilla is one of the medicines used for coffee withdrawal when the characteristic emotional state is present. *Nux vomica* is prescribed just as commonly.

In women's health, *Chamomilla* is most renowned for treatment of dysmenorrhea, metrorrhagia, and premenstrual syndrome. Each of these conditions is accompanied by a childish, whiny, and irritable mood. The menstrual cramps are often knife-like, aggravated by anger, and alleviated by warm compresses. The hemorrhage is coagulated and comes on after anger. The premenstrual syndrome includes the onset of dysmenorrhea *before* the menses and an absence of breast swelling or tenderness.

Adult men rarely need *Chamomilla*. However, an old homeopathic medical journal, *The Homeopathic Recorder,* in 1934 reported the following comment from a panel discussion at a conference: "Dr. Tyrell said once to me, 'When the husband complains of the wife's being cross and irritable, and he can't get along with her, give *him* a dose of *Chamomilla* . . .'" (Tyler, 1980).

Although not commonly prescribed for asthma, *Chamomilla* should be considered when an exacerbation follows anger.

Chamomilla may be prescribed for unbearable toothache pain that is aggravated by cold air, anything warm in the mouth, and drinking coffee. Homeopathic medicines can reportedly palliate dental pain although people may postpone needed dental work.

Main food desires: Cold drinks, bread, and sour food
Main food aversions: Beer, coffee, and warm drinks
Aggravated by: Anger, cold air, damp air, music, wind, lying in bed, eructations, night, heat, warm food, covering, touch, and being looked at
Alleviated by: Warm, wet weather and being carried around

COMPARISONS

- *Cina*—Irritable children with anger from being touched or looked at
- *Rheum officinale*—Impatient, asks for many things, teething, and diarrhea
- *Tuberculinum*—Aggression with otitis media

KEY SYMPTOMS OF *CHAMOMILLA*

- Whiny, restless, and irritable
- One cheek red, the other pale
- Generally alleviated by being carried
- Children's ailments (e.g., teething, otitis media, and colic)
- Green stool

Typical Symptoms

The following are symptoms reported in the nineteenth-century trial or in accidental poisonings (Allen, 1875), annotated with related modern medical diagnoses.

Recorded Symptoms	Modern Diagnoses
Cognition, Emotions, and Affect	
Pitious moaning of a child because he cannot have what he wants	Restless
Irritable, easily impatient	Capricious
	Whining irritability
The pains sometimes made him very peevish	
Peevish about everything	
Whining restlessness; the child wants this and that and, when it is given, he will not have it, or pushes it from him	
The child can only be quiet when carried on the arm	
General	
Excessive thirst	
Appearance	
Redness of one cheek	Fever
Nose	
Epistaxis	
Mouth	
Toothache, especially severe after a warm drink	Teething
	Dental pain
Slight discomfort in the back teeth, makes him very peevish	
Abdomen	
Gripping, tearing colic in the region of the navel and lower down on both sides, with pain in the small of back as if it were broken	Colic
	Flatulence
Colic rather cutting than sticking with accumulation of saliva in the mouth	
Gastrointestinal System	
Green watery diarrhea	Diarrhea, especially after anger
Diarrhea smelling of rotten eggs	

continues

continued

Recorded Symptoms	Modern Diagnoses
Female Reproductive Tract	
Drawing from the sacral region forward, gripping and pinching in the uterus, followed by discharge of large clots of blood	Metrorrhagia Dysmenorrhea
Profuse discharge of clotted blood with severe pains like labor pains in the uterus	
Dreams	
Fantastic	

CHAPTER 7

Ferrum phosphoricum

Common Name: Iron Phosphate

OVERVIEW

Ferrum phosphoricum is unusual in homeopathic medicine in that it has proven to be a very useful medicine in primary care practice despite the fact that the number of subjects in the clinical trial was too small to provide a distinctive profile of symptoms. The clinical use was determined primarily from clinical experience based on educated guesses regarding the symptomatology of iron phosphate, which were based on the extensive trials of both iron (*Ferrum metallicum*) and *phosphorus* (see Chapter 13, *Phosphorus*).

Ferrum phosphoricum is used primarily for nondescript inflammatory and febrile conditions. In local inflammation, it is useful when there is redness and mild pain with few other symptoms. An example would be an inflamed tympanic membrane, without pus, and with very little or no pain. If given early, *Ferrum phosphoricum* may prevent the onset of a true otitis media.

This homeopathic medicine is indicated for febrile conditions of unknown origin, usually with red face, tachycardia, increased thirst, and no other distinctive symptomatology. *Ferrum metallicum* falls into a group of three common medicines for the first or second day of fever, which can be useful for Fridays in pediatric or primary care practices when parents bring children in with the beginnings of fever, hoping something can be done to prevent illness over the weekend. *Aconitum napellus* should be used for fevers that come on the most suddenly, and are accompanied with anxiety, restlessness, and in-

67

creased thirst. *Belladonna* should be used for fevers that come on slightly less rapidly with a red face, glassy eyes, and *decreased* thirst. Fevers needing *Ferrum phosphoricum* come on like those for *Belladonna*, or a bit more slowly, with red face, and *increased* thirst. A few doses of a 30C potency *Ferrum phosphoricum* at the onset of such illnesses can often cure the illness while it is still mild.

Like *Phosphorus* and *Ipecacuanha*, *Ferrum phosphoricum* is used to check epistaxis or other hemorrhages of bright red blood. The nosebleed should stop within a couple of minutes of administration of the medicine.

A more controversial use of this medicine is to treat mild anemia in people whose intake of iron-containing foods seems to be adequate, and there is no excessive bleeding. The 3X or 6X potency is given three times a day for an appropriate period of time, such as 6 weeks, and then the hemoglobin and reticulocytes are rechecked. Some clinicians use *Ferrum proto-oxalatum* the same way for anemia, instead. No research has yet been conducted to confirm the effectiveness of this treatment.

Main food desires: Alcohol
Main food aversions: Meat and milk
Aggravated by: At night (4 to 6 a.m.), from touch, being jiggled or jarred, and motion, on the right side
Alleviated by: Cold compresses

COMPARISONS

- *Belladonna, Aconitum napellus,* and *Phosphorus*—In fever and inflammation
- *Aconitum napellus, Phosphorus, Ipecacuanha,* and *Millefolium*—In hemorrhage of bright red blood (see Chapter 17, Injuries and Emergencies)

KEY SYMPTOMS OF *FERRUM PHOSPHORICUM*

- Early inflammation and fever
- No distinctive symptoms
- Increased thirst
- Epistaxis of bright red blood
- Iron deficiency anemia

Typical Symptoms

The following are symptoms reported in the nineteenth-century trial or in accidental poisonings (Allen, 1875), annotated with related modern medical diagnoses.

Recorded Symptoms	Modern Diagnoses
Cognition, Emotions, and Affect	
A feeling of "letting down," inertia, indifference to ordinary matters	Anemia Viral illness
General	
Heat and dryness of face and palms while sitting; also the throat and upper chest	Fever
Head	
While reading, headache from right brow to right ear	Febrile headache Right otitis media or otalgia
Ears	
Sticking in the right ear, as if a large pointed stick were lodged deeply therein, extending as a dull headache over that side	Right otitis media or otalgia
Gastrointestinal System	
Most intense heartburn, with rising so irritating it made me cough . . . for some time	Pyrosis Esophagitis
Extremities	
After writing, rheumatic feeling in right wrist, extending downward in the course of the dorsal tendons, most when resting it; then the pain seems to ebb and flow at short intervals	Nerve entrapment conditions of the wrist Overuse injuries of the wrist
When writing, pain occasionally extends up the forearm, mostly in the dorsal and ulnar aspects; on rising, felt in little finger to first phalynx; better by external warmth and wrapping	
Sleep	
4:30 p.m. drowsy; eyes feel it much; the feeling extends upward into the head; soon after had to lie down and take a nap	Fatigue

CHAPTER 8

Gelsemium sempervirens

Scientific Name: *Gelsemium sempervirens*
Scientific Family Name: Loganiaceae
Common Names: Yellow Jessamine, Carolina Jasmine, Evening
  Trumpet Flower, and Woodbine

OVERVIEW

Gelsemium sempervirens is an extremely poisonous climbing plant
that is native to the southern United States. It bears brilliant yellow,
fragrant, tubular flowers in the summer. It is so toxic that it can even
poison the bees that pollinate it.

The illnesses that are treated with *Gelsemium sempervirens* come on
slowly over period of days. Gradually, the patient begins to droop like
a rag doll. Even the eyes droop. He or she lies in bed with the head
propped up high, which seems to help. When rising, the patient must
take an arm or a railing for support and, trembling and weak, make his
or her way to the bathroom, for example, where pale urine is mictur-
ated in quantities that can appear to exceed the fluid intake. The thirst
is actually reduced. There may be dizziness. A low temperature pre-
vails throughout the illness.

The above is the typical picture of a *Gelsemium* illness. Not surprisingly, it is one of our leading medicines for influenza. It should be
considered for other infectious diseases, such as acute prostatitis,
when the general symptoms described above are present. Chills are
felt up and down the spine. There is some aching, but not as severe as
in influenza; that should be treated by *Eupatorium perfoliatum*.

70

Gelsemium can be useful for upper respiratory infection or seasonal allergies as well when the weakness seems disproportionate to the illness. It can also be used to treat postinfluenzal fatigue and was historically used for polio. It is one of the medicines homeopathic specialists use for multiple sclerosis and myasthenia gravis (Morrison, 1993).

On the cognitive level, the mind is dull, and the patient cannot concentrate. On the emotional level, *Gelsemium* is known for treating illnesses that begin after hearing bad news. It is a medicine for performance anxiety (compare with *Picricum acidum, Aethusa cynapium*, and *Argentum nitricum* in Chapter 22, Emotional Health and Chemical Dependency Recovery) with mental dullness and frequent urination.

Gelsemium has associated with it many symptoms of the eye, such as:

- One pupil dilated, the other contracted
- Both pupils dilated
- Diplopia (especially during pregnancy)
- Intermittent blindness
- Dim vision or swimming
- Glaucoma
- Hazy vitreous
- Retinitis
- Orbital neuralgia with contraction and twitching of ocular muscles
- Aura preceding migraine
- Red, sore, and aching eyes. It is reputed to help discomfort from adjustment to new prescription glasses or contacts.

A key symptom of *Gelsemium* is a headache with a sensation as if there were a band around the head. Pain in the occiput may also be present. The head feels heavy, and the discomfort radiates to the neck and shoulders. The patient may suffer from a migraine headache preceded by blindness or visual aura, alleviated by profuse urination (compare with *Iris versicolor* and *Sanguinaria canadensis* in Chapter 26, Brain and Nervous System). The headache is aggravated by exposure to the sun or tobacco smoke.

Painless involuntary diarrhea from receiving bad news has been treated with *Gelsemium*. The stool may be yellow, clay-colored, cream-colored, or like green tea.

Main food desires: None

Main food aversions: None

Aggravated by: Emotional shocks; bad news; motion; humid and warm weather; or damp, cold, and foggy weather; and thunderstorms

Alleviated by: Reclining with head held high, profuse urination, perspiration, shaking, alcoholic drinks, trying to concentrate, stooping, and arrival of afternoon

COMPARISONS

- *Baptisia tinctoria*—Great weakness with slow onset of low-grade febrile illness (see Chapter 25, Infectious Disease)
- *Bryonia alba*—Influenza with slow onset; patient wants to remain in bed (see Chapter 25)
- *Scutellaria laterifolia*—Postinfluenzal fatigue, anxiety, clouded thinking, and dizziness

KEY SYMPTOMS OF *GELSEMIUM SEMPERVIRENS*

- Generalized weakness with ptosis of the eyelids
- Sensation of a band around the head
- Profuse pale urination
- Apathy
- Low-grade fevers of slow onset
- Visual symptoms

Typical Symptoms

The following are symptoms reported in the nineteenth-century trial or in accidental poisonings (Allen, 1875), annotated with related modern medical diagnoses.

Recorded Symptoms	Modern Diagnoses
Cognition, Emotions, and Affect	
Dullness of all the mental faculties, alleviated by profuse emission of watery urine	Performance anxiety Influenza
Incapacity to think or fix the attention	
General	
Complete relaxation of the whole muscular system with entire motor paralysis	Postinfluenzal fatigue Ataxia Labyrinthitis
Weakness and trembling through the whole system	Febrile illness
Chilliness, especially along the spine	
Head	
Heaviness of the head alleviated by profuse emission of watery urine	Headache
Eyes	
Dizziness of the head and blurred vision returned and gradually increased so that all objects appeared very indistinct	Blurred vision Labyrinthitis Migraine
Dimness of sight and vertigo	
Mouth	
Numbness of the tongue, feels too thick to speak	
Extremities	
Fatigue of the lower limbs after slight exercise	Fatigue and weakness Ataxia
He tried to walk, but staggered as if drunk	

CHAPTER 9

Hepar sulphuris calcareum

Common Name: Calcium Sulfide

OVERVIEW

Hepar sulphuris calcareum should always be considered for illnesses that have a component of pus formation, when accompanied by extreme chilliness and sensitivity of the affected area of the body to cold and touch. These three symptoms are a reliable guide to its prescription. It is one of the main medicines for bacterial tonsillitis, pharyngitis, bronchitis, nongonorrheal prostatitis, abscesses almost anywhere in the body (e.g., skin, rectum, breast, lungs, axilla, liver, and teeth), as well as suppurative infections of the skin, ear, and mucous membranes.

The sinusitis, for which *Hepar sulphuris* is prescribed, has a yellow purulent (and sometimes bloody) discharge from the nose. Pain is felt at the root of the nose or in the bones of the nose. The membranes of the nostrils are sensitive to inspired air.

Hepar sulphuris calcareum is a common medicine for otitis media or otitis externa. Purulent material may be visible in the middle ear or auditory canal, or there may be suppurative otitis media. Cool compresses on the ear will elicit pain, and warming the ear externally will alleviate.

When deciding whether to prescribe *Hepar sulphuris calcareum* for pharyngitis, the clinician should note whether the patient has a sensation as if a fishbone or needle were in the throat, which is a characteristic symptom of this medicine. There is usually exudate at

74

the site of inflammation (e.g., tonsils, pillars, or pharynx). The patient may be observed wincing on swallowing because of the sharp pain. This pain often extends to the ear on swallowing, turning the head, or yawning. In keeping with the general pattern, cold food or drinks aggravate the pain, and warm things alleviate.

This is also a medicine for certain viral illnesses, such as influenza and other viral syndromes, when generalized emotional and physical sensitivity are present. The patient may wear a hat and lie completely under the covers to afford protection from the slightest cool draft.

Hepar sulphuris calcareum is a common cough medicine and is one of the three most commonly prescribed medications for croup. The child sits up in bed and extends the neck with a feeling of suffocation. The cough is usually dry and hoarse and stimulated by exposure of any part of the body to cold air. (There may be rattling in the lungs in bronchitis.) It typically worsens in the morning.

Although the effect of the patient is usually normal, on occasion there may be depression with intense sensitivity. Occasionally, a patient is encountered who has outbursts of anger, which are on rare occasions violent.

Hepar sulphuris must not be forgotten for infected wounds, furuncles, abscesses, and impetigo when pus has formed and the area is extremely tender.

Main food desires: Sour food, vinegar, alcohol, brandy, spicy food, pungent food, and wine
Main food aversions: Strong cheese
Aggravated by: Cold, touch, night, and lying on the painful part
Alleviated by: Heat, moist heat, and damp weather

COMPARISONS

- *Calcarea sulphurica* (calcium sulphate)—Tendency to fistula formation with suppuration, with yellow bloody discharge; not as tender as with *Hepar sulphuris*; wounds that do not heal (see Chapter 17, Injuries and Emergencies)
- *Myristica sebifera*—Paronychia and skin infections (see Chapter 17)

- *Silica*—Paronychia, abscesses, and ulcers (see Chapter 17)
- *Arsenicum album*—Very chilly and irritable; warmth in general alleviates (see to Chapter 17)

KEY SYMPTOMS OF *HEPAR SULPHURIS CALCAREUM*

- Depressed mood and extreme sensitivity
- Chilliness with a striking sensitivity to cold air
- Pus formation
- Abscess
- Fishbone-like pains in the throat

Typical Symptoms

The following are symptoms reported in the nineteenth-century trial or in accidental poisonings (Allen, 1875), annotated with related modern medical diagnoses.

Recorded Symptoms	Modern Diagnoses
Cognition, Emotions, and Affect	
Discontent with himself	Depression
Depressed, sad, apprehensive	
The slightest thing made him break out into the greatest violence	
General	
Perspires easily on every, even slight, motion	
Great desire for vinegar	
Head	
Tensive headache above the nose	Sinus headache
Constant pressive pain in one half of the brain as from a plug or nail	
Blowing of offensive mucus from the nose	
Ear	
Violent stitches in the ear on blowing the nose	Suppurative otitis media and otitis externa
Purulent discharge from the ear	
Cracking in the ears	
Face	
Great swelling of the upper lip	
Pharynx	
Sticking in the throat as from a splinter, on swallowing, and extending toward the ear on yawning, or on turning the head	Pharyngitis Tonsillitis
Pain in the throat on swallowing as from an internal swelling	
Respiratory System	
Paroxysms of cough as from taking cold, with excessive sensitiveness of the nervous system as soon as only the slightest part of the body becomes cold	Croup Bronchitis

continues

continued

Recorded Symptoms	Modern Diagnoses
Genitourinary System	
He is obliged to wait a while before the urine passes, then it flows slowly	Urinary retention (not a major medicine for benign prostatic hypertrophy)
Never able to finish urinating, it seems as though some remains behind in the bladder	
Skin	
Unhealthy suppurating skin, even slight injuries mature and suppurate	Various kinds of suppurative processes (e.g., abscesses, suppurating glands, infected wounds, acne, skin ulcers, paronychia, and impetigo)
Soreness and moisture in the fold between the scrotum and thigh	
Bleeding of an ulcer, especially on wiping	
Great sensitiveness of the skin to touch and to the slightest cold	Herpes simplex
A red itching spot beneath the lower lip, which soon becomes covered with many yellow blisters, which change to a scurf	
Dreams	
Anxious dreams of conflagrations	
Falling from a precipice	
Danger, fright, anxiety	
Flying from danger	
Full of strife	
Expectorating blood and pus	
Hearing shouting	
Broken windows	

CHAPTER 10

Ignatia amara

Scientific Name: *Strychnos ignatia bergius*
Scientific Family Name: Loganiaceae
Common Name: St. Ignatius Bean

OVERVIEW

Ignatia amara is a large, woody climbing shrub, native to the Phillipines, that bears 1-inch-long brownish-black hard beans that have silvery hair. These contain more strychnine and brucine than *Nux vomica*.

This homeopathic medicine is most commonly used in primary care for acute grieving or shock following a death, relationship breakup, parental divorce, forced relocation, job loss, rape, accident, or physical assault. Shock and denial is a normal component of grieving in the early stages, but when a patient seems not to be progressing to acceptance as the weeks and months progress, this medicine will often help. It can also treat somatic symptoms that develop as a result of dysfunctional grieving, especially convulsions, twitching or tics, muscular cramps, jerking on going to sleep, irregular menses, amenorrhea, headaches, anorexia, loss of voice, syncope, numbness, hiccup, and paresthesias.

Those who have not yet accepted the suffering and loss inherent in human life due to youth or a protected environment face disillusionment when the first major loss occurs. *Ignatia amara* is used for this painful conflict brought about by clinging to a romantic or idealistic world view. Like a child whose parents are divorcing, he or she feels,

"This can't really be so" or "This can't possibly be happening to me." The patient believes his or her pain is somehow special and unique, and there is an element of disillusionment with the world or God.

Sometimes real physical pathologies develop such as pharyngitis (alleviated by swallowing), rectal fissures, severely painful hemorrhoids, or rectal prolapse. There are reports of cases where *Ignatia* appeared to actually cure epilepsy and even encephalitis that appeared to arise from grief.

The patient usually presents with excessive sighing or the need to take deep breaths frequently. There is a strong aversion to crying in front of anyone, including the clinician. Tears may come to the eyes during the interview, and then be suppressed. The patient may try to disguise the tears or ascribe them to allergies. Sometimes the patient can cry only when alone, or he or she may note the inability to cry at all since the loss or shock. When weeping starts, it is often uncontrollable, spasmodic, and atypical crying. The patient may alternate laughing and crying when recovering from a trauma. Disproportionate anger may arise when the person is contradicted.

There is usually some kind of tension visible in the neck and throat. The patient may feel a lump in the throat that is alleviated by swallowing solid food, but comes back after swallowing. The patient may bite the inside of his or her cheek.

Ignatia amara may be indicated when there are somewhat strange symptoms that have been described by homeopathic clinicians as contradictory, changeable, paradoxical, or opposite of each other (Morrison, 1993).

Many varieties of head pain were elicited in the clinical trial that mimicked tension, cluster, or migraine headaches. Smoke aggravates the headache and makes the patient indignant.

Perspiration on the face, especially in a small spot, has been clinically noted to be a significant finding. The patient may generally have a diminished appetite, with only the desire for cheese and special little gourmet foods or treats remaining. The patient may demonstrate a desire or aversion to fruit.

The patients who require *Ignatia amara* feel inwardly guilty and self-critical, but are outwardly critical of others, especially clinicians. Often, when the adult patient leaves the office, it is clear that they feel misunderstood and possibly misdiagnosed. The patient may show feelings of indignation toward friends and family, who the patient feels have not "been there" in his or her time of need. These feelings may manifest themselves to the clinician in a gentle way or in a hardened way, depending on the patient.

Main food desires: Fruit and sour food

Main food aversions: Fruit, smoking, tobacco, meat, milk, warm food, and wine

Aggravated by: Coffee, smoke and other odors, morning, postmealtime, open or cold air, touch, yawning, stooping, walking, and standing

Alleviated by: Eating (especially sour foods), changing position, being near a heater, lying (or other pressure) on the affected body part, urinating, being alone, deep breathing, and swallowing

COMPARISONS

- *Aconitum napellus*—Effects of fright and shock (see Chapter 22, Emotional Health and Chemical Dependency Recovery)
- *Moschus*—Globus hystericus, "hysterical" fainting, convulsions, spasms, and desire for cheese
- *Natrum muriaticum*—Grief with aversion to consolation; no crying (see Chapter 22)
- *Staphysagria*—Effects of assault and rape (see Chapter 22)

KEY SYMPTOMS OF *IGNATIA AMARA*

- Sighing
- Functional disorders from grief or shock
- Globus hystericus
- Situational depression
- Aversion to smoke, which aggravates the condition
- Contradictory symptoms

Typical Symptoms

The following are symptoms reported in the nineteenth-century trial or in accidental poisonings (Allen, 1875), annotated with related modern medical diagnoses.

Recorded Symptoms	Modern Diagnoses
Cognition, Emotions, and Affect	
If she is refused even gently what she wishes, or if others wish something different from what she wishes, then she cries aloud	Acute grief Posttraumatic stress Situational depression
Finely sensitive mood, delicate conscientiousness	
Slight blame or contradiction excites him to anger, and this makes him angry with himself	
Involuntary weeping for 3 days	
Quiet earnest melancholy; cannot be induced to talk or be cheerful; with flat, watery taste to all food, and little appetite	
Inconstant, impatient	
Irresolute	
Incredible changes of mood (e.g., joking merriness alternating with weeping every 3–4 hours)	
Inappropriate feelings of guilt	Posttraumatic fear
Fear of thieves, on waking after midnight	
Unusual tendency to be frightened	
Dread of every trifle, especially of things coming near him	
General	
Aversion to tobacco smoking	Hypersensitivity to tobacco smoke
Mouth and Pharynx	
He easily bites the inside of the cheek near the orifice of the salivary duct while chewing	Globus hystericus Pharyngitis Dysphagia
Retching (constrictive) sensation in the middle of the throat as if there were a long morsel of food or a plug sticking there; felt more not swallowing than when swallowing	

continues

continued

Recorded Symptoms	Modern Diagnoses
Sticking low in the throat disappears on continuing to swallow and returns when not swallowing	
If he swallows anything solid, like bread, it seems as though the sticking entirely disappears	

Gastrointestinal System

| Hiccough after eating and drinking, or from smoking tobacco in one accustomed to smoking | Persistent hiccup |
| A peculiar sensation of weakness in the region of the upper abdomen and pit of stomach | |

Rectum

Prolapse of the rectum	Hemorrhoids
Pain in the rectum as from blind piles	Rectal prolapse
Sharp pressive pain in the rectum	
Pain in the anus without reference to the stool	

Respiratory System

| Uninterrupted provocation to a hacking cough in the larynx . . . in the evening after lying down; it does not disappear on coughing, but only on suppressing the cough | Cough from suppressed emotions |
| Cough . . . more excited, the more he allows himself to cough | |

Extremities

Single jerkings of the limbs on falling asleep

Shaking chill with redness of the face

Sleep

Stamps with the feet in sleep

Dreams

Full of mental exertions and scientific investigations

Reflection and deliberation

Frightful things

Disappointments, miscellaneous plans and efforts

He had fallen into the water and cried

Buried alive for a month or more

CHAPTER 11

Mercurius vivus or Mercurius solubilis

Scientific Name: Elemental Mercury or *Dimercurous Ammonium Nitrate*
Common Name: Quicksilver (Elemental Mercury)

OVERVIEW

There were two thorough trials of mercury in the nineteenth century (Allen, 1875), one of elemental mercury (*Mercurius vivus*) and one of a mercury made soluble through a process invented by Samuel Hahnemann, the founder of homeopathy, using nitric acid and ammonia (*Mercurius solubilis*). The experiments produced such similar symptoms in subjects that the substances are used interchangeably in clinical practice.

At the time of homeopathy's origin, the toxic symptoms of mercury poisoning were well-known. It was widely used in medical treatment of the time. Therefore, the toxic symptoms were well-known and indexed alongside the functional symptoms that emerged in the trial.

Because *Mercurius* causes so much symptomatology and pathology of the ear, nose, throat, and mouth, it is an absolutely irreplaceable medicine in primary care. As the clinical trials below demonstrate, it is a major medicine for otitis media, upper respiratory infection, pharyngitis, dental and gum disease, and sinusitis. If the person is generally ill, in addition to the local symptoms, it can be distinguished from other medicines for these conditions based on the following general symptoms.

The person who is ill enough to demonstrate generalized symptoms will have excessive and foul salivation and perspiration, as well as

84

perhaps be trembling and weak. The clammy perspiration is noticeable on examination. There is usually a metallic taste in the mouth, a coating on the tongue, and indentations of the teeth on the tongue no matter where the local symptomatology manifests. There will be adenopathy and increased thirst. The most characteristic symptom of *Mercurius* is a distinctive sensitivity to slight variations in ambient heat *and* cold, with an inability to become comfortable with the temperature. The patient repeatedly adjusts the covers of the bed to try to find comfort. All symptoms are typically aggravated at night. There may be a desire to eat buttered bread.

For otitis media, *Mercurius* is usually used when the patient presents with the tympanic membrane already suppurated and a green, yellow, yellow-green, bloody, and/or foul-smelling otorrhea. The otitis media can be on either side.

Mercurius is the most common medicine for pharyngitis and tonsillitis, usually accompanied with adenopathy. There is a metallic taste in the mouth and salivation with drooling during sleep. It is one of the homeopathic medicines used to treat mononucleosis.

Upper respiratory infection with much sneezing, watery discharge, a distinct metallic taste in mouth, increased salivation, thirst, and sensitivity to heat and cold responds to *Mercurius*. This can progress to sinusitis with an acrid, purulent nasal discharge; the prescription is based once again on the general symptoms of *Mercurius*.

Mercury is present in the metal amalgams used to fill cavities. Interestingly, it is also a major medicine (in a homeopathic potency) for disease of the teeth and gums. When *Mercurius* is indicated, gums recede and bleed easily. Teeth are loose and feel tender and elongated to the patient. There is tooth decay and dental abscess with the pain aggravated at night. There is increased foul-smelling salivation, which has a sweetish metallic or burnt taste. Tongue feels heavy and thickened, and may have a yellow coating and a longitudinal furrow on its superior surface. Teeth leave indentations on tongue.

In men's health, *Mercurius* was historically one of the homeopathic treatments for gonorrhea. Now, it is most often used for itchy inflammatory conditions of the male genitalia, accompanied by swelling and involvement of the lymphatic vessels of the penis, with inguinal adenopathy. *Mercurius* can treat genital herpes in both men and women.

Mercurius is a medicine used for painful diarrhea with tenesmus and chills, which are aggravated at night. The stool is slimy, bloody, and/or green.

The affect and emotional state of the patient, requiring *Mercurius* at a sick visit is usually unremarkable. The speech symptoms that came out in the medicine trials (e.g., delayed answering, stammering, and hurried speech) are rarely observed.

Main food desires: Bread and butter, cold drinks, beer, lemons, liquid food, and milk

Main food aversions: Brandy, butter, strong cheese, coffee, high-fat food, salty foods, sweets, and wine

Aggravated by: At night, too cold or too warm, lying on right side, and perspiring

Alleviated by: Nothing

COMPARISONS

- *Hepar sulphuris calcareum*—Purulent and suppurative conditions (see Chapter 18, Skin)
- *Ailanthus glandulosus*—Severe tonsillitis with a foul smelling exudate, accompanied with cervical adenitis (see Chapter 20, Ear, Nose, and Throat)
- *Mercurius iodatus flavus*—Pharyngitis and tonsillitis with symptoms that resemble *Mercurius*, but on the right side only (see Chapter 20)
- *Mercurius iodatus ruber*—Pharyngitis and tonsillitis with symptoms that resemble *Mercurius*, but on the left side only (see Chapter 20)

KEY SYMPTOMS OF *MERCURIUS*

- Sensitivity to both heat and cold
- Foul odor of perspiration and all secretions
- Excessive salivation and perspiration
- Metallic taste in mouth and a coated, indented tongue
- Symptoms aggravated at night
- Adenitis

Typical Symptoms

The following are symptoms reported in the nineteenth-century trial or in accidental poisonings (Allen, 1875), annotated with related modern medical diagnoses.

Recorded Symptoms	Modern Diagnoses
Cognition, Emotions, and Affect	
Slow in answering questions	
Memory weak	
Hurried and rapid talking	
Stammering	
General	
Desire for bread and butter	Influenza
Extreme, violent thirst	Cytomegalovirus
Trembling	Mononucleosis
Weak	
Bone pains	
Weary	
Appearance	
Pale, earthy colored, and puffy (face)	
Ears	
Difficult hearing	Suppurative otitis media
Roaring in the ears	
Matter flows from both ears	
Bloody and offensive matter flows from the right ear with tearing pain	
Yellow matter discharge from left ear	
Sticking and burning pain deep in both ears, worse in left	
Eyes	
A fog before one or both eyes	Photophobia
Cannot tolerate firelight or daylight; firelight blinds the eyes in the evening	
Nose	
Constant nasal catarrh	Sinusitis
Offensive odor from nose	Upper respiratory infection
The odor of old cheese	
Acrid matter flow from the nose as in violent coryza	
Nasal bone painful when taken hold of	

continues

continued

Recorded Symptoms	Modern Diagnoses
Mouth	
Bluish mucous membrane	Stomatitis
Ulcer spreads rapidly in extent, without penetrating into the flesh, and is very painful	Gingivitis
	Periodontal disease
	Dental caries
Bad odor from mouth	Dental abscess
Disagreeable sweetish taste	Halitosis
Violent stomatitis and salivation	
Speech difficult on account of trembling of the mouth and tongue	
Teeth	
Black, loose carious teeth	
Decay of teeth; they become loose in succession	
Teeth became denuded of the gum and turn black with nightly pains in the teeth, jaws, head	
Violent toothache with swelling of the gum and salivary glands	
Looseness of the teeth	
Gums	
Red and bleeding at the slightest contact, sometimes spontaneously	
Small ulcers at intervals	
Bright red margins	
Spongy and bleeding	
Tongue	
Red, swollen	
Coated tongue, showing impress of the teeth upon the margin	
Swollen and its movements difficult	
Pharynx	
Constantly dry; it hurts as if too tight posteriorly; a pressure in it as he swallowed, yet he was constantly obliged to swallow because mouth was always full of water	Pharyngitis
	Hyperptyalism
	Tonsillitis
	Mononucleosis
Suppuration of tonsils, with sharp or sticking pain in fauces when swallowing	
Lymphatic System	
Submaxillary, cervical, and sublingual glands enlarged and indurated	Adenitis
Axillary glands swollen	

continues

continued

Recorded Symptoms	Modern Diagnoses
Gastrointestinal System	
Diarrhea with bloody stools, green diarrhea, green mucus	Gastroenteritis
	Exacerbation of ulcerative colitis
Ineffectual urging to stool every moment, with tenesmus in the rectum	
Exhausted after the stool	
Genitourinary System	
Constant desire for urination, every 10 minutes, but only a little passed	Urinary tract infection (uncommon)
	Urethritis
Burning in urethra	
Female Reproductive Tract	
Green leukorrhea; she is obliged to scratch, especially evenings and night with violent burning after scratching	Bacterial vaginosis
Extremities	
Trembling of the hands and feet so that patient was unable to write	
Perspiration	
Profuse, offensive	
Sleep	
As soon as he went to bed in the evening, the pains recommenced and banished sleep	
Dreams	
Frightful	

CHAPTER 12

Nux vomica

Scientific Name: *Strychnos nux vomica*
Scientific Family Name: Loganiaceae
Common Names: Poison Nut, Quaker Bations

OVERVIEW

Nux vomica is prepared from the apple-sized hard shell fruit of a South Asian tree, which, like *Ignatia*, contains the toxic alkaloids strychnine and brucine. It was historically used in physiological doses for surgical shock and cardiac failure, as well as paralysis of the peripheral motor nerves.

The emotional state found in conditions that respond to *Nux vomica* is very distinct. The patient is markedly impatient, irritable, and critical of others. The patient feels especially critical of people not doing work quickly and efficiently, or those who leave items in the wrong place. There is also a tremendous hypersensitivity to odors, noise, and light. People around the patient feel like they are "walking on eggshells" in order to not upset him or her. The patient feels wretched in the early morning. This state is familiar to many because it resembles a hangover from alcohol intoxication, coffee or nicotine withdrawal, and is one of the most common medicines for these periods of detoxification. These symptoms can also be commonly found in people with acute allergies, headaches, upper respiratory infections, and many digestive problems. In addition to these conditions, illnesses that respond to this medicine may arise from too much studying and other sedentary stressful work.

Nux vomica is reported by some clinicians to be the most common homeopathic medicine for tension headache and occasionally migraine. People who have an irritable sensitivity to light, odors, and noise during headache are treated with *Nux vomica*. They isolate themselves in a quiet, darkened bedroom, like those who require the homeopathic medicine *Bryonia alba*.

The allergy and upper respiratory infection symptoms are alike: a watery, fluent discharge follows much violent sneezing, especially during the day and in the open air. Discharge stops at night. In allergies, there is a crawling sensation in the nose. Occasionally, *Nux vomica* is a medicine for asthma that is aggravated by cold, hay fever, excitement, fear, anxiety, flatulence, and other digestive upsets.

Nux vomica is one of the main medicines for many diseases of the gastrointestinal tract, including, but not limited to, flatulence, colic, peptic ulcer, constipation, diarrhea, nausea of pregnancy, and general indigestion. The patient craves spicy food, beer, high-fat foods, and stimulants. Frustrated effort is the general theme of the medicine. There is nausea with an inability to vomit even though the patient feels the need to, and may retch violently. There is constipation with straining. Food feels like it lies heavily in the stomach and cannot pass. Stomach pains extend to the back and chest. Hemorrhoids or rectal fissures may be present (from straining or sedentary work) with itching and bleeding that is alleviated by cool bathing. *Nux vomica* is indicated for infantile hernia from constipation or crying in babies annoyed by draft when the diaper is changed.

Spasmodic urethral stricture causes patients to strain to urinate. *Nux vomica* is indicated for the patient with cystitis or kidney stones when the general symptoms listed above are present.

The patient may have insomnia with hypersensitivity to noise, odors, and light during sleep. In addition, the patient may be sleepless from thoughts, especially related to work, success/failure, thwarted plans, and ambitions. He or she may wake very early (3:00 to 4:00 a.m.) and not be able to get back to sleep.

Cervicobrachial neuralgia may be present with stiff neck and pain radiating to the right shoulder, which is aggravated by touch. The patient may suffer from aching lumbar pain that has a distinctive characteristic; the patient must sit up in order to turn in bed. The patient may have a lame feeling in the sacral region, especially after parturition.

Main food desires: Alcohol, beer, brandy, coffee, fat, spicy food, lime, and milk

Main food aversions: Ale, beer, bread, coffee, meat, tobacco, and water

Aggravated by: Tobacco, drugs, alcohol, coffee, spices, overeating, studying too much, being sedentary, anger, noise (including music), odors, touch, drafts, and both the pressure of wearing clothes and uncovering

Alleviated by: Napping or simply resting, wrapping the head up, hot drinks, milk, fats, humidity, and lying on either side

COMPARISONS

- *Arsenicum album*—Irritable, fastidious, thirsty, and chilly
- *Bryonia alba*—Irritable, thirsty, wants to lie down in dark quiet room during headache or influenza (see Chapter 25, Infectious Disease, and Chapter 26, Brain and Nervous System)
- *Ignatia amara*—Sensitive to cigarette smoke, rectal pathology, and indignation (see Chapter 23, Gastrointestinal System)
- *Sepia*—Irritable, alleviated by engaging in his or her occupation, constipated, and sensitive to noise, and dysmenorrhea (see Chapter 23 and Chapter 27, Gynecology and Primary Care for Pregnancy and Childbirth)

KEY SYMPTOMS OF *NUX VOMICA*

- Impatient and irritable
- Sensitive to noise, odors, light, and touch
- Frustrated straining
- Chilliness
- Illnesses from stress, sedentary work, and use of stimulants or intoxicants
- Wakes at 3:00–4:00 a.m.; cannot get back to sleep.

Typical Symptoms

The following are symptoms reported in the nineteenth-century trial or in accidental poisonings (Allen, 1875), annotated with related modern medical diagnoses.

Recorded Symptoms	Modern Diagnoses
Cognition, Emotions, and Affect	
Quarrelsome, even to violence	Hangover
Oversensitive to impression upon the senses; he cannot tolerate strong odors or bright light	Cigarette and caffeine withdrawal
	Irritability and anger
He cannot tolerate a noise; talking, music, and singing affect him	
Ill-humored and very hypochondriac, and affected by the slightest thing, after eating	
Dread of the kind of literary work at which one must think and employ the ideas, whether to be elaborated by writing or delivered orally in the morning	
Intoxicated dizzy heaviness in the morning	
General	
Aversion to the usual food and drink and their customary tobacco and coffee	
Violent contractive painful sensation	
Coldness of whole body	
Head	
Headache . . . on waking in the morning	Tension headache
• worse after eating	
• with nausea and very sour vomiting	
• heaviness and pressure, after dinner, especially on moving the eyes	
• morning in bed as if . . . beaten with an ax	
• morning as if he had not slept at night	
• tensive headache in the forehead	
Eyes	
Intolerant of daylight in the morning	Photophobia
Nose	
Profuse discharge of mucus from one nostril that seems obstructed by a dry fluent coryza	Allergic rhinitis
	Upper respiratory infection
	Sinus headache
• in morning	

continues

continued

Recorded Symptoms	Modern Diagnoses
• fluent by day, stopped at night	
• coryza in morning and after dinner	
• coryza and scraping in the throat, crawling and creeping in the nose, and sneezing	
Catarrh (sinus congestion) with headache, heat in face, and chilliness	
Frequent sneezing	
Sneezing in the morning in bed, but after rising, fluent coryza	
Mouth and Pharynx	
Bad taste in the mouth in morning though food and drink have a natural taste	Postnasal drip
Throat rough from catarrh	
Gastrointestinal System	
Eructations of bitter and sour liquid	Flatulence
Nausea after dinner	Nausea
Smoking makes him nauseated	Vomiting
After a meal, he is . . . anxious, nauseated and sick as after a violent purge	Threatening hernia
	Indigestion
Vomiting of sour smelling and sour tasting mucus	
Retching . . . while hawking mucus from the pharynx	
Pressure as from a stone in the upper abdomen or stomach	
Flatulent distension of the abdomen after eating	
Pain in the abdominal ring, in the morning, in bed as if hernia would be incarcerated	
Rectum	
Sharp pressive pain in the rectum after a stool and after a meal, especially on exerting the mind or studying	Hemorrhoids
	Rectal fissures
	Constipation
Tearing, sticking, and constricting pain as from aggravated [hemorrhoids]	
After a stool, it seemed as if some remained behind and could not be evacuated with a sensation of constriction in the rectum	
Discharge of bright red blood with the feces . . . anxious desire for stool	
Ineffectual desire for stool	

continues

continued

Recorded Symptoms	Modern Diagnoses
Respiratory System	
Roughness or scraping in the larynx that provokes cough	Cough from postnasal drip or upper respiratory infection
Violent cough before rising in the morning	
Dry cough midnight to daybreak	
Genitourinary System	
Frequent desire to urinate	Urinary retention
Painful ineffective desire to urinate	Urinary tract infection
Violent straining . . . efforts to urinate constant and most painful without being able to pass a single drop	
Female Reproductive Tract	
During menses, nausea in the morning with chilliness and attacks of faintness	Dysmenorrhea
Back	
Pain in the small of back as if beaten and bruised	Lumbar pain
Dreams	
Frightful	
Very much engaged in absorbing occupations	
All teeth fell from mouth or are falling out	
Fillings falling out	
Sick or mutilated people	
Wild beasts	
Lice and vermin	

CHAPTER 13

Phosphorus

Scientific Name: Elemental Phosphorus

OVERVIEW

The clinical trials of *Phosphorus* produced such a rich array of symptoms that it is difficult to pick out a few that show the characteristics of the medicine. The most common uses for *Phosphorus* in integrative practice are for respiratory illnesses, such as coughs and bronchitis, as well as digestive illnesses that include nausea and vomiting. But this medicine should not be forgotten in any ailment when the characteristic mental/emotional state and general physical symptomatology of the person are present.

While the depressive symptoms predominated in the clinical trials, the affect that accompanies an illness that responds to *Phosphorus* is more commonly an anxious one. The anxiety is accompanied with restlessness and is easily calmed by the clinician's reassurances. A cardinal symptom is poor concentration. Americans usually use the term "spacy" to describe this state. The patient startles easily from unexpected noises, such as the telephone or thunder. The patient wants to be in the company of others when he or she is sick. Patients are hypersensitive to all sensory input, including odors, light, vibrations, touch, changes in barometric pressure and weather, as well as the emotional atmosphere.

Physically, they can be sensitive to cold when ill. An increased thirst, preferably for ice-cold drinks, is an important symptom, although sometimes the thirst will vanish during the fever. There may be a craving for dark chocolate, cold foods like chocolate ice cream and salads, and salty food when ill. The patient cannot comfortably lie on the left side.

Viral illnesses of almost all kinds have been treated with *Phosphorus*, including influenza, gastroenteritis, mononucleosis, cytomegalovirus, and hepatitis. The patient's temperature can be moderately elevated or high. The febrile patient has a circumscribed redness of one (usually the left) or both cheeks. *Phosphorus* is the most common medicine prescribed when the person looks and acts well despite a high temperature. Vomiting or vertigo accompany many illnesses treated with *Phosphorus*.

Phosphorus and *Ipecacuanha* are the two main medicines indicated for nausea and vomiting when there are no other symptoms. *Phosphorus* should be used when the patient is very thirsty for cold drinks during the nausea, and ice water may actually initially alleviate the nausea. Then, when presumably the water has become warm in the stomach, everything is vomited.

The lung ailments that benefit *Phosphorus* often begin with an upper respiratory infection, then descend. Bronchitis with any kind of cough or expectoration will respond to *Phosphorus* if the general symptoms of the patient fit. While the integrative clinician who is beginning to use homeopathic medicines may not feel comfortable using it for this purpose, *Phosphorus* is a major medicine for pneumonia. The symptoms mimicking left lower-lobe pneumonia clearly emerged in the proving, and yet, clinically, it is equally useful for right-sided pneumonia when the general symptoms match.

Historically, *Phosphorus* was one of the main medicines used for tuberculosis with hemoptysis. In India, there are still hospitals that use homeopathy to treat tuberculosis. The combined hemorrhagic and lung symptoms guided homeopaths to this clinical use, as did public health reports about workers in nineteenth-century match factories, where toxic exposure to phosphorus was common. A high percentage of workers in any given match factory would typically develop tuberculosis, often preceded by typhus, bronchitis, and pneumonia. The prevalence of these diseases was disproportionate to other low-income factory workers of the era. *Phosphorus* has also been used to treat malignancy, especially brain tumors, skin cancers, leukemias, and lymphomas.

Phosphorus is a common medicine for bright red bleeds of the uterus, rectum, eye, nose, and bladder when the general symptoms of the person correspond to those described above. *Phosphorus* is also still used to treat hepatitis and alcoholic cirrhosis. Also, among homeopathic specialists, it is used in the treatment of multiple sclerosis, diabetes, and hypoglycemia.

Main food desires: Cold drinks, cold food, spicy food, ice cream, salty food, wine, alcohol, brandy, carbonated drinks, cheese, chicken, chocolate, cold milk, cucumbers, milk, refreshing things, dry rice, sour food, sweets, and whisky

Main food aversions: Fruit, warm drinks, warm food, beer, bread, butter, coffee, fish, flour, garlic, meat, milk, onions, oysters, pudding, sweets, tea, tobacco, tomatoes, and vegetables

Aggravated by: Sudden changes in weather, windy or cold weather, thunderstorms, lightning, lying on the painful side, lying on the left side, lying on the back, talking, touch, odors, light, cold, open air, hypovolemia, and ascending stairs

Alleviated by: Cold food, water, washing face with cold water, sleeping, eating, rubbing, sitting, and darkness

COMPARISONS

- *Arsenicum album* and *Phosphoricum acidum*—Influenza with increased thirst and exhaustion (see Chapter 25, Infectious Disease)
- *Ferrum phosphoricum* and *Aconitum napellus*—Fever with increased thirst (see Chapter 25)
- *Ferrum phosphoricum, Ipecacuanha, Cinnamomum, Millefolium,* and *Aconitum napellus*—Hemorrhage of bright red blood (see Chapter 17, Injuries and Emergencies)
- *Arsenicum album*—Bronchitis, increased thirst, restlessness, and anxiety (see Chapter 21, Lower Respiratory System)

KEY SYMPTOMS OF *PHOSPHORUS*

- Poor concentration ("spacy") with anxious restlessness, responds to reassurance
- Hemorrhages, usually of bright red blood from any orifice
- Fevers with vomiting
- Increased thirst for ice-cold drinks
- Cough

Typical Symptoms

The following are symptoms reported in the nineteenth-century trial or in accidental poisonings (Allen, 1875), annotated with related modern medical diagnoses.

Recorded Symptoms	Modern Diagnoses
Cognition, Emotions, and Affect	
Apathetic; he answers very slowly, moves very sluggishly	Anxiety
	Poor concentration
Very much depressed in spirits, with disinclination to work, without cause	Apathetic when depressed
Anxious oppression	
Disinclination to study	
Inability to think	
Could not study or keep his mind on any particular subject long at a time	
Slow flow of ideas, absence of mind	
General	
Emaciation	Bacterial or viral infection (e.g., influenza)
He lay only on the right side at night	
Lying on the left side at night causes anxiety	Blood coagulation disorders
Mucous membranes pale	Hemorrhage with anemia
	Fatigue states
The blood of the hemorrhages was very fluid and difficult to coagulate	Hypovolemia and electrolyte imbalances secondary to hemorrhage, or vomiting and diarrhea
Small wounds bleed very much	
Excessive thirst	Diabetes
Lax muscular system	
Great weariness	
Weakness	
Flushed cheeks, the left one much more than the right	
Chilliness, every evening with shivering, without thirst	
Coldness in the knees constantly at night in bed	
Heat at night without thirst, and sweat from which he frequently woke	
Febrile heat and sweat at night with ravenous hunger that could not be appeased, followed by chilliness with chattering of teeth and external coldness; after the chill internal heat, especially in the hands with constant external coldness	

continues

continued

Recorded Symptoms	Modern Diagnoses
Head	
Heavy pressing downward of the forepart of the head	Headache
Ears	
Vertigo; he was obliged to lie down for several days because as soon as he made any effort to rise, the vertigo returned	Labyrinthitis Hearing impairment Ménière's disease
Hearing difficult	
Eyes	
A green halo about the candlelight in the evening	Intraocular hemorrhage with floaters
Black floating points before the eyes	
Nose	
Swelling of the nose, which is painful to touch	Epistaxis
Epistaxis	
• Slow bleeding of the nose	
• Frequent blowing of blood from the nose	
• Frequent and profuse nosebleed	
• Nose swollen and dry, cannot draw air through it	
Larynx and Trachea	
Rawness with frequent hacking cough and hawking	Laryngitis Cough
Rough, husky, hoarse voice	
Voice nearly lost	
Abdomen	
Liver enlarged	Hepatitis
Spleen enlarged	Flatulence
Abdomen distended, tympanic	Mononucleosis
Incarceration of flatus beneath the ribs with oppression of the chest	
Very loud rumbling in the abdomen	
Emptiness and a feeling of weakness in the abdomen	
Gastrointestinal System	
Ulcers bleed on the appearance of the menses	Gastritis Nausea and vomiting
Nausea that disappears on drinking water	Hyperemesis gravidarum Gastric or duodenal ulcer

continues

continued

Recorded Symptoms	Modern Diagnoses
Frequent nausea and vomiting of everything that he ate	Hepatitis
Hematemesis	Gastroenteritis
Burning in the stomach	
Violent pain in the stomach, gradually spreading over the whole abdomen, with vomiting	
Sensitiveness to pressure over the pylorus	
Epigastric region became exceedingly painful to pressure, with enlargement of the liver	
Pressure as from a hard substance, above the pit of the stomach	
Diarrhea	
Involuntary stool the moment anything entered the rectum	
Whitish gray stool	
Watery stools mixed with whitish yellow and cheesy matter	

Genitourinary System

Turbid and high colored	Urinary sediment
Urine deposits a white sandy sediment	
Urine brown with a red sandy sediment	

Female Reproductive Tract

Hemorrhages	Irregular menses
Unusual irritability of the genital organs	Increased libido
Menses early	Uterine hemorrhage
	Uterine myoma

Male Reproductive Tract

Frequent, painful erection	Increased libido
Extreme irresistible desire for coition	Erectile dysfunction
Ineffectual erections during coition	

Heart and Lungs

Suffocative pressure on the upper part of the chest	Bronchitis
Spasmodic cough with oppression of the chest and some expectoration of mucus	Croup
	Pneumonia
	Asthma
	Cough
Violent dry cough on reading aloud	Heart palpitations from anxiety
Frequent dry cough with scanty expectoration	Hepatization of lungs

continues

continued

Recorded Symptoms	Modern Diagnoses
Percussion showed slight dullness on the right lower portion posteriorly, with diminished respiratory murmurs and fine vesicular rales . . . accompanied by expectoration of tenacious purulent mucus	
Cough in the morning after rising with expectoration of transparent mucus	
Cough caused tickling in the throat	
Bloody expectoration with mucus	
Short respiration	
Respiration anxious, panting, oppressed, very labored	
Great dyspnea	
Great oppression of the chest so that the patient, during the attack of cough and in order to expectorate, must sit up in bed when she experiences great pain, with a constrictive sensation under the sternum	
Distressing anxiety and pressure in the chest amounting to real suffocation so that deep inspiration was difficult, but not impossible	
Heaviness of the chest as if a weight were lying upon it	
Anxiety about the heart, associated with nausea and a peculiar sensation of hunger, somewhat relieved by eating, distressing her even in bed	
Violent palpitation	
Back	
The spinous processes of the dorsal vertebrae between the scapulae became exceedingly sensitive to pressure; also the muscles between the spinous processes and the left scapula were sensitive, much worse on the left side	Thoracic muscle spasm, sprain/strain, and subluxation
Burning pain between the scapulae	
Extremities	
There was a sensation of numbness in the hands	Thoracic outlet syndrome Neuropathy
Falling asleep of the hands in the morning on waking	
My fingers were all thumbs	

continues

continued

Recorded Symptoms	Modern Diagnoses
Perspiration	
Profuse perspiration over the whole body on the slightest exertion	
Perspiration and a feeling of anxiety toward morning	
Sleep	
Constant sleepiness	Insomnia
Very restless nights, constant dreaming	
He cannot fall asleep before midnight	
Dreams	
Vermin	
Biting animal	
• ferocious black horse	
• insect stinging behind the ear	
Vivid	
Scientific	
Philosophical	
Historical	
Fighting	
Violent physical exertion	
Restless work and business	
Robbers	
Dead people	
Lascivious with emissions	
Hemorrhage	
Fire	
Pinched on the back and breast and tickled on the soles	

CHAPTER 14

Pulsatilla

Scientific Name: *Anenome pulsatilla*
Scientific Family Name: Ranunculaceae
Common Names: Wind Flower and Pasque Flower

OVERVIEW

Pulsatilla is a small dull violet-purple flower native to the nonwooded areas of Europe, especially in calcium-rich soils. The whole plant is covered with silky hairs. It is used in herbal medicine for asthma, bronchitis, conjunctivitis, diarrhea, headaches, and neuralgia. At one time, it was in the United States Pharmacopoia.

Pulsatilla is without question one of the top five most commonly used medicines in homeopathic primary care. This medicine is useful in virtually all children's illnesses and is also a major medicine for women's health care, especially around the perinatal time.

During an illness that will respond to treatment with *Pulsatilla*, the patient's affect often changes. There is easy weeping, a clingy quality, and a strong desire for company and consolation. In children, the clinician will often have to choose between *Pulsatilla* and *Chamomilla*. Children needing either of these medicines may stay in the parents' arms during an office visit and will probably be crying. But the resemblance between them ends there. *Pulsatilla* fits the child who behaves as softly and sweetly as possible, given his or her discomfort. They may have times of anger, but the mood is highly changeable so that the anger gives way to weeping or good cheer. These patients respond to sympathy and loving attention not only with improved mood, but the symptoms of the illness may actually improve. *Chamomilla* fits the patients who are unrelentingly miserable and give the impression that they would like everyone around them to share in that state. The angry crying is alleviated only while they are being carried.

The *Pulsatilla* patient feels better in general in the open air (e.g., with the windows open or outside). The clinician may be told by the parents that the child is much better since they left the house on the way to the office visit. There may be a general aggravation in the evening or at twilight. Since thirstlessness is an uncommon characteristic in a sick person, it is an important guide to the prescription of *Pulsatilla* as it is for *Belladonna* and *Gelsemium sempervirens*. The patient may have an aversion to meat fat and pork, which may also aggravate symptoms. The patient may desire cheese, peanut butter, creamy desserts, and whipped cream. There may be a desire or aversion to butter.

The clinician should consider prescribing *Pulsatilla* when the patient adopts a particular posture when he or she is asleep; on his or her back with the hands over the head.

This medicine was used for the treatment of many infectious diseases of childhood. Since most of these diseases have been virtually eliminated through immunization, its use for this purpose has declined. Since many parents still decline the varicella vaccination, clinicians still use *Pulsatilla* to treat varicella.

The nasal discharge indicating *Pulsatilla* is thick, copious, and usually green, yellow, or changeable in color. Unlike many nasal discharges, this one does not irritate the area under the nose. *Pulsatilla* is a common medicine for the treatment of established upper respiratory infection, allergic rhinitis, or after either of these ailments has progressed to sinusitis.

Discharges from any orifice having this characteristic thick, bland quality can be treated by *Pulsatilla*. Expectoration in bronchitis, nasal discharge, vaginal discharge, and even (historically) gonorrhea, usually have the same thick, bland quality. If the patient has no general or affective symptoms accompanying the illness, the medicine can be prescribed based only on this symptom (compare *Kali bichromicum* in Chapter 20, Ear, Nose, and Throat). On the other hand, if the discharge is clear or acrid, and the general symptoms of the patient fit *Pulsatilla*, the medicine will still be effective.

The medicine is one of the top four medicines for otitis media, especially, but not exclusively, of the left ear, often occurring at the end of an upper respiratory infection.

The main use of *Pulsatilla* in nonpregnant patients for gastrointestinal illnesses is for fat intolerance. Dyspepsia or vomiting may follow long after a meal of fatty foods, ice cream, or pork.

During pregnancy, *Pulsatilla* is used for nausea and vomiting, inflamed varicosities, pyrosis, constipation, and delayed labor. It should be noted that the naturally increased thirst of pregnancy does not contraindicate a prescription of *Pulsatilla*. During labor, the woman seems exceptionally dependent on her partner or loved ones. The woman may state "I can't do it" and cease to work at labor; then effort resumes when she is told that she can do it. Midwives have noted that women who respond to this medicine in labor tend to invite many people to the birth for support. It has been prescribed for fetal malposition, with claims made that its use can turn the fetus to correct positioning. Homeopathic specialists who treat chronic health imbalances use *Pulsatilla* to treat menstrual dysfunction, including amenorrhea, irregular menstruation, metrorrhagia, and dysmenorrhea. Occasionally, *Pulsatilla* is useful in cystitis, when the general symptoms fit, and for vaginitis with a creamy discharge.

The most common medicine for joint pain and stiffness that are alleviated by motion are *Pulsatilla* and *Rhus toxicodendron*. But unlike with *Rhus toxicodendron*, joint problems where *Pulsatilla* is indicated are aggravated by warm compresses and baths. There are often wandering pains in the body (e.g., arthritis pains that flare in one joint, then recede in that joint and flare in another joint). The patient gets hot in bed at night and uncovers the feet.

In men's health, there can be orchitis or epididymitis usually on the left side, after antibiotic treatment for gonorrhea or historically from mumps. Because adult men require *Pulsatilla* prescription less commonly than women and children, it is sometimes overlooked.

Main food desires: Cold food, alcohol, beer, eggs, herring, ice cream, refreshing things, sour foods, sweets, tea, and tonics

Main food aversions: Butter, eggs, fruit, meat, warm drinks, warm food, bread, drinks, milk, oil, pork, smoking, tobacco, and water

Aggravated by: Closed, warm rooms; bedrest; clothes; getting feet wet; onset of evening; rest; beginning motion; high-fat foods; ice cream; eggs; letting the extremities hang; and sun

Alleviated by: Uncovering; gentle motion; erect posture; continued motion; lying with head high; pressure; massage; and cool, fresh, open air.

COMPARISONS

- *Kali bichromicum* and *Mercurius vivus*—Thick green or yellow discharges
- *Kali sulphuricum*—Yellow nasal discharge that is aggravated when overheated (see Chapter 20, Ear, Nose, and Throat)
- *Phosphorus*—Symptoms that are alleviated by consolation and dependence
- *Sulphur*—Warmth that is alleviated by cold; puts feet out of covers
- *Argentum nitricum*—Indigestion, warmth that is alleviated by cold, desires for ice cream, and aversion to pork (see Chapter 23, Gastrointestinal System)

KEY SYMPTOMS OF *PULSATILLA*

- Soft, gentle weeping or changeable demeanor
- Symptoms alleviated by consolation
- Symptoms alleviated by the open air
- Thick, nonacrid, yellow, green, or changeable discharges
- Aversion to meat fat with desire for milk fat or nut butters
- Decreased thirst

Typical Symptoms

The following are symptoms reported in the nineteenth-century trial or in accidental poisonings (Allen, 1875), annotated with related modern medical diagnoses.

Recorded Symptoms	Modern Diagnoses
Cognition, Emotions, and Affect	
Anxiety at night, as from heat	Anxiety from hot and poorly ventilated rooms
Hypochondriac moroseness, out of sorts with everything	Crying with the slightest provocation
Breaking out into weeping	
General	
During the menses, it became black before the eyes, and she felt worse on going into a warm room	Syncope in a warm, closed room
	Decreased thirst
	Fever
Feeling of discomfort over the whole body in the morning after rising, disappearing on moving about	Chills
	Febrile childhood diseases (e.g., mumps, measles, rubella, and varicella)
He longs for fresh air	
Symptoms alleviated in the open air	
When lying upon the back, the pains decrease and disappear	
Loss of thirst	
Chilliness, yawning, and stretching before the appearance of the menses	
Chilliness the whole evening before bedtime, even while walking	
Chilliness over the abdomen, extending around even to the lower portion of the back	
Anxious heat	
Intolerable burning heat in bed with uneasiness	
Sensation of heat at night without thirst	
External warmth is intolerable; the veins are enlarged	
Head	
Dullness of the head and headache, like a bruised sensation in the forehead	Sinus headache
	Dyspeptic headache
	Migraine headache
Headache in the evening	Tension headache
Headache as if one had eaten too much or as if the stomach had been disordered by being overloaded from too much fat meat	

continues

continued

Recorded Symptoms	Modern Diagnoses
Headache extending to the eyes so that they ache in the evening	
Throbbing pressive headache, relieved by external pressure	
Pressive or tensive drawing pain in the forehead above the orbits, aggravated on raising the eyes	

Ears

Vertigo, especially while sitting	Labyrinthitis
Vertigo in the morning on rising from bed on account of which he was obliged to lie down again	Otitis media
	Suppurative otitis media (usually left ear)
Violent pain in the ear as from something forcing outward	Otitis externa
Heat, redness, and swelling in the outer ear	Serous otitis media
Discharge of matter from the left ear	
Itching deep in the ear	
Difficulty of hearing as if the ears were stopped . . . with roaring in it like the sound of a distant noise	

Eyes

Burning and itching in the eyes that provokes rubbing and scratching	Conjunctivitis
The margin of the lower lid is inflamed and swollen with lachrymation in the morning	Hordeolum
	Lachrimation
Sty on the lid with inflammation of the white of the eye	Allergy
The inner canthus seems agglutinated with matter in the morning	
Itching and burning in the lids in the evening	
Lachrymation in the cold open air	
The eyes are full of water in the wind	
Transient obscuration of vision	

Nose

Sneezing	Upper respiratory infection
Stoppage of the nose, as from catarrh in the evening, on going to bed, and in the morning, a thick yellow opaque mucus, as an old catarrh, is blown from the nose	Allergic rhinitis
	Sinusitis

continues

continued

Recorded Symptoms	Modern Diagnoses
The nasal mucus is offensive	
Bad smell in the nose	
Constant tickling in the nose	
Mouth	
Toothache immediately on taking anything very warm into the mouth	Dental and periodontal pain
Fine sticking gnawing toothache in the gum, especially toward evening, aggravated by the warmth of the bed, relieved by uncovering and by a draft of cold open air	Halitosis
In the morning, the mouth and pharynx are dry and covered with a tasteless insipid mucus with an offensive odor from the mouth that is not perceptible to himself	
Abdomen	
Flatus moves from one part of the intestines to another with loud rumbling and gurgling and with gripping sensation, especially in the evening in bed	Colic
Sensation of heaviness like a stone in the abdomen, just before menses	Flatulence
Pressive constrictive pain, like a stone, in the lower abdomen, extending down to the bladder	Cystitis
	Dysmenorrhea
Gastrointestinal System	
Frequent eructations tasting of food	Pyrosis
Nausea water brash,* disagreeable risings	Nausea of pregnancy
Qualmish nausea in the morning	Esophagitis
Vomiting of food that had been eaten a long time before	Nausea and vomiting
Sensation in the stomach as if one had eaten too much; food rises up into the mouth as if one would vomit	Gastritis
Pain in the stomach an hour after eating	Dyspepsia
Scraping sensation in the stomach and esophagus, like a heartburn	Gastroenteritis

*Water brash is the regurgitation of an excessive amount of saliva from the lower part of the esophagus with some acid material from the stomach.

continues

continued

Recorded Symptoms	Modern Diagnoses
Gnawing sensation in the stomach, like ravenous hunger	
Diarrhea as green as bile once or twice a night with movement in the intestines before every stool	
Watery diarrhea at night	
Frequent evacuations of only mucus with colic	
Rectum	
Painful protruding blind hemorrhoids	Hemorrhoids
• with itching in the evening	
• with itching in the anus	
Genitourinary System	
Frequent desire to urinate	Urethritis
Involuntary micturition in bed at night	Enuresis
Profuse flow of urine	Orchitis
Right side of scrotum swollen	Prostatitis
Painful drawing pains in the spermatic cords, lasting a long time	Epididymitis
Swelling of the testicles	
Female Reproductive Tract	
Painless leukorrhea with swelling of the pudenda	Candidal vulvovaginitis
	Bacterial vaginosis
Acrid thin leukorrhea	Delayed labor
Leukorrhea with burning pain	Amenorrhea
Contractive pain in the left side of the uterus like labor pains, obliging her to bend double	Irregular menses
Suppression of the menses	
Delayed menses with coldness of the body; chilliness and trembling of the feet	
Heart and Lungs	
Violent tickling and scraping of the larynx, bringing tears to the eyes and causing dry cough	Asthma
	Cough
	Bronchitis
Constant cough in the evening on lying down	Heart palpitation
Cough with expectoration of yellow mucus	
If she lies on the left side, she complains of anxiety and rapid palpitation and want of breath	
Back	
Pain in the small of back, as if sprained, on motion	Lumbar sprain/strain
	Back labor
Pain in the small of back like labor pain	

continues

continued

Recorded Symptoms	Modern Diagnoses
Extremities	
Simple pain in the limbs, especially in the joints, obliging him to stretch the body with heat of the whole body without thirst in the morning in bed	Osteoarthritis
	Connective tissue disease
	Inflamed varicose veins
	Rheumatoid arthritis
The hip joint is painful as if dislocated	
A drawing pain in the muscle of the thigh at night that obliges him to move; he does not know what to do; together with sleeplessness, tossing about the bed, even when there is no pain, and coldness all over	
Painless swelling of the knee	
Cracking in the knees	
A painful stiffness in the right knee while walking whenever the thighs are stretched out straight	
Tearing and drawing in the knee	
The varicose veins swell up	
Skin	
A burning itching over the whole body on becoming warm in bed . . . there is no appearance of an eruption	Eczema
	Urticaria
Biting itching here and there in the skin	
Intolerable itching in the evening in bed	
Sleep	
Irresistible in the afternoon	Insomnia
He can scarcely keep awake in the evening	Fatigue
	Menopausal hot flashes
Sleep before midnight prevented by a fixed idea or an anxious sensation of heat	
Sleep at night restless; on account of an intolerable sensation of heat he was obliged to throw off the cover	
Dreams	
Quarrels	
Frightful things	
He had been beaten and was unlucky	
Sobbed and wept aloud in his sleep	
Fright and disgust	
Lascivious	
Amorous	
Dread of men (in women)	

CHAPTER 15

Rhus toxicodendron

Scientific Names: *Toxicodendron radicans* and *Toxicodendron toxicarium*
Scientific Family Name: Anacardiaceae
Common Name: Poison Ivy

OVERVIEW

Toxicodendron radicans (climbing poison ivy) and *Toxicodendron toxicarium* (eastern poison oak) are combined to prepare the homeopathic medicine *Rhus toxicodendron*. These plants are notable for their three leaves, the central one being longer than the other two. It was used in herbal medicines historically for skin conditions, paralysis, and arthritis, despite its obvious hazards. The effects of the acrid oil of the *Toxicodendron*s is well-known by North Americans: itching and burning fluid-filled vesicles on an inflamed base. The homeopathic medicines prepared from this plant family should therefore always be considered for vesicular dermatoses, such as varicella, erisipelas, herpes simplex, impetigo, contact dermatitis, and herpes zoster.

Rhus toxicodendron is actually prescribed more often for conditions that have no rash at all than for those that do. *Rhus* is the preeminent medicine in homeopathy for the musculoskeletal system. As illustrated by the selected symptoms from the trial (see below), there can be painful conditions in almost any muscle, tendon, and joint in the body. The pain must have certain alleviating and aggravating factors to be relieved by *Rhus*. The pain and stiffness (and the well-being of the patient as a whole) is exacerbated on first motion and relieved on

113

continued motion. This is the cardinal characteristic of the medicine. For this reason, *Rhus toxicodendron* has been called the rusty gate medicine. When the patient rests in one position for a while, the stiffness resumes. There is improvement from warmth and aggravation from cold, damp weather. It is indicated for illnesses that come on in cold, damp weather or when camping.

Arthritis is an example of an illness where the pain has the above characteristics. Indeed, *Rhus* can palliate the pains of arthritis. It is one of the most common medicines for sprains and back injuries, usually 3 or more days after the injury when the swelling has subsided, but the pain and stiffness remain. It can be a medicine for cervical strain and acceleration/deceleration injuries. It has been reported that this medicine can even ease the stiffness of Parkinson's disease (Morrison, 1993). Tendonitis more often responds to *Ruta graveolens*, but occasionally *Rhus toxicodendron* is the indicated medicine.

The patient displays a physical restlessness that arises from discomfort. He or she cannot get comfortable in any one position, which leads to insomnia with tossing and turning. *Rhus* can be effective for influenza or bronchitis with this kind of restless aching that is alleviated by continued motion.

There can be a hoarse voice or sore throat that improves as the speaker talks.

Rhus toxicodendron is one of the main medicines prescribed for enuresis of school-aged boys.

There are two important symptoms that should be memorized. First, the patient often has a red triangle on the tip of the tongue (the apex facing the tip). Second, the patient craves cold milk.

The patient requiring *Rhus toxicodendron* uually presents no striking psychological symptoms, but occasionally will be inexplicably cheerful. Uncommonly, a depression can occur as the patient declines with progression to compulsive behavior, such as rigid ritualistic or superstitious routines.

Main food desires: Milk, beer, cold drinks, cold milk, oysters, sweets, and tonics

Main food aversions: Alcohol, beer, meat, soup, and wine

Aggravated by: Cold dampness, becoming chilled when hot and perspiring, resting, beginning to move, before storms, after exertion, after midnight, being jarred, and ice-cold drinks

Alleviated by: Continued motion, heat in any form (e.g., hot bath, warm wraps, and warm weather), being massaged, holding the painful part, stretching extremities, and changing position

COMPARISONS

- *Arsenicum album*—Restlessness, sensitivity to cold, increased thirst, and fever
- *Calcarea carbonica*—Arthritis pains that are aggravated by cold, damp weather and by overexertion
- *Cimicifuga racemosa*—Whiplash or pain in the joints of the hands or feet, depression that is aggravated by cold, damp weather (see Chapter 17, Injuries and Emergencies)
- *Dulcamara*—Illnesses with achiness from cold, damp weather or hot days with cool nights
- *Phosphorus*—Bronchitis or influenza with chilliness and restlessness, desire for cold milk (see Chapter 21, Lower Respiratory System, and Chapter 25, Infectious Disease)
- *Radium bromatum*—Restless aching and stiffness that is aggravated by warmth
- *Rhododendron chrysanthum*—Arthritis pain at the approach of a storm or in wet weather
- *Ruta graveolens*—Stiffness and pain from sprains and tendonitis alleviated by warmth (see Chapter 17)

KEY SYMPTOMS OF *RHUS TOXICODENDRON*

- Aching pain aggravated by cold and damp, and in the morning before moving around
- Aggravated on first motion and alleviated on continued motion
- Stiffness
- Sprains and strains
- Red triangle on the tip of the tongue
- Desire for cold milk

Typical Symptoms

The following are symptoms reported in the nineteenth-century trial or in accidental poisonings (Allen, 1875), annotated with related modern medical diagnoses.

Recorded Symptoms	Modern Diagnoses
Cognition, Emotions, and Affect	
Sad, begins to weep without knowing why	Depression
Melancholy, ill-humor, and anxiety as if a misfortune would happen, or as if she were alone and all about her were dead and still, or as if she had been forsaken by all her friends; worse in the house, relieved by walking in the open air	Restlessness
	Delirium
Very restless mood	
Great apprehension at night, cannot remain in bed	
General	
Great thirst	Arthritis
Desire for cold milk	Fibromyalgia
She could not sit still on account of internal uneasiness, but was obliged to turn in every direction on the chair and move all her limbs	Influenza
	Connective tissue disease
She feels stiff on rising from a seat	
Soreness in every muscle, which passes off during exercise	
Fever at 6 p.m.	
High fever	
Ears	
On rising such dizziness that it seemed as if she were going to fall forward and backward	Labyrinthitis
	Orthostatic hypotension
Eyes	
The eyes are closed or greatly swollen and inflamed from swollen lids	Conjunctivitis
The eyes are red and agglutinated with matter in the morning	*Rhus* dermatitis around the eyes
Heaviness and stiffness of the lids, like a paralysis as if it were difficult to move the lids	
Face	
Great swelling of the face	Facial *Rhus* dermatitis

continues

continued

Recorded Symptoms	Modern Diagnoses
Mouth, Parotid Glands, and Pharynx	
Sore sensation with redness at the apex of the tongue	Mumps
Maxillary and parotid glands much enlarged	
Swelling of the submaxillary glands	
Respiratory System	
Short cough, from severe tickling and irritation behind the upper half of the sternum, followed by the feeling of discouragement and apprehension	Viral or allergic tracheobronchitis
Back	
Stiffness in the small of the back, painful on motion	Back sprain/strain, especially lumbar
While sitting, the small of the back aches as after long stooping and bending the back	Muscular stiffness and pain from overuse
Pain, as if bruised, in the small of the back whenever he lies quietly upon it or sits still; on moving around, he feels nothing	Arthritis Connective tissue disorders Contusion
Extremities	
All the limbs feel stiff and paralyzed, during and after walking with a sensation of . . . weight upon the nape of the neck	Cervical strain Whiplash injury Arthritis Connective tissue disease
Sensation of stiffness upon first moving the limb after rest	Fibromyalgia Sprain
Violent tearing pain in the arm, most violent when lying still	Muscle soreness and stiffness Tendonitis
Pain in the left upper arm as if the muscles or tendons were unduly strained	Sciatica
Jerking tearing in the elbow and wrist joints during rest, better during motion	
Sensation in the upper surface of the left wrist on bending it as if it had been sprained	
Aching pains in the legs, inability to rest in any position but for a moment	
Tension in the hip joint while sitting	
Stiffness of the knees and feet	

continues

continued

Recorded Symptoms	Modern Diagnoses
Tearing in the knee and ankle, worse during rest	
The legs seem weary and heavy as if he had walked a long distance	
Pain, like tingling in the tibia at night, while the feet are crossed; she is constantly obliged to move the feet back and forth, and on this account, is unable to sleep	
The feet painful as if sprained or wrenched in the morning on rising	
Unusual weariness of the limbs while resting	
Skin	
Numerous vesicles that burst and secreted for 8 days a slimy liquid	Chickenpox Eczema
Swelling . . . with violent itching and burning increased on touching or moving the parts affected as if pierced by hot needles; white transparent vesicles appeared on the highly red and inflamed skin	Erysipelas Erythema nodosum Herpes Impetigo Contact dermatitis Shingles
Covered from head to foot with a fine red vesicular rash, itching and burning terribly, especially in the joints; worse at night, causing constant scratching with little or no relief, and which felt very hard upon pressure with the finger; skin burning hot	Pemphigus Pemphigoid
The face became red, enormously swollen and edematous, then also the hands and skin of the whole body became covered with a scarlet-like exanthema, with intolerable itching, biting	
The backs of the hands and legs became covered with blisters that burst and slowly desquamated; violent vesicular erysipelas of the face and hands attended with a high state of fever	
Vesicular eruption on the cheek with intense itching and burning	

continues

continued

Recorded Symptoms	Modern Diagnoses

Sleep
Sleeplessness 4 whole nights; she could not remain in bed

Restless sleep with tossing about, rising, and throwing off the bed covers

As soon as he wished to fall asleep, his business came to him in anxious dreams

(Modern Diagnoses): Insomnia

Dreams
Things that had been talked about the previous evening

Fire

Accomplishing plans that had been projected the day previous, associated with occurrences with which she had been busy

CHAPTER 16

Sulphur

Scientific Name: Elemental Sulfur

OVERVIEW

The symptoms of *Sulphur* occupy 138 pages of one of the encyclopedic books of data from the nineteenth-century clinical trials (Allen, 1875). Many clinicians, both contemporary and historical, have reported that *Sulphur* is the most commonly prescribed medicine in their practices. Many of the clinical applications of *Sulphur* are in the realm of chronic disease, but it is also very useful at the sick visit, especially when a minor illness has lingered longer than expected. A vast range of human ills has been successfully treated by this medicine when the general symptoms fit.

If any new emotional change is seen in acute disease, it is that an irritable criticalness arises, especially toward the ideas of others. The patient may have a rush of ideas, which he or she believes are very significant and profound and have wide implications for society. There is physical laziness and untidyness, which the patient is unconcerned about. Often, however, new emotional symptoms are absent, and the clinician prescribes *Sulphur* based on the patient's general or local symptoms.

The patient may present in wrinkled or inappropriately casual clothes, in clothes that have been worn for days, or with personal hygiene slightly under par. The hair, for example, may appear unwashed. The lips, rims of the eyelids, or anus may be reddened, and various kinds of rashes and exanthemata may accompany the illness.

The perspiration, mouth, or stool may have an exceptionally offensive odor. The patient is sensitive to heat, especially the heat of the blankets at night even if he or she feels chilly. Since the illness started, she or he may have begun to uncover one or both feet while in bed. The feet or hands may actually feel a burning discomfort from the heat.

The patient may be suddenly hungry and weak at 11 a.m. There may be a desire for sweets and spicy food, or unusual beliefs about nutrition (e.g., a completely uncooked vegan diet is best or prolonged fasting is excellent for the health). He or she is thirsty, especially for sweet drinks. Symptoms are aggravated by standing and bathing.

Sulphur is indispensable in almost every kind of skin disease, specifically acne, impetigo, pemphagoid, pemphigus, seborrhea, tinea, herpes, and eczema. The eruptions itch, and are aggravated by heat, especially under the covers in bed and from a warm bath. The itching can be so severe that the patient scratches until the eruptions bleed or until there is burning. There may be itching or burning skin without any rash. Scratching aggravates the itching. There is intolerance of wool clothing. The rashes may arise from exposure to perfumes or synthetic materials.

The digestive system is another main focus of symptoms. *Sulphur* is one of the main medicines used to treat diarrhea, especially when the patient runs directly from the bed to the bathroom early in the morning. The stool is irritating and exceptionally foul smelling. Interestingly, the stool and flatus can have a sulfurous odor (like rotten eggs).

Sulphur can be used to treat peptic ulcer, hiatal hernia, or esophagitis when the general symptoms fit. Rectal fissures, abscesses, and fistulae; proctitis; and hemorrhoids are commonly treated with *Sulphur* when there is burning, redness of the anus, and, most importantly, rectal itch.

In the respiratory system, *Sulphur* is an important medicine for bronchitis and cough. It should be considered for lingering cough after an acute respiratory infection. The patient may have a deep, hoarse voice. A violent cough may be triggered by tickling in the larynx or by lying on the back, and a headache may accompany it. In bronchitis, there may be much rattling of mucus and heat in the chest, aggravated at 11 a.m., with greenish, sweet-tasting, and purulent expectoration. The patient may describe a sensation of burning or coldness in chest that extends to the face.

Low back pain, with or without sciatica, that is aggravated by standing often responds to *Sulphur*, especially when the patient cannot stand fully erect. The back pain is aggravated from standing, and the patient has trouble lowering into a chair and must drop part of the way.

Main food desires: Alcohol, beer, fat and sweets together, spicy food, raw food, sweets, whisky, wine, ale, brandy, claret, chocolate, cucumbers, cereals, fat, liquid food, meat, oysters, pickles, sour food, vegetables, and warm drinks

Main food aversions: Eggs, meat, olives, beer, strong cheese, chicken, high-fat foods, milk, sour food, sweets, tobacco, and wine

Aggravated by: Emotional upsets and ordeals; motion; humid weather; spring; fog; cold, damp weather; thunderstorms; heat of sun; summer; tobacco; and emerging dentition (Note: subject observed becoming aggravated at regular intervals, e.g., every 4 hours or 24 hours)

Alleviated by: Profuse urination, perspiring, alcohol, thinking, stooping, continued motion, and reclining with head propped up (Note: The person's symptoms or the person as a whole were observed to be worse in the afternoon)

COMPARISONS

- *Argentum nitricum*—Desire for sweets, esophagitis, and becomes easily overheated (see Chapter 23, Gastrointestinal System)
- *Nux vomica*—Criticalness, love of spicy foods, and low back pain (see Chapter 17, Injuries and Emergencies)
- *Phosphorus*—Thirst, burning pains, desire for sweet and spicy foods, hypoglycemia, and bronchitis (see Chapter 21, Lower Respiratory System)
- *Pulsatilla*—Uncovering feet in bed, beliefs about diet, sinusitis, and intolerance of heat (see Chapter 20, Ear, Nose, and Throat)

KEY SYMPTOMS OF *SULPHUR*

- Irritability, criticalness, and rush of ideas that patient believes are important

- Disinterest in undertaking mundane tasks, such as physical labor or cleaning
- Burning pains
- Intense pruritus of the skin and rectal itch
- Red orifices
- Uncovering of one or both feet at night in bed
- Desire for sweets, fats, spicy food, and alcohol
- Aggravation from standing up

Typical Symptoms

The following are symptoms reported in the nineteenth-century trial or in accidental poisonings (Allen, 1875), annotated with related modern medical diagnoses.

Recorded Symptoms	Modern Diagnoses
Cognition, Emotions, and Affect	
Irritable mood, easily excited, and always absorbed in himself	Self-absorbed affect
Ill-humored and fault finding	Criticalness
Irritated cross temper	Unconcern about basic activities of daily living
Anxiety with heat of the head and cold feet	Theorizing
Great anxiety in the evening after lying down so that she cannot fall asleep for an hour	
She destroys her things, throws them away, thinking she has a superfluity of everything; (and) she wastes to a skeleton	
Numerous morbid ideas, extremely disagreeable, causing rancor, though with also joyful thoughts (and melodies), mostly from the past, take possession of her; they throng one upon the other so that she cannot free herself from them during the day, with neglect of business; worse in the evening and in bed when they prevent falling sleep	
She fancies that she has become emaciated	
She fancies that she has beautiful clothes; old rags look like fine things, a coat like a beautiful jacket, a cap like a beautiful hat	
Greatly inclined to philosophical and religious revelries	
Indolence of mind and body through the day; disinclination for any work or movement	
When spoken to, he seems absorbed as if walking in a dream	
General	
She is obliged to drink much	
Vasomotor instability	
Burning	

continues

continued

Recorded Symptoms	Modern Diagnoses
Itching	
Offensive odors	
Emaciation	
Weak and prostrated in the afternoon	
Weariness and sleepiness all day	
Head	
Sensation of fullness and heaviness in the head as if filled with blood	Muscle tension headache
Pressure in the head immediately after rising	Migraine headache
	Acne
	Seborrhea or impetigo on the head
Hammering headache on vivacious talking	Tinea capitis
Aching pain in the forehead	
Itching pimples on the scalp	
Pimples on the forehead painful to touch (vertex, occiput, nape)	
On the forehead, complete patches and groups of black points like comedones	
A humid eruption on the top of the head, like tinea capitis, small grain-like pustules filled with pus, and drying up into honey-like scabs	
Itching on the head with impatience	
Ears	
Vertigo while walking in the open air; she did not dare to stoop, nor to look down; was obliged to steady herself to avoid falling	Vertigo
Eyes	
Redness of the eyes during the day; violent itching in them in the evening	Allergy
Purulent mucus in the eye	Conjunctivitis
Burning of the eyes	Migraine
Agglutinated eyes in the morning	
Itching on the borders of the eyelids	
Vision as through a veil	
Flickering before the eyes	
Dark points and spots before the eyes	
Nose	
Inflammation in the nose	Acne
Black comedones on the nose	Allergic rhinitis
Frequent sneezing	Sinusitis
Violent coryza	
Offensive odor of the nasal mucus on blowing the nose	
Itching in the nose	

continues

continued

Recorded Symptoms	Modern Diagnoses
Mouth and Pharnyx	
Swelling of the lower lip with eruptions upon it	Dental caries
Drawing toothache	Abscess
Throbbing and boring in the teeth	Postnasal discharge from sinusitis
Coated tongue	Allergic rhinitis
Great dryness of the palate with much thirst	Upper respiratory infection
Scraping in the throat with hawking and clearing the throat	
Gastrointestinal System	
Ravenous hunger which obliges him to eat frequently; if he does not, he has headaches and great lassitude and is obliged to lie down	Hypoglycemia
	Diabetes
	Pyrosis and reflux esophagitis
	Diminished appetite
He is hungry; but as soon as he only sees his food, his appetite vanishes and he feels full in the abdomen; when he begins to eat, he is averse to it	Flatulence
Sour eructations frequently during the day	
Tension and pressure in the umbilical region	
Distension of the abdomen, rumbling in the bowels	
Emission of much flatus smelling of rotten eggs	
Anus and Rectum	
Pressure toward the anus	Diarrhea especially in early morning
Burning in the rectum during a stool	Hemorrhoids
Violent itching in the rectum	Rectal fissures
Crawling and biting in the rectum as from worms while sitting in the evening	Parasites (especially nematodes)
Hemorrhoids	
Violent burning in the anus	
Desire for stool with some colic woke him about 5 a.m.	
Straining before and after stool	
In the morning after waking, great tenesmus in the anus followed by a copious fluid stool	
Diarrhea with rumbling in the abdomen	

continues

continued

Recorded Symptoms	Modern Diagnoses
Genitourinary System	
Burning in the urethra while urinating	Urethritis
Frequent sudden desire to urinate	
Female Reproductive Tract	
The menses, after lasting 10 days and a half and flowing profusely, stopped immediately	Prolonged menstruation
Male Reproductive Tract	
Itching in the glans penis	Fungal infection of the glans
Respiratory System	
Hoarseness in the morning	Anxiety expressed in cardiac and
Dry cough woke him from sleep at night	chest symptoms
Weakness of the chest when talking	Cough
Pressure upon the chest with anxiety	
Anxious palpitation	
Back	
Violent pain in the back for several nights with bruised sensation in the small of the back, on account of which she could not fall asleep, with great (flushes) of blood	Lumbago
Extremities	
Burning of the hands	Impetigo
Burning in the soles of the feet	
Skin dry eruption with burning itching	
Itching vesicular eruption on the back of the hand	
Skin	
A scaly eruption . . . with violent burning itching after scratching	Eczema
	Urticaria
Repeated burning in various parts; after scratching it hurts as if sore	Dry skin
	Contact dermatitis
Prickling in the skin of the whole body in the evening after getting warm in bed	
The itching spots are painful after scratching	
Itching, now here, now there	
Perspiration	
Very disgusting offensive sweat in the axilla	Offensive perspiration

continues

continued

Recorded Symptoms	Modern Diagnoses
Sleep	
At night profuse sweat and restless sleep	Insomnia
Irresistible sleepiness during the day	Fatigue
Sleepless and wide awake all night	
Could not get to bed before midnight	
Contrary to habit, he woke very early and could not fall asleep again	
Dreams	
Comical	
Vivid	
Anxious	
Dead people	
Erotic	
Murder	
Disgust	
Strange grimaces appeared to her	
Danger from fire and water	
Murders	
Been bitten by a dog	
Stretched out number a quarter of a yard long	

PART III

Clinical Prescribing

The chapters that follow provide helpful differentials for clinical application of homeopathy. Primary care clinicians are very familiar with the concept of a differential diagnosis; this term is used to describe the various diagnoses that should be ruled out in the process of analyzing the data that the patient presents. In homeopathy a second "diagnosis" is made; the homeopathic medicine that is most similar to the patient's symptoms. Medicines will need to be compared in a homeopathic differential.

Although the medical diagnosis rarely determines the prescription in homeopathic medicine (with a few notable exceptions such as *Agaricus muscarius* for frostbite, or *Arnica montana* for hematoma), there is a group of medicines that are far more commonly indicated for each of the specific conditions that are seen in a primary care sick visit than the other thousand (or so) medicines that are used in homeopathy. Actually, 240 medicines comprised 98% of the homeopathic medicines prescribed for all conditions at one American homeopathic pharmaceutical laboratory that had statistically analyzed its sales (Hahnemann Laboratories, personal communication, 1995).

Differentials have been developed between medicines commonly prescribed for certain diagnoses by experts in the field. These have evolved over the years as these protocols were published, then refined and updated by other authors over the past two centuries (e.g., Bruning & Weinstein, 1986; Cummings & Ullman, 1984; Gibson, 1981; Jonas & Jacobs, 1996; Jouanny, 1980; Royal, 1923; Shepherd, 1982). These, the foundational materia medicas, and computerized homeopathic databases are the foundation of Part III.

A genre of homeopathic texts called *repertories* should be mentioned. A repertory is an advanced tool used for data analysis during or after a patient consultation. It is a list of single symptoms that are paired with all the medicines that were demonstrated to have that symptom in those medicines' trials, or symptoms that have been cured by a medicine in the repeated clinical experience of expert homeopathic clinicians (van Zandvoort, 1997; Schroyens, 1998). Originally large books, they are now available on disk. The use of these tools is an art in itself, and they are not necessary for the level of practice addressed here.

There has been a paucity of high-quality studies on all but a few of the conditions addressed in Part III. The implications of this are that the efficacy of most of these homeopathic clinical differentials has not been scientifically established, and that there is some subjectivity in making recommendations regarding posology. The approach to potency and repetition of the dose as well as the duration of treatment that this text recommends is too high, often repeated, and continued for too long according to some homeopathic experts. On the other hand, the potencies recommended are too low, repetition too infrequent, and treatment too short according to other homeopathic experts. The author has taken the middle ground with regard to potency, preferring to use the 30C potency whenever possible so that the new prescriber of homeopathic medicines can become thoroughly acquainted with the efficacy of that potency before exploring the entire range. In determining frequency of dosing and the duration of treatment, the author has relied on her own clinical experience and the literature, with the intention of providing a safe schedule without requiring the clinician to check in with patients too frequently about minor health issues. Patient education materials are provided in Appendix D; these may help reduce the frequency of phone calls and can be adapted to suit individual practices.

When the clinical differential involves a number of medicines, the author has labeled certain ones as "most commonly indicated," based on the literature, her own practice, and the work of other homeopathic clinicians she has collaborated with. Symptoms and sensations that are italicized have been repeatedly emphasized in the homeopathic literature as being highly characteristic of the medicine being profiled.

CHAPTER 17

Injuries and Emergencies

Homeopathic first aid is commonly practiced in the home by parents who prefer natural ways to cope with life's bumps and bruises. A walk down the homeopathy aisle at the local health food store will often bring encounters with people ready to give testimonials to the effectiveness of *Arnica montana* for bruises and *Cantharis* for burns. This section will show how simple it can be to use homeopathy for injuries. Some differential for homeopathic medicines for true emergencies will be presented for those who want to go further.

The first aid information in self-care books comes from several sources. The original clinical trial of the substance may have demonstrated symptoms that mimic those of injury, such as the bruised feeling of *Arnica*. Homeopaths staffed acute care hospitals and many free dispensaries in England and the United States in the late nineteenth and early twentieth century (Shadman, 1958). They even provided care on or near the battlefield in World War I (Shepherd, 1982). From this clinical experience, protocols for emergency homeopathic treatment, including life-threatening situations, evolved. Many of the simple protocols could easily be subjected to scientific investigation to objectively test their utility.

ABRASIONS

The traditional external dressing for abrasions in homeopathic medicines are *Calendula officinalis*–based products. These are believed to speed wound healing, lower the occurrence of infection, and reduce inflammation when appropriately applied. There is no significant body of research to support or refute this claim, and the effects of this flower (the pot marigold) have not been proven to be more effective than bactericidal creams and ointments or even other herbs.

That being said, *Calendula* has been used externally by many homeopathic physicians and surgeons on the battlefield and in the hospital with very satisfactory results (Shadman, 1958; Shepherd, 1982). *Hypericum perforatum* herbal preparations have also been used alone or in combination with *Calendula*. Since most homeopathic pharmaceutical manufacturers have their own *Calendula* and *Hypericum* preparations, their instructions should be followed in applying wound dressings.

ANGINA

It is unlikely that clinicians will be interested in prescribing a homeopathic medicine instead of conventional therapies for angina. However, a remote locale or a patient unwilling to take any "unnatural" medicines can present an opportunity to do so.

The main distinguishing characteristics among medicines for angina are the quality, location, and radiation of the chest pain. Give 30C, wait 2–5 min, and change medicines if relief is not obtained. If relief is felt, repeat the medicine every 10 min for three doses, and then wait to see if discomfort returns.

Apis mellifica—Needle-like pains radiate *posteriorly* from the heart in patients with kidney failure or mitral valvular disease. The patients experience tachycardia with intermittent pulse.

Argentum nitricum—The patient is anxious about what might happen with *palpitation* and throbbing throughout the whole body. There is a sensation of fullness in the cardiac region that is alleviated outdoors and aggravated at night. The pulse is irregular and intermittent. The patient may avoid medical attention, saying he or she is fine.

Arnica montana—Severe angina pain is felt in the *elbow* of the left arm. These are needle-like pains in the heart or sudden pain like an electrical shock or like the heart is being squeezed. The patient presents with an irregular pulse and congestive heart failure with cardiac hypertrophy. Heartbeats shake the whole body. The patient fears death, with cardiac distress at night. The patient's angina is aggravated by physical overexertion (see Chapter 2, *Arnica montana*).

Arsenicum album—Heart pains radiate to the *neck and occiput* with anxiety, dyspnea, and syncope. Standing alleviates the symptoms; drinking water aggravates them. The patient has accelerated heart rate in the morning; is *restless,* chilly, thirsty for sips; and fears he or she will *die* (see Chapter 3, *Arsenicum album*).

Aurum metallicum—*Aurum metallicum* is indicated for hypertensive arteriosclerotic patients with a serious, business-like affect. Symptoms are tachycardia and an irregular pulse with the subjective sensation that the heart *stops beating* for 2–3 sec, then resumes tumultuously, accompanied by a "sinking" feeling at the epigastrium. Angina pectoris is present in patients with cardiac hypertrophy, aortic disease, or valvular disease. Carotids and temporal arteries pulsate visibly. The patient may be clinically *depressed* with suicidal ideation. There is a less frequently indicated medicine, *Convallaria majalis,* whose symptoms include tachycardia and the sensation of the heart's stopping and suddenly resuming. It should be considered in heavy *smokers* with no cardiac hypertrophy. (Also compare *Chininum arsenicosum* and *Magnolia grandiflora* below.)

Aurum muriaticum—The patient describes a sensation of weight on the chest near the heart. Symptoms may include *violent palpitations;* sore aching, heaviness, and rigidity in heart; and *hyperemia* from heart disease. There may also be piercing pains above the heart.

Cactus grandiflorus—The patient presents with severe, *constricting* pain in the heart, sensation of weight on the chest, anxiety, dyspnea, and coldness of extremities. The pain is aggravated by lying on the left side and from exertion. The pain radiates to the *left arm.*

Chininum arsenicosum—Angina comes on after acute *infection.* The patient may have bradycardia and describe a sensation as if his or her heart had stopped. The patient is short of breath on ascending and may have cardiac dyspnea.

Crataegus Oxyacantha—There is pain in the region of the heart and under the *left clavicle.* The patient may present with congestive heart failure, aortic disease, extreme dyspnea on slight exertion, dilated heart, and an irregular pulse that is intermittent tachycardia and valvular murmurs. Patient is cold to the touch with cyanosis of fingers and toes.

Kalmia latifolia—The patient presents with chest pain that radiates to *left hand and arm* and is aggravated by lying on the left side and feels better lying on the back. There may be cardiac hypertrophy;

valvular disease, especially following treatment of arthritis; or advanced congestive heart failure. Patient might also have intense palpitations with visible lifts and loud murmurs.

Latrodectus mactans—This is the most common medicine for angina because the effect of the poison of this spider (the black widow) mimics the most common kind of angina. Chest pain radiates to the axilla or *down the arm* (more commonly the left) causing *numbness and coldness* of the hand. The patient is anxious and restless and believes he or she will not be able to breathe and will die. She or he may scream with the pains.

Magnolia grandiflora—The patient has *cramp-like* pain in the heart. (Cardiac lesions may be present in patients with concurrent rheumatic disease.) There may be pain around the heart accompanied by itching of the feet or alternating pains between the spleen and the heart. The patient is tired and stiff, and sore when quiet. The patient may have asthma or dyspnea when walking fast or lying on the left side. The patient may describe a sensation as if his or her heart had stopped beating.

Naja tripudians—The patient may present with violent pain, shooting to the *left scapula, shoulder, or neck* with anxiety and fear of death; the patient holds his or her hand over the painful area. There may be needle-like pain in the region of the heart and cardiac hypertrophy. The patient's history may include valvular damage from bacterial disease or mitral valve prolapse. Other possible symptoms are bradycardia, irregular pulse, frontal or temporal headache accompanying the angina, and cardiac cough.

Oxalicum acidum—The patient presents with sudden, sharp, and piercing pains in the *left lung*, thereby causing dyspnea. There may be precordial pains that dart to the left shoulder. In patients with organic heart disease, there may be palpitation and dyspnea. Heart symptoms alternate with aphonia. The patient's heart may have aortic insufficiency.

Phosphorus—Pains radiate to the *right arm*. The heart is weak and dilated. Other symptoms include tachycardia, feeling of warmth in the heart, and violent palpitation with anxiety, while lying on the left side. The patient is anxious, "spaced-out," and thirsty for large quantities of ice-cold drinks. (See Chapter 13, *Phosphorus*).

Rhus toxicodendron—The patient's heart feels tired, with pains radiating down the *left arm*. There is uncomplicated hypertrophy from violent exertion. There may also be tachycardia with irregular intermittent pulse and numbness of the left arm. The left arm aches with heart disease. (See Chapter 15, *Rhus toxicodendron*).

Spigelia anthelmia—The patient experiences violent precordial sticking or compressing pains, radiating to *throat, arms,* and *scapula* that are aggravated by the least *motion,* inspiration, or by lying on the left side, or bending double. The patient craves hot water, which alleviates the pain. There are frequent attacks of palpitation; these are usually accompanied by foul odor from the mouth. Pulse may be intermittent, irregular, and accompanied by anxious palpitation. There is pulsation of the carotids and subclavian arteries.

Spongia tosta—The patient describes waking suddenly from cardiac pain and dyspnea *after midnight;* he or she was flushed, faint, anxious, perspiring, hot, and frightened to death. There is tachycardia and violent palpitation with dyspnea. The heart feels as though it is forced upward with blood surging up toward the neck, head, and face, accompanied by closure of eyelids and lachrimation. Valvular disease in the patient causes cardiac insufficiency. The patient may present with aortic aneurysm or cardiac hypertrophy with asthmatic symptoms. If *Spongia tosta* fails to alleviate symptoms in this kind of scenario, especially if the cardiac pain is felt in the left shoulder, the clinician should prescribe *Aconitum napellus*, which is used for sudden illnesses accompanied with fear.

APPENDICITIS

There are anecdotal twentieth-century stories of patients being treated with homeopathy for acute appendicitis on the way to the hospital, and the symptoms completely subsiding by the time those patients arrived. It goes without saying, however, that surgical treatment should not be delayed for results from homeopathic treatment. The local symptoms of the top three medicines used for appendicitis are similar. The 200C or 1M potency should be given every 6 hr for three doses; then its effectiveness should be evaluated.

Belladonna—The pain is markedly aggravated by touch, for example of the bedclothes (like with *Lachesis mutus*), and general firm pressure alleviates the pain. The pain is aggravated by being *jarred.* The patient has a fever with a *red face.* (See Chapter 4, *Belladonna*).

Bryonia alba—There is violent pain in the abdomen, which may be accompanied by severe vomiting. The patient is thirsty, but vomits water immediately. The patient is generally aggravated by motion and lies *perfectly still* with the limbs flexed and knees drawn up. The pain is alleviated by *firm pressure*. (See Chapter 5, *Bryonia alba*).

Iris tenax—There is a painful spot over the *ileocecal* region, the size of a coin.

Lachesis mutus—The patient presents with swelling in the cecal region and must lie on back with knees drawn up. The abdomen is hot and sensitive. There is knife-like or tearing pain in the right side of the abdomen. There may be peritonitis.

ASPHYXIA OR RESPIRATORY DISTRESS OF THE NEWBORN

The homeopathic literature and contemporary midwives who use homeopathy in birthing have reported dramatic results in neonatal crises. This differential should be memorized by the clinician to be useful in an emergency. The following medicines in the 30C potency are kept in an emergency tray immediately at hand. A single dose is administered. The infant should revive within 5 seconds, precluding the need for resuscitation in many cases. If the child improves after the medicine, and then declines again, another dose of the medicine is given.

The following is primarily from lectures by Ananda Zaren and the written works of Moscowitz (1992) and Perko (1997), all of whom have had extensive experience with births and/or homeopathic supervision and teaching of midwives. Table 17–1 provides a comparison between medicines.

Aconitum napellus—There is a sudden loss of consciousness with *respiratory arrest and cardiac arrest* (or very faint pulse) from asphyxia. The infant is hot and purplish.

Antimonium tartaricum—Rarely is any other medicine needed than this one for *meconium aspiration*. The infant should respond by immediately coughing up the meconium, even if the infant appears lifeless. *Antimonium tartaricum* is indicated for respiratory distress syndrome (i.e., the infant is pale, gasping, and breathless although the cord still feebly pulsates). There may be trembling of the chin and lower jaw.

Arnica montana—*Arnica montana* is not a respiratory remedy per se, but is used for dyspnea from swelling of the throat or trachea

Table 17–1 Indicated Homeopathic Medicines for Asphyxia in the Neonate

	Meconium	Pallor	Gasping	Trauma	Cyanosis	Flaccidness	Unresponsive to warming	Cold to touch	Red or purple color	Rigidity
Aconitum napellus									✓	✓
Antimonium tartaricum	✓	✓	✓							
Arnica montana				✓						
Arsenicum album		✓	✓							
Camphora	✓							✓	✓	
Carbo vege-tabilis						✓	✓	✓		
Digitalis purpurea					✓			✓		
Laurocerasus		✓			✓		✓	✓		
Opium		✓		✓				✓		✓

secondary to *contusions* from face presentation. It can be the medicine for trauma from shoulder dystocia. *Aconitum napellus* is given first to a neonate with reddish purple face after shoulder dystocia. (See Chapter 2, *Arnica montana*).

Arsenicum album—This medicine is indicated when the neonate takes a *gasp* before respiratory arrest. (When *Carbo vegetabilis* and *Laurocerasus* are indicated, there is no gasp.) The infant is limp, pale, and lifeless, not cyanotic. (See Chapter 3, *Arsenicum album*.)

Camphora—This medicine is indicated when there is icy coldness in *dying* neonates with sinking strength. The upper lip may twitch. In rare cases neonates may respond to this medicine for meconium aspiration instead of *Antimonium tartaricum* when this marked *coldness* is present and the child is clearly dying. There may be hard places on the skin of the abdomen and thighs, which rapidly become more indurated. At times, there is a deep redness spreading over the same area of the thighs and abdomen.

Carbo vegetabilis—The infant is *flaccid* and cold to touch. The heart sounds are barely audible and the pulse is intermittent. There is no response to stimulation or warmth. The neonate may have Cheyne-Stokes respiration.

Digitalis purpurea—There is *compression* of the lungs, irregular heart rate, and bradycardia that improves from any sort of motion. The neonate is cyanotic and icy cold. *Digitalis purpurea* is especially indicated in babies with congestive heart failure or congenital heart disease.

Laurocerasus—The infant is *cyanotic*, has a sunken face, and is gasping for breath. The muscles of the face twitch. The skin is cold to touch (compare with *Carbo vegetabilis*). There is no reaction to warmth. Bradycardia is present, and the heart rate drops further on exertion.

Opium—There is pallor and *rigidity*, and the trunk is curved in the form of an arch. The neonate has the appearance that he or she is *dreaming*, sleepy, or stuporous. The infant is breathless although the cord still pulsates.

BITES AND STINGS

For bites and stings, the indicated medicine can be given in the 30C potency. The frequency of doses should be determined by the acuity of the patient's reaction. In mild reactions, a dose every hour for three doses would be indicated; in more severe situations, the medicine can be repeated as often as every 5 min.

Apis mellifica—The area around the bite or sting is *puffy and warm*. In light skinned people, the swollen area will be pink. There is a stinging or itching sensation. There may be swelling around the eyes as well. This medicine is usually used for bee and jelly fish stings that have these qualities. (*Medusa* is indicated when the face is edematous, and there is numbness; there may be burning and/or prickling heat.)

Ledum palustre—The area around the bite is *hard, blanched, and cool* to touch. Usually hornet, mosquito, and wasp stings have these qualities.

Less Commonly Indicated Medicines

Anthracinum—This medicine is indicated for deep *blue* or black lesions with very intense burning. Brown recluse spider bites can have this quality.

Cantharis—The bite area is very erythematous, and there is a *burning* quality to the pains.

Carbolicum acidum—When a patient has an anaphylactic reaction, this medicine in a 30C potency is indicated every 10 min while seeking help. The standard first aid measures must be taken as well. The patient has a dusky face and peri-oral pallor.

Hypericum perforatum—This medicine is indicated for stings or bites with *shooting* pains.

Vespa crabro—Since yellow jackets sometimes forage in garbage, bacteria may be injected under the skin when a person is stung. In these cases, the usual medicines may fail as an erythematous, wheal-like cellulitis develops and gradually spreads. The area may itch, burn, and/or sting. The patient lacks concentration, literally *staring into space*. The pains feel like the sting is being pierced with red-hot needles. The indicated medicine for these cases is *Vespa crabro*, which is made from a member of the wasp family.

If snake and scorpion bites are common in the region, homeopathic medicines may be available that are manufactured from the offending animal. It is also wise to check with other homeopathic clinicians in the area about what they have found effective.

BURNS

With burns, the sooner that the medicine is administered, the more effective it will be. As a general guideline, a 30C dose should be given every 2 hr for three doses, then as needed for the pain. As more experience is gained, the clinician will be able to adapt the schedule of repetition to match the circumstances.

Belladonna—*Belladonna* is indicated for hot, swollen, and scarlet-red sunburn.

Cantharis—This medicine is indicated for second- and third-degree burns.

Causticum—*Causticum* is used in the burn treatment protocol to promote good healing after *Cantharis* eases the initial pain of the third-degree burn. The clinician should begin with a 30C dose three times a day for 3 days, then twice a day for 3 days, and finally, once a day for a few more days.

Phosphorus—*Phosphorus* is indicated for electrical burns.

Urtica urens—This medicine is used to treat first-degree burns.

CEREBROVASCULAR ACCIDENTS

There have been many medicines mentioned in homeopathic literature to aid in the recovery of stroke patients. None has been studied. It is commonly assumed that *Arnica montana* would help the body resorb the blood. Likewise, *Aconitum napellus* may calm the patient's initial fright about the cerebrovascular accident.

CONTUSIONS AND HEMATOMAS

The first medicine to be considered in contusions is always *Arnica montana* (see Chapter 2, *Arnica montana*). It is the treatment of choice, except in the specific situations that are described below.

Bellis perennis—The first medicine to use for contusions of the *pelvic organs*.

Conium maculatum—If *Arnica* fails to relieve bruising, swelling, and pain from injury of the *male genitalia*, or induration and bruising of the *breast* after a blow, *Conium maculatom* is indicated.

Hamamelis virginiana—This medicine should be used for contused *veins* with ecchymosis.

Hypericum perforatum—*Hypericum perforatum* is indicated for bruises around nerves that result in sharp or *shooting* pains, usually extending proximally.

Ledum palustre—This medicine is used to speed the resolution of the discoloration of *black eyes*.

Ruta graveolens—Bruises of the *periosteum* respond to *Ruta graveolens*.

Symphytum officinale—This medicine should be used when injuries of the *cartilage* or the periosteum do not respond to *Ruta graveolens*.

DISLOCATED JOINTS

Bryonia alba—There are anecdotal reports that *Bryonia alba* in high potency can relieve the pain of a dislocated joint. When there is severe pain on motion, 200C potency is indicated (or a 1M or 10M) and repeated every hour for three doses, and then p.r.n. if it has been effective. (See Chapter 5, *Bryonia alba*).

EYE INJURIES

Abrasions

Small corneal abrasions, such as commonly occur in contact lens wearers, are reputed to respond to one or two doses of *Euphrasia officinalis* 30C. Refer to the section on foreign bodies in the eye, below.

Blunt Trauma Eye Injuries

Arnica montana—*Arnica* should be the first medicine prescribed for blunt trauma to the eye. In cases where a black eye is anticipated, 200C can be given every hour for three doses, then every 6 hr while awake for 3 days. (See Chapter 2, *Arnica montana*.) In cases where the patient seems especially anxious and restless, then he or she should be prescribed *Aconitum napellus* 30C every 15 min for several doses, which the homeopathic literature suggests will help heal the contusion, as well as calm the patient.

Hamamelis virginiana—If *Ledum* and *Arnica* fail to complete resorption of blood from a *subconjunctival bleed*, *Hamamelis* 30C can be prescribed twice a day for a week.

Ledum palustre—After 2–3 days of treatment with *Arnica* for *black eye* or subcutaneous hemorrhage, *Ledum* is indicated to speed the resorption of blood and restore normal color, especially if the eye feels cold and numb to the patient.

Symphytum officinale—If *Arnica* does not alleviate the *pain in the eyeball* itself, *Symphytum officinale* is indicated.

Foreign Bodies

The usual protocols should be followed for removal of a foreign body. Traditional antibiotic ophthalmic ointments have not been reported to interfere with homeopathic medicines. If a foreign body has penetrated the eye, *Aconitum napellus* or *Sulphur* are indicated, or *Sulphuricum acidum* if the major feature is intraocular hemorrhage. The usual treatment protocols must be used in addition because of the risk of blindness from bacterial infection.

Aconitum napellus—*Aconitum napellus* is indicated for agitation and *anxiety* that accompanies corneal abrasion from contact lenses or after removal of a foreign body.

Euphrasia officinalis—This medicine is indicated for corneal abrasions with much *tearing*. A corneal ulcer may or may not be present.

Conjunctival Inflammation from Trauma

This type of inflammation may occur after the removal of a foreign body or as a result of chemical exposure. In addition to the usual first aid measures, such as fluorescing the eye, flushing the eye, and using ointments, the following medicines may be helpful in the 30C potency. Each medicine may be given every hour for three doses, and then three times a day for 3 days.

Calcarea carbonica—This medicine is used to treat spots and *ulcers* on the cornea, photophobia, and lachrimation in the open air. The vision is dim, as if looking through a mist.

Hamamelis Virginiana—This medicine is used to treat sore eyes when the blood vessels are injected.

Hepar sulphuris calcareum—This medicine is indicated for corneal ulcers with sore eyeballs, and great *sensitivity* to touch and air. Eyes and lids are red and inflamed. The patient's eyes are painful with a sensation as if they are pulled back into the head. (See Chapter 9, *Hepar sulphuris calcareum*.)

Pulsatilla—This medicine is used to treat *purulent* conjunctivitis, in which the discharge does not irritate the skin and there is much tearing. (See Chapter 14, *Pulsatilla*.)

Sulphur—Heat, burning, and redness of the eyes is treated with *Sulphur*. (See Chapter 16, *Sulphur*.)

FRACTURES

In addition to the usual medical protocol for fracture, there is a homeopathic protocol that is reported to speed healing. The first medicine to be administered is *Arnica montana* 200C every 4 hr for three doses to reduce bruising and swelling. If there is sharp pain persisting after this, as from nerve injury, *Hypericum perforatum* 30C should be given three times a day for 3 days, shorter if the pain subsides sooner. In any fracture, *Symphytum officinale* 6C (or *Calcarea phosphorica* 6X, which is available in any health food store) can be prescribed twice a day until the follow-up X-ray, which may encourage union of the bone although there is no research to support this claim.

FROSTBITE

Agaricus muscarius is the traditional treatment for frostbite or chilblain. 30C should be prescribed every 3 hr for three doses, and then twice a day for 3 days if symptoms persist.

HEAD INJURIES

Arnica montana is the first medicine for concussion. For a recent injury, 200C every 6 hr should be given for three doses. If symptoms persist, the medicines that follow are the most common for sequelae. The indicated medicine should be given in the 30C potency three times a day for 3 days, whereupon improvement should be noted from the correct medicine. Treatment can begin with any of these medicines instead of *Arnica*, if the symptoms match. Conventional emergency treatment should not be delayed.

A randomized, double-blind, placebo-controlled clinical trial of homeopathic treatment of mild traumatic brain injury (MTBI) was funded by the National Institutes of Health, conducted at Spaulding Rehabilitation Hospital in the Boston area, and published in the *Journal of Head Trauma Rehabilitation* (Chapman, Weintaub, Milburn, Pirozzi, & Woo, 1999). The 50 subjects in the trial had a mean duration of symptoms of 2.93 years and were assessed pre- and posttreatment with a battery of functional and cognitive/linguistic tests that the hospital routinely used to establish therapy goals. The physicians were limited to a group of 18 homeopathic medicines, which were prescribed in the classical homeopathic manner. Analysis of covariates suggested that homeopathic treatment was the only significant or near significant predictor of improvement in the functional subtests ($p = .009$, $p = .058$, $p = .027$), which translated into clinically significant outcomes such as several subjects' returning to work who had been unable to work for years. The cognitive/linguistic battery did not show significant differences among groups, which could be ascribed to limitations within the study, such as the number and potency of homeopathic medicines, or the duration of treatment (4 months). Adverse reactions to the homeopathic medicines were rare (10%) and minimal. The results suggested that homeopathy—alone or used concurrently with conventional drugs and rehabilitation therapies—may be effective in treating people with persistent MTBI, a clinical entity for which conventional treatment has limited effectiveness.

While this study focused on the chronic effects of brain injury, many of the same medicines used in the study are also used for acute closed head injury in the prescribing differential that follows.

Cicuta virosa—This medicine is used for postconcussion *spasms, seizures, amnesia, or behavior disorder*. There may be opisthotonos; jerking of the head to one side; and twitching of various parts, such as the arms and fingers. Spasms move violently downward accompanied with sudden shocks through the body or head, followed by rigidity or shrieking, and then prolonged unconsciousness. There may be facial distortions or bloody foam from the mouth and then prostration. The spasms are stimulated by *touch, by noise*, or loud talking. The patient has amnesia for what has occurred for hours or days and does not recognize anybody, but answers questions well. The patient feels this is a terrible and strange place and confuses the present with the past. The patient may display strange behaviors such as shouting, singing, silly gestures, dancing, moaning, howling, and crying. The patient may fall to the ground and roll around with or without a seizure.

Helleborus niger—The patient presents with *delayed and dulled* reaction to sensory input (e.g., vision, hearing, and taste). He or she has lost control over muscles (e.g., ataxia, or dropping of objects from the grasp). Thumbs may be adducted. Muscular weakness progresses to complete paralysis. There may be seizures with twitching of muscles and *involuntary behavior* such as motion of one arm and leg, with paralysis of the contralateral side. The patient may roll, strike the head, or bore it into the pillow. The patient may describe a sensation as if water were swishing inside the head. There may be cephalalgia-like electric shocks that pass through the brain, followed by spasms and vomiting.

Natrum sulphuricum—This medicine is used to treat clinical *depression* following concussion, especially when there is suicidal ideation of shooting oneself. *Natrum sulphuricum* can also treat asthma, headaches, or epilepsy following concussion when the other medicines in this section are not appropriate.

Opium—This medicine is indicated for coma from head injury, *stertorous* respirations, and contracted or dilated pupils that may not react to light. *Opium* may also be used for noncomatose patients who are lightheaded, have a placid and apathetic affect, and are indifferent even to pain. The patient is *dreamy*, slow, with dull cognition. The patient states a desire to go home, even though he or she is at home. The patient may demonstrate carphology and errors in perception. Other symptoms include glassy, half-closed, and staring eyes, a hot head, and severe constipation.

HEMORRHAGE

The following guide is provided to assist with quick clinical prescribing for hemorrhage. The general symptoms of the patient, if present, will be of great value in effective prescribing. What follows are the most common medicines for hemorrhage with the usual characteristics of the blood, followed by the patient's specific words used to describe the pain. More in-depth review of the main medicines for epistaxis as well as more specific differentials are available in Chapter 20, Ear, Nose, and Throat.

This material should be memorized, and the medicine should be available on an emergency tray. The hemorrhage should subside in a few seconds following administration of the correct medicine in the 30C potency; if not, it is assumed to be an incorrect selection.

General Medicines for Hemorrhage

Arnica montana—This medicine is indicated when the blood is dark and fluid, but can be of any kind. The patient's soreness is aggravated by touch. The patient who will benefit from *Arnica montana* may have uterine or nasal hemorrhage from injury.

Belladonna—*Belladonna* is indicated for copious, bright red blood with clots. In uterine hemorrhage, a clot is passed followed by a gush of hot blood. Blood coagulates quickly, and the clots can be large. The patient may experience throbbing pains that are aggravated by jarring and fly all over the body. The patient is sensitive to touch, light, or being jarred.

Bryonia alba—This medicine is indicated when the hemorrhage is dark red. Pains are aggravated by motion; the patient is irritable and wants to be alone.

Carbo vegetabilis—*Carbo vegetabilis* is indicated when there is a passive hemorrhage of pale blood. Other symptoms include weakness, faintness, hot head, cyanosis, cold extremities, and a desire for open air.

Chamomilla—The patient presents with a dark fluid hemorrhage that coagulates when exposed to air, with bright red gushes. The patient complains of tearing and unendurable pain, and is irritable, whiny, and hypersensitive to that pain.

Cinchona officinalis—This medicine is indicated when the patient presents with dark blood and very dark clots. Pain is aggravated by the slightest touch and alleviated by firm pressure. Other symptoms include hypovolemia, weakness, and pallor from hemorrhage.

Ferrum metallicum—The patient has a hemorrhage with bright red blood with clots. He or she is also weak and anemic (compare with *Cinchona officinalis* above), and has gushes of blood (*Ipecacuanha* below). The patient may have yellowish or orange cheeks.

Ferrum phosphoricum—This medicine is used to treat hemorrhage of bright red blood. Like *Phosphorus*, it is used routinely.

Ferrum proto-oxalate—*Ferrum proto-oxalate* is effective for treating painless uterine hemorrhage (similar indications as *Belladonna* and *Sabina*, but painless). Nondescript. (Compare with *Kali ferrocyanatum*; see under "Remedies Specifically for Uterine Hemorrhage" below.)

Ipecacuanha—The patient is experiencing gushes of bright red blood with no clots. In uterine hemorrhage there is a pain from the navel to the uterus. Nausea and/or vomiting usually accompanies bleeding.

Lachesis mutus—When *Lachesis mutus* is indicated, the blood is dark or even black. The patient may be talkative and suspicious with darting eyes and tongue.

Phosphorus—The patient has a bright red and profuse hemorrhage. Small wounds also bleed profusely. Blood may have clots or be fluid. The patient has unquenchable thirst for ice water and desires company.

Remedies Specifically for Uterine Hemorrhage

Aletris farinosa—There is heavy bleeding with black clots, oozing in between menses, and anemia. The patient describes the uterus as feeling heavy.

Cinnamomum—The hemorrhage in patients requiring *Cinnamomum* is bright red with no clots, either profuse or continuous. The patient may be suffering from abruptio placentae. The patient may experience a bearing-down sensation.

Crocus sativus—The hemorrhage that should be treated with *Crocus sativus* consists of strings of clots with no fluid. The feet are ice cold and there may be a sensation that there is something alive in the abdomen even though the patient is not pregnant.

Crotalus horridus—This medicine is indicated for oozing dark blood. Other symptoms include dry skin and mouth, and palpitations during menses.

Erigeron canadensis—Hemorrhages requiring this medicine are bright red with black dark strings. They are aggravated by the least motion and are accompanied by tenesmus.

Hamamelis virginiana—Patients who would benefit from *Hamamelis virginiana* are suffering from a continuous, painless, steady, slow, and dark red flow. Women with many varicosities and hemorrhoids are most likely to present with these symptoms.

Kali ferrocyanatum—Symptoms that can be treated with this medicine include passive, painless, and thin uterine hemorrhage. Other indicators are debility, anemia, pallor, crying over little things, and aversion to consolation.

Kreosotum—Hemorrhage that should be treated with this medicine flows intermittently. The vagina burns and is sore.

Millefolium—This medicine is indicated for gushes of bright red blood in the beginning, followed by continuous bright red dribbling. It is especially useful after instrumented delivery. The hemorrhage may be painless.

Sabina—*Sabina* is indicated when liquid bright blood is intermingled with clots. It is watery and then coagulates. There are shooting pains from back to front and from below upwards (sacrum to pubis). These pains resemble bearing-down pains, as if to expel a clot.

Secale cornutum—Hemorrhage that benefits from *Secale cornutum* is black, coagulated, passive, and offensive; leaves a dark tarry stain; and is aggravated by motion. The hemorrhage can be copious or continuous. The patient feels chilled during the pains, but may have a burning sensation. The hemorrhage may be painless. *Secale cornutum* is usually indicated for multiparous women who are sensitive to heat and want to be uncovered.

Thlaspi bursa-pastoris—The patient presents with unclotted, dark hemorrhage. There is cramping, aching, and sore pain. This medicine is useful in women who have nosebleeds all through pregnancy and then hemorrhage at birth.

Trillium pendulum—This medicine should be used to treat active hemorrhage with thick, dark, and clotted blood. *Trillium pendulum* is useful in women who hemorrhage at each delivery. Normal lochea becomes watery; the patient feels as if her bones are broken.

Ustilago maidis—This medicine is indicated for treating passive, slow bleeding with huge clots. Blood may be half clots, half fluid blood; or oozing dark clotted material with black strings. The patient experiences bearing-down pain.

LACERATIONS

Since the differential for homeopathic treatment of lacerated wounds is very similar to that of surgical incisions, the reader can refer to Chapter 28, Postsurgical Care.

OVERUSE INJURIES

Repetitive stress injuries, so common in workers in the meat and computer industries, including carpal tunnel syndrome, have not been adequately addressed in the homeopathic literature as yet. However, there are several medicines that have been mentioned for repetitive stress injuries of the wrist, which are profiled below.

Ordinary muscle soreness following exercise might be alleviated by *Bellis perennis*, a member of the daisy family, which has been anecdotally reported to help the aches and pains of gardeners and laborers. This has not been studied. One large study showed *Arnica montana*, 30X is ineffective for muscle soreness following long-distance running (Vickers, Fisher, Smith, Wylie, & Rees, 1998).

Actaea spicata—This drug is prescribed when the patient suffers from tingling and tearing pains in the wrists aggravated by touch and motion. The joint may be swollen.

Causticum—The patient has *contractures* of the muscles and tendons as well as thickened and indurated tendons.

Ferrum phosphoricum—There is pain in the right wrist after writing that extends distally along the dorsal tendons and is aggravated when resting the joint. When the patient writes, the pain will occasionally extend proximally along the forearm, mostly in the dorsal and ulnar aspects. The pain is alleviated by warm compresses and wrapping. (See Chapter 7, *Ferrum phosphoricum*.)

Guaiacum—The patient complains of *left wrist* pain, possibly with contracture that is alleviated by cold applications.

Ruta graveolens—The patient presents with *tendonitis* with no distinctive symptoms.

Viola odorata—This medicine is indicated for pain and numbness of the *right wrist*, which may extend to the hand and fingers.

PUNCTURE WOUNDS

Ledum palustre, 30C is routinely prescribed for puncture wounds, including for *infiltration* from a blood draw or IV.

SCIATICA

Acute back pain is addressed in the sections on Sciatica, Spinal Injuries, and Sprains and Strains.

Data gathering for sciatica should include location, sensation, radiation, alleviating and aggravating factors, and accompanying symptoms. Patients who are experiencing moderate sciatic pain can be prescribed the 30C potency three times a day for 5 days; the drug can then be taken ad lib for pain if it has been effective.

Aconitum napellus—This medicine is indicated when the patient has suffered a *sudden* onset of shooting pains after exposure to cold, dry wind.

Ammonium muriaticum—The patient's pain is aggravated by *sitting* and relieved somewhat by walking or entirely by lying down. The patient may complain of having the sensation that the hamstrings are too short.

Colocynthis—Classic sciaticas with no unusual symptoms usually respond to *Colocynthis* if bilateral or left-sided, or *Magnesia phosphorica* if right-sided. The patient describes sharp, shooting pain alleviated by *pressure* and aggravated by cold, damp weather; motion; walking; and breathing. The patient may have drawing muscle contractions followed by numbness in the limb into which the sciatica extends. Symptoms also include irritability.

Dioscorea villosa—The patient presents with tearing pain in the *right* leg, from the point of exit of the sciatic nerve; the pain is only felt when *moving* or *sitting* up.

Gelsemium sempervirens—This medicine is indicated when there are burning pains aggravated at night, thereby preventing sleep. Pains are also aggravated at rest, and especially when *beginning to walk*. *Gelsemium sempervirens* is especially indicated for anterior crural neuralgia. (See Chapter 8, *Gelsemium sempervirens*.)

Gnaphalium polycephulum—The patient complains of *numbness* alternating with intense pain down the back of the leg that is aggravated by lying, moving, and stepping. Sometimes the numbness and pain are simultaneous. There may also be muscular cramping.

Hypericum perforatum—There is a sharp *shooting* pain, especially after injuries to the spine such as spinal surgery or coccyx injury during childbirth. The pain is aggravated by raising the arms and by touch.

Ignatia amara—*Ignatia amara* is indicated when the sciatica's onset is during *grieving*. Other symptoms include numbness, muscle cramps, and sharp pains along the nerve. (See Chapter 10, *Ignatia amara*.)

Kali iodatum—Severe pain is aggravated by being still; therefore, the patient is *restless*. The pains are aggravated when the patient warms up in bed, or lies on the affected side, and are alleviated by flexing the legs. The patient may have the sensation as though he or she is warmer than usual.

Lac caninum—This medicine is indicated when the pain *alternates* sides.

Lachesis mutus—The patient complains of right-sided sciatica that is aggravated by *slight touch* or after sleep.

Magnesia phosphorica—This medicine has similar indications as *Colocynthis*. The pain is alleviated by *heat* and hard pressure (often right-sided). The pains can be lightning-like. Compare with *Rhus toxicodendron*, which is aggravated by cold damp.

Natrum muriaticum—The patient presents with lumbago and sciatica that is alleviated by *lying on something hard*. The patient has a bruised feeling; the pillow feels too hard.

Natrum sulphuricum—The pain is only present when *stooping* or rising from a seat.

Nux vomica—*Nux vomica* is indicated for sciatica with the usual *Nux vomica* general etiologies and emotional states (see Chapter 12, *Nux vomica*). The pain is alleviated by heat, and aggravated by *passing stool* or urging at stool. The pain is usually right-sided, an indication similar to that of *Tellurium*.

Plumbum metallicum—The patient complains of cramping extending down the legs during severe *constipation* with colic.

Rhus toxicodendron—*Rhus toxicodendron* is indicated when the patient describes a lame feeling that is aggravated on first motion, and by cold and damp. *Continued motion* alleviates the pain (see Chapter 15, *Rhus toxicodendron*).

Ruta graveolens—When *Ruta graveolens* is indicated, the pain is directly in the *spine*, as if the patient had been beaten. The patient is more weak and lame than those who need *Rhus toxicodendron*. Lower extremities can give way. The patient's history includes injury or overuse. Symptoms are alleviated by rest and aggravated by motion, touch, sitting, breathing, and stepping.

Sepia—The patient has a weak sensation in the lower back, with sciatica that can extend to the heels. The sciatica is aggravated by sitting, and alleviated by pressure or lying on the right side. The pain is more often on the right side even though the general symptoms of this medicine are usually left-sided.

Tellurium metallicum—*Tellurium metallicum* is prescribed for patients with right-sided sciatica that is aggravated by lying on the leg, coughing, jarring, laughing, sneezing, pressing to pass stool, and stooping. This medicine may palliate pain of a ruptured disk.

SPINAL INJURIES

This protocol is for recent spinal injuries. Chronic pain of any kind is best addressed collaboratively, with a homeopathic specialist as part of the team. If the injury has occurred in the past 6 weeks, one of the following medicines can reputedly ease pain and speed healing. There has been no research done to support or refute these claims.

The 30C potency can be prescribed three times a day for a week, then p.r.n. for pain if the drug has been effective. The more severe the injury, the more beneficial it would be to use a higher potency, such as 200C (once a day for 5 days) or a 1M (once a day for 3 days), then p.r.n. for pain.

Bellis Perennis—This medicine is used to treat pain from spinal injuries from sudden deceleration accidents or near accidents (when the patient grabbed onto something). The pain is experienced up and down the entire back. *Bellis perennis* is sometimes helpful for the pain of compression fractures.

Hypericum perforatum—These pains arise after injury and may *shoot* up and/or down the spine, or be described as tearing. This medicine can be prescribed for injury to the *coccyx*, sacral pain after instrumental delivery, and cervical pain that extends to the arm and is aggravated by moving the head.

Natrum sulphuricum—This medicine is used to treat spinal pain after injury, especially *spinal concussion*, that is aggravated by sidelying, sitting, retention of urine, and motion. The pain worsens at night. There are piercing pains between the scapulae. The patient may describe a sharp knife-like pain in the back spreading upwards like a fan. There may be violent pains in the cervical spine and occiput. The pain is accompanied by gloomy *depression*. The patient isolates him- or herself and is loathe to talk about his or her problems.

Thuja occidentalis—The patient presents with bruised pain in the spine, especially lumbar, as if he or she has been beaten. The pain is aggravated by the *jar* of taking a step, or accidentally making a false step that jiggles the patient. The pain is also aggravated during menstruation, or by *straightening* the back.

SPRAINS AND STRAINS

Sprains and strains are commonly self-treated by homeopathic self-care enthusiasts. A typical schedule would be to give the medicine in the 30C potency three times a day for 3 days and then with gradually decreasing frequency until the discomfort and stiffness have resolved.

Cervical Sprain and Strain

Bryonia alba—*Bryonia alba* is indicated when there is a painful stiffness in the neck, with pain on every *motion*, and when the patient is irritable.

Cimicifuga racemosa—This medicine should be prescribed when the neck is very stiff and sore following an injury, especially acceleration/deceleration injuries (e.g., whiplash). The pain is aggravated by *pressure* and can cause nausea and vomiting. Pain may be present in the angle of the left scapula. The patient is depressed, yet talkative, and may describe the impression that a *black cloud* has enveloped him or her; the patient's thinking is foggy; or the patient may fear that he or she is going insane.

Rhus toxicodendron—The neck is stiff and achy, but improves from *continuing to move* and stretch it, and from a *warm* shower or heating pad. There may be cracking and popping sounds in the neck on motion. Pain frequently extends to the left shoulder. (See Chapter 15, *Rhus toxicodendron*.)

Sanguinaria canadensis—This medicine is indicated for neck pain that extends to the *right* shoulder.

Extremities

Ledum palustre—The tissue around the joint is *cool*, indurated, and bluish or *blanched* (in light complected people). Ice packs and cool compresses alleviate the pain.

Rhus toxicodendron—The joint is stiff and achy, but improves from *continuing to move* it, and from *warm* bath, shower, or heating pad.

Ruta graveolens—The patient presents with *residual* mild pain in an ankle weeks after a sprain. The patient may have a swollen aching joint, tendonitis, or sprained *ocular muscles* from overuse.

Lumbar and Lumbosacral Sprain or Strain, and Lumbago

Agaricus mescarius—Back pain is aggravated by sitting, exerting, sexual intercourse, or bending forward. (The patient complains of the sensation that the spine will break when stooping.) Symptoms are alleviated by lying down. The patient demonstrates obsessive *anxiety about health* and is focused on the back.

Bryonia alba—The patient stays in bed, *not moving*. Pain is alleviated by placing something hard under the patient's back, and by having him or her stand still. Other symptoms include *irritability*, thirst, and wanting to be left alone. (See Chapter 5, *Bryonia alba*.)

Calcarea carbonica—This medicine is used to treat weakness of the back that follows injury from *lifting or overexertion*. The weakness is aggravated in cold, damp weather. This is more commonly seen in obese people.

Calcarea fluorica—Back pains resemble those treatable with *Rhus toxicodendron*. Patients easily *overheat* and may suffer from *severe scoliosis*.

Calcarea phosphorica—*Calcarea phosphorica* is indicated for people with scoliosis who have *sacroiliac injuries* from lifting. The sacrum is numb and lame, or sacroiliac area feels broken to the patient. The pain may make the patient scream and is aggravated by *cold and damp*. The patient's hands and feet are cold and clammy.

Nux vomica—There is pain in the big muscles, usually from becoming chilled after overexertion. The pain is alleviated by *warmth*. The patient is *irritable*, impatient, and possibly constipated. (See Chapter 12, *Nux vomica*.)

Rhododendron chrysanthum—The symptoms are very much like those of *Rhus toxicodendron* (i.e., aggravated by cold and damp, alleviated by motion and warmth), with tearing pain in the lower back. Sacral pains are aggravated by sitting. Pain may intensify *before* a storm. This medicine may be useful when *Rhus toxicodendron* is not effective, even though it seemed indicated.

Rhus toxicodendron—The pain is alleviated by *warmth* and *motion*, and aggravated by cool, damp weather.

Sulphur—The patient cannot rise from the chair without great difficulty, and cannot sit down in the chair without dropping the last few inches. Back pain is aggravated by *standing*. The patient cannot sit up straight. (See Chapter 16, *Sulphur*.)

SUNSTROKE AND HEAT EXHAUSTION

A 30C potency medicine can be prescribed once an hour for three doses in addition to the usual first aid measures.

Belladonna—Like the symptom associated with *Glonoinum*, there is a *throbbing headache* and red face. In patients who will respond to *Belladonna*, however, there is more likely to be dilated pupils, dry skin, and possibly outright delirium with hallucinations. (See Chapter 4, *Belladonna*.)

Glonoinum—This is the most common medicine for heatstroke. It should be prescribed when the patient has a severe, *throbbing*, and *bursting* headache with a hot red face and perspiration. Patient is disoriented and becomes lost in familiar locations.

Veratrum album—*Veratrum album* is indicated for the collapsed patient with *vomiting and diarrhea* and cold perspiration on the forehead.

SYNCOPE

Syncope can have many etiologies. The following are medicines for syncope and faintness caused by common emotional situations or minor acute illness. A single dose of 30C may be given in addition to the usual positioning strategy. Noticeable relief will be felt immediately if the prescription is correct. More doses may be given as needed if the faint feeling returns.

Aconitum napellus—This medicine is used for syncope after a fright; the patient is restless, *anxious*, and thirsty.

Arsenicum album—*Arsenicum album* can be used to treat syncope before or after vomiting or stool, or during asthmatic crisis. The patient's frequent fainting is aggravated in the morning and from motion. This medicine can be used to treat syncope in pregnancy and labor. Other symptoms include anxiety, desire for company, and sipping of (preferably) warm drinks. (See Chapter 3, *Arsenicum album*.)

Carbo vegetabilis—This medicine can be used to treat people debilitated from dehydration or a previous illness, who have faintness, bluish skin, a hot head, and cold extremities. The patient craves moving *air*, fans him- or herself, stands in front of a fan or air conditioner.

Coffea cruda—Syncope from *good news* should be treated with *Coffea cruda*.

Ignatia amara—Syncope from *bad news*, such as a disease diagnosis or news of a death, should be treated with *Ignatia amara*. (See Chapter 10, *Ignatia amara*.)

Moschus—This medicine is indicated for syncope of anxious women, who are emotionally highly reactive (i.e., historically known as *hysteria*). Symptoms intensify in the open air, at menopause, before or during the menses, or from anemia.

Nux vomica—Syncope from the sight of *bloody* wounds responds to *Nux vomica*.

Opium—*Opium* should be used to treat syncope after a fright that is accompanied by general lethargy, *sleepiness*, and disorientation.

Pulsatilla—Syncope from a *stuffy* room can be alleviated with *Pulsatilla*.

CHAPTER 18

Skin

The approach to the treatment of skin disease is very different in homeopathic medicine than in conventional medicine. All but the most transient rashes and infections are viewed by the classically trained homeopath as manifestations of deeper health imbalances of the whole person. The routine treatment of an even minor skin condition by steroid or antibiotic creams, minor surgery, or chemical ablation is believed to intensify, or even create, more serious concurrent chronic disease in the patient. This theory of health and disease will be discussed in Chapter 29, History and Conceptual Framework of Homeopathic Medicine.

Because many skin disorders are considered to have deep roots physiologically, the prognosis of treatment with primary care homeopathy is often provisional, and depends on the patient's overall health. The prognosis is good if the patient as a whole is healthy and happy, and the skin problem is of recent onset. More chronic, multifaceted cases would best be referred to a homeopathic specialist.

ACNE

Acne is an example of a condition viewed as an expression of an internal health imbalance by most homeopaths. Therefore, its treatment is complex, and there are dozens (if not hundreds) of different homeopathic medicines that could be prescribed for it. That being said, there are a handful of medicines that are the most frequently indicated, and if the patient matches some key characteristics of one of these medicines it may very well benefit them. The clinician should prescribe the 12C potency twice a day for 6 weeks. Because of its chronic nature, improvement is most often not noted for several weeks. The patient should be educated that the eruptions may intensify somewhat at the beginning, before subsiding.

Most Commonly Indicated Medicines

Calcarea silicata—This medicine should be used to treat *pustular* acne in very chilly and constipated patients, who are nonetheless intolerant of heat. The patient is fearful, irritable, and indecisive.

Calcarea sulphurica—*Calcarea sulphurica* is the most common medicine for moderate to severe acne; it is highly effective for infected abscesses that have a lumpy *sanguinopurulent* discharge.

Hepar sulphuris calcareum—This medicine is indicated for pimples on the face and the forehead, in particular, that are very *painful* to touch. (See Chapter 9, *Hepar sulphuris calcareum*.)

Natrum muriaticum—For the patient whose skin is even more *oily* than most acne patients, *Natrum muriaticum* is most effective. He or she may have a history of multiple losses (e.g., deaths of loved ones, loss of home) and become withdrawn and noncommunicative. The patient has a desire or aversion to salty foods, and a strong thirst.

Nux vomica—This medicine is prescribed for the acne of lively, *irritable*, and hard-driving adolescents who work and play hard, like spicy foods, and are attracted to drugs and/or alcohol. (See Chapter 12, *Nux vomica*.)

Sulphur—*Sulphur* works well for the acne of intellectually active patients with strong self-esteem who are sensitive to heat. They kick the covers off at night because they cannot tolerate the warmth. They may have a history of other skin problems. Teenagers who love pizza and soda and have untidy habits may benefit from this medicine. (See Chapter 16, *Sulphur*).

ATOPIC DERMATITIS, SEBORRHEA, AND PSORIASIS

Eczema, seborrhea, psoriasis, and dry skin are chronic health problems that people commonly seek help for from a homeopathic specialist. They cannot be effectively treated within the time limits and skill level of a typical integrative primary care practice.

BACTERIAL INFECTIONS OF THE DERMIS

Abscesses, Infected Wounds, and Suppurative Processes

The safe resolution of treatment of inflammatory and suppurative processes is reputedly hastened by homeopathic medicines. It is not yet established whether homeopathic medicines are effective when antibiotics are given concurrently. In the early stages of inflammatory processes or in very small abscesses, the healing process will be sufficiently accelerated by a routine prescription of a 30C potency, like that described in Chapter 1, An Introduction to Homeopathic Medicine. Special instructions will follow for more advanced infected wounds and abscesses.

Early Inflammatory Stage

Apis mellifica—The patient presents with a soft, warm, and pinkish (in the light-skinned) swelling that stings and is sensitive to contact with anything warm or hot, and is alleviated by cool compresses. This will respond to *Apis mellifica*, a medicine made from honeybees.

Belladonna—*Belladonna* is indicated when there are all the signs of inflammation: redness, swelling, heat, and throbbing pain. This prescription should be in the early part of the suppurative process, preceding or at the onset of pus formation. (See Chapter 4, *Belladonna*.)

Localization Stages

Calcarea sulphurica—On other occasions, discharges continue from abscess via a *fistula*, continuing for weeks or even months. The discharges are yellow, lumpy, and bloody and full of pus. *Calcarea sulphurica* is expected to complete the healing of the abscess and stop the discharge.

Hepar sulphuris calcareum—When pus has clearly formed, and has either consolidated in a subdermal abscess, or is venting freely from a wound or fistula, the preferred medicine is *Hepar sulphuris calcareum*. *Hepar sulphuris calcareum* 4X has been studied for its effects on pyoderma in general, in terms of days to resolution, by a German researcher (Mossinger, 1980) and found to be only slightly more effective than placebo in a small study with fair to poor internal validity. In North America this would be considered too low a potency to have optimal effect in suppurative processes. A 30C potency should be used for a small, mildly purulent wound or abscess, given three times a day for 3 days, then with decreasing frequency until the pus has cleared. For larger, more quickly advancing purulent conditions, treatment should begin with a 30C every hour for three doses, then continue every 3 hr for three doses. Improvement should be visible at this time, and from the beginning of treatment, there would be no extension of involvement noted. Repetition of the dose can then continue with gradually decreasing frequency, and then stop when the pus has cleared. A 200C potency is believed to exert a more powerful effect, and can follow the 30C in these cases two to three times a day for a few days, when the patient seems to be improving but more rapid healing or less frequent dosing is desired. The clinician must closely monitor the patient and leave him or her with a prescription for an appropriate antibiotic in case it is needed. (See Chapter 9, *Hepar sulphuris calcareum.*)

Silicea—Occasionally, after the inflammation and flow of pus have subsided from treatment with *Hepar sulphuris calcareum*, painless pockets of pus remain behind. *Silicea*, 30C once a day for up to 1 week, is expected to bring the infection to resolution either through resorption or venting. A rarely used medicine called *Myristica sebifera* is said to hasten suppuration when *Silicea* fails.

Lymphatic Involvement

Bufo rana—When the septic process—with or without cellulitis—has traveled though the lymphatic ducts to the local lymph nodes, causing a localized *lymphangitis*, especially axillary, the medicine that should be prescribed is *Bufo rana*. It can be prescribed in the 200C potency three times a day for 3 days, and then with decreasing frequency until the lymphangitis has resolved. Obviously, in mainstream health settings there would be great haste to prescribe antibiotics, and again it is unknown how beneficial homeopathy is when prescribed concurrently with antibiotics.

Generalized Sepsis*

Again, a primary care clinician in the modern medical climate would not prescribe a homeopathic medicine without an antibiotic if

---

*Homeopathic physicians served at the front in World War I. A low-potency homeopathic medicine, still containing a significant amount of the original substance, was made out of the gunpowder of the time. This was prescribed in the 3X potency administered orally for soldiers with wounds, and was anecdotally reported to protect against wound infection. It has not been studied and is still used primarily in England in various potencies.

there were the suspicion of sepsis. Therefore, the classical treatment for the onset of generalized sepsis is only briefly discussed below.

Arsenicum album—The local symptoms are accompanied by anxiety, chilliness, restlessness, and thirst for sips of warm drinks. (See Chapter 3, *Arsenicum album.*)

Echinacea angustifolia—So commonly used in botanical medicine, *Echinacea angustifolia* has a very rare, circumscribed use in homeopathic medicine for sepsis and lymphangitis. The patient feels weak and tired and has muscular aching. He or she speaks and ambulates slowly. The patient feels worse in general from eating and exposure to cold air, and better from lying down and resting. The affect is depressed and irritable, especially from being contradicted. Other symptoms include headache, flushed or bluish face, burning hot forehead from fever, and chilliness accompanied with nausea and perspiration. The patient may also have an irregular fever and chills, sour-tasting hematemesis, and perspiration on the upper body and on the forehead.

Mercurius vivus or *Mercurius solubilis*—These medicines are used to treat sepsis with profuse perspiration, sensitivity to both heat and cold, drooling, and foul odor and metallic taste in mouth. These general symptoms and others are presented in Chapter 11, *Mercurius vivus* or *Mercurius solubilis.*

Pyrogenium—*Pyrogenium* is prescribed for sepsis with fever during which the chill stage predominates. Pulse and fever are disproportionate (e.g., high fever with normal pulse, or low fever with tachycardia). Patient is restless; the tongue is red and shiny. The patient has body aches and generalized soreness. There is a febrile flush of the face starting around 3:00 or 4:00 p.m. that lasts until midnight, and is followed by large drops of cold perspiration on the skin.

Historically, septic shock, disseminated intravascular coagulation, and gangrene were treated with such medicines as *Crotalus horridus*, *Lachesis mutus*, *Tarentula cubensis*, and *Anthracinum*. These medicines are manufactured from venomous snakes, spiders, and disease products that mimic the end stages of a patient decompensating from bacteremia. Needless to say, a solely homeopathic approach would be unethical today.

Erysipelas

This condition may be prescribed the 30C potency every 4 hr for three doses. If there is improvement, the medicine can be repeated twice a day until the lesions have resolved. The patient who opts for homeopathic treatment should be written a prescription for an antibiotic that should be started if the condition worsens or does not rapidly improve from the homeopathic medicine.

Aconitum napellus—Eruptions come on very *rapidly*, and are red, hot, swollen, dry, and burning, and accompanied with high fever, anxiety, and thirst. Lesions sometimes extend toward the patient's left.

Apis mellifica—This is used to treat erysipelas with sensitiveness, *puffiness,* and a rosy hue. The lesions sting and can progress to gangrene.

Belladonna—Like when *Aconitum napellus* is being prescribed, the eruption is bright *red*, dry, and hot, and comes on quickly. The general symptoms help one distinguish erysipelas that should be treated with one or the other. When there is red face, dilated pupils, high fever, throbbing and thirstlessness, *Belladonna* should be administered. The patient's eyes look glassy and he or she seems mentally unfocused or may even hallucinate with the fever. (See Chapter 4, *Belladonna*.)

Croton tiglium—This medicine is indicated for vesicular clusters with *severe pruritis*, followed by burning, especially on the face and genitals. Area becomes sore if scratched, and is alleviated by gentle rubbing. Vesicles burst and form crusts.

Euphorbia officinarum—The patient presents with bullous or vesicular erysipelas of the *mucous membranes* that are red and swollen and cause stinging pains. The vesicles are filled with yellow exudate.

Graphites—*Graphites* is used to treat erysipelas that changes location or recurs, with a moist crusty eruption. There is a sticky, thin, and *honey-colored* exudate. Lesions extend or move to the left. The patient is afebrile.

Lachesis mutus—This medicine is best used to treat mottled or *dark* lesions in elderly patients who are talkative and heat/sun intolerant. These lesions can turn gangrenous.

Mercurius vivus—The patient has moist and crusty eruptions. Scratching aggravates them. The patient *perspires* heavily, is sensitive to heat and cold, drools in his or her sleep, has an offensive odor, and is thirsty. (See Chapter 11, *Mercurius vivus* or *Mercurius solubilis*.)

Rhus toxicodendron—Lesions with marked swelling with burning, itching, and stinging are best treated with *Rhus toxicodendron*. Scratching aggravates the itching. Lesions move or extend left to right and may turn gangrenous. There is generalized *stiffness and achiness* that is alleviated by warmth and aggravated by cold damp. The patient desires milk. The clinician should note a red triangle at the tip of the tongue. (See Chapter 15, *Rhus toxicodendron*.)

Furuncles and Carbuncles

All the medicines for suppurative processes in general are important medicines for furuncles. In addition, there are several special medicines for furuncles that tend to progress to carbuncles, or to recur. The 30C potency may be prescribed three times a day for 5 days, then with diminishing frequency if effective. If not effective, the medicine should be discontinued, and another appropriate medicine given a trial.

Anthracinum—The patient has successions of indurated blue or black furuncles and carbuncles, with tremendous *burning*, especially above the scapula or on the back of the shoulder. *Burning* furuncles are reputed to respond to one of the following medicines: *Anthracinum, Apis mellifica, Arsenicum album, Crotalus cascavella, Hepar sulphuris calcareum*, or *Tarentula cubensis* (van Zandvoort, 1997).

Arsenicum album—This medicine is used to treat burning furuncles alleviated by warm compresses that are more likely to arise on the right side of the body. (See Chapter 3, *Arsenicum album*.)

Crotalus horridus—The patient presents with bluish or *dark*, blood-filled boils or carbuncles that are surrounded by purplish mottled skin and edema. They are more likely to occur on the *right* side of the body.

Lachesis mutus—Carbuncles with a *bluish-purplish* appearance and with small vesicles surrounding them are best treated with *Lachesis mutus*. These lack the burning pains of several of the carbuncles treated with other medicines, and are more likely to occur on the *left* side of the body. The manner of the patient may be loquacious or suspicious.

Secale cornutum*—Secale cornutum* is for gradually progressing furuncles with *green* pus, especially in thin elderly people with claudication and burning feet, twitching or quivering in skin, and formication under the skin.

***Sulphur*—**The boils come up in crops. Furuncles are *recurring*, periodical, or come in succession. These furuncles are often seen in intellectually active and sloppy people prone to skin problems who are sensitive to heat. The patient kicks off the covers at night. (See Chapter 16, *Sulphur*.)

***Tarentula cubensis*—**This medicine is for indurated, bluish carbuncles with severe *burning stabbing pains*. The patient is very *weak* and perspires profusely.

Impetigo and Folliculitis

The standard prescribing instructions, as presented in Chapter 1, may be given. The medicine selected may be given in the 30C potency, three times a day for up to a week. The usual patient education about hygiene should be given (e.g., clipping the nails very short).

Most Commonly Indicated Medicines

***Antimonium crudum*—**Vesicles and scaly pustules with *thick, honey-colored* scabs that burn and itch are best treated with *Antimonium crudum*. The itching is aggravated when warm in bed (like with *Mercurius*). The patient's skin may be dry.

***Dulcamara*—**The vesicular eruptions become thick, *brown-yellow* crusts that bleed when scratched, and then they become sensitive bleeding ulcers. There are moist eruptions on the face, genitals, and hands. The associated glands may be enlarged. The eruptions are aggravated in damp, cold weather.

***Hepar sulphuris calcareum*—**The patient has offensive moist eruptions in folds, such as papules that are prone to *suppurate* and extend. There is impetigo in patients for whom every slight injury of the skin becomes infected. (See Chapter 9, *Hepar sulphuris calcareum*.)

Mercurius vivus—Vesicular and pustular eruptions with pruritis are aggravated from getting too warm in bed. These may become irregularly shaped ulcers with undefined edges. There are pimples around the main eruption. The patient *perspires* heavily. (See Chapter 11, *Mercurius vivus* or *Mercurius solubilis*.)

Rhus toxicodendron—The eruptions markedly burn, itch, and sting. Scratching aggravates the itching. Lesions move (or extend) left to right. There is a red triangle at the tip of the tongue. (See Chapter 15, *Rhus toxicodendron*.)

Less Commonly Indicated Medicines

Arsenicum album—The patient with vesicles that cause severe *burning* pain that are alleviated by warm applications. (See Chapter 3, *Arsenicum album*.)

Arum triphyllum—Bright red eruptions that stay red as though the skin is stained are best treated with *Arum triphyllum*. There is itching of fingers and toes and denuded raw bloody surfaces. The child *picks* the nose and lips.

Juglans cinerea—There are pustules on the *thighs, hips, and buttocks* that itch and burn, with a few pustules on the trunk and arms.

Kali bichromicum—These lesions are pustules with black apices, often beginning as folliculitis, that later may leave ulcers with a *"punched out"* appearance and sticky exudate. There may also be vesicular eruption with itching. After healing, round depressed scars remain behind.

Mezereum—The lesions ooze an acrid glutinous exudate and form *thick crusts* with pus or a *chalky white* material underneath. There may be severe itching that moves after it is scratched.

Nitricum acidum—Impetigo becomes ragged or *fissured* easily; there are bleeding ulcers with plugs of pus and *splinter-like* pain. Long continued suppurative processes.

Viola tricolor—The patient presents with very itchy impetigo on the *face and head*, with burning and itching that is aggravated at night. There are thick scabs that crack and exude a sticky, yellow pus.

CONTACT DERMATITIS

Rhus Dermatitis

Oil of urushiol is the central dermatitis producing chemical of poison ivy and poison oak. After exposure to the oil, the patient needs to remove it with rubbing alcohol poured over the area, or with commercial products like Technu. It usually takes 1–2 days after exposure for the rash to appear. However, the most highly sensitive (10%) will get symptoms in 4–8 hr. Typically, the whole process of erythema and vesicles is completed in 10–14 days (Epstein, 1998).

Homeopathic medicines can be prescribed concurrently with oat meal (Aveeno) bath for poison ivy and poison oak rashes. The homeopathic medicine is unlikely to be effective when corticosteroids are administered concurrently. Patients that present with severe dermatitis over much of the body, or dermatitis approaching the eye should be treated with steroids exclusively.

It is best to treat *Rhus* poisoning early with homeopathy. Poison oak of the western *diversaloba* type nearly always presents initially with indurated striated lesions, which are blanched in light-skinned people, surrounded by erythema. If the medicine *Ledum palustre* is given at this stage, it is believed that the painful vesicular rash that erupts later can be greatly diminished in size and severity. Sensitive people should carry a vial of *Ledum palustre* on hikes and camping trips to be taken as soon as symptoms begin. The clinician should prescribe a 30C potency once every 3 hr for three doses, then three times a day until symptoms are mostly resolved (up to 5 days). There has been no research done on homeopathic treatment of *Rhus* dermatitis. The eastern poison oak more often presents initially with reddened dots; this will sometimes respond to the medicine *Urtica urens*, prescribed as *Ledum* would be.

Soon the papulovesicular or vesiculobullous lesions begin, and the homeopathic treatment must be individualized. It may seem strange that the differential between medicines includes the location of the rash, because that is believed to be an artifact of where the patient was exposed to the plant. But clinically, the location does seem to be important.

Most Commonly Indicated Medicines

Anacardium orientale—The patient has tremendous itching that is relieved by scalding water (like the medicines manufactured from the *Rhus* genus) and aggravated by scratching. There is much swelling and yellow vesicles from the size of a pinhead to a pea that sometimes burn and are often scarlet red. The clinician may need to choose between prescribing *Anacardium* and *Rhus* based only on the main seat of the *Anacardium* rash being the *forearm and face*, and not significantly elsewhere on the body.

Graphites—Moist vesicles ooze a sticky, *honey-colored* exudate. They are aggravated at night, and unlike most of the medicines for this dermatitis, by warmth. The vesicles are found on the fingers, buttocks, feet, toes, face, vulva, penis, back, and bends of joints.

Sulphur—*Sulphur* is used to treat *Rhus* poisoning accompanied by itching that is aggravated at *night in bed*, and from bathing or scratching. The patient is sensitive to heat and tosses the covers off the feet at night. He or she craves sweets, fat, spicy foods, and alcohol. The rash may be located almost anywhere: the hands, forearms, wrists, legs, feet, toes, elbows, face, and vulva. (See Chapter 16, *Sulphur*.)

The Toxicodendron genus

The three main members of the *Toxicodendron* genus family in North America have each been made into homeopathic medicines. The itching associated with two of the three is temporarily relieved by showering in very hot water. There are subtle differences between the three, and the patient's symptoms may correspond to the species the patient was exposed to.

Rhus diversiloba (Toxicodendron diverisiloba, or Poison Oak)—The patient presents with violent skin symptoms, with severe heat, burning, and itching. There is a vesicular rash on the face with great *edema* and swelling of the glands of the neck. Vesicles dry to a crust that makes movements of the face and mouth painful. There may be heat and itching of the scrotum and adjacent surface of the thigh. Unlike other members of the *Rhus* genus, the itching is alleviated by cold and aggravated by heat, warmth, rubbing, or scratching. The rash may be found on the face, hands, and genitalia. Eruptions may return annually without further exposure to the plant.

Rhus toxicodendron (Toxicodendron radicans and T. toxicarium, or Poison Ivy)—The patient suffers intense, burning pruritus that is *alleviated by heat* and scratching, and aggravated at night from exposure to open air. The skin swells and forms multiple small yellow vesicles, which break open and leave crusts. The patient is very *restless* and cannot get comfortable in bed. There may be lymphatic enlargement. The rash may be found almost anywhere: hands, joints, inner aspect of joints, forearms, wrists, fingers, thighs, knees, legs, face, eyelids, vulva, scrotum, and back. (See Chapter 15, *Rhus toxicodendron.*)

Rhus venenata (Poison Elder)—There are clusters of fine vesicles with severe pruritus that is relieved by hot water. The involved skin turns *dark red*. There are red, indurated lesions, especially on the face, neck, and chest. The patient complains of much itching of the face and genitalia at night. The rash may be located on the forearms, wrists, back of the hands, thighs, feet, toes, ankles, face, eyelids, penis, and scrotum.

Less Commonly Indicated Medicines

Anagallis arvensis—*Anagallis arvensis* is indicated for dry, *grouped*, vesicular eruptions on the hands and fingers, especially the palms. New vesicles appear on the hands after the first crop has healed.

Bryonia alba—Toxicodendron exposure makes the patient feel ill in general; he or she wants to lie down alone, and be perfectly still. The local symptoms are relatively mild. He or she desires large amounts of water at long intervals. The patient is *irritable* and averse to consolation. (See Chapter 5, *Bryonia alba.*) The vesicles are on the face or back.

Croton tiglium—The patient has intensely itching *confluent* vesicles, followed by painful burning. Scratching is painful, especially for rashes of the *male genitalia*. The rash may be found on the thighs, face, eyelids, penis, and scrotum.

Sanguinaria canadensis—This medicine is best used for *prickling* heat that has spread over the body with red blotchy eruptions and no vesicles. The burning and itching are aggravated by heat.

Sepia—*Sepia* is indicated when there is a vesicular rash in the *bends of the elbows and knees*, with itching that is not relieved by scratching. Patient may become chilly and apathetic during the rash, which may be located on the back, fingers, knees, hollows of knees, calves, feet, upper arms, face, vulva, and penis.

FUNGAL INFECTIONS

Tinea infections of recent origin may respond to one of these medicines. The clinician should give the 30C potency once a day for a week; if the patient improves, the medicine should be stopped unless relapse occurs, and then repeated as needed. If there is no improvement, the clinician should prescribe the next most likely medicine. Applying apple cider vinegar externally one to three times a day is also beneficial.

General

Arsenicum album—The patient presents with very dry eruptions with *rough scales*, which may become wet on scratching. Scratching also aggravates the pruritus. The patient may pick at the scales until they bleed. The general symptoms of *Arsenicum album*, such as burning pains alleviated by warmth, may be present as well. (See Chapter 3, *Arsenicum album*.)

Graphites—*Graphites* should be used to treat eruptions in the folds of the skin that ooze thick, *amber* exudate. The skin is generally dry, thickened, and cracked.

Mancinella—*Mancinella* is used to treat tinea pedis with vesiculobullous eruptions that ooze a sticky exudate, and may also have brown crusts and scabs (compare with *Graphites*). This medicine is commonly indicated for adolescents with depressed affect.

Mezereum—The patient has burning, intolerably itchy eruptions that ulcerate and form *thick scabs*. Beneath the scabs, there is purulent material.

Sepia—The patient has isolated, brown, or white, slightly scaly spots on the upper part of the body. The rash is dry, but the skin becomes moist after scratching. *Sepia* is more commonly indicated at times of hormonal transitions, such as pregnancy and menopause.

Silicea—This medicine is used to treat tinea pedis with vesicles between the toes. The patient shows none of the distinctive features of the other medicines.

Sulphur—*Sulphur* can be used to treat very itchy eruptions. The pruritus is aggravated by *warmth or bathing* as well as by scratching, which makes the area burn. The general symptoms of *Sulphur* may be present. (See Chapter 16, *Sulphur*.)

Tellurium metallicum—The patient has red and itchy ringworm that becomes wet with tiny blisters.

Onychomycosis

Hyperkeratosis subungualis and distal onychomycosis with the resulting nail dystrophy such as from infection with *Trichophyton rubrum* or *Tinia unguinum* have reportedly been successfully treated with homeopathic medicines. A daily dip in apple cider vinegar has also been gradually curative of nail fungus. The differential below is for onychomycosis of recent origin in healthy people. The 12C potency can be prescribed twice a day for 6 weeks. If the nails are improving, the patient may continue taking the medicine until the nail dystrophy has resolved.

Antimonium crudum—This medicine is indicated for thickened, hard, and possibly deformed nails that tend to *split longitudinally*. This is the most important medicine for *horny growth* under the nails. There is hyperkeratosis, cracking of the skin, and hard warts on the hands and feet. The patient often has digestive complaints as well.

Graphites—The patient presents with thick, discolored, and deformed toenails that peel or fall off. The patient may be chilly, mentally dull, and sad; he or she may also suffer from constipation, dyspepsia, and dry skin.

Silicea—The patient has thickened, ridged, brittle, and yellowed nails with white spots. The feet are cold and damp with offensive perspiration. The patient is chilly, mild-mannered, and obstinate.

HERPETIC INFECTIONS

Herpes Simplex

The duration and discomfort of herpetic eruptions are reportedly diminished by treatment with appropriate medicines. While some homeopathic specialists make claims of complete remission of outbreaks with long-term treatment, the integrative clinician is more likely to see symptomatic relief of the current episode. If outbreaks are recurrent, the patient should obtain the appropriate medicine in the 30C potency in anticipation of the next episode because the maximum benefit can be gained from beginning treatment early during an outbreak. The patient can begin taking the medicine every 3 hr for three doses when the prodromal symptoms are noticed. If the medicine seems to be helping, it can be continued twice a day for the remainder of the outbreak. Possible signs of improvement include diminished discomfort and diminished constitutional symptoms (e.g., malaise). If treatment begins later in an outbreak, quicker drying up and healing of lesions will be noted with the correct medicine.

Most Commonly Indicated Medicines

Apis mellifica—This medicine is indicated for puffy, warm, *stinging*, and rosy eruptions that are aggravated by warmth and alleviated by cool compresses.

Arsenicum album—The patient has severely burning lesions that feel better from *warmth*. He or she is chilly, febrile, restless, anxious, and thirsty for sips of water or warm tea. Less commonly, there may be black, blue, or blood-filled vesicles. (See Chapter 3, *Arsenicum album*.)

Hepar sulphuris calcareum—Herpetic lesions of the oral cavity that are *hypersensitive* to cold food and water are best treated with this medicine. (See Chapter 9, *Hepar sulphuris calcareum*.)

Mercurius vivus or Mercurius solubilis—*Mercurius* is indicated for genital herpes with the usual local symptoms and swelling of the local nodes. Patient is febrile, sensitive to heat and cold, *perspires* heavily, and has an offensive odor. Outbreaks commonly occur during menstruation in women. (See Chapter 11, *Mercurius vivus* or *Mercurius solubilis*.)

Natrum muriaticum—*Natrum muriaticum* is used to treat herpes simplex in any location that flares during periods of grief. The patient is reserved and averse to consolation. The patient's thirst is increased, and there is marked desire or aversion to salt. There are pearly herpes around the *lips* and fissure down the center of the lower lip. The lips may tingle or feel numb.

Rhus toxicodendron—This medicine is indicated for small vesicles of the anogenital area, lips, or oral cavity with a red base, that itch and burn. The outbreak is accompanied by generalized achiness that is alleviated by moving around and warmth, and aggravated by cold and damp. The pains of this genital herpes shoot down to the legs. *Natrum muriaticum* and *Rhus toxicodendron* are reputed to be the most common medicines for herpes on the lips, face, and around the mouth. (See Chapter 15, *Rhus toxicodendron*.)

Sepia—*Sepia* is used to treat itchy genital herpes that extends up the *vagina*. Outbreaks occur during the menses in female patients.

Less Commonly Indicated Medicines

Borax—*Borax* is used to treat herpetic lesions about the lips with concurrent apthae of the mouth and tongue, especially in children. The patient fears downward motion (e.g., an infant being put in a crib, or an elevator ride). He or she is also greatly sensitive to noise.

Croton tiglium—Genital herpes with formication and itching of the clustered vesicles is best treated with *Croton tiglium*. Scratching is painful. The rash is alleviated by gentle rubbing. The vesicles burst and form crusts.

Dulcamara—The patient presents with moist, oozing eruptions and brown-yellow crusts aggravated by contact with *cold water*; they bleed when *scratched*. In female patients, outbreaks are more likely to occur before or during the menses.

Graphites—Anogenital herpes with vesicles that break and exude a sticky, *honey-colored* fluid are best treated with *Graphites*. The vesicles are aggravated during or after the menses. The patient has dry, cracked skin in general.

Nitricum acidum—The patient has vesicles under the foreskin or at the *mucocutaneous* junction of the anus, which bleed easily and sting.

Petroleum—*Petroleum* is used to treat itchy genital or perianal herpes in chilly, anxious patients with extremely *dry* skin (compare with *Arsenicum album*).

Thuja occidentalis—*Thuja occidentalis* is helpful for genital herpes in patients with a history of gonorrhea or chlamydia, and whose specific symptoms do not quite fit any of the other medicines.

Herpes zoster

This herpetic infection is addressed in Chapter 26, Brain and Nervous System.

URTICARIA

More than 10% of children get hives; in most cases, the hives come and go for a few days and then disappear (Schmitt, 1992, p. 100). These medicines are reported to ease discomfort and shorten the episode. The clinician should give the 30C potency every 2 hr for three doses, and again if the symptoms recur. If there is no improvement after the first three doses, the medicine should be stopped.

Apis mellifica—This is a common medicine for urticaria that is *puffy*, pink, warm, itching, and stinging. The rash is sensitive to touch, aggravated by warmth and perspiration, and alleviated by cold compresses. The medicine is indicated for urticaria that arises during asthma attacks and fevers.

Dulcamara—Dulcamara is used to treat hives that come on at night, especially when it is cool, damp, or when the weather changes from warm to cool and damp; after scratching; and before or during the menses.

Pulsatilla—The rash *changes location* on the body. It is aggravated in the evening and at night, and alleviated by cold. The patient may be weepy, clingy, and thirstless, and may feel better in the open air (See Chapter 14, *Pulsatilla*.)

Urtica urens—The patient has a large, itchy, and blotchy rash that burns and stings, especially after eating *shellfish*. It is aggravated by cold, general warmth, after bathing, or after physical exercise.

WARTS AND MOLLUSCUM

Warts, genital condyloma, and molluscum contagiosum must be treated over a period of at least 10 weeks. The clinician should prescribe the 30C potency twice a week or the 12C potency twice a day. Children's warts are much more responsive to this sort of treatment—quite frequently falling off in less than a month. Genital warts, caused by human papilloma virus, in adults are reputed to be curable with homeopathy, but may require treatment by a homeopathic specialist when treatment with the following quick differential fails. Plantar warts of many years' duration in adults may or may not respond to homeopathy; the chances of a positive result are much greater if the patient is referred to a homeopathic specialist.

There have been three studies on the homeopathic treatment of warts. The first (Labrecque, Audet, Latulippe, & Drouin, 1992) randomized, double-blind, placebo-controlled trial of 162 patients used a polypharmacy approach to the treatment of plantar warts. The medicines used were *Thuja occidentalis*, 30C; *Antimonium crudum*, 7C; and *Nitricum acidum*, 7C. *Thuja occidentalis* was given once a week, and the other two medicines were given once a day. The trial lasted 6 weeks. The results showed no difference between the control and treatment groups. A smaller contemporaneous study found it took a longer treatment period for homeopathic treatment to be effective for warts; in fact, 18 of 19 people in this descriptive study were completely cured of their plantar warts in 2.2 months on average, with the classical individualized approach to prescribing (Gupta, Bhardwaj, & Manchanda, 1991). In this study, *Ruta graveolens* was the most commonly prescribed medicine, prescribed to 12 of the 19 patients. *Thuja occidentalis* was prescribed for only 3 patients, and *Antimonium crudum* was prescribed for 2 patients.

Smolle, Prause, & Kerl (1998), researchers whose reference to homeopathy as "superstition and quackery" in their published report raises the question of a possible bias, conducted a double-blind, placebo-controlled study on 60 children with warts. They state that a homeopathic physician individualized a homeopathic medicine for each child. The basis of the individualization, the qualifications of the physician prescribing, and the identity of the medicines used in the study were not identified. Neither were the potencies of the homeopathic medicines. The study took place over an 8-week period, again possibly too short a treatment period to be effective. There was no significant difference in efficacy between placebo and homeopathy.

Antimonium crudum—This medicine is indicated for *hard* warts (especially planter warts) that are horny or smooth and found anywhere on the body.

Calcarea carbonica—The patient presents with warts on the face and/or hands. These kinds are especially common in obese people with cold hands and feet, who wear socks to bed and crave eggs and sweets. Other symptoms include brittle peeling nails and perspiration on the occiput and neck during sleep.

Causticum—Easily bleeding warts are treated with *Causticum*. Warts on the *tip of the nose, subungual* warts, or warts on the back of the glans penis are reputed to respond to *Causticum*. It is also commonly indicated for warts on other locations of the face.

Dulcamara—*Large, flat* warts on the back of the hands, fingers, or on the face or the back are best treated with this medicine. The warts are brown, smooth, and soft. They are more commonly indicated in people with a domineering affect, who feel generally worse in damp weather.

Mercurius sulphuratus ruber—The patient presents with *fan-shaped* condyloma in the rectum, or anywhere on the penis, especially the prepuce and frenum. The condylomata may bleed when touched. This medicine was formerly named *Cinnabaris*.

Natrum sulphuricum—These are soft, *red*, and fleshy genital condylomata, in patients who have an emotionally closed affect and like to eat yogurt.

Nitricum acidum—Warts at *mucocutaneous* junction of the genitals, anus, or lips respond well to *Nitricum acidum*. The warts may be fissured, jagged, and irregularly shaped (like *cauliflower* or a coxcomb); or pediculated, soft, and moist; or simply flat. They may easily bleed, burn, or sting. A yellow discoloration, if present, is a good indicator that *Nitricum acidum* will be effective. The warts are more commonly seen in chilly patients who have strong anxiety about their health.

Ruta graveolens—This medicine is indicated for inflamed, flat, and sore warts, especially on the palms of the hands. A subject in the nineteenth-century clinical trial of *Ruta* reported "small epithelial swellings on the joints of toes." This statement might have been the key that led to the successful treatment by Gupta et al. (1991) of plantar warts with this medicine, which is not commonly prescribed by North American homeopathic clinicians for plantar warts.

Sabina—Genital warts that *itch and bleed* in women with uterine disorders, dysmenorrhea, or epistaxis are treated with *Sabina*.

Sepia—The patient presents with large and jagged or flat, hard, and *brown* warts on the face, neck, arms, or soles of the feet. There may be a genital condyloma inside the *vagina* or on the *penis*. Sometimes, the warts itch. These are more commonly seen in chilly, irritable, and apathetic people, with low libido, who cry easily.

Thuja occidentalis—This medicine is used to treat human papilloma virus infection anywhere on the genitalia (male and female) or anus, when other medicines are not appropriate. It is also used for warts on the hands (especially the left) and chin; less commonly elsewhere on the face or the body. The warts are moist or dry, like a coxcomb or cauliflower, bell-shaped, or flat.

Molluscum Contagiosum

Molluscum is not broadly addressed in the homeopathic literature, and there has been no research to confirm if the following differential for recently acquired cases is effective (van Zandvoort, 1997). Therefore, this differential is very incomplete. Since the lesions are always similar in appearance, the prescription is based on the symptoms and characteristics of the person as a *whole*. The clinician can prescribe one of the following in the 12C potency twice a day for 6 weeks, longer if the lesions are only partly resolved at that point.

Bromium—The patient presents with a hoarse voice, dry cough, and enlarged glands.

Bryonia alba—*Bryonia alba* is indicated for irritable patients who want to be alone, are thirsty for large amounts of water at long intervals, and feel generally worse from motion. (See Chapter 5, *Bryonia alba*.)

Calcarea arsenicica—Clinicians should prescribe this for chilly, obese, and perimenopausal women with heart palpitations from the slightest emotions.

Kali iodatum—Patients will respond well to this medicine who have a harsh temper, are generally sensitive to heat, wake at 5 a.m., and are prone to allergic rhinitis, sinusitis, goiter, severe sciatica, or recurring pneumonia.

Lycopodium clavatum—Those patients prone to performance anxiety, flatulence, and other digestive problems do well with *Lycopodium clavatum*. They desire sweets, warm food, and drinks. They experience low energy or digestive troubles from 4–8 p.m.

Mercurius sulphuricus—Patients who have the general *Mercurius* symptoms outlined in Chapter 11 as well as lung disease that causes dyspnea should be prescribed *Mercurius sulphuricus*.

Natrum muriaticum—This medicine is best for reserved patients who need a lot of time alone, are thirsty, and have a craving for or aversion to salt. They are prone to headaches during the day and from exposure to sunlight. Herpetic lesions are common among them, and they probably have oily skin and often a central fissure on the lower lip.

Silicea—Patients needing *Silicea* to treat their molluscum are thin, delicate, chilly, and mild-mannered and may have constipation with no urging, white spots on their nails, and offensive perspiration on their feet.

Sulphur—Patients who have a history of itchy skin problems react well to *Sulphur*. They are sensitive to heat, especially in bed at night; they stick their feet out of the covers. (See Chapter 16, *Sulphur*.)

Teucrium marum—Patients with concurrent nasal or rectal polyps and rectal itch should be prescribed *Teucrium marum*.

Thuja occidentalis—This medicine is indicated for patients with poor self-esteem who seem to evade the clinician's questions and who are prone to warts and polyps in addition to the molluscum. These patients are generally aggravated by eating onions and by damp weather.

WENS

Wens, sebaceous or epidermal inclusion cysts, are chronic health problems that cannot be prescribed for quickly in a primary care setting. Referral to a homeopathic specialist is recommended.

CHAPTER 19

Eye

This chapter will address ailments of the eye and lid likely to be encountered by the primary care clinician. The treatment of eye injuries is covered in Chapter 17, Injuries and Emergencies.

CONJUNCTIVITIS

Conjunctivitis is reputedly easy to treat with homeopathic medicines, but there is no body of research to confirm this. There is a large selection of medicines for conjunctivitis mentioned in the large homeopathic texts, but in clinical practice, one of the following 10 medicines will be indicated. If conjunctivitis accompanies an upper respiratory infection, one medicine should be selected in such a way that it covers all of the symptoms of the patient. The clinician should prescribe the 30C potency three times a day for 5 days; improvement should begin within 12 hr; often it starts immediately. A conventional prescription can be written for ointment if the medicine is not effective. The usual patient education information about hygiene should be done.

Most Commonly Indicated Medicines

Belladonna—The conjunctivae are *dry, red, and burning*, and they may throb. The eyelids are swollen. These symptoms come on rapidly. (See Chapter 4, *Belladonna*.)

Hepar sulphuris calcareum—The conjunctivitis is purulent with marked chemosis and profuse discharge. The eyes are very sensitive to touch and air. The eyes and lids are inflamed. There may (or may not) be purulent bacterial infection elsewhere, such as the pharynx or skin. (See Chapter 9, *Hepar sulphuris calcareum*.)

Mercurius vivus* or *Mercurius solubilis—There is a profuse, acrid, and burning discharge. The eyelids are red and swollen and may appear thickened. The patient may feel generally ill during this conjunctivitis with, for example, pharyngitis, lymphatic swelling, metallic taste in mouth, foul body odor, and excessive perspiration and salivation. (See Chapter 11, *Mercurius vivus* or *Mercurius solubilis*.)

Pulsatilla—This is reputed to be the most common medicine for conjunctivitis in primary care. The ocular discharge is *thick*, profuse, yellow, and *not* acrid. There is itching and burning in the eyes, and much lachrimation. The patient's eyelids are inflamed and adhere to one another with crusty material, especially *on waking* in the morning. Or there can be a very mild conjunctivitis, with the general symptoms indicative of *Pulsatilla*. (See Chapter 14, *Pulsatilla*.)

Less Commonly Indicated Medicines

Aconitum napellus—Like with *Belladonna*, the *Aconitum* conjunctivitis comes on *rapidly* with a hot dry feeling in the eyes, as though there is sand in them. The eyelids become swollen, indurated, and red. The conjunctivitis may be caused from cinders or other foreign bodies. The clinician may detect a feeling of *anxiety* and fear in the patient, as if this were a life-threatening condition. The symptoms may have come on after being out in the cold wind. The thirst may be increased.

Apis mellifica—The main distinguishing characteristic of the conjunctivitis requiring this medicine is the significant *edema* of the eyelid or the area around the eye. Other symptoms include redness; chemosis; hot lachrimation; and a burning, stinging, or shooting pain in the eye.

Arsenicum album—The patient presents with very painful *burning* in the eyes with acrid tearing. The eyelids are red, ulcerated, scaly, scabby, and granulated. There is edema around the eyes. Like with *Aconitum*, the patient is chilly, thirsty, and anxious, but this conjunctivitis does not come on as rapidly. The ulceration makes it more serious medically. (See Chapter 3, *Arsenicum album*.)

Euphrasia officinalis—Called eyebright in the herbal lore, euphrasia is occasionally indicated in conjunctivitis with *profuse* watery hot or acrid lachrimation; the patient feels as though he or she is swimming in tears. There is a sensation as if there were a hair before the eyes, with a desire to wipe it away. The symptoms are aggravated in the open air, or on lying or coughing. The tears leave a varnish-like mark that may progress to a thick, acrid, and yellow discharge from the eyes.

Rhus toxicodendron—The conjunctivae are inflamed, and the eyelids agglutinated, and there may be a pustular rash on the lids. The conjunctivitis may resemble a case of ocular toxicodendron dermatitis, even if the patient has had no exposure. There is photophobia with profuse flow of yellow pus. The eyes gush hot, scalding tears upon opening. (See Chapter 15, *Rhus toxicodendron*.)

HORDEOLUM

Single incidents of stye are reputed to respond to treatment with a few doses of a 30C potency of the indicated medicine. Although there has been no homeopathic research on this condition, recurrent styes are reputed to be very responsive to treatment by a homeopathic specialist.

Most Commonly Indicated Medicines

Graphites—*Graphites* should be prescribed for styes in patients who have *fissures* of the outer canthi or eyelids, as well as styes from ingrown eyelashes. The tears are inflamed, dry, scaly, and pale. There may be phlyctenae or cystic tumors of the eyelids. This medicine is used to treat styes of the lower lid.

Pulsatilla—The patient has styes with inflamed lids that stick together from *crusty* material. The patient presents as weepy, clingy, and desirous of consolation. Reputedly, this is the most common medicine for styes in children. (See Chapter 14, *Pulsatilla*.)

Sulphur—*Sulphur* is used to treat styes and tarsal tumors that are associated with *burning* itchy lids, aggravated by heat. Like *Pulsatilla*, there is agglutination of lids. There may be oily tears. *Sulphur* is more commonly indicated for styes of the left eye. *Sulphur* is used to treat styes in both the upper and lower lids. (See Chapter 16, *Sulphur*.)

Less Commonly Indicated Medicines

Lycopodium clavatum—Styes on lids near the inner canthi are treated with *Lycopodium clavatum*.

Sepia—*Sepia* is best for styes in people, especially women, at times of *hormonal transitions* (e.g., pregnancy or menopause). The tarsi are red and prone to tumors. The eyelids droop and are prone to epithelioma.

Staphysagria—Recurrent styes and nodules on the eyelids are best treated with *Staphysagria*. These styes occur at times when the patient is suppressing strong *anger* (e.g., abused women or children who feel ashamed). They are more common on the left side. *Staphysagria* is indicated for styes of the upper lid.

DIABETIC RETINOPATHY

One major study has been concluded on diabetic retinopathy (Zicari, Ricciotti, Vingolo, & Zicari, 1992). This double-blind, randomized, and placebo-controlled study on 60 patients used *Arnica montana*, 5C (administered orally) as the sole homeopathic treatment. The study showed that 47% of patients given *Arnica montana*, 5C experienced improvement in central blood flow to the eye, while only 1% of patients given the placebo experienced this improvement. Further, 52% of patients given *Arnica montana*, 5C experienced improvement in blood flow to other parts of the eye, while only 1.5% of those given the placebo experienced a similar degree of improvement.

CHAPTER 20

Ear, Nose, and Throat

EAR

Eustachian Tube Obstruction

The following medicines are indicated when eustachian tube obstruction follows an upper respiratory tract infection, sinusitis, or otitis media. The 30C potency may be prescribed twice a day for 7 days.

Causticum—The patient complains of ringing and roaring sounds accompanied by pulsating sensation and deafness. Words and steps *reecho* in the ears. Erythematous ears *burn* inside. The patient may crave smoked meats. The patient may cough, but with difficulty expectorating the phlegm, or experience stress incontinence on coughing.

Dulcamara—*Dulcamara* is indicated when obstructed tubes cause earache, especially left-sided, with buzzing, needle-like pains, and occasionally swelling of parotid glands. The middle ear is full of mucus. These earaches typically arise during damp weather, or after sleeping on the ground in a cool, damp climate. The patient's joints may be stiff and achy. He or she may have herpes around the lips.

Graphites—There is a thick, *glue-like* mucus in the eustachian tube, with associated deafness that is usually left-sided. The patient may have eczema, mental dullness, and chilliness.

Hydrastis canadensis—This medicine is used to treat a blocked eustachian tube during sinusitis. Refer to the section on sinusitis for details.

183

Kali bichromicum—This medicine is used for a blocked eustachian tube during sinusitis. Refer to the section on sinusitis for details.

Kali muriaticum—This is the most common medicine for deafness from white or clear effusion and crackling noises on blowing the nose or swallowing. There is snapping, itching, or a sensation that there are plugs in the ears. The eustachian tube is sore. There may be periauricular adenopathy.

Mercurius delcis—Deep-toned roaring is heard in the ear. The tympanic membrane is thickened, retracted, and immovable. The patient may have general symptoms indicative of *Mercurius*, as noted below under "Otitis Media."

Silicea—*Silicea* is used as indicated under "Otitis Media."

Furuncle

Refer to Chapter 18 for homeopathic medicines for furuncles in general. In addition, homeopaths have traditionally used *Plantago major* (plantain) botanical tincture specifically for furuncle of the ear. It is diluted one to one with water, warmed, and dropped into the meatus, or applied with cotton balls, as a local measure.

Motion Sickness

Begin by giving the medicine in the 30C potency once every .5 hr for three doses, and then decrease the frequency of the dose as symptoms subside.

Cocculus indicus—This medicine is indicated for train and seasickness, and vomiting with a profuse flow of saliva, accompanied by headache or syncope. The vomitus has an offensive, sour, or bitter odor. Nausea that may be perceived as *rising to the head* is felt. Retching, hiccuping, spasmodic yawning, and cramps may be experienced in the epigastrium. The patient is repulsed by all food and drink, including the odor of food, but craves beer. The patient may be bloated and may have vertigo with nausea that is aggravated by raising the head, which feels heavy. The patient's symptoms are aggravated by the motion of boats and motor vehicles; swimming;

exposure to cold, open air; touch; noise; being jarred; kneeling; stooping; exertion; eating; or from pain or anxiety.

Tabacum—This medicine has a reputation of being the leading medicine for motion sickness, especially severe seasickness. The patient suffers from *severe nausea* and violent vomiting with retching that is aggravated by the slightest motion and alleviated by uncovering the abdomen. The patient spits frequently. There is a very distressing faint, sinking feeling in the epigastrium. The patient may have severe vertigo with copious cold perspiration, which is aggravated on opening the eyes. There is a tight, band-like sensation in the head, and the face is deathly pale, bluish, pinched, and sunken. One cheek may be hot and flushed, the other pale. Affect is morose, forgetful, and apathetic. The symptoms are aggravated by the motion of a boat, horseback riding, lying on the left side, opening the eyes, the onset of evening, and extremes of heat or cold. These same symptoms are alleviated by cold compresses, fresh air, twilight, uncovering the abdomen, weeping, vomiting, sitting, staying indoors, and lying in a side position.

Otitis Externa

The common approach of instilling water and white vinegar (1:1) three to four times a day in the ear for a few days, while otherwise keeping the ear dry, is a valid one. The following are the most common homeopathic remedies if symptoms persist. The homeopathic medicine may be prescribed in the 30C potency twice a day for a week.

More Commonly Indicated Medicines

Belladonna—*Belladonna* is indicated when there is *throbbing* pain and a very red, swollen ear canal. The pain is aggravated when the person is jarred. The patient may have a flushed face. The symptoms were of sudden onset. (See Chapter 4, *Belladonna*.)

Ferrum phosphoricum—*Ferrum phosphoricum* is prescribed when there is nondescript inflammation of the ear canal with no pus and no general symptoms. (See Chapter 7, *Ferrum phosphoricum*.)

Hepar sulphuris calcareum—Reputedly the most common medicine for otitis externa. Ear is extremely sensitive to air and touch, more painful at night, and relieved by covering. The sensitivity to touch is more localized than in *Mercurius*. (See Chapter 9, *Hepar sulphuris calcareum*.)

Mercurius vivus or Mercurius solubilis—There is an offensive, green exudate and may be swelling of the periauricular glands. Infections treated with *Mercurius* are more often aggravated at *night* than those treated with *Hepar sulphuris calcareum*. (See Chapter 11, *Mercurius vivus* or *Mercurius solubilis*.)

Pulsatilla—A circumscribed redness is noted on exam, or the general symptoms of *Pulsatilla* may be present. Weepiness, desire for sympathy, desire for open air, and thirstlessness are the guiding symptoms. (See Chapter 14, *Pulsatilla*.)

Less Commonly Indicated Medicines

Aconitum napellus—The infection has a sudden onset with restlessness, *fear*, and increased thirst. The medicine is less commonly indicated than *Belladonna*, which also has a red face and a sudden onset.

Chamomilla—The patient demonstrates extreme intolerance to the pain, with the general symptoms of *Chamomilla* such as *irritability* and desire to be carried. (See Chapter 6, *Chamomilla*.)

Tellurium metallicum—The meatus *itches*, swells, and throbs. The ear may have offensive discharge, with the odor of pickled fish.

Otitis Media

The current standard of care for the treatment of otitis media in North America is universal treatment with antibiotics. A recent study of 100 children diagnosed with persistent otitis media with effusion showed that bacterial pathogens were isolated from only 35 of the children's middle ear effusion, while 30 children had virus DNA (9 of these cohabitating with bacteria) (Pitkaranta, Jero, Arruda, Virolainen, & Hayden, 1998). The authors of the study were interested in the possibility that viruses play a larger role in otitis media than had been previously thought. Equally intriguing is that 65% of these children, whose samples were collected when their PE tubes were put in after more than 2 months of suffering with otitis media with effusion had no detectable bacteria, yet the main treatment for them up to that point would have been antibiotics.

In addition, it is common for the slightest injection of the tympanic membrane to be diagnosed as otitis media, without the presence of mucopurulent or mucoid effusion of the middle ear. Many cases of otalgia from upper respiratory tract infection are, therefore, being prescribed antibiotics, in addition to those prescribed for true otitis media cases without bacterial present.

There is among many parents of children with recurrent otitis media and their alternative medicine providers a belief that frequent antibiotic use can reduce the children's immunity to infection in general. Certainly, no clinician who works with children is happy that many of his or her young patients suffer from multiple or chronic ear infections. In the face of such frustration, doctors sometimes declare that this sad state of affairs is an inevitable result of juvenile ear anatomy.

Friese, Kruse, and Moeller (1997) conducted a prospective study that compared conventional and homeopathic treatment of acute childhood otitis media in five German otolaryngological practices. Factors compared were otoscopic findings, fever, results of therapy, intensity and duration of pain, duration of therapy, and frequency of recurrences. The parents of 131 children in the study chose freely between homeopathic or conventional medical care from their ear, nose, and throat doctors. Of those, 103 children underwent homeopathic treatment, while 28 underwent conventional care. The homeopathic group was initially treated exclusively with homeopathic single remedies (*Aconitum napellus*, 30X; *Apis mellifica*, 6X; *Belladonna*, 30X; *Capsicum annuum*, 6X; *Chamomilla*, 3X; *Kali bichromicum*, 4X; *Lachesis mutus*, 12X; *Lycopodium clavatum*, 6X; *Mercurius solubilis*, 12X; *Okoubaka*, 3X; *Pulsatilla*, 2X; and *Silicea*, 6X), which were given either every 2 hours or three times a day, depending on the severity of the illness. All but one of these medicines is addressed in the sections in this chapter entitled "Otitis Media" and "Otorrhea." *Okoubaka* is not in the Homeopathic Pharmocopoeia of the United States, and is little known in North America. The median duration of treatment for the homeopathic group was 4 days. The conventionally treated group was prescribed nose drops, antibiotics, secretolytics, and/or antipyretics. Median duration of treatment was 10 days. Fifty-six percent of the conventionally treated group experienced no recurrences within 1 year of treatment, and 43.5% had a maximum of six recurrences. Of the children treated homeopathically, 70.7% experienced no recurrences within 1 year of treatment and 29.3% had a maximum of three recurrences. Five were eventually prescribed antibiotics; 98 were completely cured by the homeopathic treatment. No lasting harmful effects of therapy were observed in either group.

These findings confirm the impression of homeopathic clinicians that homeopathic medicines can resolve almost all cases of otitis media (and otalgia) without any other treatment, and that recurrences are less likely than with conventional treatment. By memorizing only the indications of the top five medicines and prescribing them when the indications are clear, primary care clinicians can test the validity of homeopathy in their own practices. The protocol would be to prescribe a 30C potency to be given every hour while the child is awake. If there is no improvement in the pain after three doses, another homeopathic medicine should be given. If there is no relief from pain after three doses of the second medicine, have the patient fill the prescription for the antibiotic. If pain is relieved by either medicine, have the patient take that medicine three times a day for 7 days of treatment, or shorter if the subjective symptoms have completely resolved. A minor otalgia should completely resolve after 24 hours; otitis media with effusion usually resolves in 4 days. The patient should return for an ear check in 1 week.

The discomfort of otitis media is almost always aggravated when lying down; this symptom does not help in the selection of the medicine. Patients with recurrent otitis media may be referred to a homeopathic specialist.

There are many other homeopathic medicines that have been used to treat otitis media. Below are the medicines one is most likely to prescribe for acute otitis media before rupture of the tympanic membrane has occurred. Long-term preventive treatment by a homeopathic specialist is believed to be of benefit to children who are already established in a pattern of chronic ear infections.

Most Commonly Indicated Medicines

Apis mellifica—This medicine is prescribed when the external ear is red, inflamed, and sore with stinging pain.

Belladonna—The tympanic membrane is very red and bulging, often associated with reddened throat, cold extremities, and pounding throbbing pain in the ear. This is more commonly (but not exclusively) a right-sided otitis media that comes on suddenly. A high fever with a bright red face and glassy appearance of the eyes may be present. The patient has diminished thirst and is sensitive to being jiggled and jarred, which aggravate the ear pain. These middle ear infections may occur concurrently with difficult dentition of childhood. (See Chapter 4, *Belladonna*.)

Chamomilla—The pain from otitis media makes the child scream, cry, or whine irritably. The earache often appears to be the result of teething problems. The only relief comes from being carried around, and the child screeches with anger as soon as he or she is put down. The child asks for various things, which are rejected when offered. This otitis media, like that treated with *Belladonna*, often comes on during teething. Thirst may be increased. There may be a clear nasal discharge and green stool. Sometimes, the child may be observed to have one red and one pale cheek. (See Chapter 6, *Chamomilla*.)

Ferrum phosphoricum—There is otalgia with a reddened, or partially reddened, tympanic membrane (compare with *Belladonna*). There is no purulent effusion in the middle ear or any other symptoms—simply fever with red face and increased thirst. (See Chapter 7, *Ferrum phosphoricum*.)

Hepar sulphuris calcareum—Severely painful otitis media with yellow purulent effusion is present. The tympanic membrane may suppurate. The person has become chilly, and the otalgia increases from exposure to cold air. Pharyngitis is often, but not always, present concurrently. Pain may shoot from the throat to the ear on swallowing. Other bacterial infections with purulent exudate, such as impetigo, may be present concurrently elsewhere. (See Chapter 9, *Hepar sulphuris calcareum*.)

Pulsatilla—Usually the ear infection follows upper respiratory tract infection with a thick, nonirritating, yellow, green, or changeable nasal discharge. More commonly, there is a very painful, left-sided otitis media accompanied by fever, but *Pulsatilla* is indicated in any case when the patient has the general symptomatology of *Pulsatilla*: decreased thirst, weepy, clingy, desirous of open air. (See Chapter 14, *Pulsatilla*.)

Less Commonly Indicated Medicines

Calcarea carbonica—A nondescript otitis media is found on physical exam. Child is not in acute distress and may not have noticed pain. General symptoms associated with *Calcarea carbonica*: cold hands and feet, desire for milk and eggs, sedentariness, chubbiness, and perspiration on occiput or vertex at night. If otorrhea is present, it is offensive.

Capsicum annuum—In contemporary practice, this medicine is used for otitis media that has lasted more than 2 days with high fever and severe stabbing, stinging, and burning pains. The face is hot, and the cheeks are red. Other symptoms include hot feeling in the fauces, pain and dryness in the throat that extends to the ears, and an inflamed uvula and palate, which are swollen and relaxed. Historically, this medicine was the leading homeopathic medicine for threatened or actual mastoiditis with sensitive inflammation in and behind the ear.

Gelsemium sempervirens—This medicine is indicated when there is otalgia during an upper respiratory tract infection or influenza that has *Gelsemium* symptomatology. (See Chapter 8, *Gelsemium sempervirens*.)

Kali bichromicum—The patient presents with *stringy or globby* yellow nasal discharge, moderate ear pain, sinus headache, and fever.

Lachesis mutus—Otitis media begins on the left side and then appears on the right. There is a persistent high fever.

Lycopodium clavatum—Otitis media begins on the right side and then appears on the left, or starts on the right side and remains there. Humming and roaring are heard in the ears, which impairs hearing. Sounds echo in the ear. If tympanic membrane has ruptured, there will be a thick yellow offensive discharge with deafness. The patient may have the sensation that hot blood is rushing into the ears. The general symptoms indicative of *Lycopodium* may be present: thirst for warm drinks, flatulence, fear of being alone, and controlling behavior. The symptoms are aggravated in the late afternoon and early evening.

Mercurius vivus or Mercurius solubilis—Otitis media in conjunction with *suppurative* tonsillitis, severe sore throat, and fever are best treated with one of these medicines. Refer to section entitled "Otorrhea" and Chapter 11, *Mercurius vivus* or *Mercurius solubilis*.

Tuberculinum or Tuberculinum aviare—The clinician should treat otitis media with either of these medicines when the following general symptoms are clear and distinct. The child is easily bored, restless, calculatingly destructive of property, and malicious toward people. He or she finds it amusing to strike siblings, especially surreptitiously, and is indifferent to parent's reprimand. The child desires milk and smoked meats.

Otorrhea

If the patient presents after rupture of the tympanic membrane has already occurred, any of the above medicines for otitis media may still be indicated, or the following specific remedies may be useful. (See Exhibit 20–1 for a summary.)

Borax—The discharge is mucopurulent. Patient is easily *startled*, and the pain makes him or her anxious. There may be *herpetic eruptions* around the mouth.

Calcarea sulphurica—The patient has thick, lumpy, yellow, purulent, and possibly sanguinous otorrhea. General symptoms are similar to those indicative of *Calcarea carbonica* (refer to "Otitis Media" above), but the person is not chilly.

Mercurius vivus or Mercurius solubilis—Otorrhea is a thick, yellow, and purulent discharge, which may contain some blood. More

---

Exhibit 20–1 Qualities of Otorrhea and the Appropriate Homeopathic Medicines

Right—*Lycopodium clavatum* and *Silicea*
Left—*Graphites* and *Psorinum*
Bloody—*Belladonna, Calcarea carbonica, Calcarea sulphurica, Causticum, Ferrum phosphoricum, Graphites, Hepar sulphuris calcareum, Lycopodium clavatum, Mercurius, Psorinum, Pulsatilla, Silicea,* and *Sulphur*
Brownish—*Psorinum*
Cheesy—*Hepar sulphuris calcareum* and *Silicea*
Green—*Hepar sulfuris calcareum, Mercurius, Tuberculinum,* and *Lycopodium clavatum*
Ichorous (watery pus)—*Lycopodium clavatum, Psorinum, Silicea,* and *Tellurium metallicum*
Mucous—*Belladonna, Calcarea carbonica, Graphites, Hepar sulphuris calcareum, Lycopodium clavatum, Mercurius, Pulsatilla, Silicea,* and *Sulphur*
Offensive—*Calcarea carbonica, Calcarea sulphurica, Causticum, Hepar sulphuris calcareum, Hydrastis canadensis, Kali bichromicum, Lycopodium clavatum, Mercurius, Psorinum, Pulsatilla, Silicea, Sulphur, Tellurium metallicum,* and *Tuberculinum*
Thick—*Calcarea carbonica, Calcarea sulphurica, Hepar sulphuris calcareum, Hydrastis canadensis, Kali bichromicum, Lycopodium clavatum, Mercurius, Psorinum, Pulsatilla,* and *Silicea*
Thin—*Graphites, Mercurius, Psorinum, Silicea,* and *Sulphur*
Watery—*Calcarea carbonica, Mercurius, Silicea,* and *Tellurium metallicum*
White—*Hepar sulphuris calcareum* and *Kali muriaticum*
Yellow—*Calcarea carbonica, Calcarea sulphurica, Hydrastis canadensis, Kali bichromicum, Lycopodium clavatum, Mercurius, Psorinum, Pulsatilla,* and *Silicea*

often than not, the otorrhea is right-sided. The pain extends to the ear, from the teeth or throat. General symptoms of *Mercurius* may be present such as *offensive perspiration*, halitosis, drooling, metallic taste in mouth, swollen indented tongue, and sensitivity to both heat and cold. (See Chapter 11, *Mercurius vivus* or *Mercurius solubilis*.)

Psorinum—An *offensive* discharge from the ears may be accompanied by pustules on the face. The patient is generally very *chilly* and may feel despair that he or she will not recover from the illness.

Silicea—*Silicea* is indicated for protracted illness, when suppurative otorrhea appears. There is a mild earache, which may have a shooting quality, but usually no fever. There may be perforations of the tympanic membrane that are slow to heal or protracted otorrhea that is thin and has an offensive odor. Before antibiotics were introduced, this medicine was used to treat otorrhea that had progressed to such a degree that it contained tiny bone fragments. The general symptoms indicative of *Silicea* may be present (e.g., chills, perspiration on the neck and occiput, and offensive foot sweat). Caution should be exercised in prescribing this medicine when PE tubes are in place because *Silicea* is known for hastening the expulsion of foreign objects.

Sulphur—The patient presents with an offensive irritating discharge from the ears, which leaves the external ear raw and erythematous. These local symptoms may be accompanied by the general symptoms indicative of *Sulphur*: feels warm; uncovers feet in bed; is thirsty; and desires sweets, salt, and fat. (See Chapter 16, *Sulphur*.)

Tellurium metallicum—This medicine is used to treat otorrhea that smells *like fishy saltwater*. There may be eczema behind the ears, with thick crusts. The otorrhea may be accompanied with symptoms of otitis externa: itching, swelling, and throbbing in the meatus. The patient may complain of constant pain deep in the ear.

Vertigo

A double-blind study of 116 patients with various types of vertigo showed therapeutic equivalence between a complex homeopathic medicine for vertigo and betahistamine (a common treatment for vertigo in Europe), in terms of frequency, duration, and intensity during a 6–week trial period (Weiser, Strosser, & Klein, 1998). Another nonplacebo-controlled descriptive study (*n* = 31) evaluated the effectiveness of *Vertigoheel*, a complex homeopathic medicine, in treatment of patients with vertigo of various etiologies. The majority of patients in this group had regression of clinical symptoms (Morawiec-Bajda, Lukomski, & Latkowski, 1993).

Vertigo can be caused from many underlying disease processes, and its individualized classical homeopathic treatment is too vast a topic for the busy integrative clinician to master. However, there is a manageable group of medicines for vertigo due to *vestibular hypofunction* in the elderly, presented below. Given that treatment by complex homeopathic medicines for vertigo have shown promise, this approach is worth investigating for other etiologies such as Ménière's disease, traumatic origin, and vestibular neuronitis.

Vertigo of the Elderly

The 12C potency can be prescribed for 12 weeks, evaluated for efficacy, and continued on a p.r.n. basis if effective.

Ambra grisea—This is used to treat vertigo accompanied by the early stages of senile *dementia*. There is deafness in one ear, and roaring and whistling heard in the other. The patient presents as bashful and shy, or silly and talkative. The patient asks questions, but does not wait for the answer before going on to another topic. Other symptoms include declining reading comprehension, great sensitivity to noise and music, desire to be alone, and insomnia from anxiety.

Arsenicum iodatum—*Arsenicum iodatum* is indicated for vertigo with tremulous feelings in elderly patients with chronic obstructive pulmonary disease and chronic bronchitis with greenish yellow, *purulent expectoration*. There is profound prostration, emaciation, and tendency to diarrhea. The heart is weakened by chronic lung disease and is tachycardic. The tympanic membrane is thickened. There is deafness from hypertrophy of eustachian tubes, intense thirst for cold drinks, and possibly nausea with vomiting an hour after eating.

Baryta carbonica—Vertigo with nausea aggravated by *stooping*, and by lifting the arms up is best treated with this medicine. There may be a sensation as though the brain is loose in the skull, which is alleviated by cold air. The patient exhibits child-like behavior and is timid, cowardly, and indecisive. There is increasing cognitive and memory impairment and shyness with strangers (compare with *Ambra grisea* above). There are commonly concurrent cardiovascular symptoms such as aneurysm, bradycardia, hypertension, or arteriosclerosis. In the male, there are commonly genitourinary symptoms such as benign prostatic hypertrophy, indurated testicles, impotence, or premature ejaculation.

Conium maculatum—This medicine is used to treat vertigo, especially in *smokers*. The patient experiences a whirling feeling (when looking at an object, it appears to turn in a circle). This symptom is aggravated by *rising*, going down the stairs, or the slightest motion of the eyes or head. There is a "numb" feeling in the brain that is aggravated by turning over in bed. Other symptoms include progressive weakness, incoordination or paralysis, unsteady gait, trembling of extremities, and sudden loss of strength while walking. There may be concurrent arteriosclerosis. In men, there may be genitourinary symptoms such as benign prostatic hypertrophy and impotence.

Cuprum metallicum—The patient presents with vertigo with internal *tremors*. The head drops toward the chest, which is alleviated by voiding *stool* and *lying down* and aggravated by looking up. The patient may have concurrent angina pectoris or frequent muscle cramps. There may also be cramping in the chest; behind the sternum; and in the toes, fingers, soles, or calves that is alleviated by *stretching*. Cramps in the calves prevent coition. There is jerking during sleep.

Granatum—Very persistent vertigo with nausea and *salivation* is best treated with *Granatum*. The patient has sunken eyes, dilated pupils, weak vision, and an insatiable appetite.

Iodium—*Iodium* is for vertigo that is aggravated by *stooping* and by being in a *warm room*; it is for restless, lean, and elderly people prone to chronic headaches who always feel too hot.

Rhus toxicodendron—When vertigo comes on as soon as the patient *rises* from a sitting position and the extremities feel heavy, *Rhus toxicodendron* should be prescribed. There may be concurrent arthritis that is aggravated by first motion, and is alleviated by continued motion. Symptoms are generally worse in cold, damp weather.

Sinapis nigra—Vertigo with *allergic rhinitis* and halitosis is best treated with *Sinapis nigra*.

NOSE

Allergic Rhinitis and Seasonal Allergies

Individualizing a medicine for acute allergic rhinitis can be difficult because the symptomatology of one medicine is so similar to the next (Shore, 1994). Many substances in nature can stimulate the common symptoms of allergy: runny nose, itchy eyes, and so on. Therefore, according to the basic tenets of homeopathic prescribing, many should be useful therapeutically for these conditions. Not surprisingly, common allergens such as *Ambrosia artemisiaefolia* (ragweed) have their place in the homeopathic treatment of allergies, as do mucous membrane irritants such as *Allium cepa* (red onion). Further reflection on pharmacology and toxicology will suggest the use of a few minerals as well, such as *Kali iodatum* (potassium iodide, which is used in substantive doses in conventional medicine as a liquifier of nasal secretions), and, indeed, these are homeopathic medicines for allergy symptoms.

For this reason, many clinicians prescribe complex homeopathic medicines for hay fever. Each homeopathic pharmaceutical manufacturer makes its own formula for allergy relief that is sold over the counter to consumers. Clinicians have reported that regional variations occur in the effectiveness of a certain formula according to the local climate and vegetation. Therefore, clinicians and consumers should experiment with different brand names and determine which work best for them. In general, it is best to begin therapy with homeopathic medicines when symptoms are mild. When treatment is begun when the histaminic reaction is at its peak, it is often impossible to see any therapeutic effect.

One double-blind study investigated the effectiveness and tolerance of one allergic rhinitis complex that is marketed to integrative physicians by a homeopathic pharmaceutical manufacturer in comparison with cromolyn sodium therapy. One hundred forty-six outpatients with symptoms of hay fever were enrolled in the clinical study (randomized, double-blind, equivalence trial). The time of treatment was 42 days. The homeopathic remedy (Luffa Comp.—Heel trademark nasal spray, dosage: 0.14 ml per application, four times per day/naris) consisted of a fixed combination made up of *Luffa operculata, Galphimia glauca, Histaminum hydrochloricum*, and *Sulphur*. The main outcome measure of the efficacy was the quality of life as measured by means of the Rhinoconjunctivitis Quality of Life-Questionnaire (RQLQ). The tolerance of the trial medication was registered by means of global assessment, rhinoscopy, and recording of adverse events, and with the aid of vital and laboratory parameters. The results of the study demonstrate a quick and lasting effect of treatment. The RQLQ global score changed significantly in the course of the treatment.

Another method is to use an isopathic approach instead of a homeopathic one. Isopathy is treating the person with the same substance that causes the illness, in this case the allergen. Homeopathic pharmaceutical manufacturers make medicines from the most allergenic pollens, molds, or dust mites. Mattress dust, house dust, molds, and mixed grass pollens are the commonly used isopathic preparations, which are available by mail. Reilly et al. (1994) demonstrated the effectiveness of homeopathy for allergic conditions at the level of ($p = 0 \cdot 0004$) in a meta-analysis of three studies. These studies used an isopathic model of homeopathic immunotherapy in allergy. In two of the studies, a homeopathic preparation of grass pollens was compared to placebo in the treatment of 144 patients with active allergic rhinitis (Reilly, Taylor, McSharry, & Aitchison, 1986). The homeopathically treated patients showed a significant reduction in patient and physician assessed symptom scores. The significance of their responses increased when results were corrected for pollen count, and the response was associated with halving the need for antihistamines. The third study was on 28 patients with allergic asthma, using a homeopathic medicine made from their principal allergen (usually house dust mite). They continued with their usual conventional care during the trial. A daily visual analog scale of overall symptom intensity was the outcome measure. A difference in visual analog score in favor of homeopathy appeared within 1 week of starting treatment and persisted for up to 8 weeks ($p = 0 \cdot 003$). There were similar trends in respiratory function and bronchial reactivity tests. A fourth study by this group has now been submitted for publication, which the researchers report has again shown a result favorable to homeopathy in the treatment of allergies.

Eleven studies published in German language publications (Wiesenauer & Gaus, 1991; Wiesenauer & Ludtke, 1996) compared the medicine *Galphimia glauca* in very low potency (4X, 6X, and 2C) to placebo in the ocular symptoms of pollinosis, with a somewhat favorable effect found in the treated group. The studies' internal validity was ranked high on two scales by independent reviewers (Linde et al., 1997). This effect could be ascribed to the herb itself since a small but significant amount of the herb would remain at such a low concentration. This medicine is not well-known in North America, but it is one of the ingredients in a complex over-the-counter medicine sold in health food stores.

When taking a classical approach, individualizing a medicine for the specific symptoms of the patient with allergies, the following data should be gathered from the patient:

- the color of nasal or ocular discharge
- whether the discharge is irritating to the area over which it flows
- specific areas that itch (e.g., canthi, lids, conjunctivae, roof of mouth, nose, or throat)
- environmental conditions, such as dry or damp air, or occupying a closed versus well-ventilated room

If the rhinitis has progressed into sinusitis, the appropriate prescription will be found later in this chapter. Careful examination of the eyes, nose, and throat is important.

Repetition of the medicine will continue as long as exposure to the allergen continues. Frequency can be determined by the patient, but taking a dose before symptoms are expected to begin is best. Long-term treatment by a homeopathic specialist is reputed to reduce or eliminate allergies.

Allium cepa—The patient presents with streaming eyes and nose. The nasal discharge *irritates* the area beneath the nose; lacrimation is not irritating, however. Symptoms worsen in the spring and in August.

Ambrosia artemesiaefolia—This medicine is used to treat lachrimation with intolerable *itching of the eyelids*.

Apis mellifica—Very *edematous*, red eyelids that are almost swollen shut. Conjunctivae may be red and puffy. The symptoms are alleviated by cool compresses. *Rhus toxicodendron* should be considered when the same symptoms are present, but instead the patient's eyes are helped by warm compresses.

Aralia racemosa—The patient *sneezes* frequently with a copious, watery, and excoriating discharge that is aggravated by drafts. The patient may have a dry cough from tickling in the throat that comes on between 11:00 p.m. and 12:00 a.m., or after about 2 hr of sleep. There may be asthmatic symptoms.

Arsenicum album—The patient has an irritating, watery nasal discharge and is *chilly, restless, anxious*, and thirsty for frequent sips, especially of warm drinks.

Arsenicum iodatum—The patient either has a very irritating and watery nasal discharge, or a thick and yellow one. Mucous membranes are thick and swollen. The patient is *warm and restless*. There is a constant irritation and tingling of the nose with a constant desire to sneeze.

Arum triphyllum—There is severe *tingling and itching* in nose, pharynx, and mouth. The patient picks at the lips and puts finger into nose in an attempt to relieve it. Very irritating discharges are present, like with *Allium cepa, Arsenicum iodatum*, and *Bromium*, and the lips are cracked and painful. Discharge is left-sided and worsens in the evening and at night. The person may be hoarse.

Arundo mauritanica—There is *itching and burning of the nose* (primarily), palate, mouth, skin, and conjunctivae. The lids and canthi are spared. The patient experiences excessive salivation. Compare with *Wyethia helenioides*.

Bromium—Frequent *sneezing* is the predominant symptom, which differentiates *Bromium* from *Allium cepa*, with which it shares many common symptoms. There is copious, watery nasal discharge that *irritates* the skin beneath the nose, the lips, the opening of the nostrils, and the inner nostrils. There is burning, itching, and rawness inside the nostrils. The patient may describe a sensation of coldness inside the nose or hoarseness or asthma, which accompanies the allergies. The person feels generally worse from hot weather and being overheated. Lacrimation is not present.

Carbo vegetabilis—The patient is *weak*, apathetic, and desirous of having the fan directed toward him- or herself. The patient sneezes from irritation in the larynx or tickling in the nose, which is aggravated by blowing the nose.

Dulcamara—The flow of mucus from rhinitis becomes completely stopped during a *cold rain* without sinusitis.

Euphrasia officinalis—The eyes and nose are streaming, and the *tears are irritating*, but the nasal discharge is not (the opposite *Allium cepa*). The canthi and lids itch. Sneezing aggravates the lacrimation; it and the cough are both worse in the morning after rising, and accompanied by the need to expectorate mucus. The patient is photophobic. Symptoms are alleviated by lying down. Compare with *Nux vomica*, which is indicated for very similar physical symptoms, but the sneezing is the most intolerable.

Gelsemium sempervirens—The patient presents with dullness, *fatigue*, and heaviness, violent paroxysms of sneezing, and headache. The eyes do not itch. Allergies appear in the spring and in August. There is an irritating nasal discharge and later an obstruction.

Histaminum hydrochloricum—This medicine has generic histaminic reactions without any distinguishing symptoms.

Kali iodatum—The patient suffers an irritating discharge with nasal obstruction in a warm room (compare with *Arsenicum iodatum, Carbo vegetabilis*). Nose becomes red and swollen and produces a profuse, irritating, hot, and watery discharge that is aggravated in cool air, and accompanied by *salivation and dyspnea*. There is burning, throbbing, or tightness at the root of the nose with cool, greenish, irritating discharge as rhinitis begin to ascend to sinuses. The patient sneezes violently.

Naja tripudians—*Asthma* accompanies seasonal rhinitis and worsens at night. The eyes do not itch. The allergies appear in the spring and again in August. There is a sensation of the thoat's constricting. The patient may have a left frontal or temporal headache.

Nux vomica—Allergies make the person *irritable and impatient*, and may possibly be accompanied by constipation. There are episodes of violent *sneezing* or unsuccessful attempts to sneeze that are stimulated by formication in the nostrils, especially the left. The nose feels obstructed, but watery mucus flows from one side. Nose runs freely in the open air and during the day, yet feels dry at night.

Pulsatilla—The patient's eyes burn and itch and the patient feels that he or she must rub them. The watery nasal discharge changes to yellow and green as the rhinitis continues. The patient feels generally uncomfortable in a warm room. All symptoms are alleviated in the *open air*. The patient may have other general symptoms indicative of *Pulsatilla*, such as weepiness and desire for consolation.

Sabadilla—*Sneezing* is the most distressing symptom to the patient and worsens in the *open air*. There are paroxysms of 10 or more sneezes. Lacrimation may also be present, and is aggravated by yawning. The patient is generally chilled, which is alleviated by warm food and drinks. The left side of the patient's throat may be sore. Soreness is alleviated by warm drinks.

Sinapis nigra—Scanty and irritating mucus from the posterior nares feels *cold*. *Left* nostril is blocked or the nostrils can be alternately blocked. Symptoms include a dry, inflamed, and hot nose and sinuses with lacrimation, sneezing, hacking cough, and asthmatic breathing. There are loud coughing spells with barking expiration.

Wyethia helenioides—Itching of the *palate* is the most distressing symptom to the patient; the throat feels dry and swollen as though something needs to be cleared from it. These symptoms usually arise in the fall.

Epistaxis

One dose of 30C potency of the indicated medicine is reputed to stop the bleeding of an ordinary bloody nose within 2 min. The clinician should repeat the medicine if the bleeding returns and change the medicine if the bleeding does not stop.

Arnica montana—*Arnica montana* is indicated when the epistaxis is from injury. (See Chapter 2, *Arnica montana*.)

Belladonna—Epistaxis during fever or throbbing headache with glassy eyes, dilated pupils, and red face is best treated with *Belladonna*. Compare with symptoms indicative of *Ferrum phosphoricum*. (See Chapter 4, *Belladonna*.)

Ferrum phosphoricum—The patient presents with epistaxis of bright red blood during fever, possibly with red face. Compare with *Belladonna*. (See Chapter 7, *Ferrum phosphoricum*.)

Ipecacuanha—Gushes of bright red blood with nausea and sometimes perspiration are best treated with *Ipecacuanha*.

Phosphorus—*Phosphorus* is the general medicine for epistaxis, particularly a profuse, bright red nosebleed caused by vigorous nose blowing.

Upper Respiratory Infection

In a conventional medical practice, it is considered normal and healthy for children to contract six colds a year (Schmitt, 1992). In the community of homeopathic medical practices, such frequent infections are considered a sign that a child's immune system is not up to par. Homeopathic doctors and nurses, based on clinical experience, believe constitutional treatment of such children reduces the frequency of upper respiratory infections by strengthening the resistance of the host. One very well-done study demonstrated a very small advantage to homeopathy compared to placebo in this regard (de Lange de Klerk, Blommers, Kuik, Bezemer, & Feenstra, 1994). This randomized, double-blind study in the pediatric outpatient department of a university hospital studied 175 children with frequently recurring upper respiratory tract infections. The evaluative outcome criteria were:

1. mean score for daily symptoms
2. number of antibiotic courses
3. number of adenoidectomies and tonsillectomies over 1 year of follow-up

The results showed the mean daily symptom score was 2.61 in the placebo group and 2.21 in the treatment group (difference 0.41; 95% confidence interval –0.02 to 0.83). In both groups the use of antibiotics was greatly reduced compared with that in the year before entering the trial (from 73 to 33 in the treatment group and from 69 to 43 in the placebo group). The proportion of children in the treatment group having adenoidectomies was lower (16%, 8/50) than in the placebo group (21%, 9/42). The proportion having tonsillectomies was the same in both groups (5%).

The expected course of an untreated cold consists of a fever for less than 3 days, and nose and throat symptoms continuing for 4–10 days. A cough may last for 2–3 weeks. Treatment of a common cold is not necessary, but is frequently demanded by patients who are uncomfortable and need to get back to work, school, or daycare. Patients should be educated that resting during the early part of the cold is likely to shorten its duration and help treatment. The improved comfort from the decreased achiness and congestion from homeopathic treatment may result in sleepiness. Increased fluid intake should be encouraged.

To treat a patient with a cold, the patient should first be educated to abstain from decongestants, antihistamines, expectorants, and cough suppressants. Self-treatment with echinacea, garlic, and vitamin C is not contraindicated during homeopathic treatment, but eucalyptus cough drops and chest rubs containing camphor are believed by some in the profession to negate the benefits of homeopathic treatment.

The expected response to a correct homeopathic medicine is for the patient to become more comfortable (e.g., reduced nasal discharge and general discomfort, lowered fever, more quickly resolved and fewer sequelae). The earlier in the illness the correct homeopathic medicine is given, the better the result. A person might require one homeopathic medicine in the early stages of a cold and another in the later.

There has been one published randomized, double-blind, and placebo-controlled study on treatment of upper respiratory tract infection with a complex over-the-counter homeopathic medicine (Davies, 1971). The effect of this medicine was insignificant. The classical homeopathic treatment of upper respiratory infection, presented in this chapter, has not yet been given a research trial.

There are four symptoms categories that are key to selecting the indicated prescription among this group of common medicines for the treatment—not prevention—of upper respiratory infections. These are, from most significant to least:

1. Affect and behavior
2. Thirst
3. Subjective temperature
4. Nasal discharge

These lines of inquiry should never be neglected when gathering data from the patient.

Most Commonly Indicated Medicines

Aconitum napellus

- Affect and behavior: The onset of the cold is accompanied with anxiety disproportionate to the symptoms. The patient has insomnia with restlessness at night in bed from fear or anxiety.
- Thirst: The patient has an intense burning thirst and desires beer.
- Subjective temperature: The patient is usually chilly with hot hands and cold feet. There are waves of chills that alternate with heat. The patient may have the sensation of dry burning heat with fever.
- Nasal discharge: The nose is dry and stopped up or runs hot, scanty, watery discharge.

Characteristic symptoms—The first sign of a cold is after exposure to cold, dry wind. Rapid onset of symptoms is a key indicator for *Aconitum napellus*, which is rarely indicated after the first 24 hours of a cold. There is frequent and violent sneezing and heavy, hot, and bursting headache. There may be a burning or undulating sensation in the head or a sensation as if there were a hot band about the head or boiling heat in the brain. The eyes may feel dry and hot as if there were sand in them. Eyelids may be swollen and red and the cheeks hot and red. One cheek may be red and hot, and the other, pale and cold. The throat is red, dry, hot, and constricted. The tonsils are swollen and dry. There may be a hoarse, dry, croupy, painful cough or a short barking, whistling cough aggravated by every inspiration, the night, or drinking. The cough is alleviated while lying on back. Laryngitis or tingling in chest after coughing may be present. There may be a nose bleed during the cold. Symptoms are aggravated by teething, lying in bed at night, and cold, dry weather. They are alleviated by open air and rest.

Allium cepa

- Affect and behavior: The affect is unremarkable, or the patient may be slightly frightened or gloomy.
- Thirst: Thirst has increased.
- Subjective temperature: This is unremarkable.
- Nasal discharge: A profuse, clear, and fluent discharge irritates the skin below the nostrils and the upper lip, with burning and smarting in the nose. The nose drips. Discharge from the eye, if present, is clear, streaming, and bland. (The converse eye and nasal characteristics indicate *Euphrasia officialis*.)

Characteristic symptoms—The person feels generally better in the open air (compare with *Pulsatilla*.) Coughing hurts the larynx. There is frequent violent sneezing. Symptoms move from the left side to the right side. There is aching in the forehead that extends to the eyes and face, which is alleviated when the nose runs and returns when the flow ceases.

When a profuse bland lacrimation is present, it is aggravated by coughing. The person wants to rub the eyes. There may be rawness of the throat, which extends from the throat to the ear (compare with *Hepar sulphuris calcareum*.) There is dripping from the uvula and a lump in the throat. (If this symptom is present in a case where there is a true pharyngitis, *Hepar sulphuris calcareum* or *Lachesis mutus* should be considered before *Allium cepa*. If the lump is a somatization of grief, consider *Ignatia amara*.) The person may desire raw onions.

The hacking tickling cough can be constant and accompanied by hoarseness. This cough is aggravated from inspiring cold air, and so uncomfortable that the person wants to hold it back. The patient grasps the throat while coughing. The larynx is painful when talking. Symptoms are aggravated by damp weather, warm rooms, wet feet, and evening. Symptoms are alleviated by bathing, cool open air, and motion.

Arsenicum album

- Affect and behavior: The patient is anxious, irritable, distressed by disorder, and restless, wanting to go from one bed to another. The corresponding state in children makes them want to be carried, and then be passed from father to mother.
- Thirst: The patient wants sips of warm drinks frequently.
- Subjective temperature: The patient is chilly.
- Nasal discharge: A thin, watery, and acrid nasal discharge irritates the nostrils and upper lip. The nose is stopped up indoors and at night; it feels stopped up even during a fluent nasal discharge.

Characteristic symptoms—The person who needs *Arsenicum album* seems like they have *Allium cepa* symptoms, except that there is a higher fever and more burning in the nose, and the patient is chilly and thirsty. There may be a postnasal drip that feels hot and burning. The patient is prone to burning pains that are relieved by warm compresses. The sore throat is relieved by hot drinks. The patient feels better indoors although the nose is stopped up while there. Head colds tend to go down to the chest. There may be a dry cough that is generally aggravated after midnight. Cold sores may be found in the nose. Sneezing is unsatisfactory. Symptoms, which worsen between midnight and 2:00 a.m. are aggravated by cold drinks, cold and damp air, and exertion. They are alleviated by heating pad or hot water bottles, hot drinks, warm covers, motion, lying with the head elevated, company, and open air.

Gelsemium sempervirens

- Affect and behavior: The patient is apathetic, drowsy, and mentally dull.
- Thirst: The thirst is decreased or absent.
- Subjective temperature: The patient has chills up and down the spine and may be generally chilly or warm.
- Nasal discharge: The nose is stuffed or produces a thin, hot, acrid, and watery discharge.

Characteristic symptoms—A patient has a cold with fever and aching, tiredness, heaviness, and weakness, and sometimes dizziness. Soreness is especially felt in the muscles of the extremities. The patient wants to lie down quietly, in a half-reclined position or wants to be held. These symptoms are most commonly found in spring or summer colds.

If there is a headache, it is dull, heavy, and band-like and extends from around the occiput to over the eyes. The eyelids droop, and the ears are stopped up. The patient sneezes in the early morning and has a dry cough with sore chest. There is a burning in the larynx and chest when coughing. Symptoms are aggravated by humid weather, especially in the spring or summer, motion, and thunderstorms. Symptoms are alleviated by alcoholic drinks, mental effort, bending forward, continued motion, onset of afternoon, and lying supine with head elevated.

Mercurius vivus or Mercurius solubilis

- Affect and behavior: Affect is unremarkable.
- Thirst: The patient is thirsty for cold drinks or beer.
- Subjective temperature: The patient is only comfortable in a very narrow temperature range. He or she uncovers from heat, then gets chilled and covers up, then uncovers, and so on.
- Nasal discharge: Nasal discharge is acrid, purulent (green or yellow), thick, or profuse. It makes the nose and upper lip sore.

Characteristic symptoms—The cold starts with an irritation in the throat, and often pain or burning in the tonsils, which is followed by a profuse nasal discharge. Or conversely, the patient is prone to having every cold end in a sore throat. Lachrimation is profuse, burning, and acrid. There is much sneezing and the nostrils are raw and ulcerated. The infection may progress to sinusitis. The patient may have offensive perspiration, spongy swollen tongue with indentations from teeth, metallic taste in mouth, and drooling. Colds tend to evolve into bacterial sinus or eye infections. There is a sick odor to perspiration and breath. Symptoms are aggravated by becoming too hot or too cold; onset of night; perspiring; changeable, cloudy, damp, or cold weather; a warm room; and lying on the right side. Symptoms are alleviated by moderate ambient temperature.

Nux vomica

- Affect and behavior: Affect is irritable and impatient.
- Thirst: Thirst is unremarkable.
- Subjective temperature: The patient is chilled.
- Nasal discharge: Nose is dry at onset with stuffed-up feeling in the sinuses, sore throat and watery eyes. Then the nose begins to run;

it is especially fluent in the morning and in a warm room. It is dry at night. One nostril may be stopped, and one running with a watery discharge.

Characteristic symptoms—Like *Aconitum napellus*, *Nux vomica* is most commonly indicated at the beginning of a cold. Hence, when there are few distinctive symptoms at the beginning of a cold, *Nux vomica* can be prescribed initially, in the absence of the anxiety that is characteristic of an *Aconitum* cold. There may be violent sneezing from intense crawling in nostrils (especially the left). Newborns have the snuffles. Nosebleeds may arise from coughing. Small ulcers appear in the throat; the pain is aggravated by empty swallowing. There are needle-like pains in the ears when swallowing, and itching in the eustachian tubes. Symptoms, which are worse in the early morning, are aggravated by cold, ambient air; dry, open air; drafts and wind; and uncovering. Symptoms are alleviated by naps and resting, hot drinks, moist air, and lying on the side.

Pulsatilla

- Affect and behavior: The patient is weepy, wants consolation, and often suddenly changes to being happy. A child wants to be held and carried slowly, and gently cries when put down.
- Thirst: Thirst is reduced or absent.
- Subjective temperature: The patient may be chilled, but feels generally worse in a stuffy warm room.
- Nasal discharge: There is a green, yellow, orange, or changeable nasal discharge that can have an offensive odor, but is always nonirritating to the skin. The nose is stuffed up at night, when lying down, or in a warm room. It is better in the open air.

Characteristic symptoms—The patient loses sense of smell and taste (compare with *Natrum muriaticum*). Conjunctivitis may develop from colds with yellow or green discharge. The patient craves refreshing things, pungent things, cheese, peanut butter, and creamy foods. The patient is averse to meat fat. Symptoms are aggravated by warm rooms and lying in bed, and the onset of evening. Symptoms are alleviated by cold, fresh, open air; uncovering; gentle motion; and lying with head high. They are also alleviated after a good cry.

Less Commonly Indicated Medicines

Ammonium carbonicum

- Affect and behavior: Affect is depressed, cross, troubled, weepy, or normal.
- Thirst: Thirst is unremarkable.
- Subjective temperature: The patient is very sensitive to cold air.
- Nasal discharge: Discharges are hot, irritating, and sometimes sticky. A profuse, protracted, and watery discharge is present during the day, but the nose may be stopped up at night. Children are unable to blow their noses.

Characteristic symptoms—These are the frequent colds of obese, fatigued, and sedentary people, especially those with heart failure, wheezing, and a suffocative feeling or for babies with the snuffles. There is a continuous urging to sneeze. The eyes are dry and burning. The patient is very sensitive to cold air and stormy weather. Symptoms are aggravated by cold, damp, and cloudy weather. They are alleviated by eating, dry weather, and lying on the right side.

Dulcamara

- Affect and behavior: Affect can be normal, or restless and impatient with desire for many things that are rejected when offered. The patient is confused, cannot find the right word, and cannot concentrate. He or she scolds without being angry.
- Thirst: The patient is very thirsty for cold drinks.
- Subjective temperature: This is unremarkable.
- Nasal discharge: There is profuse, watery discharge from the nose and eyes; nose runs more in a warm room than in a cold one. It stuffs up in cold air or cold rain.

Characteristic symptoms—The cold comes on when the weather changes from hot to cold suddenly, or from going from hot weather into cold air conditioning, or when camping outdoors in wet weather. Summer colds may be associated with diarrhea. Prolonged coughing fits are stimulated by tickling in the back of throat with copious loose easy expectoration. Symptoms include stiffness, numbness, aching, soreness of muscles, and a stiff neck. The cold is accompanied by inflammation of the eyes and herpes on the lips (compare with *Natrum muriaticum*), as well as a winter cough. Symptoms are aggravated by cold, damp weather; cold drinks; ice cream; and rest. They are alleviated by motion, warmth, and dry weather.

Eupatorium perfoliatum

* Affect and behavior: The affect is unremarkable, except that the patient may moan from the aching pain.
* Thirst: The patient thirsts for cold water.
* Subjective temperature: The patient is chilled and shivers in the cold air.
* Nasal discharge: The nasal discharge is clear and watery.

Characteristic symptoms—This medicine is more commonly indicated in influenzas, but occasionally encountered in the treatment of extremely uncomfortable colds. The patient suffers from fever, weakness, and aching throughout the body; it is painful to move. He or she is sensitive to change of temperature. The most characteristic symptom of this medicine is that there is an aching that feels as if it is in the bones. There is pain in the back of the neck, between the shoulders, in the back, and in the muscles of the lower limbs, with a bruised pain in the calves. These are similar to indications for *Gelsemium sempervirens*. Shivers extend up and down the spine. There is a sore, heavy, and throbbing pain in the occiput after lying down. The head feels like it has a metal cap on it. Sore, aching eyeballs accompany the headache. The patient coughs from laryngeal tickling accompanied by soreness of chest, which he or she must hold (compare with indications for *Bryonia alba* in bronchitis and influenza). The cough hurts the head as well. The patient craves ice cream. Symptoms, which are worse from 7:00 to 9:00 a.m., are aggravated by cold air, coughing, and motion. They are alleviated by perspiration, lying on the face, and conversation.

Euphrasia officinalis

* Affect and behavior: Affect is normal.
* Thirst: Thirst is unremarkable.
* Subjective temperature: Subjective temperature is normal.
* Nasal discharge: The nasal discharge is profuse, watery, and non-irritating.

Characteristic symptoms—This medicine is indicated for mild colds. Eyes are watery from profuse, hot, and acrid tears. Conjunctivitis can develop with a thick, acrid, and yellow discharge from the eyes. The patient is photophobic. Nasal discharge is sometimes accompanied by cough and much expectoration of mucus in throat from postnasal drip. The patient may complain of congestive headache. Symptoms are aggravated by wind, sunlight, onset of evening, warmth, and being indoors. They are alleviated by open air, winking, and wiping the eyes.

Ferrum phosphoricum

- Affect and behavior: Affect is normal.
- Thirst: The patient is thirsty.
- Subjective temperature: Subjective temperature is unremarkable.
- Nasal discharge: Nasal discharge is clear.

Characteristic symptoms—Ferrum phosphoricum is indicated when the beginning of a cold is accompanied by a slight fever; bruise-like soreness of chest, shoulders, and muscles; deafness from a cold; and pallor alternating with redness. The patient avoids meat and milk and desires sour foods and drinks. He or she may have laryngitis with hoarseness. The patient suffers a short, painful, tickling, hacking, tormenting, and spasmodic cough that is worse in the morning and evening. The chest is heavy, sore, or congested. The patient is restless, sleepless, and drowsy. Symptoms are worse at night, and at 4:00 to 6:00 a.m. They are aggravated by motion, noise, being jarred, cold air, touch, and cold drinks. They are alleviated by lying down and cold compresses.

Hepar sulphuris calcareum

- Affect and behavior: Affect is sad, touchy, argumentative, irritable, and dissatisfied.
- Thirst: Thirst may be unremarkable or increased.
- Subjective temperature: The patient is very chilly.
- Nasal discharge: Nose is congested and painful with sneezing and running in the cold, dry wind.

Characteristic symptoms—This medicine is indicated for the later stages of a cold. The patient is chilly and sensitive to the slightest draft. Colds that begin after exposure to damp, cold weather respond well to *Hepar sulphuris calcareum*. The patient has a low fever and profuse perspiration that is sour, sticky, offensive, and aggravated by the slightest exertion (compare with *Mercurius*). The patient has yellow, thick expectoration; every one of his or her colds seems to turn to bronchitis. There is pain in the larynx when inhaling cold air, accompanied by loss of the voice and a cough. The patient may cough when uncovering any part of the body. He or she desires fat, spicy and pungent foods, and sour foods, especially vinegar and pickles. Symptoms are aggravated by cold, dry air; drafts; having any part of the body uncovered; touch; noise; exertion; and onset of night. They are alleviated by heat and warm wraps.

Hydrogen

- Affect and behavior: The patient is tranquil, serene, and calm. He or she is confused when trying to concentrate (e.g., studying and reading). The patient avoids company (compare with *Phosphorus*).
- Thirst: Thirst is unremarkable.
- Subjective temperature: The patient is sensitive to cold.
- Nasal discharge: Nasal discharge at night and in the morning on waking can be viscid, frothy, tough, thin, and almost any color—yellowish green, yellow, white, egg white–colored, reddish yellow, orange, green, clear, or brownish.

Characteristic symptoms—There is tingling and formication inside the nose, which stimulates ineffectual efforts to sneeze. The tingling is worse in cold air, or during the chill. There may be a peppery sensation or a one-sided blockage of the nose, which alternates sides and is alleviated in the open air. Nasal discharge is accompanied by a sore throat and/or a cough that can progress to sinus infection. There is weakness, trembling internally, and aversion to condiments. Symptoms are aggravated by riding in a car and walking. They are alleviated by open air.

Kali iodatum

- Affect and behavior: Affect is normal.
- Thirst: The patient possesses a violent thirst.
- Subjective temperature: The patient alternates between hot and cold; symptoms are generally aggravated by heat.
- Nasal discharge: There is profuse, acrid, hot, and watery discharge that becomes cool, greenish, and irritating.

Characteristic symptoms—The nose is red and swollen. Nasal discharge is worse in cool air and accompanied by salivation and dyspnea. The patient feels tightness at the root of the nose. There is burning, throbbing in nose and sinuses on inhaling, and violent sneezing. The watery eyes produce profuse hot or acrid tears that are aggravated in the open air, and from lying or coughing; they leave a varnish-like mark. The patient is photophobic. The cold may progress to conjunctivitis with thick, acrid, and yellow discharge. There is a cough with easy expectoration during the day only; less on lying down and at night. Symptoms are aggravated by heat, pressure, touch, late night (2:00 to 5:00 a.m.), damp, changing weather, jarring, and cold foods (especially milk). They are alleviated by cold, open air, and motion.

Natrum muriaticum

- Affect and behavior: Affect is unremarkable, or may be sad, weepy, or self-isolating. The patient is averse to consolation.
- Thirst: The patient is thirsty for large quantities of water.
- Subjective temperature: The subjective temperature is unremarkable.
- Nasal discharge: This medicine is useful in all stages of a cold. In the early stages, there is a violent, gushing, and fluent nasal discharge. This lasts 1–3 days without treatment, followed by thickening of the mucus so that it resembles raw egg white. This may continue as a copious, thick, clear to whitish, and nonirritating discharge, or as postnasal drip with stoppage of the nose, thereby making breathing difficult.

Characteristic symptoms—There is acrid lacrimation, with redness and burning of the eyes that is stimulated by sneezing, coughing, and laughing. The patient sneezes early in the morning; there are little ulcers in the nose. There may be loss of smell and taste, pearly herpes vesicles on or near the lips or at the edge of hair, and a crack in the middle of the lower lip. The patient desires salt, bitter things, sour things, grains and cereals, oysters, fish, and milk. He or she is averse to coffee, meat, tobacco, and bread. Symptoms, which are worse from 9:00 to 11:00 a.m., are aggravated by heat, dampness, exertion, and sympathy. They are alleviated by rest, open air, perspiring, before breakfast, massage, and lying on the right side.

Phosphorus

- Affect and behavior: The patient lacks concentration, is anxious and restless, fears being alone especially at twilight, and wants sympathy. He or she also seeks reassurance from the clinician (compare with *Arsenicum album* and *Hydrogen*).
- Thirst: The patient craves cold drinks with ice.
- Subjective temperature: The patient is chilly or warm and sensitive to cold.
- Nasal discharge: The nose is free-flowing or dry on alternating sides.

Characteristic symptoms—Sneezing causes pain in the throat. There may be epistaxis. Colds may rapidly become bronchitis. The patient craves salt, sour foods, and spicy foods. Symptoms are aggravated by lying on the left side or back; talking; touch; odors; light; cold, open air; sudden changes in weather; morning and evening; and especially twilight. They are alleviated by eating, sleeping, washing face with cold water, massage, sitting, and the dark. (See Chapter 13, *Phosphorus.*)

Sinusitis

Homeopathy is reputed to be successful in treating sinusitis, often curing the illness sooner than antibiotics would be expected to. If improvement is not seen in the patient's comfort after 24 hours, the medicine is incorrect. As the sinuses become less inflamed and secretions become thinner, increased nasal discharge and postnasal drip will be noted as the sinuses clear. The patient must be urged to increase fluid intake. Goldenseal and echinacea herbal preparations will not interfere with homeopathic treatment, and may even expedite it.

Sinusitis is one of a few common conditions in primary care that may require a higher potency than 30C to resolve successfully. Five days of a 30C potency of the indicated medicine may resolve milder sinusitis without fever or intense pain (with relief felt after one day if the medicine is correct). Moderate intensity sinusitis may call for the 200C potency three times a day for at least 3 days, with decreased frequency of repetition as symptoms lessen in the days that follow. The medicine is discontinued only when symptoms are completely resolved. Severe sinusitis, with intense pain and fever, may require the use of a 1M potency three times a day for 3 days, and then once a day until symptoms resolve. When using higher potencies such as the 200C and 1M, patient education must be precise as to when to discontinue the medicine. Continued repetition of an incorrect medicine is reputed to be more likely to generate the characteristic symptoms of a medicine when it is given in a higher potency.

Most Commonly Indicated Medicines

Hepar sulphuris calcareum—The patient has soreness at the root of the nose and a painful obstruction in the nose or there may be a thick, offensive nasal discharge that smells like old cheese. The patient is intensely *chilled* and sensitive to drafts. The sinusitis may be accompanied by pharyngitis that extends to the ears on swallowing.

Kali bichromicum—The patient feels pressure-like pain and obstruction at the root of the nose. The discharge has a characteristic thick and tough *stringiness* or globbiness. The color is green or yellow. Expired air feels hot. The patient can smell purulent material in the nose. The septum may be ulcerated and the patient may have nasal polypi.

Mercurius vivus or Mercurius solubilis—The patient has green or yellow nasal discharge, a *metallic* taste in the mouth, offensive perspiration, and offensive breath. He or she is alternatively chilly and warm, and the tongue holds indentation marks from teeth. (See Chapter 11, *Mercurius vivus* or *Mercurius solubilis*.)

Pulsatilla—The mucus is thick with yellow, green, or changeable *copious, bland* discharge. The person may have general symptoms indicative of *Pulsatilla:* weepiness, desire for consolation, symptoms alleviated in open air, no thirst, etc. (See Chapter 14, *Pulsatilla*.)

Silicea—The nose is dry and *obstructed*, with loss of olfactory sense. The nasal discharge is frothy. Dry hard crusty material in the nostrils causes bleeding when loosened. The patient may have a perforated septum or fissures in the nostrils and may feel generally chilly. The clinician should compare with *Sticta pulmonaria* in cases where an obstructed nose is present, and with *Hepar sulphuris calcareum* in cases where chilliness is notable.

Less Commonly Indicated Medicines

Bovista—The patient becomes physically *awkward* during the sinusitis; his or her speech seems awkward with possible stuttering. Especially notable is the patient's tendency to drop objects. *Bovista* is a more common remedy for sinusitis than *Kali bichromicum* for patients with moderate to severe chronic asthma. There is a stringy and tough discharge from the nose. The nose is obstructed, especially when lying down. Crusty dried mucus is observed around the nostrils. Cheeks may be swollen; lips may be cracked.

Hydrastis canadensis—The patient presents with a thick, *yellow, and ropy* mucus, with no other characteristics. If *Kali bichromicum* fails, *Hydrastis canadensis* should be prescribed.

Mercurius sulphuratus ruber—Heavy pressure is felt at the root of the nose; the pressure is aggravated by the pressure of glasses. The discharge from the nose is acrid, offensive, burning, watery, lumpy, or

214 AN INTRODUCTION TO HOMEOPATHIC MEDICINE IN PRIMARY CARE

dark. The patient may describe being awakened from sleep by *dry mouth and throat*; he or she must rinse the mouth. The patient expectorates stringy mucus from throat or has lumpy mucus from postnasal drip.

Sticta pulmonaria—The patient complains of pressure or stuffy *fullness* at the root of the nose. He or she feels a constant need to blow the nose, but there is *no discharge*. There is also painful dryness of mucous membranes. The nose is dry, but the patient has a postnasal drip. There is tickling high in the pharynx. Incessant, dry, hacking cough prevents sleep; coughing stimulates more coughing. The neck is stiff and sore; pain extends to the shoulder.

Sulphur—The nose is obstructed on *alternate sides*. The tip of the nose or alae nasi are red and swollen. The patient can smell the old mucus in the nasal passages. The patient is generally hotter than usual, and consequently averse to ambient heat. The patient is thirsty and desires spicy, salty, and fatty foods. (See Chapter 16, *Sulphur*.)

THROAT

Pharyngitis

Pharyngitis is reputed to be easy to treat with homeopathy. The choice of medicine is not affected by whether the streptococcal culture is positive or negative, but a good diagnosis is still necessary. The differential among homeopathic medicines for pharyngitis is usually clear; hence, viral infections are believed to respond well to homeopathic treatment. Streptococcal infections are often treated by homeopathic specialists who have established faith in the effectiveness of homeopathic medicines and serve a patient population who has as well. Given concern about dangerous sequelae, the best approach for those integrating homeopathic treatment protocols into conventional practices is to treat streptococcal pharyngitis with antibiotics.

The most important symptoms in distinguishing among homeopathic medicines are the distribution of the throat pain or tonsillar swelling, whether the throat is alleviated or aggravated by cold or warm drinks, whether empty swallowing or swallowing of food is painful, and any distinctive symptoms that have occurred concurrently in the person as a whole. The exact quality of the pain is helpful, but often impossible for children (and some adults) to describe. These areas of inquiry should not be neglected during data gathering. A 30C potency can be repeated every 2–3 hr for three doses at first. If there is no improvement after the third dose, as measured by reduced discomfort, another medicine should be selected. If the pain has improved, the clinician should instruct the patient to reduce the frequency of repetition to three times a day and continue for 3 days.

Most Commonly Indicated Medicines

Arsenicum album—Pharyngitis that is alleviated by *warm drinks*, which the patient desires to sip often, is indicative of *Arsenicum album*. The patient is generally chilly, restless, and anxious, and desires company. (See Chapter 3, *Arsenicum album*.)

Hepar sulphuris calcareum—The pharyngeal pain often feels sharp, like a *splinter* or splinters are caught there, and extends to the ear on empty swallowing or yawning. The pain is alleviated by warm drinks (compare with *Arsenicum album*) and aggravated from being touched, drinking cold drinks, and eating cold food. The pharyngitis may be accompanied by tonsillitis. There is tender cervical adenitis. (See Chapter 9, *Hepar sulphuris calcareum*.)

Lachesis mutus—The pharyngitis is *left-sided*, or starts on the left and goes to the right, and severe. Grayish discoloration of the pharynx progresses toward purple. The patient may describe the sensation of a lump or ball in throat, which ascends and is swallowed back again. He or she may experience a choking sensation, or be intolerant of snug clothing around the neck. The throat pain extends to the ear (compare with *Hepar sulphuris calcareum*, *Lac caninum*, and *Mercurius*). Swallowing is most painful when the throat is empty, less so from liquids, and alleviated by solids. The patient may become talkative during the illness, and is generally intolerant of heat.

Lycopodium clavatum—The patient presents with *right-sided* pharyngitis, or it begins on the right and moves to the left. The pain is alleviated by *warm drinks*, and aggravated by cold ones. The patient may also have the general symptoms indicative of *Lycopodium clavatum* such as increased flatulence and bossiness; the symptoms may worsen from 4:00 to 8:00 p.m.

Mercurius vivus or Mercurius solubilis—Almost any pharyngitis may be alleviated by *Mercurius vivus* or *Mercurius solubilis*; it will only palliate the symptoms (thereby prolonging the illness) unless the true symptomatology of *Mercurius* is present (Voegeli, 1981). There is a constant desire to swallow. The sore throat exudes a putrid or metallic taste. There may be ulcers present and needle-like pains extending to the ear on swallowing. Fluids may return through the nose. Pus has formed. The throat is sore, raw, smarting, and burning. The patient may lose his or her voice completely. The tongue is swollen and bears indentation marks from the teeth. Frequently, drooling will be reported by the patient, and breath and perspiration are *offensive*. In general, the patient is sensitive to both heat and cold, and is very thirsty for cold drinks. (See Chapter 11, *Mercurius vivus* or *Mercurius solubilis*.)

Less Commonly Indicated Medicines

Aconitum napellus—This sore throat comes on very *suddenly*, often after exposure to *cold, dry air*. The pharynx is red, hot, and dry. It feels constricted, with a choking sensation on swallowing. The tonsils are dry and swollen. The patient is thirsty and anxious.

Belladonna—The patient presents with a *scarlet* throat and tonsils that are swollen. The infection usually starts on the right and moves to the left. There is tender cervical adenitis of the neck. The patient may have spasms of the throat leading to food being forced up through the nose. There is a clear exudate on the tonsils. The patient's thirst is decreased, and he or she has a red face. *Belladonna* and *Aconitum napellus* are more often indicated on the first or second day of a pharyngitis, and onset is always sudden for both medicines. (See Chapter 4, *Belladonna*).

Lac caninum—*Lac caninum* is indicated for pharyngitis with pain on *alternating* sides. There may be pearly white exudate on the pharynx. The neck and tongue are stiff. The throat feels burned raw. Throat pain extends to the ears and is soothed by cold drinks.

Mercurius iodatus flavus—Pharyngitis that is treatable with *Mercurius vivus* or *Mercurius solubilis* can be right-sided, but that treated by *Mercurius iodatus flavus* is very distinctly *right-sided* and accompanied by a thickly coated tongue, which is yellow at the base. The tip and edges may be red and take the imprint of teeth, and a constant impulse to swallow may be observed (compare with *Mercurius*). There may be cheesy tonsillar exudates and offensive breath. There are small ulcers on the posterior pharynx.

Mercurius iodatus ruber—Symptoms resemble those indicative of *Mercurius vivus* or *Mercurius solubilis*, but are *left-sided*. Fauces are dark red. The muscles of the throat and neck are stiff.

Phytolacca decandra—The patient presents with follicular pharyngitis and tonsillitis. The pharynx is red, dark red, or bluish red and puffy. The pharynx is sore, and the pain on swallowing *extends to the ears*. The *right* tonsil throbs. The pain may be a burning and sticking sensation or like a ball or lump, and is aggravated by *warm drinks* and alleviated by cold drinks. The soft palate is sore and there are white-gray spots on the fauces. The person may be restless, weak, shivering, and achy in general. The patient may clench the jaw. There is profuse, hot lacrimation. This pharyngitis may occur during difficult dentition (compare with *Belladonna*), or during an exacerbation of rheumatic disease in adults.

Rhus toxicodendron—The patient describes sore, burning, or needle-like pains after *straining* the throat or in damp weather. The pain is alleviated by warmth in general, and warm drinks specifically. The pain is aggravated by empty swallowing, but alleviated afterwards. The throat is more painful in the *morning*, and is more likely to be left-sided. The tongue may be *reddened* at the tip. (See Chapter 15, *Rhus toxicodendron*.)

Tonsillitis

Any of the medicines used for pharyngitis may also be used for tonsillitis. In addition, the medicines that follow are more commonly indicated in tonsillitis, and their use in simple pharyngitis is rare.

Ailanthus glandulosus—*Ailanthus glandulosus* is indicated for follicular tonsillitis, streptococcal infection, or virulent viral infection. The throat is swollen and discolored purple or dark. The fauces feel dry, and the tonsils are studded with many *deep ulcers* (worse on the left), with loose pulpy discharge. There is irritation and itching of the posterior pharynx. The pain on swallowing extends to the ear. The neck is tender and swollen. Other symptoms may also include frontal headache with drowsiness, dilated pupils, photophobia, hoarse voice, and a dry, brownish tongue. Light-complected patients will show dusky, purplish, or mahogany-toned darkening of integument. Materia alba may be present. In the most severe cases, the patient becomes weak and delirious (compare with *Lachesis mutus* and *Arsenicum album*).

Apis mellifica—The patient presents with a stinging pain with swelling in the throat. There is edema of the uvula and small patches of white exudate. The patient is thirstless and is adverse to touch. He or she is talkative and busy.

Baryta carbonica—*Baryta carbonica* is used to treat an exacerbation of chronic enlargement of the tonsils, in which the tonsils nearly occlude the throat, and appear inflamed, with swollen veins visible. The tonsillitis comes on after exposure to cold and wind, or after upper respiratory infection. The tonsils may suppurate. The patient experiences smarting pain when swallowing and may only be able to swallow liquids. The patient feels as though there is a plug in the pharynx. There is a stinging pain in the tonsils or pharynx.

Baryta muriatica—The tonsils are enormously enlarged, and the submandibular and cervical glands are enlarged as well, especially on the right side (Morrison, 1993). Pain on the right side is alleviated by cold drinks. The patient has difficulty swallowing. The uvula is elongated.

Kali muriaticum—This medicine is indicated when there is follicular tonsillitis accompanied by blocked eustachian tubes. Tonsils are so *enlarged and inflamed* that there is concern that the airway will become obstructed. There are grayish patches or spots or crusty adherent exudate on the pharynx and tonsils.

Nitricum acidum—Sticking pain feels as if *splinters* are in the throat, extending into ears when swallowing (like *Hepar sulphuris calcareum*). The tonsils are red and swollen with small ulcers. Swallowing is difficult, even for small amounts. The patient expectorates mucus from posterior nares. The patient is anxious about the illness, and has a fear of death. The patient is irritable, cursing, or depressed and uncommunicative (compare with *Arsenicum album*).

CHAPTER 21

Lower Respiratory System

ACUTE ASTHMA

Acute asthma is usually well managed by bronchodilators, but an integrative clinician might like to try the classical homeopathic approach as well, especially when a child seems slow to respond to the nebulizer during an acute episode. The effectiveness of homeopathic medicines is not diminished by concurrent bronchodilator treatment. Steroid-based inhalers are believed to interfere with successful long-term, advanced treatment by specialists working to cure asthma. Homeopathic specialists anecdotally report that childhood asthma *is* generally curable with advanced constitutional treatment, while adult onset asthma is often not. The approach that follows is not aimed at cure; it is a palliative treatment for exacerbations of asthma. It is not known whether steroids reduce the effectiveness of this approach.

Integrative clinicians are advised not to use more than a 30C potency in asthmatic patients. The rationale is that lower potencies are more gentle in their action, thereby providing a smooth yet effective recovery. The clinician should give the 30C potency of the indicated medicine every 10 min in a severe attack, with a nebulizer, or on the way to the emergency room. If not improved by the third dose, the clinician should try another homeopathic medicine in addition to whatever other treatment is being implemented. In mild to moderate attacks a dose can be given every half hour for three doses; if the patient has not improved after three doses, the medicine should be changed. Patients must be told to continue their current conventional treatment plans in addition to the homeopathic medicine. The clinician should carefully document this education.

Arsenicum album—The patient presents with great dyspnea, and with possible cyanosis. He or she displays great *anxiety and restlessness*. The patient is *exacting* and demands everything in the environment be just so. Other symptoms may include profuse, cold perspiration; burning or coldness in the chest; whistling, wheezing respirations; chills; and frequent thirst for sips of warm drinks. The patient is unable to lie down and must sit up or get out of bed. Symptoms are aggravated by odors, laughing, at 12:00–2:00 a.m., and while ascending stairs and inclines. They are alleviated by coffee. This medicine is indicated for asthma during an upper respiratory infection. (See Chapter 3, *Arsenicum album*.)

Kali carbonicum—The patient presents with dyspnea that is aggravated by the least motion or walking; the dyspnea may alternate with diarrhea or vertigo. The distinguishing feature is that the asthma is aggravated at at *3:00 a.m.*, and in the very early morning in general. The patient is weak, irritable, and quarrelsome.

Naja tripudians—Clinicians use this medication for asthma brought on by spring *allergic rhinitis*, or for cardiac patients. The patient describes a sensation of a weight on the chest as if a hot iron rod had pierced the chest. The asthma is aggravated at *night* and by lying down, and improved by sitting up.

Pulsatilla—*Pulsatilla* is indicated for shortness of breath that is aggravated by lying on the left side, by becoming *warm*, after eating, and in the evening. Like most *Pulsatilla* complaints, the asthma is alleviated in the *open* air. Other symptoms include dry, hacking cough; feeling of a weight on the chest; and being thirstless, weepy, and desirous of consolation. (See Chapter 14, *Pulsatilla*.)

Asthma Attacks from Molds and Damp Environments

Blatta orientalis—Sturdy obese patients with asthma from *moldy*, damp environments, or decomposing leaves are best treated with this medicine. There is much wheezing, dyspnea, and shortness of breath from slight exertion. Symptoms are generally aggravated from exertion and ascending stairs or inclines.

Natrum sulphuricum—*Natrum sulphuricum* is used to treat asthma in people who live near water or in *basements*. They have dyspnea that is aggravated in the early morning. Acute asthma arises during a cold or exertion. Patients are short of breath while walking with an urge to take deep breaths. The asthma may be associated with *early-morning diarrhea*. Symptoms are alleviated by warm, dry air. The patient is averse to talking or being spoken to.

Asthma with Nausea

Ipecacuanha—The patient presents with asthma and is gasping for breath. There is constant constriction in the chest and larynx that is aggravated by the least motion, and much violent suffocative coughing with *retching*. During the cough, the child stiffens and can become cyanotic and *nauseous*, culminating with gagging and vomiting. Symptoms are alleviated by open air, warmth, and rest.

Lobelia inflata—Mild asthma with anxiety and hyperventilation that causes weakness, cold perspiration, and prickling all over is best treated with this medicine. There is constriction in the chest, or a sensation like a wedge in the larynx or throat pit. Intense *nausea and vomiting* and a spasmodic cough may accompany the asthma. The patient sits with his or her elbows on the knees. The patient has become very sensitive to the odor of tobacco, even if he or she smokes.

Asthma with Perspiration

Sambucus nigra—Sudden dyspnea especially on *falling to sleep*, or dyspnea that wakens the patient at midnight with copious perspiration. This medicine is also used to treat an asthma attack after a fright. There may be whistling respirations, and the hands become cyanotic, and the feet are icy cold. The patient may be cyanotic in general and feel *hot* subjectively. These symptoms are aggravated by dry, cold air; drinking cold drinks when feeling hot; and lying down. They are alleviated by moving, wrapping up, and sitting up in bed.

Silicea—Silicea is indicated when there are recurring upper respiratory infections that settle in the chest and stimulate asthma attacks. The patient experiences dyspnea from a *draft* on the neck, or after becoming overheated during exertion. He or she is short of breath from exertion and cold air. The patient is chilly, often (but not always) lean, and has *offensive perspiration* on his or her feet.

Sulphur—The patient has asthma with a suffocating feeling as though there were a plug, valve, or leaf in the larynx, thereby compelling the patient to throw the head back. Symptoms include loud and whistling inspirations at bedtime, dyspnea with perspiration that *wakes* the patient at night, and anxious, gasping breathing. There is a dry, tight cough that wakes the patient, followed by burning in the chest and throat. The symptoms are aggravated by cold drinks or excitement, sweets, and drinking cold milk. They are alleviated by drinking or eating, especially warm things. (See Chapter 16, *Sulphur*.)

BRONCHIOLITIS

The clinician should consider the medicines below and prescribe according to the instructions for asthma. Because of the similarities among bronchiolitis, asthma, and bronchitis, there will be some redundancy here with those sections.

Arsenicum album—Dyspnea prevents reclining and is aggravated by odors, laughing, drinking any liquid that is not warmed, and turning in bed. The patient has whistling, wheezing respirations, and asthma around midnight. The patient's cough alternates between dry and loose, (more dry at night) and is alleviated by sitting up. Expectorations are scant and frothy. There is great dyspnea; the face may be cyanotic and covered with cold perspiration; and the patient has great anxiety. The patient is chilly, restless, and exacting. (See Chapter 3, *Arsenicum album*.)

Belladonna—The patient has a tickling, short, and dry cough that is aggravated at night and from yawning. The child cries before the cough and moans at every breath. The voice is high and piping. The patient experiences dyspnea with short, quick respirations, especially with a red face, cold hands and feet, and a hot head. (See Chapter 4, *Belladonna*.)

Cuprum metallicum—The bronchiolitis that *Cuprum metallicum* is used to treat is characterized by a *spasmodic* quality. The cough is spasmodic with constriction of the chest; it can alternate with spasmodic vomiting. The cough may have a gurgling sound. While the symptoms of most children who have this condition will be alleviated by warm water, this cough is alleviated by drinking cold water. There may be cramps and twitching elsewhere in the body as well (e.g., in the calves, soles, or extremities). There may be cyanosis or a marbled appearance of the skin. Symptoms are generally aggravated around 3:00 a.m. like with *Kali carbonicum*.

Ipecacuanha—Ceaseless violent cough with *retching* is best treated with *Ipecacuanha*. During the cough, the child stiffens and can become cyanotic and nauseous, culminating with gagging and vomiting. There is unrelenting constriction of the chest and larynx that is aggravated by the slightest motion. The patient gasps for breath. The lungs have coarse, loose crackles, yet there is *no expectoration* (compare with *Antimonium tartaricum* and *Causticum* in the section entitled, "Acute Bronchitis"). Symptoms are alleviated by open air, warmth, and rest.

Lycopodium clavatum—Shallow and rattling respiration are aggravated by lying on the back. Cough can be dry, tickling, teasing, deep, and hollow; it is aggravated by deep breathing and cold air. If it can be expectorated, the sputum is greenish yellow, lumpy, or offensive. Although this state can occur in any child, it is especially common in small boys with failure to thrive. There may be *fanning* of the alae nasae. The patient desires open air. The symptoms are generally alleviated by warm drinks and are aggravated in the *late afternoon and early evening*. His or her mood is domineering, but he or she is afraid to be alone.

Mephitis mephitica—While all bronchiolitis is characterized by difficulty exhaling, this medicine is called for when the child is suffocating from this difficulty. The child gets cyanotic. There are rales in the upper chest. There is an extremely *violent, paroxysmal* spasmodic cough mainly at night. The cough causes *vomiting* after eating.

Phosphorus—There is dyspnea from the slightest motion. Tight, suffocative breathing is aggravated by coughing. The voice is *hoarse* especially in the morning and evening. The cough causes *pain in the abdomen* and is aggravated by *cold drinks*, which the child craves. The sputum is easy, frothy, rusty, bluish, salty, sour, sweet, or cold. The patient is generally anxious, lacks concentration, likes company, and has an increased thirst for cold drinks. (See Chapter 13, *Phosphorus*.)

Nux vomica—The patient presents with a violent paroxysmal cough with shallow respirations. He or she is hoarse with painful roughness in the larynx and chest. There is dyspnea that is alleviated by eructations. *Constipation* with straining may accompany the illness. The patient wants to eat during the cough, and desires spicy food and stimulants. The patient is irritable, impatient, and generally chilly. (See Chapter 12, *Nux vomica.*)

Pulsatilla—There is a loose cough in the morning, and a dry one in the evening and at night; the patient must be propped up in the crib or bed to get relief. The sputum is thick, purulent, slimy, sweet, salty, and/or bitter as it loosens up. The cough is dry, hacking, and stimulated by tickling in the epigastrium. The patient is intermittently hoarse. The patient's shallow respirations are aggravated by lying on the left side. There is dyspnea on lying down that is aggravated by heat and that is alleviated in the open air. The patient is weepy, clingy, and thirstless. (See Chapter 14, *Pulsatilla*.)

ACUTE BRONCHITIS

Acute bronchitis is regarded by homeopathic clinicians as easy to treat with homeopathic medicines. The 30C potency may be prescribed three times a day for 5 days and then with gradually decreasing frequency as the symptoms continue to subside. If the treatment is begun after there is bacterial involvement with yellow or green expectoration, there will be a slow, but steady healing process of at least 5 days. A 200C potency may be prescribed twice a day during this time. Rest is of the utmost importance in lung ailments; the patient should be sternly warned that premature return to work or school may result in a long illness or pneumonia. If the patient feels he or she needs to continue working, despite the risk, the clinican should prescribe antibiotics for bacterial bronchitis. Ample hydration should be stressed.

Homeopathic treatment of pneumonia is a common occurrence in the offices of homeopathic specialists, but the topic is being omitted from this book because it is beyond the comfort zone of most integrative clinicians to treat pneumonia without antibiotics.

Antimonium tartaricum—This medicine successfully treats severe bronchitis primarily in children, with coarse rales. The child may become somewhat cyanotic, with a coating on the tongue. It seems as though the children are *drowning* in their own secretions. If the symptoms are less severe, and the illness is in its early stages, *Ipecacuanha* is indicated.

Bryonia alba—The patient is irritable, wants to be *still*, and wants to be left *alone*. He or she is thirsty for large amounts of water at long intervals. There is a dry, hard, and painful cough, which causes the patient to hold his or her sides, chest, and head, thereby controlling the pain. Pains can be sharp and needle-like in the chest, right side, sternum, or near the right scapula. They are aggravated during fever, chills, or perspiration. There may be intercostal chondritis. A friction rub may be heard over the lung. The patient must sit up in bed at night to cough. Since deep inspiration stimulates a cough, the patient breathes shallowly. Not surprisingly, laughing aggravates the cough and the pain; fortunately, the patient is not in a joking mood. The patient may expectorate rusty, blood-streaked sputum or tough sputum. The symptoms are aggravated in general by the least motion; becoming overheated; eating, especially acidic foods; being touched; and at 9:00 p.m. They are alleviated by pressure with the hand or by lying on the painful part of the chest or back; cool, open air; cold food and drink; and quiet. The chest pain may be alleviated by pressure applied to the middle of the hand. (See Chapter 5, *Bryonia alba*.)

Causticum—There are two key features of the *Causticum*-indicated bronchitis that, if present, can ensure a correct prescription. The first is that when attempting to expectorate sputum, the patient gets it part way up, then it slips back down. The patient feels like he or she cannot cough deeply enough. The second is that the patient is newly experiencing some stress incontinence (i.e., losing a small amount of *urine* with the cough). There may be *hoarseness* during the bronchitis.

Ipecacuanha—*Ipecacuanha* is indicated in children at the *beginning* of bronchitis that has increasing mucus, distressing cough, significant fever, and rales throughout all fields (Borland, 1982).

Phosphorus—Bronchitis that is best treated with *Phosphorus* can have any kind of cough and any kind of sputum. One characteristic symptom is *burning* in the air passages. This symptom is especially frequently seen in the bronchitis of children after croup. The cough is aggravated by reading aloud, change of weather, being in the company of strangers, laughing, exertion, or singing. Most important in the selection of *Phosphorus* as a medicine for bronchitis are the general symptoms of the patient. The patient is *thirsty* for ice-cold water, *anxious*, and "spaced out"; he or she desires company. (See Chapter 13, *Phosphorus*.)

Pulsatilla—The cough is loose in the morning, but becomes dry in the evening and at night. The cough compels the patient to sit up in bed, thereby alleviating it. The sputum may be almost any color, or changeable. The cough may be stimulated by a tickling sensation in the epigastric region. The chest feels like it has a weight on it. The typical *Pulsatilla* general symptoms will usually be present: weepiness, dependent behavior, thirstlessness, and desire for open air. The cough improves in the open air. (See Chapter 14, *Pulsatilla*.)

Silicea—Clinicians use *Silicea* to treat *lingering* bronchitis; the patient never seems to rouse the defenses to oust the illness. The patient is chilly in general. There are coarse rales with profuse, *yellow, and lumpy sputum*. The patient expectorates little granular balls that taste and smell offense when broken up. There is rattling and sharp or needle-like pains in the chest through to the back (like with *Bryonia alba*).

Sulphur—The patient experiences coarse rales and a sensation of burning, heat, or coldness in the chest that extends to the face. A tickle in the larynx stimulates a violent cough, which may aggravate a headache. There is a sensation of a weight on the chest, or a band around it. There is a *greenish* purulent sputum with a sweetish taste. Talking makes the chest feel weak. Shooting pains in the chest that extend to the back are aggravated by coughing, lying on the back, and deep inspiration. The patient feels hot; his or her feet are so hot that the patient sticks them out of the covers. He or she is thirsty. Symptoms are worse at 11:00 a.m. (See Chapter 16, *Sulphur*.)

Bronchitis Accompanied by Disproportionate Anxiety

Arsenicum album—*Arsenicum album* is used to treat the chilly, restless patient who is anxious as though this bronchitis would kill him or her. An exacting irritability accompanies the anxiety. The patient is thirsty for sips of warm drinks frequently. The patient desires company. (See Chapter 3, *Arsenicum album*.)

Phosphorus—See under "Acute Bronchitis."

Bronchitis Accompanied by Sinusitis

Kali bichromicum—*Stringy*, thick, globby, and yellow sputum and postnasal drip are the most important symptoms of bronchitis that should be treated with *Kali bichromicum*. The patient describes a feeling of rawness or pain under the *sternum*, with pains that extend through to the back and shoulders with a cough or when undressing. There is pain at the bifurcation of the trachea on coughing. There may be a sensation as though a bar is across the chest. The patient may at times have a dry, metallic, and hacking cough.

Hepar sulphuris calcareum—Intense *chilliness* is always expected in a *Hepar sulphuris calcareum* illness, with sensitivity to the slightest cool *draft*. The bronchitis patient has coarse rales; the sputum is yellow and thick, feels loose, and yet is surprisingly difficult to expectorate. The patient may have the sensation that there are drops of hot water in the chest. Sometimes difficult to distinguish when *Hepar sulphuris calcareum* is needed and when *Silicea* is needed. (See Chapter 9, *Hepar sulphuris calcareum*.)

Mercurius vivus or Mercurius solubilis—Usually *Mercurius* is prescribed for bronchitis based on the general symptoms of the patient (e.g., feels *too chilly or too warm*, exudes *offensive* perspiration and halitosis, and has an indented tongue). The specific lung symptoms from the proving are as follows. Respiration is difficult especially when lying on the left side, but the cough is exacerbated by lying on the right side. The cough is dry at night with a yellow-green sputum by day. There are paroxysms of cough at night that are brought on by the warmth of the bed. There are needle-like pains that start in the lower-right chest and go through to the back, which are aggravated by sneezing or coughing. The patient may have a sensation of bubbles or hot steam in the chest. (See Chapter 11, *Mercurius vivus* or *Mercurius solubilis*.)

Pulsatilla—See under "Acute Bronchitis."

Silicea—See under "Acute Bronchitis."

Frequent Bouts of Bronchitis Following Upper Respiratory Infection

Arsenicum album, Bryonia alba, Hepar sulphuris calcareum, Phosphorus, Pulsatilla, and *Sulphur* can all be used for people whose colds always seem to end in bronchitis.

Tuberculinum—This medicine is usually indicated for children who become malicious during a cough, striking others surreptitiously, and then laughing about it. There is a mucous rattle in the chest with or without expectoration and thick, yellow or yellow-green sputum. The child craves cool air, and even likes to stick his or her head out of the window of the car, or in front of a fan.

Bronchitis with Great Weakness

Antimonium tartaricum—See under "Acute Bronchitis."

Muriaticum acidum—The patient is completely physically exhaused from prolonged bronchitis and sleeps most of the day. The distinctive symptom is that he or she is too weak to remain sitting up under the covers and *slips down* into the bed. The ambulatory patient lies down on the seats in the waiting room before an appointment.

Stannum metallicum—The patient feels weak in the chest. The cough is aggravated by laughing, singing, talking exertion, or lying on the right side. There is retching with the coughing and much mucus in the trachea. The patient easily expectorates copious sweet, salty, sour, or purulent material on balls of mucus. The chest feels raw or hollow with sharp or needle-like pains in the left side or below the left axilla, when breathing or lying on that side. The patient has night sweats that force him or her to loosen the clothes.

Bronchitis in Older Persons

Older people are not prescribed different medicines than young people simply by virtue of their age. These medicines are for people who are fragile and have signs of physiological decay, such as heart disease, lung disease, or diabetes from extreme old age, chronic tobacco, alcohol, or drug use, or a lifetime of poor nutrition or high living. Since the concurrent chronic diseases of the patient can be important in prescribing, a quick review of the chart is helpful with the new patient. Potency selection and repetition of the dose is not different from the general instructions for bronchitis. Since the response will be slower, however, the clinician needs to ensure to continue the patient on a medicine until the symptoms are completely gone, as long as the person is clearly slightly better each day.

Ammonium carbonicum—This medicine is prescribed for rattling in the chest with scanty expectoration in exhausted seniors with *weak hearts*, especially for those who are *sedentary and obese*. It can also be used for any adult with chronic bronchitis and for the winter exacerbation of bronchitis. The patient is forgetful, gloomy, and hard of hearing. He or she has chronic rhinitis with mouth breathing. Dyspnea wakes the patient and is aggravated by the slightest exertion or entering a warm room. Cool air alleviates the dyspnea. The sputum can be of the watery and profuse kind, and/or the sticky, tough, and difficult-to-exporate sputum of those with chronic bronchitis (Borland, 1982). The patient may have chronic obstructive pulmonary disease, angina, or pulmonary edema. The patient is very sensitive to cold air. Symptoms are aggravated by cold, cloudy weather and motion; they worsen at 3:00–4:00 a.m. Symptoms are alleviated by eating, lying on the abdomen, dry weather, and lying on the right side.

Carbo vegetabilis—That patient presents with wheezing and rattling of mucus in the chest. There are occasional long coughing spells with burning in the chest that are aggravated in the evening, in the open air, and after eating and talking. An old person who needs *Carbo vegetabilis* to recover from bronchitis may also present with one of the following: cyanosis, ecchymosis, varicosities, mottled cheeks, venous overdistention, senile gangrene beginning in the toes, or bed sores. There may also be pallor and *icy coldness*. The patient is exhausted from medicines, diseases, or dehydration. The patient is very weak and faint, but is better from being fanned hard or being exposed to the open air. The breath may be cool and the perspiration cold or hot. The head may feel hot. The pulse is almost imperceptible and is tachycardic; there is also tachypnea. There are eructations and *flatulence*. The hair falls out from a generally weakened condition.

Hippozaeninum—This medicine is used to treat bronchitis in the aged where, like with *Antimonium tartaricum*, the person seems on the verge of suffocating from his or her own secretions, and suctioning is called for. The respirations are noisy, short, and irregular. The medicine is also used to treat patients who have chronic sinusitis with papules and ulcerations in the frontal sinus and pharynx. There may be adenopathy and concurrent skin diseases, such as pustules, abscesses, ulcers, and eczema.

Hydrastis canadensis—One of the foremost medicines for exhausted, emaciated older persons is *Hydrastis canadensis*. The distinctive feature is that the sputum is copious; comes up easily; and is thick, yellow, and possibly bloody. There is dyspnea that is aggravated by lying on the left side.

Lycopodium clavatum—See under "Bronchiolitis."

Senega officinalis—There are coarse rales with great difficulty expectorating the viscid and copious sputum. The coughing hurts the back, and the chest walls are sore. The coughing often ends with a *sneeze*. There is heaviness in the chest, especially when ascending an incline or a staircase. Patients with chronic obstructive pulmonary disease or asthma find this medicine especially effective for their bronchitis.

LARYNGITIS

There are only a handful of medicines for the homeopathic treatment of laryngitis, which seem to be effective in most cases. A day of not speaking is recommended at the onset of treatment, if possible. The 30C potency may be prescribed twice a day for 3 days, or may be discontinued sooner if no longer needed.

Argentum nitricum—This medicine is used to treat hoarseness in professional speakers and singers, coupled with performance anxiety.

Arum triphyllum—Occasionally, one will encounter a postinfluenzal laryngitis where the loss of voice begins with a change in the voice to a *higher or lower* tone. It may progress to total aphonia.

Causticum—The patient has hoarseness in the *morning* that usually improves later in the day. The patient coughs violently and cannot seem to expectorate the mucus in the larynx. The patient may *lose urine* during the cough. Symptoms are aggravated by cold, dry weather. There may be a sudden and complete loss of the voice. Along with *Argentum nitricum*, *Causticum* is one of the few medicines for loss of voice in singers.

Carbo vegetabilis—The patient presents with a husky voice that is the result of a prolonged cold; it is aggravated in the evening. The person is generally run down, and the larynx feels raw.

Phosphorus—With the hoarseness, there is a very painful raw feeling in the larynx. The patient cannot speak from the pain in the larynx. The hoarseness and/or aphonia are aggravated in the *evening*. There may be a velvety sensation or a violent *tickling* in the larynx while speaking. The patient thirsts for ice-cold drinks. (See Chapter 13, *Phosphorus*.)

Rhus toxicodendron—The patient has lost his or her voice. Loss of voice may be from overuse (e.g., in speakers). The voice gets stronger as the person *continues* to speak. He or she has a dry, tormenting, and paroxysmal cough. There are aching pains around the ribs, and the patient is physically *restless*. (See Chapter 15, *Rhus toxicodendron*.)

ACUTE LARYNGOTRACHEOBRONCHITIS (VIRAL CROUP)

Homeopathic clinicians have claimed croup to be an easy condition to treat for over 100 years. In the last century, one famous practitioner of homeopathy sold kits with three medicines in numbered vials to families for home treatment of children with croup. The instructions were to give one medicine; and if that did not work, give the next; and if that did not work, give the next. These medicines were *Aconitum napellus, Hepar sulphuris calcareum,* and *Spongia tosta.* Contemporary clinicians report that these are still by far the most frequently indicated medicines for croup.

The clinician should prescribe a 30C potency every hour for three doses, and give the usual advice about bringing the child into a steamy bathroom. If there is not significant improvement, the medicine is incorrect and should be changed.

Most Commonly Indicated Medicines

Aconitum napellus—The child wakes up suddenly in the *early part* of the night (before midnight) with the typical hoarse, dry, and barking cough and dyspnea of croup. Fear is written on the child's face, and there is an *anxious* restlessness. On reflection, it is often noted by the parents that the child had been in a *cold, dry* wind during the day that preceded the onset of symptoms.

Hepar sulphuris calcareum—The child is very *chilly* and wants to be completely covered up. The exposure of any part of the body to cold aggravates the cough, which worsens in the morning and the evening. (See Chapter 9, *Hepar sulphuris calcareum.*)

Spongia tosta—This is the classic medicine for the hoarse, barking cough and dyspnea of croup. Onset is typically later in the night than when *Aconitum napellus* is indicated, but the onset is slower and accompanied by some *fright*. Respirations may sound like the noise of *sawing* a pine board by hand. The cough resembles the sound of a seal *barking*.

Less Commonly Indicated Medicines

Bromium—The patient presents with a dry cough with hoarseness. Inspired air feels *cold*, even when it is not. It feels like there is *smoke* in the lungs when there is not. There is a burning pain behind the sternum.

Iodium—The patient has a *painful*, choking hoarseness; the child grasps the throat while coughing (compare with *Aconitum napellus*). The cough is dry and tickling. The patient is short of breath, especially when ascending stairs. The child feels *hot*.

WINTER COUGH

An annoying dry cough in an otherwise well person of any age is an unwelcome feature of winters in cold climates. Homeopathic medicines are reputed to easily resolve such coughs. *Rumex crispus* or *Spongia tosta* will successfully treat most.

Aconitum napellus—A tickling cough accompanied by anxiety and a sense of suffocation plagues the patient. The attack comes on after exposure to *cold, dry* air, accompanied by marked chilliness, and often followed by a high fever. The patient is restless and intensely thirsty.

Hyoscyamus niger—The patient has a dry, incessant cough when *lying* down that is alleviated by sitting up, warm air, and bending forward. It is aggravated by lying down, eating, talking, drinking, and inspiring cold air. The cough worsens at night. *Sips of water* aggravate the cough.

Rumex crispus—The inspiration of *cold air* causes tickling at the suprasternal notch, which leads to coughing. A dry cough prevents sleep.

Spongia tosta—The patient has a dry, hollow, and *barking* cough with no other symptoms.

Sticta pulmonaria—The patient presents with a cough from tickling high up in the pharynx. A ceaseless, dry, and hacking cough interferes with sleep. Coughing stimulates more coughing, as does inspiring. The cough worsens towards evening and from fatigue.

CHAPTER 22

Emotional Health and Chemical Dependency Recovery

Homeopathic clinicians report that adjustment reactions to transitions, losses, stresses, or crime can be greatly smoothed by the use of a relatively small group of medicines. The most common remedies for these transitions are summarized below. The treatment of chronic affective disorders requires the complete training of a homeopathic specialist as well as a practice structured to have at least 1-hour patient visits. There is a dirth of double-blind, placebo-controlled research on homeopathic treatment of psychological disorders; the only study thus far is a pilot study that showed a positive effect for homeopathy over placebo in the treatment of depression (Davidson, Morrison, Shore, Davidson, & Bedayn, 1997).

ACUTE GRIEF

Aurum metallicum—The patient who is helped by *Aurum metallicum* feels *responsible* in some way for the loss. There is an unshakable belief that a duty has been neglected. The patient presents with intense *hopelessness*, self-condemnation, and loathing for life. He or she may talk about *suicide* or make secret plans to commit suicide, usually with a gun or by crashing a car. The patient is depressed, brooding, and irritable, and has a desire to be alone and an aversion to sympathy or touch. He or she feels worse from sunset to sunrise, and during the winter. The patient feels better from walking or listening to music.

Calcarea phosphorica—The grief of school-age girls with late afternoon headaches is best treated with *Calcarea phosphorica*. The children moan, groan, and cry in their sleep, and sigh when awake.

233

They may feel *discontent* and wish to travel. They crave smoked meat, like bacon or sausage. This medicine is less commonly indicated than *Ignatia amara*.

Cocculus indicus—This medicine is used to treat very sad people who cannot stop thinking about what happened. The patient sits dazed, absorbed in these thoughts, and observes nothing around him or her. The patient may experience sudden and severe anxiety attacks. There is a feeling that things are unreal. The patient is easily offended, cannot stand being contradicted, takes everything the wrong way, and is very anxious about the *health of others*. At times, that patient is talkative, witty, joking, dancing, and gesticulating. There may be vertigo, numbness, or paralysis during the period of mourning. The persons who suffers from this type of depression are frequently the caregivers for loved ones with serious illnesses. This medicine is less commonly called for than *Ignatia amara*.

Ignatia amara—*Ignatia amara* is the most common medicine for situational depression from acute grief, and the somatization of grief. It is normal to be depressed from losses. Patients are prescribed *Ignatia amara* when they seem to be unable to really accept the loss; thus they have *difficulty crying* especially in front of others, or display a difficult, spasmodic kind of weeping. They feel the grief in their throats, with difficulty swallowing, or a sensation of a lump's being there. There may be twitching, hiccups, or spasms. Frequent *sighing* is a key symptom. There is a new sensitivity to odors, especially smoke. These patients are prone to headaches, which may come on from exposure to cigarette smoke. The headaches are aggravated by stooping. Because patients often present with physical complaints that are the result of grief, clinicians should note excessive sighing (a symptom of grief) during patient consultations. (See Chapter 10, *Ignatia amara*.)

Natrum muriaticum—This medicine has symptomatology very similar to that of *Ignatia amara*. Like with the latter, the patient has a strong *aversion to consolation*, and usually finds it difficult to cry in front of others; at other times, the weeping is uncontrollable, much to the patient's embarrassment. Unlike when *Ignatia amara* is indicated, there is not the sensitivity to smoke or frequent sighing. The patient strongly desires to be isolated from other people. The patient's thirst is usually increased, and there is a craving or aversion to salt. There may be many kinds of physical symptoms that arise during mourning, most commonly they include tension headache; herpetic eruptions; or mild, but lingering, sinusitis with thick, white or clear postnasal discharge, like the uncooked white of an egg. The patient feels generally worse 9:00–11:00 a.m., and from being out in the sun.

Phosphoricum acidum—The patient displays *weakness* and apathy, as though he or she has given up. Typically, this state results from an unhappy love situation. The cognition is slow. He or she cannot find the right word; memory is impaired; the patient answers slowly. The patient may weep from homesickness and hopelessness. Painless diarrhea and increased perspiration often occur during mourning. The patient is thirsty for refreshing drinks like fruit juice.

ANTICIPATORY ANXIETY

Aethusa cynapium—This medicine is prescribed for students whose cognitive processes become impaired from overstudying. They can no longer *think* or fix the attention. They are anxious and restless; they cry and may possibly vomit.

Argentum nitricum—*Performance anxiety* and fear of failure that may be accompanied by diarrhea, sore throat (splinter-like sensation), and/or flatulent distension is best treated with *Argentum nitricum*. There may be problems with the pharynx and larynx in singers and public speakers. In more extreme cases, there are strange new impulses and phobias emerging concurrently. The patient may believe that he or she will fail at the task at hand. *Phobias* may be of crowds, driving, bridges, heights, church, open spaces, looking up at tall buildings, certain street corners, or small enclosed spaces. The patient desires sweets and sugar, but feels generally worse from eating them. The patient also feels generally worse in hot weather or rooms.

Gelsemium sempervirens—Commonly known as a medicine for influenza, *Gelsemium sempervirens* also helps people who enter a state of anticipation that *mimics a viral syndrome*. The person becomes weak, sleepy, dull-minded, and apathetic. He or she urinates more than the usual amount of pale urine, and yet his or her thirst is diminished. The patient has a feeling of dread, and that this experience is an ordeal. There may be vertigo as well. (See Chapter 8, *Gelsemium sempervirens*.)

Lycopodium clavatum—Symptoms are similar to indicators for *Argentum nitricum* with bloating from *anticipatory anxiety* and desire for sweets. A lack of self-confidence is compensated for with a boastful and haughty demeanor. Other symptoms include fear of being alone, anger on waking, and fullness from eating only a small amount of food. Anxiety is alleviated by drinking warm drinks.

Picricum acidum—Like with *Aethusa cynapium*, there is mental exhaustion from *overstudy*, especially before a big examination, such as medical or legal boards. The patient experiences anxiety and foreboding that he or she will fail. The patient loses the will to even undertake the task and may give up the attempt. He or she may sit still and listless, and take no interest in his or her surroundings.

BUSINESS FAILURE AND FINANCIAL LOSS

Arnica montana—The patient is morose and filled with regrets; he or she feels like a good-for-nothing. The patient feels emotionally *bruised* from the experience, and so has a fear of being struck, touched, or even approached. He or she also fears crowds and public places. The patient is apathetic and hopeless, but physically restless. He or she claims there is nothing wrong and refuses professional help. (See Chapter 2, *Arnica montana*.)

Aurum metallicum—This medicine is thought of by homeopaths as one that might have helped the stockbrokers that jumped out of windows on Wall Street when the stock market crashed in 1929. The patient may feel a heavy *responsibility* for what has happened, and is experiencing a very serious depression. The patient feels happy when contemplating death and suicidal thoughts, but claims he or she will not go through with it because of their responsibilities to others. There may be a brooding depression with irritability and self-blame that he or she neglected a duty. The patient does not want to talk.

Cimicafuga racemosa—The patient is despondent, morose, and dejected. Negative and pessimistic, the patient may use the metaphor of a heavy, black cloud to describe his or her state. The patient sits and mopes in great sadness, and when questioned, breaks into tears. Other symptoms include a sense of foreboding, disconnected thoughts, fear of insanity, and wild behavior that may make the clinician wonder whether the fear is well-founded. The patient is agitated, with coarse and jerky involuntary movements (e.g., chorea, athetosis, and grimacing). The patient is talkative, jumping from one subject to another, and takes no interest in housework. In the end, the patient may not take medicine because of paranoia it will harm him or her (Moscowitz, 1992).

Colocynthis—The patient presents with *anger and indignation* over a business failure. The patient is easily offended, impatient, and yet greatly affected by the misfortunes of others. He or she wants to walk around, and not interact with anyone, including friends. He or she has had painful bouts of irritable bowel syndrome or flatulence that cause him or her to double up, and apply pressure to the abdomen.

Natrum muriaticum—This medicine should be used to treat the strong, silent type who wants to hide depression and feelings of humiliation about this issue from others. Refer to the section entitled, "Acute Grief."

Nux vomica—This patient is angry and frustrated from *blocked ambition*. There is impatience and *irritability* and physical symptoms such as tension headaches, migraines, and constipation. The patient craves stimulants such as cocaine, caffeine, and nicotine. There may be alcohol abuse and outright alcoholism exacerbated by the failure or financial loss. (See Chapter 12, *Nux vomica*.)

Rhus toxicodendron—Anxiety and depression with a feeling of restlessness, helplessness, and profound despondency is best treated with *Rhus toxicodendron*. The patient cannot identify why he or she is *crying alone* each evening. The patient may even fear being poisoned. He or she has "had it" with life, and the thoughts turn to suicide by drowning. Memory becomes impaired for recent events. A sense of fear is exaserbated at night, and the patient cannot lie in bed. Physical stiffness and achiness is alleviated by continued motion and warmth, and aggravated by cool, damp weather. (See Chapter 15, *Rhus toxicodendron*.)

Sarsaparilla—Urinary tract infections, or idiopathic problems with *urination* after a business loss, should be treated with *Sarsaparilla*. The patient is easily offended, uncommunicative, and despondent.

Staphysagria—For people who were *abused* in their work or business, and they feel ashamed for allowing it to happen, this is the main medicine. These include passive patients with low self-esteem and suppressed anger, which eventually may lead to violent outbursts. The patient is gloomy and petulant, throws things, and shreds clothes. The libido is high with frequent masturbation. The patient feels insulted, indignant, and sensitive to rudeness, and believes his or her partner will leave as a result of the business failure.

FEAR REMAINING AFTER A FRIGHTENING EVENT

Aconitum napellus—Panic attacks with *agonizing* fear, restlessness, and terror are treated with *Aconitum napellus*. There is fear of *dying* (and a delusion that he or she might suddenly do so), crowds, crossing the streets, and the future. He or she may have chest pain or fever accompanying the fear. The patient screams, moans, gnaws the fists, bites the nails, and wants to die. The patient may have agoraphobia. There is also increased thirst.

Opium—The cognitive and emotional state of the opiates is familiar to nearly all health care providers. This state mimics a state of *shock* following a severe fright. The patient does not want anything; he or she is *indifferent* to pain and pleasure, and claims that nothing is wrong (like with *Arnica montana*). The patient is *dreamy*, sluggish, dull, and stuporous. He or she states the desire to go home even when at home.

INSOMNIA

The treatment of insomnia with homeopathy is very difficult, and reputedly has mixed results. However, acute episodes of insomnia that fit one of the two medicines that follow may gradually respond to one of the following medicines. The clinician should prescribe the medicine in the 30C potency: one dose in the morning for 3 days, then one dose a week for as long as it is needed.

Coffea cruda—This should be prescribed for sleeplessness after *good* news or fun when the thoughts are racing. The patient is awakened by every sound.

Nux vomica—*Nux vomica* is a medicine for hard-driving people who are sleepless from a rush of ideas about *work, business, or projects*. The patient awakens too early and cannot get back to sleep. He or she may weep and talk in his or her sleep, and be irritable and impatient during the day. (See Chapter 12, *Nux vomica*.)

INSULTS, WOUNDED HONOR, SHAME, AND EMBARRASSMENT

There are six main medicines prescribed for illnesses following wounded honor, or prolonged feelings of indignation and anger after being humiliated or shamed. These medicines are profiled elsewhere in this chapter. They are *Chamomilla, Colocynthis, Ignatia amara, Natrum muriaticum, Phosphoricum acid,* and *Staphysagria.*

AILMENTS FROM BAD NEWS

Gelsemium sempervirens—This medicine is indicated for the patient who falls into an apathetic, mentally dull, and *weak* state after receiving bad news (e.g., the diagnosis of an incurable illness) and cannot seem to rally. (See Chapter 8, *Gelsemium sempervirens.*)

DRUG AND ALCOHOL ADDICTION

Homeopathic medicine has been used as a support for drug and alcohol withdrawal and chemical dependency treatment. In 1987 the government of India established six drug detoxification clinics in New Delhi police stations that used homeopathic medicines coupled with yoga. These clinics conducted a clinical trial of homeopathic medicines on heroin withdrawal symptomatology. This was a double-blind placebo-controlled study on 60 patients, 30 of whom received placebo and 30 took individualized homeopathic medicines (Bakshi, 1990). Subjects were visited twice a day, and the determination was made at each visit to maintain the patient on the same medicine or change it. The number of days until the resolution of symptoms of withdrawal was reduced in the homeopathically treated group. Symptoms significantly shortened included lachrymation, body ache, pain in the legs, rhinorrhea, sneezing, yawning, vomiting, nausea, diarrhea, abdominal pain, loss of appetite, chill, piloerection, nocturnal emissions, daytime emissions, sleep restlessness, agitation, irritability, and lassitude. The most commonly used medicines were *Aconitum napellus, Arsenicum album, Belladonna, Bryonia alba, Camphora, Chamomilla, Coffea cruda, Impecacuanha, Mercurius solubilis, Nux vomica, Opium, Pulsatilla, Rhus toxicodendron,* and *Sulphur,* but the report did not discuss the specific withdrawal symptoms that these commonly used homeopathic medicines would be indicated for, or the potencies that were prescribed. The general indications for each of these medicines are discussed throughout this book.

The following information was shared with the author by Janet Zand, OMD, who has had extensive experience with the use of homeopathy with the chemically dependent people in her private practice in the United States.

For most patients who make a decision to, or are forced to discontinue their substance abuse, the initial reaction is anxiety and fear. This acute phase usually lasts between 24 hr and 1 week. The presenting problem is usually twofold: heightened *anxiety* and physiological *craving*. The primary medicines for this stage are summarized below. The medicine should be given in the 30C potency every 1–6 hr depending on the intensity of symptoms.

Phase 1: Acute Stage

Aconitum napellus—The patient experiences *fear* with awareness of heart palpitations. This is reportedly common among cocaine users.

Antimonium tartaricum—The patient is delirious, with stomach pain and vomiting accompanying the withdrawal pain. There is *much mucus*. This medicine is most commonly used among heroin addicts.

Arsenicum album—The patient is anxious, *restless,* and strongly agitated. *Arsenicum album* is most commonly used for people psychologically dependent on marijuana. (See Chapter 3, *Arsenicum album.*)

Belladonna—The patient demonstrates sudden and *violent* behavior with an inclination to bite. The patient is feverish and in a world of his or her own. He or she is disinclined to talk. Red face, dilated pupils, and thirstlessness may also accompany these symptoms. *Belladonna* is useful in withdrawal from heroin and hallucinogenic drugs. (See Chapter 4, *Belladonna.*)

Crocus sativa—The patient experiences sudden mood changes, especially anger leading to *violence,* which is followed quickly by *apologies.* These symptoms are common in alcohol withdrawal.

Hyoscyamus niger—This medicine is often very effective with alcohol withdrawal and *aggressive* behavior. The patient has toxic gastritis, combative mania, and intense insomnia. The patient picks at the bedcovers, and may be sly, dishonest, or manipulative about attempts to obtain alcohol. The patient may expose his or her genitalia or engage in inappropriate sexual talk.

Ipecacuanha—*Ipecacuanha* is used to treat persistent nausea, *vomiting*, and irritability due to withdrawal.

Moschus*—Moschus* is used for what was once termed "hysterical" behavior, with *fainting* fits and pseudoconvulsions from emotional causes. The patient has fits of anger with scolding and uncontrollable laughter. The patient is aggravated by cold and is greatly sensitive to open air. Other symptoms include flatulence, anxiety, abdominal distention, and muscular tension (even the skin feels tense). The patient desires black coffee, and is averse to food. The chest feels oppressed. There may be sudden, severe asthma, or *pseudoasthma* from emotions with difficult respiration.

Nux vomica*—The patient is irritable and *hypersensitive* to all stimulation, such as noise and light. The patient may suffer from occipital or ocular headaches and is easily chilled. This medicine is very effective for many types of addiction; it is most often used for alcohol, cocaine, and coffee withdrawal. (See Chapter 12, *Nux vomica*.)

Staphysagria*—The patient is *passively angry* that he or she has to stop using. He or she *suppresses* his or her anger and indignation, which can lead to tormenting headaches.

Stramonium*—The patient presents with delirium: visual *hallucinations* of animals, insects, and ghosts, and audio hallucinations of creatures, spirits, and voices. He or she may talk continuously. The patient is terrified, and may strike out at others. He or she must have company and the lights on. He or she is very thirsty. This medicine is most commonly used in alcohol and heroin withdrawal.

Valeriana officinalis*—The clinician should consider this medicine when the patient is withdrawing from sleeping medication, or had been using alcohol to help with sleep. The patient is experiencing an excited *sleeplessness* and irrational mood changes.

Veratrum album*—This medicine is indicated for *collapse,* extreme coldness, and weakness. There is a *cold perspiration* on the forehead, the face is pale, and the pulse is tachycardic. There may also be vomiting. The patient may show sullen indifference and notices nothing. He or she may wish to cut and tear things. He or she may describe the sensation as if there were ice on the vertex of the head. The tip of the nose and face are icy cold.

Sulphuricum acidum*—Sulphuricum acidum* is to be considered during withdrawal when *debility,* especially in the digestive tract, is the most obvious presenting symptom. The patient is fretful, weak, debilitated, and easily bruised. He or she has indigestion and heartburn. The patient is averse to the smell of coffee.

Phase 2: Detoxification

The following medicines are used to bring increased comfort, and to help the organ systems that are most affected during the detoxification stage after the initial shock and stress has subsided. The clinician should give the 30C potency of the indicated medicine three times a day for 3 days, then p.r.n. when symptomatic. For relapse prevention in the later stages of recovery, treatment by a homeopathic specialist is recommended. The medicine can be changed if noted to be ineffective after the third dose.

Arnica montana—The patient suffers body aches as if he or she had been *beaten*. The patient fears the touch or approach of anyone. He or she is agoraphobic. (See Chapter 2, *Arnica montana*.)

Arsenicum album—Nausea and vomiting after eating, sometimes accompanied with diarrhea are best treated with *Arsenicum album*. The patient cannot bear the sight or smell of food. He or she is very thirsty, but drinks only a little at a time. The patient craves acidic foods and coffee. Other symptoms include diarrhea, dyspepsia, chills, restlessness, and *anxiety* that is alleviated by company. (See Chapter 3, *Arsenicum album*.)

Asclepias tuberosa—This medicine is used to treat bronchitis, pleurisy, and irritation of the larynx with huskiness of voice during detoxification.

Baptisia tinctoria—*Baptisia tinctoria* is indicated for *sepsis* resulting in great myalgia as well as fetid stools, breath, urine, and perspiration. The patient demonstrates mental confusion, wandering, muttering, and a sense of suffocation.

Berberis vulgaris—This medicine is especially effective in older alcoholics and excessive coffee drinkers with *kidney inflammation* and frequent urination. They may be nauseous before breakfast.

Bryonia alba—The clinician should treat older alcoholics with *arthritis-like* pains with this medicine. The patient is irritable and constipated, and has dry mucous membranes. The symptoms are aggravated by motion. The patient is thirsty for large quantities of water at long intervals. (See Chapter 5, *Bryonia alba*.)

Butyricum acidum—A constant state of fear and nervousness with insomnia and *impulsive thoughts of suicide* should be treated with

Butyricum acidum. The patient has a poor appetite and low back pain. Symptoms are aggravated in general by rapid motion.

Cantharis—*Cantharis* is good for treating intolerable urinary symptoms, especially *raw burning* pain and painful urge to urinate. The patient is anxious and restless.

Carbo vegetabilis—The patient has had difficulty regaining digestive function and has many *eructations* during eating. He or she has pain in the center of the abdomen from *flatulent* distension. Other symptoms include sudden memory loss as well as fear of the dark and ghosts.

Carduus marianus—Pain is in the *liver* region in alcoholics. Constipation and chest pain may also be present. The patient presents as despondent, forgetful, and apathetic.

Chelidonium majus—This medicine is indicated for jaundice from hepatic gallbladder obstruction. The pain is under the *right scapula*.

Chimaphila umbellata—Alcohol detoxification leads to depressed *urinary output* and mucus in the urine. There may be prostate enlargement.

Chionanthus virginica—*Chionanthus virginica* is used to treat headaches associated with liver problems. The patient is *jaundiced* and has yellow conjunctiva, and an enlarged spleen. The patient may have *diabetes* mellitus.

Colocynthis—Intense abdominal cramping and pain is best treated with *Colocynthis*. The patient *doubles up*. The pain is aggravated by anger and indignation.

Gambogia—The patient has dyspepsia with abdominal rumbling and diarrhea. The ileocecal region is very tender to pressure. The patient has a sensation of feeling coldness in the teeth. The tongue and throat are dry. The patient is averse to food.

Gelsemium sempervirens—This medicine is used to treat *listlessness* following drug withdrawal, particularly from cocaine and amphetamines. Other symptoms include reduced thirst, dizziness, drowsiness, trembling, and ptosis of the eyelids. (See Chapter 8, *Gelsemium sempervirens*.)

Gentiana lutea—The patient has lost his or her *appetite* and has acid reflux. There may be aching in the eyes.

Hydrastis canadensis—The patient has sinus congestion and blows his or her nose frequently, and has poor digestion with constipation during detoxification. The tongue shows imprints of teeth. The patient believes he or she will die soon, and, because of depression, wants to.

Iris versicolor—*Iris versicolor* is prescribed for the patient with frontal *headache*, nausea, ringing in the ears, and burning throat. There may be constipation especially when the stool is green. The patient may have herpes zoster or pancreatitis concurrent with dyspepsia.

Kali arsenicosum—Anxious and anemic patients with severe pruritis from eczema and dry skin benefit from *Kali arsenicosum*. The patient fears heart disease.

Lobelia inflata—*Lobelia inflata* is indicated for alcohol detoxification with *nausea*, vomiting, and dyspepsia. The patient is short of breath after eating, has vertigo, and gastric headaches related to digestive problems. Symptoms are is generally alleviated by walking rapidly.

Mercurius dulcis—Drug withdrawal associated *with ear infections*, eustachian tube dysfunction, and *diarrhea* are best treated with *Mercurius dulcis*. There may be prostatitis, nausea, and vomiting as well.

Natrum phosphoricum—Alcoholics with sour regurgitation, and thick *yellow-coated* tongue respond well to this medicine. They may be mentally dull in the morning. The clinician should look for dilation of one pupil and one hot and itchy ear. There is itching, especially of the ankles. The patient is fearful and may have the illusion that he or she hears footsteps in the next room.

Quercus glandium spiritus—This medicine is reputed to reduce alcohol craving. No research has been done to verify this. The clinician should prescribe it for 3 consecutive months in the 6X potency four times a day.

CHAPTER 23

Gastrointestinal System

ESOPHAGEAL DISORDERS

Dysphagia

Dysphagia has many etiologies, and, therefore, the homeopathic treatment is complex as well, not lending itself to summary in this introductory book. That being said, *Ignatia amara* is reputed to be a medicine *par excellence* for dysphagia resulting from acute grief.

Esophageal Reflux, Esophagitis, and Pyrosis

The following are the medicines most often mentioned in the homeopathic literature for esophageal symptoms. No clinical research has been conducted on esophageal conditions and homeopathy. A 30C potency should be prescribed every 4 hr for three doses, then as needed if found to be effective.

Arsenicum album—Burning is felt in the esophagus and sternum with a feeling of *suffocation*. There is dysphagia, spasmodic constriction, and acidic eructations aggravated by alcohol, coffee, and high-fat foods. The patient may present with anxiety that is alleviated when other people are present, irritability, restlessness, and frequent sipping of liquids. Refer to Chapter 3 for the general symptomatology of *Arsenicum album*.

Asafoetida—This is a rarely used remedy that is, however, indispensable when the clearly defined symptomatology of the gastrointestinal tract is present. The clinician will always suspect a *psychosomatic* complaint when this medicine is called for. The patient complains and seems to *exaggerate* his or her symptoms, very much wanting sympathy. The patient may have globus hystericus, and clutch at the throat. There is easy syncope of emotional origin from the slightest cause. The moods are changeable and may include bursts of laughter.

The esophageal complaints are commonly described by the patient as a sensation of a *bubble* or lump in the stomach rising up to the throat. Burning may be felt in the stomach, but more commonly it is a sensation of pulsation in the stomach that is palpable, or even visible externally. The abdomen is filled and greatly *distended* with gas, but no flatus is passed, only eructations. The gas is aggravated by high-fat foods. The patient is repulsed by food. There are explosive eructations smelling like garlic and tasting rancid, or empty eructations. Liquids may be regurgitated. Symptoms are aggravated at night; indoors; while sitting, resting, and eating; and from noise or being wrapped up warmly. The discomfort may be relieved by motion in open air, pressure, or touch.

Carbo vegetabilis—Burning felt under *sternum* is aggravated by alcohol, coffee, and high-fat foods. The patient has acrid eructations or eructations of ingesta. Since eructations give the patient relief, he or she may try to stimulate them with soda. He or she feels *weak* and very *bloated*. There is much flatulence as well. The patient is chilly, but feels better sitting in front of a fan or air conditioner.

Conium maculatum—Burning felt in *esophagus and stomach* is aggravated by drinking alcohol. Acrid eructations are aggravated on *going to bed*. The pain felt in the stomach is alleviated by eating, but then worse again a few hours later; the pain is alleviated in the knee-chest position. *Conium maculatum* is useful for pregnant women experiencing heartburn. The patient craves coffee, salt, and sour things. He or she is averse to bread. Depression, weakness, and vertigo may accompany the esophageal symptoms.

Hepar sulphuris calcareum—The patient has a constant sensation of acid rising into the esophagus and burning in the stomach. He or she desires *acidic* foods (especially vinegar), condiments, and stimulants, and is averse to fatty foods. The patient is extremely chilly and sensitive to the slightest draft of cool air. (See Chapter 9, *Hepar sulphuris calcareum*.)

Lycopodium clavatum—Incomplete burning eructations rise to the pharynx and then *burn for hours*. The patient is sated from a small intake of food and experiences much *bloating* from cereals and flatulent food such as cabbage, beans, and onions. He or she noisily passes flatus. Symptoms are alleviated in general by hot drinks and worsen 4:00–8:00 p.m. The patient desires sweets, and does not want to wear belts.

Mercurius vivus or Mercurius solubilis—The burning felt in the *stomach* is aggravated by alcohol, coffee, and high-fat foods. The patient experiences acrid eructations tasting of ingesta. Pregnant patients have heartburn, especially when symptoms come on at *night.* The general symptoms of *Mercurius* may be present, such as offensive perspiration, halitosis, swelling of the lymphatic glands, thirst, and a metallic taste in mouth. (See Chapter 11, *Mercurius vivus or Mercurius solubilis.*)

Nux vomica—Pyrosis is seen in pregnant patients, alcoholics, "partiers," and people under high stress. There are sour and bitter eructations, flatulence, and dyspepsia from drinking strong coffee. These symptoms are aggravated by high-fat foods, and worsen before breakfast. The person is irritable and *impatient.* (See Chapter 12, *Nux vomica.*)

Phosphorus—The patient presents with burning in the *esophagus* that is aggravated by high-fat foods and beer. He or she desires ice-cold drinks, salty foods, and chocolate ice cream. The patient is anxious, but easily reassured by the clinician. He or she desires company. (See Chapter 13, *Phosphorus.*)

Pulsatilla—The patient presents with heartburn of pregnancy. She desires *creamy* foods, refreshing things, pungent foods, peanut butter, and/or cheese. She has aversions to water, meat fat, pork, bread, milk, smoking, warm food, and drink. There are eructations that leave a taste of the food in the mouth. There are visible pulsations of the epigastrium. The patient is thirstless, weepy, and desirous of sympathy. These symptoms are generally alleviated in the open air. (See Chapter 14, *Pulsatilla.*)

Robinia pseudoacacia—Severe hyperacidity with pyrosis that is worse at *night in bed* is commonly treated with *Robinia pseudoacacia*. It may also be used for pyrosis of pregnancy. In addition to burning felt in the stomach, there is also burning between the scapulae. The patient may also have a dull headache.

Sepia—There is burning felt in the *stomach* that is aggravated by drinking alcohol, especially beer, and coffee. The patient complains of eructations tasting of ingesta. *Sepia* is one of the main medicines for heartburn in pregnancy. The patient presents as *apathetic*, depressed, and irritable, but improves with vigorous exercise, such as dancing. He or she wants to be alone. The libido may have dropped to nil during this illness. There is a desire for sour foods, including vinegar, as well as sweets. This esophagitis may occur in women at times of hormonal change, such as during pregnancy or menopause.

Sulphur—The patient presents with eructations tasting like *spoiled eggs* that are aggravated by eating, at night, or from pressing on the stomach. There is pyrosis that is aggravated in the morning and while standing up. There is a complete loss of appetite or a ravenous appetite and great thirst. Milk causes sour taste and sour eructations. The patient is suddenly hungry and weak at 11:00 a.m., and has an empty, weak feeling at the epigastrium. The patient becomes easily over-heated and sticks feet out of the covers at night. (See Chapter 16, *Sulphur*.)

Sulphuricum acidum—*Sulphuricum acidum* is used to treat the esophagitis of *alcoholics* who crave brandy and may have hiccups. The patient experiences pyrosis with sour eructations that set the teeth on edge. He or she perspires after eating food, especially warm food. The patient is averse to the odor of coffee. The patient is hurried and talks to him- or herself.

Esophagitis from Trauma

For contusions of the esophagus, *Arnica montana* is prescribed. For burns from hot food or liquids, *Cantharis* is prescribed.

GASTRIC DISORDERS

Peptic Ulcers

In the days before the relationship between *Helicobacter pylori* and peptic ulcer was known, patient self-referral to a homeopathic specialist was not uncommon among clients dissatisfied with the noncurative results of conventional medical treatment. There are many anecdotal reports of cures with homeopathy. Whether cures were more likely with homeopathic medicines when the etiology was *Helicobacter pylori* is unknown. Now, few patients refuse antibiotic treatment when the bacteria are present. Homeopathic treatment appeals to natural medi-cine-oriented patients who have had poor symptomatic relief from conventional therapy, or test negative for *Helicobacter pylori*.

There is not a meaningful distinction between gastric and duodenal ulcers made in homeopathic medicine. Any of the following medi-cines, when indicated, are reputed to alleviate either. If the patient presents in a crisis, because of pain, vomiting, or hematemesis, the clinician may consider a quick prescription of one of the three following medicines in addition to or preceding any emergency interventions that may be called for. These are palliative medicines, and are unlikely to treat the underlying pathology. *Atropinum* is prescribed for *pain* when the region of the stomach is very sensitive, with swelling in the pyloric region. Sleep is disturbed by gastric pains. The quality of the pain is usually griping or cramping. The clinician may give the 6C potency hourly for five doses and if it alleviates, decrease the frequency to the minimum level that controls the symptoms. *Geranium maculatum* is prescribed for *hematemesis* of large quantities of blood. The clinician may start with a 30C potency every 10 min for an hour when not vomiting. If improvement is noted, the frequency can be decreased to the minimum level needed to control the symptom. *Ipecacuanha* is indicated when *nausea and vomiting* are the predominant symptoms. Vomiting does not relieve the nausea. The tongue is clean, despite vomiting. The clinician may start with the 30C potency every 20 min for an hour when not vomiting, and then decrease to the minimum level that controls the vomiting.

Since the predominant view in the homeopathic profession is that antibiotics can interfere with homeopathic treatment, homeopathic treatment concurrently with conventional treatment of *H. pylori* may be pointless. Homeopathic treatment concurrent with antacids, H2 blockers, cytoprotectants, and anticholinergics is not specifically dis-couraged in the homeopathic literature. None of these drugs is universally believed to interfere with the healing effect of homeo-pathic medicines, yet polypharmacy itself is decried by homeopaths.

The next level of treatment involves a medicine that has the ability to heal the ulcer itself. If one observes definite symptomatic improve-ment from one of the medicines in the differential below, it is likely the ulcer is truly healing. One note of caution: homeopathic medi-cines have been reported to palliate the pain of cancer. The clinician cannot assume that a diagnostic workup for gastric cancer is unneces-sary when the symptoms are alleviated by a homeopathic medicine. There are a multitude of potential medicines for chronic or recurring ulcers; referral is recommended to a homeopathic specialist for unresponsive cases if both conventional treatment and homeopathic treatment with one of the following medicines fail.

If one of the following medicines fits the specific symptoms of the person, the clinician should discontinue the palliative medicine above, and prescribe a 30C potency of the indicated medicine. This medicine can be prescribed three times a day for 5 days, then once a day for a week, and then as needed for pain. The direction of radiating pains is very useful in deciding between medicines (see Table 23–1) (van Zandvoort, 1997).

Most Commonly Indicated Medicines

Argentum nitricum—The patient presents with gastric pain aggravated by touch, pressure, eating, drinking, and deep inspiration; the pain may radiate to the back, chest, shoulders, and abdomen. The pain is alleviated by *vomiting and eructations*. The stomach swells or is distended with gas. There may be nausea with retching and vomiting. *Argentum nitricum* is a very common medicine for peptic ulcer.

Hydrastis canadensis—*Ropy yellow* is the description most commonly used for the mucus that is expectorated; it covers the stools and drips from the sinuses. The patient describes a "sinking" sensation in the epigastrium. There is vomiting, loss of appetite, and burning and soreness over the epigastrium. The patient is weak and fatigued.

Kali bichromicum—Vomiting of *stringy* white or pinkish mucus is the key symptom to guide the clinician to prescribe this medicine for ulcer. The stomach and abdomen are very tender, and there may be gastric hemorrhage. The pains are felt in a small spot in the stomach and may be burning. The patient desires sweets and beer, and dislikes meat. *Kali bichromicum* is indicated for ulcers of burn patients.

Lachesis mutus—The patient is intolerant of *tight clothing* around the waist (compare with *Lycopodium clavatum* and *Crotalus horridus*). He or she describe sticking and gnawing pains, and vomits *black* blood. The distended abdomen is aggravated by pressure. Frank blood is found in the offensive liquid stools. *Lachesis mutus* is used to treat the ulcers of *alcoholics*. Symptoms are aggravated by sleep and external pressure. The patient is generally intolerant of heat.

Lycopodium clavatum—The ulcer symptoms requiring this medicine are accompanied by much *flatulence and distention* that are aggravated in the late afternoon through the early evening. The patient is hungry, but quickly sated because of a sense of fullness. There is a churning or gnawing sensation in the stomach. This discomfort is

Table 23–1 Homeopathic Medicine Indicated for Pain Location and/or Direction It Radiates in Gastric or Duodenal Ulcers

	Alumina	Argentum nitricum	Arsenicum album	Belladonna	Kali bichromicum	Kali carbonicum	Lachesis	Lycopodium clavatum	Nitricum acidium	Nux vomica	Ornithogalum umbellatum	Phosphorus	Sepia	Ipecacuanha
Abdomen		✓								✓		✓		
Back				✓		✓						✓		✓
Backward	✓		✓	✓				✓		✓		✓	✓	
Between shoulders				✓										
Cardiac end of stomach												✓		
Into chest		✓			✓	✓				✓		✓	✓	
Heart		✓					✓				✓			
Hypochondria												✓		
Mammae							✓							
Pyloric end of stomach			✓										✓	
Rectum			✓											
Left scapula		✓												
Shoulders					✓	✓						✓	✓	
Left side		✓												
Around sides		✓												
Throat	✓													
Umbilicus							✓		✓					
Below umbilicus								✓						

aggravated by cereals and flatulent foods, such as *onions, cabbage,* and *beans.* The patient desires sweets, pastries, hot food, and drinks, and wakes at night with hunger. He or she may vomit food, bile, coagulated blood, and/or dark greenish masses after eating and drinking. He or she may describe coldness in the stomach. The patient may become domineering towards his or her family and irritable in the morning.

Phosphorus—The patient lacks concentration, is anxious, and prefers to be around people. He or she may exhibit a strong desire for ice-cold drinks, chocolate ice cream, dark chocolate candy, salty foods, and spicy foods. Gastralgia is alleviated by *cold drinks,* but if vomiting is part of the symptomatology, it will be stimulated soon after drinking. There are spasms of the esophagus at the cardiac end. There is vomiting of bile, blood, and coffee ground-like fluid. The burning in the stomach is aggravated by eating. The patient may describe the sensation of tremors, fluttering, or something rolling over in the stomach. The stomach feels cold as though it were frozen. (See Chapter 13, *Phosphorus*.)

Psorinum—*Psorinum* is for the patient who is generally *chilly*. Whether he or she has no appetite or a ravenous one, the patient grows thin. He or she experiences tremendous *hunger* in the middle of the night and needle-like pains in the stomach from that hunger. These kinds of ulcers may arise after illness. The patient may live in poverty. Skin disorders often accompany the ulcer. The patient is very thirsty and desires beer and sour things. His or her eructations smell like bad eggs, and body odor and discharges are offensive. That patient has sour vomiting, and expresses hopelessness about the illness.

Secale cornutum—*Secale cornutum* is one of the most common medicines for ulcer after *Argentum nitricum* (Royal, 1923). The patient presents with an *unquenchable thirst* with a dry mouth. He or she has a ravenous appetite and craves *sour* things and lemonade. There is nausea with debility and easy vomiting. There may be empty retching or violent vomiting of all food, drink, and medicine; the vomitus is dark brown, coffee ground-like, and/or bloody. There may be burning pain and tenderness of the epigastrium. Other symptoms include possible gangrene and sloughing of the stomach and subjective sensation of heat, while the patient's skin is objectively cool to the touch.

Sepia—A lowered or nonexistent *libido* is a key symptom indicating *Sepia*. There may be an aversion to sex concurrent with the ulcer symptoms, or even nausea at the thought of intercourse. The patient desires vinegar, sour foods, and pickles, as well as sweets and dark chocolate. In contrast, all appetite may be lost. The patient describes a *faint* or sinking feeling coming from the epigastrium. There may be a paresthesia of a twisting sensation in the stomach that seems to rise into the throat, or simply a lump in the epigastrium. There are eructations. The patient also complains of burning inside the stomach and nausea from the smell, or even the *thought* of food. These discomforts are not alleviated by eating or vomiting.

The patient is irritable and miserable, and wants to be alone. He or she seems indifferent to his or her own family, but weeps when telling the clinician about the illness. Lumbar pain, hormonal imbalances, or menstrual difficulties may accompany the ulcer symptoms. If the patient is able, vigorous exercise, such as running, aerobics, or dancing, makes him or her feel much better. This medicine is famous for its uses for women's health issues, and, therefore, is sometimes over-looked for the treatment of gastric disorders and male patients.

Less Commonly Indicated Medicines

Alumina—Gastric pain is aggravated by *potatoes*, milk, and the feeling of clothing touching the skin over the stomach. The patient can swallow only small amounts of food at a time. These symptoms may be accompanied by serious *constipation* with no urge to pass stool.

Arsenicum album—The patient presents with *violent* symptoms. He or she describes terrible gastric burning and cramping with vomit-ing that are aggravated by cold drinks and foods and worsen at 2:00 a.m. The pain and vomiting is alleviated by warm drinks and milk. The patient rapidly *emaciates*. The stools are liquidy, dark, and often bloody. The patient is fearful of the outcome of the illness. (See Chapter 3, *Arsenicum album*.)

Belladonna—*Belladonna* is used to treat pain in the stomach that extends to the back between the scapulae. A cutting pain in the epigastrium is alleviated by bending backwards. The pain is aggra-vated by the *jiggling* of walking or any other jarring motion. The pain can be violent and paroxysmal. Stomach pain may be elicited by pressing on the spine. Pallor and weakness accompany the nausea and vomiting. The abdomen may be distended and hot and aggravated by the touch of bedclothes. The patient desires *lemons* and lemonade, which may make him or her feel better in general. He or she is averse to meat, acids, coffee, milk, and beer. In general, the patient avoids drinking. (See Chapter 4, *Belladonna*.)

Crotalus horridus—The patient vomits bilious, grass-green, bloody, or *black* material. He or she cannot keep anything down, and desires pork, stimulants, and sugar. The patient is averse to clothes around the stomach (compare with *Lycopodium clavatum, Alumina,* and *Lachesis mutus*). There is vomiting from lying on the right side. Stomach pain may be of any description.

Kali carbonicum—One important characteristic of this medicine is a general aggravation from *fasting* (when hungry the patient feels anxious, nauseated, and nervous, and has tingling and palpitations), thus, the patient wants to eat frequently. Then, upon eating a small amount of food or drink, he or she feels full, sleepy, or weak, and may not be able to finish the meal. The stomach subjectively feels as if it is distended and full of water. There is a sensation of a lump deep in the epigastrium, which is sensitive to touch. The stomach itself is *sensitive*, and there is throbbing that seems to the patient to come from the posterior part of the stomach. There is *anxiety* that is felt in the stomach. Gastric pains radiate to the back, chest, and shoulders. Nausea is alleviated by lying down and worsens at night. The patient desires sweet and sour foods. Symptoms are aggravated by milk and warm food. Generally, symptoms are worse 2:00–3:00 a.m. Low back pain may accompany the gastric symptoms.

Kreosotum—The patient presents with icy coldness in the stomach and hematemesis. There is painful hard spot that is palpable over the stomach. There are eructations of hot, frothy material. The patient is nauseous and vomits food several hours after eating. The vomitus is sweet-tasting and watery in the morning, or consists of undigested food. The patient desires *smoked meat*. Symptoms are aggravated by cold food and fasting.

Mezereum—The patient has an anxious, anguished, empty feeling in the stomach as if he or she were *dying* (compare with *Arsenicum album*). Gastralgia is burning, "corroding," and alleviated by *drinking milk*, and eating. The stomach is indurated. There is a bitter taste in the mouth; beer tastes bitter and is vomited. The patient vomits a chocolate-colored substance and blood. The patient constantly desires food, especially ham, fat, coffee, and wine.

Nitricum acidum—Ulcer pains may radiate to the umbilicus. The patient feels a hopeless *despair*, has a negative attitude, and is irritable and anxious. In general, the patient is sensitive to noise, pain, touch, and jarring. There may be a striking desire for *fat and salt*. The patient is prone to fissures of the mucous membranes.

Nux vomica—The typical emotional state of irritability with *impatience* discussed in Chapter 12, *Nux vomica*, is the guide to the use of this medicine in treating ulcers. The patient desires spicy food, beer, high-fat food, coffee, and cigarettes. He or she may be hungry, but averse to food. Nausea and gastralgia are alleviated by vomiting. There is violent sour or bilious vomiting, or the patient wants to vomit, but cannot. Food lies like a heavy knot in the stomach. Eructations are difficult to get up and have a sour or bitter taste.

Ornithogalum umbellatum—Flatulence with a swollen feeling across the lower chest accompanies the ulcer. Whenever the patient turns in bed, it feels as if *a bag of water* turned also. The patient may experience sadness or even suicidal thoughts.

Uranium nitricum—*Uranium nitricum* is used to treat ulcers with burning pains in *diabetics* who are greatly emaciated. The patient may be debilitated, and have a tendency to ascites and hypertension. The symptoms are aggravated at night and alleviated by deep breathing. The patient is angry, sad, and possibly grieving from a recent loss. Insulin-dependent patients should closely monitor glucose levels during treatment with *Uranium nitricum*, because it is one of the homeopathic medicines that was historically used to lower blood sugar levels.

Gastritis/Vomiting

There are three main medicines for simple vomiting, not related to food poisoning, pregnancy, migraine, or motion sickness, or accompanied with diarrhea. They are *Ipecacuanha, Phosphorus*, and *Pulsatilla*. The clinician should prescribe the indicated medicine in the 30C potency every half hour for up to three doses. Sometimes, the patient will vomit one more time before symptoms abate. After that, there should be no more vomiting for hours if the medicine is correct. If the vomiting returns, give another dose.

Cadmium sulphuratum—The medicine most often mentioned in the homeopathic literature for palliating the nausea and vomiting from chemotherapy or stomach cancer is *Cadmium sulphuratum*. The specific symptoms are weakness, nausea from even touching the lips, vomiting on the *least motion*, hematemesis (black), extreme weakness, and epigastric tenderness.

Ipecacuanha—The patient vomits, but does not feel better, and may even feel worse. The tongue is *clean* despite the nausea and vomiting. Rarely, a patient may have generalized itching with the nausea. He or she may vomit mucus-like jelly after stooping. *Ipecacuanha* can sometimes palliate vomiting during chemotherapy (like *Cadmium sulphuratum* can). The patient may be irritable.

Phosphorus—Although persons requiring any of these medicines might vomit each time they drink liquids, the most likely medicine for this condition is *Phosphorus*. They crave ice-cold drinks, which alleviates the nausea, but then is followed by vomiting after the liquid becomes warmed in the stomach. Vomiting can be stimulated by putting the hands in warm water. *Phosphorus* is also used to treat postsurgical vomiting and postanesthesia vomiting. Emesis may have any appearance, but is especially characteristic of *Phosphorus* when it has *filaments* in it. There may be burning pains in the stomach. The patient wants company and consolation, seems anxious, and lacks concentration.

Gastritis indicative of *Phosphorus* is often indistinguishable from one that requires *Bismuthum metallicum*, a less common medicine. An illness requiring the latter is characterized by violent abdominal pain, thirst for cold drinks, great fear, and desire for company. Also like with *Phosphorus*, patients vomit after drinking. The pains may be in the stomach or abdomen, and are cramping or burning in character. Thus, if *Phosphorus* does not alleviate the symptoms even though it seems indicated, the clinician should try *Bismuthum metallicum*. (See Chapter 13, *Phosphorus*.)

Pulsatilla—The patient vomits from eating high-fat foods, wants *consolation* and company, and is thirstless. Children want to be held and weep sweetly. They feel genuinely better with the window open or outside. In women, there is sour vomiting before the menses. (See Chapter 14, *Pulsatilla*.)

Indigestion and Dyspepsia

A dose or two of a homeopathic medicine has been noted by homeopathic clinicians to rapidly relieve acute dyspepsia. It should be noted, however, that a common etiology for epigastric discomfort after meals in middle-aged adults may be that pants are too tight. Homeopathy will not cure this.

Abies nigra—There is a subjective sensation as though a *hard-boiled egg* is lodged in the cardiac end of the stomach, especially after eating. Or the sensation is that of a hard lump in the lung, which the patient wants to cough up. This dyspepsia is most common in elderly people who have functional heart symptoms, smokers, users of chewing tobacco, and people who drink black tea to excess. The mood is depressed, and there is difficulty concentrating. The appetite is lost in the morning, but strong at noon and at night.

Anacardium orientale—The patient describes the sensation of a *blunt plug* in the stomach. Gastric pain is alleviated by eating, but is worse again after 2–3 hr. The patient hastily drinks and swallows food.

There is loss of appetite, alternating with violent hunger. Dyspepsia of this sort often occurs then the patient feels pulled in two directions at once emotionally, such as between two lovers, or between good or bad conduct. The patient appears to be a calm, nice person, but in the history, there may be swearing, brawling, or simply a big choice to be made.

Ignatia amara—Dyspepsia from *grief*, with difficulty crying and much sighing is best treated with *Ignatia amara*. The patient is sensitive to cigarette smoke. (See Chapter 10, *Ignatia amara*.)

Lycopodium clavatum—The patient demonstrates a big appetite with easy *satiety*. Eating a little creates uncomfortable fullness. The patient desires sweets and warm drinks, and wakes at night feeling hungry. Onions, cabbage, beans, and oysters disagree with him or her. There may be a churning sensation in the stomach, with bloating. Gnawing in stomach is alleviated from drinking hot water.

Nux vomica—Food lies like a *heavy knot* in the stomach. Gastralgia with pains that radiate to the back and chest is alleviated by hot drinks and aggravated by food. The patient may hiccup from overeating or from cold or hot drinks. The patient is irritable, impatient, and critical. (See Chapter 12, *Nux vomica*.)

Pulsatilla—The patient complains of heaviness in the stomach from eating a *high-fat* meal or onions. He or she is weepy, desires consolation, and is thirstless. The symptoms are generally alleviated in the open air. (See Chapter 14, *Pulsatilla*.)

INTESTINAL DISORDERS

Constipation

The medicines for constipation are the same for patients from infancy to old age. No high-quality studies have been conducted on the homeopathic treatment of constipation. The clinician should prescribe the 30C potency every 4 hr while the patient is awake. If there are no results within 24 hours, another medicine can be given a trial. There is no generally agreed upon incompatibility between homeopathy and conventional medical treatments for constipation, and obviously, the patient should increase the fluids and fiber in his or her diet.

Alumina—The patient is *dry* in general. There is tremendous dryness of the intestinal tract. The mouth is dry; the tongue is irritated; and the rectum is dry, irritated, and sometimes bleeding around the orifice. The rectum's inactivity distinguishes the need to prescribe *Alumina* from the need to prescribe *Bryonia alba*. When the former is indicated, even a soft stool is passed with difficulty. Stools are small balls or hard knots, filled with bright clots of blood. Hard stools cause severe cutting. Evacuation is preceded by painful urging, long before stool, and followed by straining at stool.

Bryonia alba—The mouth, tongue, and lips are dry. Stools are large, dry, and very hard as if burnt. The patient is *irritable,* wants to be alone, and generally aggravated by moving. He or she is thirsty for large quantities of water at long intervals.

Graphites—The patient can go days without evacuating stool, then pass a stool composed of little round *balls knotted together with shreds of mucus.* There may be an anal fissure, which causes great pain on passage; burning; smarting; and itching. The anus is sore when wiped. More commonly indicated in mentally dull, depressed, and obese patients.

Lycopodium clavatum—Hard, difficult-to-pass, small stools are seen in patients with easy satiety and much *flatulence.* Discomfort worsens at 4:00–8:00 p.m. The patient fears being alone and desires sweets.

Nux vomica—The patient feels urging to *strain* hard at the stool, yet no stool emerges, or part remains unexpelled. The patient is irritable; impatient; and sensitive to noise, odors, and light. The symptoms are worse in the morning. (See Chapter 12, *Nux vomica*.)

Opium—There is a complete *absence of urge* to stool even for many days. Stools are composed of little hard balls. The patient is drowsy in the daytime and sleepless at night with acute sensitivity to noise.

Plumbum metallicum—There is urging to pass stool with colic and *retraction* of the abdomen. The stool is passed with great difficulty and consists of little round balls that are dry, hard, and black. Spasms of the anus make it feel as though the anus is drawn upwards.

Sepia—The patient has obstinate constipation with *no urging* for days. The patient describes large, hard stools with a feeling of a ball in the rectum. There is a bearing-down feeling in the pelvis. This medicine is usually indicated in adult women, especially at times of hormonal transition. Symptoms are often accompanied by an *apathetic*, irritable state in the patient. The patient desires sour foods.

Silicea—The distinctive characteristic of constipation indicative of *Silicea* is the stool starts to come out of the anus, then *retracts* back inside. There is straining with soft stools, like when *Alumina* is indicated. Stool may be retained from fear of pain. The patient is chilly. *Silicea* is commonly indicated for constipation in obstinate children and mild-mannered adults.

Sulphur—The stools are hard, dry, black, and only expelled with great effort with pain and *burning*. There is a sensation as if part of the stool had remained behind. There is an ineffectual urging to pass stool with a sensation of heat and discomfort in the rectum. The patient describes twitching, itching, and burning of the anus, which is *reddened*. The patient has a tendency to hemorrhoids. Refer to Chapter 16, *Sulphur*, for the general symptoms.

Gastroenteritis

The first homeopathic research to be published in a major American medical journal was a study done in Nicaragua on the treatment of childhood diarrhea with homeopathic medicine (Jacobs, Jiminez, Gloyd, Gale, & Crothers, 1994). This randomized, placebo-controlled, double-blind study of 81 children from 6 months to 5 years of age showed a statistically significant decrease in duration of diarrhea in the treatment group. The medicine was individualized to the child's complete symptomatology in the classical homeopathic manner. An individualized homeopathic medicine was prescribed for each child and daily follow-up was performed for 5 days. Standard treatment with oral rehydration treatment was also given. The treatment group had a statistically significant ($P < .05$) decrease in duration of diarrhea, defined as the number of days until there were less than three unformed stools daily for 2 consecutive days. There was also a significant difference ($P < .05$) in the number of stools per day between the two groups after 72 hr of treatment. The statistically significant decrease in the duration of diarrhea in the treatment group suggests that homeopathic treatment might be useful in acute childhood diarrhea. Further research of this treatment for diarrhea both by Jacobs et al. and by independent researchers have been undertaken, but not yet published.

The medicines most often called for in the Jacobs study are prioritized below as the most commonly indicated medicines. Eighty-six percent of the cases in that study received these eight most common medicines. Interestingly, study results for diarrheas where no pathologic agent was present on stool analysis was equivocal, while effectiveness was high where an agent (*Escherichia coli*, rotavirus, *Entamoeba histolytica*, *Giardia lamblia*, and other parasites) was present.

Bacterial, Viral, or Parasitic Gastroenteritis

Parents in the Jacobs study were instructed to give the child one pellet of a 30C potency medication orally after each unformed stool.

Most Commonly Indicated Medicines

Arsenicum album—This medicine is reputed to be the most common medicine for traveler's diarrhea. Stools are burning and acrid. The diarrhea worsens *after midnight,* and may occur simultaneously with vomiting. The patient is anxious, restless, exacting, and chilly. The patient feels better when not alone. The patient is weak from the diarrhea. Although the patient is generally chilly, he or she may have burning pains, and is thirsty for sips, usually of warm drinks (e.g., tea). There may be vomiting, which occurs immediately after eating and drinking. The etiology may be from ingesting game, rancid or putrid food (especially meat), or impure water.

Calcarea carbonica—This medicine is indicated for children, especially infants, with cold and clammy hands and feet, and *perspiration on the head* that wets the pillow during sleep. This is a medicine for children with functional diarrhea at the time of emerging dentition or viral gastroenteritis. They may crave eggs.

Chamomilla—The distinctive emotional state associated with *Chamomilla* is often what guides the clinician to prescribe this medicine. It is more commonly prescribed for children when the child is whining, angry, and discontented, and is comforted by being *carried.* The child asks for things that are later rejected. The stools are distinctive: green and slimy, like chopped grass. The odor of the stool resembles that of diarrhea treated with *Sulphur*—like rotten eggs. Colic may accompany the diarrhea. The child is hypersensitive to pain. (See Chapter 6, *Chamomilla.*)

Mercurius vivus or Mercurius solubilis—The stools are slimy, acrid, undigested, and perhaps bloody in a patient who is sensitive to both heat and cold. The patient cannot get comfortable from *chills alternating with heat*. He or she produces a profuse, foul-smelling perspiration. There is a metallic taste in the mouth and halitosis. The patient is thirsty for cold drinks and drools at night in bed. (See Chapter 11, *Mercurius vivus or Mercurius solubilis*.)

Phosphorus—The patient is anxious, "spacy," and wants company. Increased thirst for cold drinks is a strong feature of this medicine. *Vomiting* is usually a strong feature of the gastroenteritis after the cold drinks (which may relieve at first) have become warm in the stomach. Stool may ooze from the anus, pass forcibly, or pour out like water. The patient feels generally better from sleep. (See Chapter 13, *Phosphorus*.)

Podophyllum peltatum—The specific quality of the stool is very important in prescribing *Podophyllum peltatum*. It can be yellow or green, *profuse, painless, frequent, gushing, and watery*. It is mixed with gas, thereby dirtying the entire toilet bowl with its sputtering. This medicine is similar to a small group of other plant-based homeopathic medicines, including *Croton tiglium*, *Gambogia*, *Momordica balsamina*, and *Elaterium*, of which *Podophyllum* is the most commonly prescribed. A yellow or green sudden, gushing, and sputtering stool will doubtless require *Podophyllum peltatum*, *Croton tiglium*, or *Gambogia*. When *Elaterium* is needed, there is little sputtering, and there is likely to be vomiting as well. Since little is known about the specific indications of *Momordica balsamina*, it is used as a backup medicine, when the others in the group have failed.

Pulsatilla—*Pulsatilla* is more often indicated for children than adults; the patient is *weepy* and clings to the parent. Compared with *Chamomilla*, the patient is in a sweeter mood, not particularly angry and demanding. The patient wants consolation and thrives on it. He or she feels better in the open air. *Pulsatilla* can treat functional diarrheas from high-fat foods in addition to actual gastroenteritis. A striking symptom is that the patient is not thirsty even when losing fluids from diarrhea and vomiting.

Sulphur—There are two distinctive symptoms of *Sulphur*. The first is that the patient gets an urgent desire to pass stool at 5:00 a.m., and it sends him or her racing directly from bed to the bathroom. The anus is inflamed and a bright *red* color, and burns. The lips may be more red than usual. The stool has a very offensive odor, sometimes a sulfurous (rotten-egg) odor. The patient is very thirsty, but has little appetite.

Less Commonly Indicated Medicines

Aconitum napellus—Violent diarrhea that comes on *suddenly* with anxiety and thirst should be treated with *Aconitum napellus*.

Aloe socotrina—There is *rumbling and gurgling* in the bowels followed by sudden urging. The patient suddenly passes a gushing, watery stool. The patient is uncertain whether gas or stool will come, and, therefore, stool or flatus may escape involuntarily. The anus is weak; there is a sense of *insecurity* about involuntary stool. Diarrhea may appear after eating oysters, during the hot season, or from drinking beer. A lot of mucus is passed. The rectum is painful.

Alstonia scholaris—Diarrhea from *impure water*, accompanied with debility is treated with *Alstonia scholaris*. The diarrhea may begin on a camping trip, thus the clinician thinks of *Giardia*. There are painless watery stools or violent purging and cramping in the bowels. The patient describes a "gone" sensation in the stomach with sinking in the abdomen. There is heat and irritation in the colon, and diarrhea immediately *after eating*.

Colocynthis—There are violent, knife-like pains in the abdomen, which make the patient *double up*, and press on the abdomen. There is diarrhea with abdominal pain after anger. There may be jelly-like stools. The patient describes the sensation as if the intestines were being ground together by stones in the abdomen, or as if they would burst.

Croton tiglium—There is sudden profuse, gushing, yellow, and watery diarrhea preceded by *gurgling* and splashing. The diarrhea may be from bad meat (e.g., *Staphylococcus aureus, Bacillus cereus,* or *Clostridium perfringens*). Pressure on the navel causes pain in the rectum or urging for stool. There is pain in the anus as if a plug were forcing outwards, which is aggravated by drinking a small amount or *while eating*. Diarrhea is followed by prostration. Diarrhea is also caused by hot summer weather. The patient may be morose and dissatisfied, or have the feeling of anxiety that something bad is going to happen to him or her.

Dulcamara—*Dulcamara* is indicated for diarrhea while *sleeping outdoors* in the summer, when the days are hot and the nights are cold and damp. There is a cutting pain at *navel* followed by painful diarrhea. Emotionally, the patient may find him- or herself scolding others when not even angry. The patient may ask for something, then immediately reject it, like with *Chamomilla*. There many be some mental confusion, with the inability to find the right word, or depression.

Elaterium—This is an invaluable remedy in treating violent vomiting and purging during *damp weather*, especially if the evacuations are copious and watery (compare with *Dulcamara*). Symptoms include forceful, *squirting* diarrhea, squeezing pains in the bowels, and much yawning and stretching. Emotionally, the patient desires to wander or travel, especially at night, yet also may be homesick. There may be starting in the sleep and a fear of disaster or impending disease. The patient is anxious and sad.

Gambogia—Diarrhea in the hot season is best treated with *Gambogia*. There is pinching and gurgling in bowels, then a *sudden gush* of yellow or green diarrhea with a burning anus and much relief. The patient is irritable and sad, and has anxious dreams.

Momordica balsamina—It is difficult to identify when this medicine is needed in dysentery because it has not had an adequate clinical trial to determine the general, emotional, or cognitive symptoms that might help distinguish it from other similar medicines. The symptomatology is *yellow* and watery stool that is discharged *explosively*, colic, nausea, vomiting, great thirst, and prostration. The clinician should compare it with *Croton tiglium, Elaterium*, and *Podophyllum peltatum*.

Pyrogenium—Diarrhea and vomiting with rapidly rising *fever* is present with profuse perspiration that does not cause a fall in the temperature. The patient has chills that begin in back. Nausea is alleviated by very hot drinks. The patient is very thirsty for small quantities of cold drinks, but the least liquid ingested is instantly vomited. The stool is extremely offensive, brown-black, painless, and involuntary.

Veratrum album—In older children and adults, this medicine is as common as those on the "most commonly indicated" list, which was derived from a study on young children only. *Veratrum album* is one of the two medicines that are especially indicated when vomiting and diarrhea occur *simultaneously*, and are aggravated by drinking and motion. Symptoms are accompanied by collapse, coldness, and blueness. The patient has cold *perspiration* on the forehead and cramping in the extremities. The skin is cold to the touch and the face is sunken.

Zingiber officinale—Heaviness in the stomach and diarrhea from drinking impure water is best treated with *Zingiber officinale*. The heaviness feels subjectively like a stone that is worse on *waking*. Symptoms include rumbling flatulence with colic and cutting pain; great thirst; and *relaxation* of the anal sphincter. The patient may display mental dullness and irritability, and may fear something will happen before he or she gets home.

Dysentery

All of the medicines that follow can have the bloody mucus-filled stool common to dysentery. Because of the symptomatic similarity between amebic dysentery (*Entamoeba histolytica*), and bacillary dysentery (*Shigella*), the homeopathic therapeutics are the same. The following are some general suggestions about prescribing for dysentery. Ultimately, how quickly a patient responds (and the ideal repetition of the dose of medicine) is related to how weakened he or she has already become before seeking homeopathic treatment, and how intense the symptoms are. Treatment can be initiated with the 30C potency given every 2 hr for three doses, and then changed to three times a day.

The period of time needed to evaluate the effectiveness of the medicine depends on how long the person has been ill. If the dysentery began in the past 24 hr, improvement should be noted in the first 6 hr after treatment has begun. Some suggested guidelines are that improvement should begin within 24 hours if symptoms began in the last week, within 5 days if the illness began a month ago. When symptoms show definite improvement, the frequency of the dose should be gradually reduced until the symptoms are completely resolved. If no improvement is noted in that time period, another medicine should be given a trial.

When the characteristics of the stool are named in the descriptions below, it is intended to give the clinician an idea of the range of characteristics that can be present, not to imply that all the different qualities will be present in one bowel movement, or even one patient. A brown, liquidy stool is the norm in diarrhea, and, therefore, that characteristic will not be an important distinguishing criterion among medicines.

Most Commonly Indicated Medicines

Aloe socotrina—*Weakness of the anus* is the most distinctive symptom for this common medicine for dysentery. The anus *oozes mucus;* stools are passed involuntarily, and there is an urging to stool with the passage of flatus only. Stools may escape involuntarily with the flatus or when urinating. The rectum may prolapse during the illness.

Pain extends from the navel to the rectum. The patient describes the sensation of a plug being between the pubic symphysis and the coccyx, with urging to stool. There is a dragging-down, full, heavy, hot, and bloated sensation in the abdomen. There is borborygmus with urgent diarrhea of *undigested* food, and pain in the rectum afterward. Stool is hot, mushy, lumpy, watery, gelatinous, and/or bloody. Much mucus is passed with pain in the rectum. Pulsation may be in the rectum after eating.

Cantharis—There is violent *burning* pain through the whole intestinal tract with painful sensitivity of the abdomen to touch. Dysentery accompanies *dysuria*. The patient feels the need to pass stool, which has a shredded appearance, while urinating. Burning pains accompany stools, with tenesmus of the rectum and bladder, and shuddering of the body following the stool. Cutting pain in the rectum is partially relieved by flatus and completely relieved by passing stool. Rarely, the patient has an increased libido with lewd talk, and rages with violent impulses.

Capsicum annuum—The patient presents with bloody, mucus-filled stool with burning and tenesmus. When stool is passed, there is a *stinging* pain, and a drawing pain in the back after it passes. The patient shivers and is thirsty after stools as well. Symptoms are alleviated while eating and from heat, and are aggravated by open air, drafts, and being uncovered. Patient may be moody—alternating laughing and weeping, joking and singing, and then anger. Other symptoms include homesickness; insomnia; red face; suicidal thoughts; awkwardness; and colliding with objects.

Colchicum autumnale—Bowel movements are very *painful and offensive* and consist of shredded, bloody stool, or gelatinous mucus, followed by *tenesmus* or spasms of the anus. Nausea and an inclination to vomit caused by swallowing saliva are present. The abdomen is distended, but contracts when touched, and is accompanied by an inability to stretch the legs. Agonizing pains remain long after stool has passed.

Colocynthis—Pain is the predominant symptom in dysentery needing *Colocynthis*. Violent pains feel as though the intestines are being ground together between two rocks. Variously described as cramping, knife-like, and squeezing, the pains come in waves, causing the patient to *double up* (which temporarily alleviates the pain). Firm pressure on the painful area at first alleviates the pain; later the area becomes tender. The pains are aggravated by the smallest intake of food or liquids. Stools are watery, frothy, yellow, shredded, sour, or gelatinous and accompanied with flatulence and pain.

Ipecacuanha—Although famous for the treatment of vomiting, *Ipecacuanha* is also useful in dysentery when it is accompanied with a *hot head and cold legs*. There is a squeezing, drawing, or knife-life pain at the umbilicus that is aggravated by motion and alleviated by rest. Stools are grassy, yellowish green, brown, frothy, slimy, molasses-like, or bloody. There are lumps of mucus in the stool.

Magnesia carbonica—The characteristic that most helps the clinician determine when *Magnesia carbonica* is required is the stool itself. The diarrhea is watery and greenish, with the green material separating and floating to the top in the toilet or bedpan, like green *scum on a pond*. Less characteristically there may be steatorrhea, or the stool may be sour smelling or lienteric. There may be cutting, squeezing, and pressing colic.

Mercurius corrosivus—The incessant *severe tenesmus*, which is not relieved by stool, and hemorrhage make this the leading medicine for dysentery. The abdomen is bloated and tender. Knife-like pains are in the abdomen. The stool feels hot, and is bloody, slimy, offensive, and contains shreds of membranous material. The patient may pass pure blood, or bloody water. The patient feels a *continuous urge* to void stool and urine. The patient perspires before and after the stool.

Mercurius vivus or Mercurius solubilis—Although not as commonly indicated for dysentery as *Mercurius corrosivus* (mercuric chloride), this medicine is not infrequently indicated. The general symptoms of *Mercurius* will be present (see Chapter 11). The intestines feel bruised when lying on the right side, or as if they have fallen to the side the patient is lying on. The patient has *adenopathy*. Stools are painful, bloody, greenish, slimy, acrid, and followed by tenesmus or chills. Rectal tenesmus may be accompanied by *tenesmus of the bladder*.

Nux vomica—While well-known for its role in the treatment of constipation, *Nux vomica* is also a common medicine for dysentery. The patient must *strain*, and then passes bloody mucus with the stool, or a discharge of pure blood. There is a knife-like pain at the umbilicus during the stool. When the stool passes, the pain subsides for a while. There is bruised soreness of the abdominal wall and soreness of the intestines, which is aggravated by *coughing* and *stepping*. These local symptoms may be accompanied by the general symptoms of the medicine (see Chapter 12, *Nux vomica*), such as irritability and impatience.

Rhus toxicodendron—The patient feels as though there is a *lump* in the abdomen or as if there is water splashing there. Cramping pains in the abdomen compel him or her to adopt a *stooped* gait; the pain is alleviated by lying on the abdomen. Stools are foul, bloody, slimy, gelatinous, watery, and frothy. They may come involuntarily in sleep at night and be accompanied by tenesmus. Patient may have the general symptoms of *Rhus toxicodendron,* such as stiffness that limbers up on continued motion, alleviation by warmth, a desire for milk, or a red triangular discoloration at the tip of the tongue. (See Chapter 15, *Rhus toxicodendron.*)

Aconitum napellus, Arsenicum album, Carbo vegetabilis, Phosphorus, and **Sulphur**—These medicines can also be prescribed on the same indications as general diarrhea.

Less Commonly Indicated Medicines

Arnica montana—Cramps from the epigastrium extend inferiorly over the bowels, followed by foul stools. There are sharp pains from side to side. Stools are bloody, foamy, purulent, and acrid. There may be involuntary diarrhea during sleep, as well as dysentery with dysuria that continues all summer and autumn. The patient experiences cramps in the rectum while standing. The flatus smells of rotten eggs. The patient must lie down after every stool. *Prolapsus ani* is worse after walking for a few minutes and is alleviated by washing the whole body. (See Chapter 2, *Arnica montana*.)

Baptisia tinctoria—The patient presents with sepsis with low fever, *soreness, heaviness, and muscular aching*. There may be sudden prostration. The patient describes the bed as too hard because he or she is so sore, yet feels too weak to move. The patient's body and all its discharges have a foul odor. The cognition is dulled with confusion.

In *delirium*, the patient may wander and mutter, and there is a delusion that the parts of the body are separated. The face appears dusky. The patient suffers sudden attacks of vomiting and diarrhea, with fever and pain. Soreness of the gallbladder may accompany the diarrhea. The diarrhea is sudden; has a very offensive odor; and is described as mushy, painless, dark, or bloody. *Baptisia tinctoria* is especially useful for the dysentery of older persons that is painless or accompanied with pain in the limbs, lumbar region, or epigastrium, and with chills.

Cuprum arsenicosum—Vomiting and diarrhea with violent *colic, obstinate hiccup, and an icy cold body* are best treated with *Cuprum arsenicosum*. There are violent cramps in the chest, fingers, calves, and toes. *Leg cramps* are alleviated by pressing the affected foot on the floor. There may be a numb, paralytic sensation in the legs. The patient trembles when attempting to walk. His or her urine has an odor like garlic.

Erigeron canadensis—Burning and soreness in the *bladder* accompany the dysentery. The rectum may hemorrhage pure blood.

Eucalyptus globulus—The patient presents with dysentery with the sensation of *heat in the rectum*. He or she has chills followed by nausea and vomiting. Thin and watery stools are preceded by sharp pains. The patient describes a feeling of a weight in the bowels, throbbing in the stomach, and aching during fever.

Kali bichromicum—Dysentery that recurs every year in the summer and that appears after a flare up of *arthritis* or after antibiotic treatment for *sinusitis* is best treated with this medicine. The stools are gelatinous or gushes of brown, frothy water. There is burning and tenesmus after the stool, especially after rising in the morning. The patient describes the sensation as if something were eating inside the bowels. Symptoms worsen at 2:00–3:00 a.m. and from drinking alcohol, especially beer. They are alleviated by heat, motion, and pressure.

Kali chloricum—Squeezing cramping pain in the abdomen accompanies the shifting of flatulence and diarrhea in the bowels; followed by *continuous rectal pain*. Much blood passes with mucus or profuse, greenish diarrhea. The patient cries from the violent *knife-like* pain in the rectum. There is sudden vomiting of all the food eaten and of offensive dark green mucus.

Silphium laciniatum—An attack of dysentery is preceded by constipated stools covered with *white mucus*.

Tanacetum vulgare—The patient feels the need to void stool *immediately* after eating. The pain in the bowels is alleviated by passing stool. The patient is nervous, irritable, tired, and sensitive to noise. The patient feels "half dead." There may be roaring and ringing in the ears; the patient's own *voice sounds strange* to him or her. The ears have the sensation of having suddenly closed up.

Trombidium—Symptoms are aggravated by eating and drinking, stool passes only after eating. There is severe pain in the *abdomen* before and after stool. The patient describes a squeezing pain in the hypochondrium during morning. The stools are brown, thin, and bloody, and accompanied by tenesmus. A sharp pain in the *left* side during stool shoots downward. There is burning in the anus.

Cinchona officinalis—See symptoms under Dehydration below.

Simple Diarrheas

Sometimes diarrhea seems to be caused by functional symptoms (e.g., from eating indiscretions, teething, and hot weather). These kinds of diarrhea are reputed to be easily addressed by a small group of homeopathic medicines. A 30C potency could be prescribed every 6 hr for three doses.

Diarrhea during Emerging Dentition

Homeopathic clinicians have observed a link between mild diarrhea and teething. One of the following medicines could be given in the 30C potency every 6 hr for three doses.

Calcarea carbonica—Diarrhea of teething in chubby, placid children with cold hands and feet and heads that *perspire* while they sleep, is best treated with *Calcarea carbonica*.

Calcarea phosphorica—The child presents with hot, green diarrhea accompanied by flatus. The child is whiny and discontented (like when *Chamomilla* is indicated), but he or she is not forceful about it. The child will not strike the parent.

Chamomilla—*Chamomilla* is used to treat sour, green, or yellow-green diarrhea in children who are extremely *irritable* while teething. The child shrieks loudly unless carried, and resumes soon after being put down. He or she may *hit* the parent in pain and frustration. (See Chapter 6, *Chamomilla*.)

Rheum officinale—Teething brings on colic, with screaming and doubling up, followed by sour smelling, slimy, brown, green, fermented, or acrid stools. The child shivers while passing stools. Perspiration is aggravated by the slightest motion and smells *sour*. Like when *Chamomilla* is indicated, the child is whining, irritable, crying, and shrieking—much more so at night.

Diarrhea in Hot Weather

Some patients are prone to diarrhea during hot weather. General diarrhea medicines (e.g., *Cinchona officinalis, Croton tiglium, Gambogia,* and *Podophyllum peltatum*) are reputed to treat this, as are the medicines below.

Bryonia alba—Gushing diarrhea that is aggravated on rising in the morning is best treated with *Bryonia alba*. Diarrhea may arise from cold drinks on hot days. There is burning in the anus during the stool, which is yellow and mushy. Generally, the patient is irritable and thirsty with a desire to be alone. (See Chapter 5, *Bryonia alba*.)

Camphora—The patient had diarrhea during a *collapse* due to heat exhaustion. (See Chapter 17, Injuries and Emergencies.)

Nux moschata—This diarrhea is caused by drinking cold drinks when hot. The patient is bloated and experiences *faintness* during or after the stool. He or she is drowsy.

Oleander—Children have diarrhea of *undigested food* from the previous day passed with *flatus* in the morning.

Diarrhea from Emotions

Medicines for acute distress from emotions are discussed in Chapter 22, Emotional Health and Chemical Dependency Recovery. Please refer to that chapter for more detailed differentials among these medicines:

- Anger—*Colocynthis*
- Anticipation—*Argentum nitricum, Gelsemium sempervirens,* and *Phosphoricum acidum*
- Anxiety—*Arsenicum album*
- Performance anxiety—*Argentum nitricum*
- Fear—*Gelsemium sempervirens* and *Opium*
- Grief—*Colocynthis, Ignatia amara,* and *Phosphoricum acidum*

Dehydration

Carbo vegetabilis—The patient is weak from long lasting or severe diarrhea. The gastroenteritis was caused by impure water, game, or spoiled food. The face appears pale or bluish, and pinched and sunken from hypovolemia. The patient is cold with *cold breath*; the pulse is barely perceptible. There is much flatus. The emotional state is generally apathetic, but there may be irritability, especially in children. There may be faintness, with a desire to have a fan blowing on the patient. The stool is brown, watery, and slimy. It may pass involuntarily with flatus.

Cinchona officinalis—The symptoms of *Cinchona officinalis* are similar to those of *Carbo vegetabilis*—flatulence, weakness, pallor, and coldness from dehydration. There are three symptoms that help distinguish *Cinchona* from *Carbo vegetabilis*. The first is the characteristic of the stool: it is yellow, watery, and undigested. The second is that the pains in a case requiring *Cinchona* are alleviated by *firm pressure,* but strongly aggravated by light touch. The third is that the passing of flatus does not alleviate the pain, while when *Carbo vegetabilis* is needed, it does. There may be ringing in the ears. This medicine was formerly named *China officinalis.*

Phosphoricum acidum—The patient is weak from dehydration and craves refreshing drinks (e.g., fruity drinks). The patient is depressed, apathetic, slow to answer, and drained. This is also the most common medicine for diarrhea from acute *grief.*

Flatulence and Colic

Complaints of gaseous distension are reputedly improved by homeopathic treatment. There has been no significant research in this area. The 30C potency can be prescribed every 3 hr for three doses, and then as needed if symptoms return.

Argentum nitricum—The patient presents with a greatly distended abdomen with very *loud eructations* and discharge of flatus. The symptoms are aggravated by eating sweets, performance anxiety, or anticipating a big event.

Asafoetida—*Asafoetida* is used to treat incarcerated flatus in adult patients who seem to *exaggerate* their symptoms to get attention. The patient grasps his or her own throat. The patient's mood changes frequently. There is explosive burping with the odor of garlic.

Carbo vegetabilis—This is the general medicine for *incarcerated flatus*. There is great distension from gas, especially in the upper part of abdomen, in people of any age, and colic in the young. The gas is aggravated by rich food and lying down and alleviated by eructations. The colic may force the patient to double up. The patient cannot bear tight clothing around the waist. The flatus is hot, moist, and offensive.

Chamomilla—*Chamomilla* is the most commonly prescribed colic medicine. The whining and irritable child is only comforted by being *carried* around. The child demands things that are rejected when offered, and may strike the parent. The child is restless. One cheek is red and hot, and the other pale and cold. (See Chapter 6, *Chamomilla*.)

Cinchona officinalis—Flatulent bloating in adults is alleviated by motion, and doubling up. *Light pressure* aggravates and firm pressure alleviates the pain. The patient's mood is irritable, touchy, disobedient, and stubborn. He or she desires sweets. There are loud eructations, and flatus does pass, but the patient is unrelieved.

Colocynthis—There are violent attack of abdominal pains, usually in adults, particularly after being angry (especially when the *anger was not expressed*). The pain makes the patient *double up,* press into the abdomen, and adopt a stooped gait. Gas pains treated with *Magnesia phosphorica* and *Colocynthis* is alleviated by warm compresses to the abdomen, a heating pad, and from pressure. But in *Colocynthis*, the *pressure* causes more relief than warmth does; in *Magnesia phosphorica* the reverse is true.

Lycopodium clavatum—The abdomen becomes bloated immediately after a light meal. The patient is generally aggravated in *the late afternoon and evening*. He or she desires sweets and warm drinks, and is intolerant of belts and clothing around the abdomen.

Magnesia phosphorica—Gas pain and colic that are greatly relieved by a *hot-water bottle* or heating pad are best treated with *Magnesia phosphorica*.

Nux vomica—The child is very irritable and *impatient* during the colic. Unlike with *Chamomilla*, he or she is not alleviated by being carried. The child strains when passing stool. The colic is aggravated in the morning in bed. The infant hates the diaper change because of the draft of cool air. There is an attack of flatulence after eating; all food seems to turn to gas. Passing flatus and moving aggravates the symptoms; applying hot-water bottle or heating pad alleviates them. (See Chapter 12, *Nux vomica*.)

ANORECTAL PATHOLOGY

Anal Fissures

Bignamini, Saruggia, & Sansonetti (1991) had a highly favorable result in a double-blind, placebo-controlled trial of *Nitricum acidum*, 9C for anal fissures, involving 31 subjects. The study received a 40 on the Jadad scale of internal validity, and 64 on a more elaborate internal validity scale (both out of a possible 100) by independent reviewers (Linde et al., 1997). This would be a simple trial to replicate and improve upon. *Nitricum acidum* is a leading medicine for fissures, but if the theory of classical homeopathy is correct, when the medicines are individualized for patients, results should be even more successful.

The clinician should prescribe the 30C potency of the indicated medicine four times a day for the first 2 days, then three times a day for 3 days, and then twice a day until symptoms are completely resolved for up to 10 more days.

Most Commonly Indicated Medicines

Chamomilla—Fissures put the patient in an *ugly mood*; he or she demands relief from the pain immediately. There is needle-like pain and soreness *after* passing the stool. (See Chapter 6, *Chamomilla*.)

Graphites—Anal fissures cause a knife-like pain during stool passage, followed by constriction and aching for several hours. The fissures bleed and ulcerate. Since there are several medicines that have within their range these exact symptoms, the clinician will need to prescribe for the general symptoms of the person. This medicine is more commonly indicated in heavyset, straight-forward, and uncomplicated people who complain of (or display) a state of mental *dullness* or fogginess. They are generally chilly and prone to abnormalities of the nails (e.g., thickened and distorted), and thickened, dry, cracked skin. They are prone to eruptions on the scalp as well as cracking of the skin behind the ears, the lips, and the corners of the mouth.

Nitricum acidum—*Nitricum acidum* is the most common medicine for anal and rectal fissures. Stools tear the anus even though they are soft. The rectum feels torn as well. The patient walks in agony, and has prolonged, splinter-like *pain after stools*. Hemorrhoids are painful and bleed easily. There is burning in the rectum after urination. The patient is very angry and makes great *demands* of the clinician. This medicine is commonly indicated in patients with a past history of gonorrhea or syphilis.

Ratanhia—The patient complains of pain in the rectum after passing stool that *persists* for minutes or hours. Stool is forced out by straining, and then followed by a severe burning, cutting, splinter-like, or "broken glass" pain in rectum. Pains are alleviated by warm bathing, lying down, or walking slowly. Hemorrhoids protrude with stool. There is rectal excoriation and oozing. This medicine is reputedly more commonly indicated for patients with *obsessive-compulsive* disorders that center on rectal hygiene or religion.

Sepia—*Sepia* is the indicated medicine for anorectal fissures in people with very *low libido* and lack of passion for life. It is especially indicated in women at times of hormonal shifts. The patient is chilled and craves sour foods. Poor muscular tone of the pelvis leads to a bearing-down or heavy feeling in that region. The rectal pain is aggravated by sitting, especially at 10:00 a.m.

Thuja occidentalis—The patient presents with a fissured anus with *condylomata* and swollen, painful hemorrhoids. There may also be oozing from the anus. Patients with a *history of gonorrhea* or chlamydia are more likely to require *Thuja occidentalis*. The stream of urine is forked. The patient may have recurrent dreams of falling.

Less Commonly Indicated Medicines

Nux vomica—*Nux vomica* has a place in every ailment of the digestive system, including anorectal fissure. In this case, however, the irritable impatience associated with this medicine is similar to that of two of the main medicines for this condition (i.e., *Nitricum acidum and Chamomilla*). The clinician should look for a history of constipation and *straining* to pass stool, or a desire for stimulants and spicy food, as corroborating symptoms in these hard-driving patients. (See Chapter 12, *Nux vomica*.)

Paeonia officinalis—The patient presents with fissures or fistula of the anus, and/or *large ulcerated hemorrhoids*. The excruciating pain in the anus continues long after the stool has passed. He or she must rise and walk about at night. The anus, which is *purple* and covered with crusty material, itches. There may be a painful anal ulcer with offensive exudate oozing onto the perineum.

Silicea—The patient has fissures or fistula of the anus with painful spasms of the anal sphincter. Intensely painful hemorrhoids protrude during passage of the stool. These are chilly patients with mild personalities; they have a history of constipation with stools that emerge from the anus while on the toilet, and then *recede* again.

Sulphur—*Sulphur* is used to treat hot patients with *red* orifices, including the anus. The rectum and anus *itch and burn;* irritating exudate oozes from the anus. The pain may pulsate. The patient may have constipation, morning diarrhea, or both. The patient desires sweets, fat, spicy food, and alcohol. He or she may display untidy personal habits, and be critical of others. (See Chapter 16 for the general symptoms of *Sulphur.*)

Pruritus Ani

The following medicines are frequently mentioned in the homeopathic literature for anal itch (without hemorrhoids). The 30C potency can be prescribed once a day for 5 days.

Petroleum—*Petroleum* is indicated for anal itch in chilly patients with extremely *dry skin*. The skin of the hands and fingers is cracked, especially in manual laborers and artisans. There may be a history of human papilloma virus infection.

Sulphur—This medicine is used to treat itching of the anus with *burning*, which may be aggravated during the day. The patients should have the general symptoms associated with *Sulphur* (Chapter 16). The itching may arouse some sexual feelings. *Scratching* exacerbates the itching.

Hemorrhoids

There is a great deal of overlap between medicines that are used to treat fissures and the medicines that are used to treat inflamed hemorrhoids. The 30C potency may be prescribed three times a day for 3 days, and gradually less frequently as symptoms subside.

Aesculus hippocastanum—*Aesculus hippocastanum* is indicated for hemorrhoids that are accompanied with lumbar or *sacroiliac pain*. The patient often has varicose conditions. The hemorrhoids feel as though the rectum were full of *small sticks*, sometimes sending sharp shooting pains up the back. The pains persist long after the stools. There may be bleeding, external hemorrhoids that are purple and painful, and aggravated by standing and walking. The patient may suffer from constipation with hard, dry stools. There is a sensation as if a bug were crawling from the anus, or as if a knife were sawing up and down in the rectum. There may be burning in the anus, with chills up and down the back, or a painful constricting feeling. Hemorrhoids are worse at menopause.

Aloe socotrina—This medicine is used to treat external hemorrhoids, like a *bunch of grapes*. The discomfort is alleviated by cold bathing. Burning and needle-like pains interfere with sleep. There is throbbing in the rectum after eating.

Belladonna—Red, hot, *throbbing*, and bleeding hemorrhoids are best treated with *Belladonna*. The patient may have a red face. (See Chapter 4, *Belladonna*.)

Collinsonia canadensis—There is the sensation of *sharp sticks* in the rectum (like with *Aesculus*), or a constricted, engorged feeling there. The anus may itch. The patient has obstinate constipation with a hard stool, or constipation alternating with diarrhea. This medicine is especially indicated in patients who have *cardiac or rheumatic* symptoms concurrently with the hemorrhoid flare-ups, or who alternate between cardiac and hemorrhoid symptoms.

Graphites—*Graphites* is prescribed for the burning hemorrhoids in obese and chilly patients with some mental *dullness*, who may desire chicken and have an aversion to sweets. They have intestinal inactivity and constipation of large, knotty-looking, and foul stools lasting for days.

Hamamelis virginiana—Sore, *profusely bleeding* hemorrhoids are best treated with *Hamamelis virginiana*. There are large quantities of tar-like blood in the stools. The patient may have varicose veins.

Kali carbonicum—Hemorrhoids are large, swollen, and painful. The patient suffers needle-like pain an hour before passing stool, and then passes large difficult stools, followed by a burning or torn feeling. Hemorrhoids are also strongly aggravated at delivery. Pain in rectum may feel like a *red-hot poker*. There is a large discharge of blood with normal stool. There may be pain in the hemorrhoids when the patient coughs. The affect of persons needing *Kali carbonicum*, interestingly, resembles the popular stereotype of the "anal retentive," with a strong sense of propriety and duty.

Nux vomica—*Nux vomica* is indicated for itching, painful hemorrhoids with an ineffectual urging to pass stool (especially after use of laxatives, or in alcoholics or drug addicts). The patient may be *impatient*, irritable, and critical. (See Chapter 12, *Nux vomica*.)

Paeonia officinalis—*Large and ulcerated* hemorrhoids are associated with excruciating pain at the anus that continues long after the stool passage. The patient walks around, or lies for minutes to hours after a stool with the buttocks held *spread apart*, to prevent any contact on the anus. The anus is covered with crusty material. Symptoms are aggravated at night.

Pulsatilla—Itching, smarting hemorrhoids in the patient, who is mild, gentle, and *weepy*, and craves sympathy are treated with *Pulsatilla*. He or she may give the impression that he or she wants to please the clinician. The patient is thirstless, has an aversion to meat fat, and desires butter, peanut butter, cream-filled pastries, and creamy foods in general. (See Chapter 14, *Pulsatilla*.)

Sepia—The patient may experience the hemorrhoids as a feeling of a ball or *fullness in the rectum*. There is rectal bleeding during the stool passage; and the rectum itches. The patient has constipation with large, hard stools, tenesmus, and pains that shoot upward from the rectum or anus. This medicine is indicated for people who present as passionless, apathetic, and undiplomatic; who complain of lowered libido; and who take pleasure only in vigorous exercise, such as running and dancing. The patient desires sour foods and dark chocolate.

Sulphur—The patient presents with large, moist, internal or external bluish, ulcerated, and perhaps strangulated hemorrhoids that are aggravated from *wiping* after stool, walking, touch, standing, and drinking beer. Symptoms are worse at night. In women, the hemorrhoids are worse during pregnancy, delivery, menstruation, menopause, and during amenorrhea. (See Chapter 16, *Sulphur*.)

CHOLECYSTOPATHY

The only placebo-controlled research on gallbladder disease and homeopathy by Mossinger in 1984 is reported to have had a highly positive result in a tiny trial (*n* = 14) of *Absinthium*, 2X for cholecystopathia in general. The results were published in a German homeopathic publication, and mentioned in Linde et al. (1997). *Absinthium* is not classically a medicine used in the treatment of gallbladder disease. Such a low potency could exert a pharmacological effect; therefore, this is not confirmation of the effectiveness of the almost inconceivable dilutions in which homeopathic medicines are usually prescribed.

The homeopathic medicines classically used for treatment of gallbladder disease vary according to the patient's symptoms, not according to whether there is a diagnosis of cholecystitis (with or without stones), biliary colic, or outright obstructive disease. Needless to say, clinicians need to follow generally accepted protocols in an emergency situation. In a typical biliary colic, the differential between homeopathic medicines is uncomplicated, and the symptomatic relief is reputed to be quick. A proper diagnostic workup must be conducted to ensure that the pain palliation provided by the homeopathic medicine does not mask important symptoms. The 30C potency may be prescribed three times a day, then as needed for return of pain if effective.

There is a difference of opinion in the homeopathic profession about whether these medicines actually encourage the passage of stones, and there is no research on which to base any conclusions (Jouanny, 1980).

Acute Biliary Colic

The Most Common Indicated Medicines

Belladonna—The pain starts and ends *suddenly;* the patient is hypersensitive to contact and movement, especially being *jarred* or jiggled. Often there is accompanying fever and congestive headaches with a red face. There is decreased thirst. (See Chapter 4, *Belladonna*.)

Bryonia alba—Pains are sharp over the hepatic region, and are aggravated by *movement* and alleviated by *pressure*. The patient may have a fever with intense thirst for large quantities of water at long intervals. Other symptoms include a bitter taste in the mouth; coated tongue; dry lips; and hard, dry, black, and bulky stools. The patient is irritable and wants to be alone. (See Chapter 5, *Bryonia alba*.)

Chelidonium majus—*Chelidonium majus* is the indicated medicine for simple biliary colic with pain that radiates to just below the *inferior angle of the right scapula*. It can also be indicated when there is concurrent liver disease with hepatomegaly and jaundice. The tongue may be discolored yellow, and shows the imprint of the teeth. The patient desires hot food and drinks, especially very hot water, which alleviates the nausea and vomiting. He or she is fatigued and lethargic. This medicine is also indicated for gallbladder dysfunction during pregnancy.

Nux vomica—There is a sensation of *constriction* around the hypochondrium with great intolerance of clothing, or of the slightest touch. There are throbbing, shooting, stinging, pressing, tensive, or needle-like pains in the region of the liver that are aggravated by *contact* or *motion*. The patient is jaundiced and has gallstones. There is swelling and induration of the hepatic region. The patient craves spicy food, beer, high-fat food, and stimulants. There may be violent, unproductive retching. Nausea is alleviated if the patient is able to vomit. Food lies like a heavy knot in stomach. The patient has the typical irritable, critical, and *impatient* demeanor of patients requiring *Nux vomica*. The patient may have concurrent viral or alcoholic hepatitis. (See Chapter 12, *Nux vomica*.)

Less Commonly Indicated Medicines

Berberis vulgaris—The patient presents with biliary colic with stones. There are needle-like pains in the region of the gallbladder that linger after the attack, *radiate* to the stomach, and are aggravated by pressure.

Chamomilla—*Chamomilla* is used to treat severe, bitter, and bilious vomiting, with griping pain in the abdomen. The biliary colic may have started after an angry episode (like with *Colocynthis*). The patient is crying and angry. He or she may ask for things that are then rejected. (See Chapter 6, *Chamomilla*.)

Cinchona officinalis—Biliary colic with stones following *dehydration* is treated with *Cinchona officinalis*. The pain is alleviated by *doubling up* (like with *Colocynthis*). There is extremely flatulent bloating that is alleviated by motion. The patient may also be jaundiced.

Colocynthis—There are violent, cramp-like pains that cause the person to *double up* (compare with *Cinchona officinalis*). Pressure alleviates the pain, as does warmth to a lesser degree. The patient may have had this attack of biliary colic after an angry episode.

Dioscorea villosa—Sharp pains from the gallbladder radiate upward to the *right*, sometimes specifically to the right nipple. Pains may also radiate to the back, chest, or arms; or shift entirely to a remote locality such as the fingers and toes. The pains are alleviated by walking; they are aggravated by *stooping* and lying down. The patient has sour or bitter eructations with hiccups.

Ipecacuanha—*Ipecacuanha* is used for palliation of continuous nausea and *vomiting* from biliary colic.

Biliary Colic in Patients with Concurrent Liver Disease

The medicines *Chelidonium majus* and *Nux vomica* in the above section can also treat biliary colic in patients with concurrent liver disease, as can the medicines below.

Baptisia tinctoria—The patient presents with constant, *severe pain* over the gallbladder. There is pain in the liver from the right lateral ligament to the gallbladder. The patient can hardly walk because the pain worsens. The pain intensifies even more ascending stairs. There may be heavy aching in the liver and soreness of the gallbladder with diarrhea. Diarrhea is painless, sudden, very foul, mushy, dark, or bloody. The patient finds thinking very difficult; the cognition seems weak and confused as if *intoxicated*.

Carduus marianus—The patient has the painful *tenderness* of an enlarged gallbladder. The concurrent liver disease, such as cirrhosis, makes the region of the liver painful; the left lobe is especially sensitive. Constipation with hard, knotty, and bright yellow stools alternates with diarrhea. Asthma or chest pain may occur concurrently with the cholecystitis.

Chionanthus virginica—This medicine is used to treat cholecystitis with stones and biliary colic in patients with hepatomegaly and jaundice, and/or diabetes. Symptoms are alleviated by lying on the *abdomen* and aggravated by being *jarred, moving, and* the *cold*. There is bile and glucose in the urine. Vomiting and cold perspiration on forehead and dorsal surface of the hands accompany the colic or passage of stool. There may be concurrent pancreatic dysfunction or disease. Stools are tarry, clay-colored, and undigested. The tongue has a thick, *greenish yellow fur*, and feels drawn up. The patient has no desire to do anything and wants to be left alone.

Hydrastis canadensis—Cutting pain from the liver radiates to the *right scapula*, and is aggravated by supine or right side-lying position. This medicine is especially suited to older persons or those who are worn out from cancer, degenerative diseases, and/or cachexia.

A ropy, yellow, mucous discharge comes from the sinuses, stomach, uterus, and/or urethra. It is also observed in the stool and urine. *Hydrastis canadensis* is good for treating jaundice and postjaundice patients if there is a suspicion of a mucous plug in the biliary tract (Jouanny, 1980).

Leptandra virginica—The patient has biliary colic with concurrent liver disease. Aching in the upper-right quadrant of the abdomen *radiates to the spine*, which itself feels chilly. The tongue is coated yellow. Great discomfort in the stomach and intestines accompanies desire to pass stool. Clay-colored stools are associated with jaundice. The patient is gloomy.

Podophyllum peltatum—This medicine is used to treat cholecystitis with stones in patients with concurrent liver disease, which causes jaundice and profuse *sputtering diarrhea*. The liver and the whole abdomen is sore, and is alleviated by rubbing.

CHAPTER 24

Genitourinary System and Men's Health

TESTICLES

Hydrocele

Hydrocele may be treated with the 12C potency of the indicated medicine, twice a day for a month. If the hydrocele has reduced at that point, the medicine can be continued until the condition has resolved.

Apis mellifica—Hydrocele in multilocular cysts can be treated with *Apis mellifica*.

Graphites—*Graphites* is indicated for hydrocele in stocky boys or men with concurrent herpetic eruptions, prurigo, or simple itching. This medicine is most often used in patients who, while not developmentally impaired, are mentally dull.

Iodium—The testes are swollen, indurated, and painful because of accompanying epididymitis and hydrocele.

Lycopodium clavatum—Hydrocele in men with gastrointestinal problems may be treated with *Lycopodium clavatum*. The patient desires to eat sweets and drink warm drinks. The patient's personality is domineering at home and charming to the outside world. The patient may have concurrent sexual dysfunction: impotency or premature ejaculation.

Pulsatilla—Hydrocele in tearful gentle boys who desire sympathy and consolation is best treated with *Pulsatilla*. The patiens are not very thirsty and have an aversion to the fat on meat. (See Chapter 14, *Pulsatilla*.)

Rhododendron chrysanthum—This medicine is used to treat left-sided hydrocele in boys.

Silicea—Itching hydrocele in shy, reserved boys or men is treated with *Silicea*. There is perspiration on the scrotum, feet, and possibly the suboccipital region.

Varicocele—In recent-onset varicocele, the clinician must investigate to rule out a retroperitoneal mass. There are too many medicines for this condition to swiftly distinguish among them in a primary care visit. If the condition began with a blow to the scrotum, the prescription most likely to be effective is *Arnica montana*, but *Hamamelis virginiana* and *Pulsatilla* have also been known to be beneficial (van Zandvoort, 1997).

EPIDIDYMITIS

Antibiotics should be prescribed because the leading cause of epididymitis in men under 35 years is chlamydia; bacilli and streptococci are the most common cause in the older group. In the days before the MMR vaccine, homeopaths treated viral (mumps-related) epididymitis primarily with *Pulsatilla, Rhododendron chrysanthum*, or *Spongia tosta*.

PENIS

Balanitis, Balanoposthitis, Phimosis, and Paraphimosis

In infections of the penis, the patient should be prescribed the 30C potency three times a day to every 3 hr depending on the severity of symptoms. The clinician will need to evaluate whether the situation is a medical emergency that requires referral. If homeopathic treatment is selected, a telephone call 24 hr after the patient's visit should confirm that improvement has begun. The patient may then gradually reduce the frequency of repetition of the medicine as symptoms resolve, and stop taking it when all symptoms are gone. If improvement is not noted, conventional treatment may be started at that time. A follow-up exam should be done in 1 week. There has been no research done on homeopathic treatment of these conditions.

Arnica montana—Phimosis from *friction* should be treated with *Arnica montana*. There is no swelling of the inguinal glands.

Calcarea carbonica—This medicine is indicated for balanitis and phimosis. The patient may have various problems with sexual functioning: burning with seminal emission, premature ejaculation, and weakness and irritability after coition. There may be itching. *Calcarea carbonica* is more commonly indicated in obese patients with *cold hands and feet*, who are partial toward *eggs* and sweets.

Caladium seguinum—The glans appears like a red rag. Prepuce remains retracted after coition. There is pruritis. The sexual organs seem *large, puffy*, relaxed, cold, and *perspiring*; the skin of the scrotum is thickened. There is no inguinal adenopathy.

Calendula officinalis—Rawness or *abrasion* of prepuce after intercourse is treated with *Calendula officinalis*. The patient may have inguinal adenopathy.

Cannibis sativa—Balanitis and phimosis in marijauna users can be treated with *Cannibis sativa*. The patient's urination stream is split (like with *Thuja occidentalis*). There is *needle-like* or zigzag pain along the urethra. There may be a urethral carbuncle. The penis has an inflamed sensation, with soreness to touch. The patient describes a dragging sensation in the testicles. The urethra may be stopped up with mucus and pus. There is no inguinal adenopathy.

Hepar sulphuris calcareum—This medicine is indicated for phimosis with *itching* of the glans, frenum, and scrotum. The patient may have concurrent herpes with friable and sensitive ulcers on the prepuce. The inguinal glands are swollen or suppurating. There may be fig-shaped warts with an offensive odor, or a history of genital condyloma. There may be a damp soreness on the genitals and between the scrotum and thigh. The patient is chilly. (See Chapter 9, *Hepar sulphuris calcareum*.)

Lycopodium clavatum—This medicine is indicated for balanitis and phimosis in men with *sexual dysfunction* (e.g., impotence, premature ejaculation, insufficient and feeble erections, and falling asleep during coition). There may be a yellow tumor behind the corona glandis. The patient may have concurrent condylomata or a history of them. The local symptoms of the patient may be accompanied by general symptoms associated with *Lycopodium clavatum* such as desire for *sweets* and *warm drinks*, feeling poorly in the late afternoon and early evening, and *flatulence*.

Mercurius vivus or Mercurius solubilis—*Mercurius* is used to treat balanitis, balanoposthitis, phimosis, and paraphimosis. *Mercurius* is a major medicine for men's genital health. The prepuce is irritated and itchy; the glans and prepuce are inflamed and swollen; and the meatus is red. There is swelling of *lymphatic vessels* along the penis, and indurated inguinal adenopathy. The testicles are swollen and hard with a shiny and red scrotum. The genitals *itch;* the patient pulls and scratches. The patient has a history of sexually transmitted disease, and may have concurrent herpes. The genitals may be cold. The patient may have some general symptoms indicative of *Mercurius*, such as metallic taste in mouth, excessive foul *perspiration,* and narrow range of comfort with ambient air temperature. (See Chapter 11, *Mercurius vivus or Mercurius solubilis.*)

Mercurius corrosivus—Balanitis, balanoposthitis, phimosis, and paraphimosis may be treated with *Mercurius corrosivus*. The key symptom is that the penis and testes are *enormously swollen*. The patient may have chordee that is aggravated by sleep. There is a history of sexually transmitted disease. Patient may have some general symptoms of *Mercurius*.

Mercurius sulphuratus ruber—This medicine is used to treat balanitis and phimosis. The prepuce is swollen and red. There are small red pimples on the glans. The corona glandis itches. The testicles are enlarged. The patient may have a history of easy bleeding from *fan-shaped* genital condylomata. The penis may *jerk* during sleep. There is a foul, acrid perspiration between the scrotum and thighs.

Nitricum acidum—Balanitis, balanoposthitis, phimosis, and paraphimosis can be treated with *Nitricum acidum*. There is soreness and burning in the glans and beneath an edematous, itchy, and burning prepuce. There may be *red spots* on the prepuce or on the corona glandis. There may be burning and stinging *ulcers* that exude offensive matter. The urine may come out in a thin stream as though there were a stricture. There may also be great *anxiety about health*, and a craving for high-fat foods. The patient may be chilled.

Rhus toxicodendron—*Rhus toxicodendron* may be indicated in balanitis, balanoposthitis, phimosis, and paraphimosis. There is intense *itching* of the genitals. The glans and prepuce are edematous, and may have dark red erysipelas. The scrotum is thick, swollen, and edematous. The patient is *restless*, and may be achy and stiff. The patient may crave cold milk, and be generally alleviated by *warmth*. (See Chapter 15, *Rhus toxicodendron*.)

Sulphur—Balanitis and phimosis with *fetid perpiration* on the genitals can be treated with *Sulphur*. The prepuce is stiff and leathery, with *copious smegma* that causes itching. The genitals itch when in bed. There are needle-like pains in the penis. The genitals are cold and flaccid. This is the leading medicine to treat inflammation from *poor personal hygiene*. Refer to Chapter 16 for the general symptoms of *Sulphur*.

Thuja occidentalis—Balanitis, and less commonly paraphimosis and phimosis, are treated with *Thuja occidentalis*. There is inflammation of the prepuce and glans; the prepuce is swollen, and there is pain in the penis. Key symptoms are a history of, or concurrent, *condylomata and skin tags* of the prepuce and glans. The genitals perspire and are offensive; the semen is *foul-smelling*. The testes feel bruised; the left one is drawn up. Chordee is aggravated at night.

PROSTATE

Acute Prostatitis

Antibiotics will be used for acute prostatitis, and homeopathy reserved for those cases that are unresponsive because of foci within the gland, or nonbacterial prostatitis. Some prolonged cases of prostatitis were historically viewed by homeopaths as having been caused by eliminating the gonococcus without curing the underlying imbalance in the person that was also caused by disease. It is arguable that this is an antiquated view from an era when antibiotics for gonorrhea did not exist, and existing medicines were not effective enough to cure the patient.

The following medicines are the most commonly indicated for prostatitis. If symptoms have persisted for many months, a referral to homeopathic specialist might be warranted. The medicine can be prescribed in the 30C potency for 5 days, then taken as needed by the patient for pain if it is effective.

Apis mellifica—There is pressing prostate pain during urination.

Belladonna—Acute *throbbing* pain in the gland is aggravated by jiggling and jarring. The prostatitis is accompanied by fever, usually high; a red face; dilated pupils; and thirstlessness. When this kind of prostatitis occurs after antibiotic treatment for gonorrhea, febrile symptoms will have been eliminated, but the discomfort from jarring remains. (See Chapter 4, *Belladonna.*)

Chimaphila umbellata—*Chimaphila umbellata* is indicated for acute prostatitis with *retention* and dysuria; the patient feels as though he is sitting on a *ball;* or the gland is painful or sore. There is smarting in the urethra from the neck of the bladder to the meatus. There may be loss of prostatic fluid. The patient may *strain* to pass urine because the prostate is swollen; the urine may be stringy, scanty, thick, turbid, and mucopurulent, or contain blood clots.

Copaiva officinalis—*Copaiva officinalis* is indicated for urinary tract infection that has *ascended* to the prostate, or that followed gonorrhea. The urethra feels wide open. The penis throbs. There is dysuria with acrid, scanty, bloody, or *flower-scented* urine. There may be purulent or acrid milky urethral discharge. The prostate is swollen.

Cubeba officinalis—The prostate swells with a feeling of pressure and heaviness in the pelvis. There is a thick, yellow, yellow-green, dark red, or stringy urethral discharge *frequently obstructing* the urethra. Cramping or knife-like pain follows urination. There may be albumin or blood in the urine.

Cyclamen europaeum—The patient complains of pressing, needle-like, or sore prostatic pain while *sitting, walking, or urging to stool.* There is a thick, yellow urethral discharge.

Gelsemium sempervirens—Prostatitis with a gradual onset, initial *low-grade fever*, weakness, and drowsiness is best treated with *Gelsemium sempervirens*. The patient wants to *lie limply* in bed with his head propped high on pillows. He may tremble or feel dizzy when he walks. His thirst is reduced. (See Chapter 8, *Gelsemium sempervirens.*)

Hepar sulphuris calcareum—Regional lymphatic glands *suppurate*. Urine is passed slowly and with difficulty; and drops out perpendicularly. The patient must *wait* to urinate. After urination, the patient feels some urine remains in bladder. There may be passing of blood or pus after urination. The patient is very *chilly;* perspiring; and hypersensitive to pain, touch, noise, odors, and drafts. (See Chapter 9, *Hepar sulphuris calcareum.*)

Iodium—*Iodium* is indicated for acute prostatitis with swelling of the gland. Urination is frequent and copious; urine is dark, yellow-green, and/or milky. A *milky white* fluid runs from the urethra *after passing stool*. The patient is restless and feels uncomfortably *hot* without fever.

Mercurius dulcis—This is one of the medicines for acute prostatitis with swelling of the gland following gonorrhea. There are burning, pressing pains and intense *dysuria*. The patient presents with fever with pallor, night sweats, tearing pains in the extremities, and weakness and trembling.

Nitricum acidum—Acute prostatitis following gonorrhea can be treated with *Nitricum acidum*. The urine has a very strong and offensive odor, like *horse urine* and feels cold on passing. The retention of urine is painless.

Pulsatilla—The patient presents with acute prostatitis with swelling and constrictive, needle-like, and pressing prostatic pain *after* urination. The patient may have the typical symptoms indicative of *Pulsatilla* such as inability to tolerate a closed room, *decreased thirst,* and moodiness. (See Chapter 14, *Pulsatilla*.)

Silicea—*Silicea* can be used to treat *abscess(es)* of the prostate or suppuration of regional lymphatic glands. The prostatitis may have followed gonorrhea. A foul prostatic discharge is aggravated by *straining* during a bowel movement. The patient is chilly and feels better in general from wrapping up.

Staphysagria—The prostatitis-associated pain extends from the *anus to the urethra*, and may follow gonorrhea. There is swelling of the prostate. The patients are generally passive ones with high libido.

Thuja occidentalis—Acute prostatitis with swelling of the gland, follows gonorrhea. There is profuse, *offensive perspiration* on the genitals that may be oily, pungent, sweet, or garlicky. This perspiration *stains* the underwear or sheets yellow. The patient has fever with shaking chills that is aggravated by urination.

Benign Prostatic Hypertrophy

The urinary symptoms are often the most valuable in determining the prescription for benign prostatic hypertrophy. Patients should be treated with the 12C potency of the indicated medicine twice a day for

6 weeks. If symptomatic improvement is noted in that time frame, the medicine can be continued for as long as it helps. If this potency helps for some months, and then the patient relapses, the medicine should be stopped, and a 15C potency of the same medicine should be given once a day for 6 weeks, and longer if it is beneficial.

Baryta carbonica—*Baryta carbonica* is indicated for prostatic hypertrophy in older men who display bashful, *childish* behavior from dementia, or in men who never mastered the adult role and behavior. The patient has chills, nocturia, involuntary *dribbling*, and an indurated prostate.

Calcarea carbonica—*Calcarea carbonica* is most beneficial for responsible, heavy-set, and hard-working men with cold hands and feet, brittle nails, and a desire to eat eggs. The urine dribbles after urination. Perspiration and facial pain accompany nocturia. The patient describes the sensation that urination is incomplete; he must wait before flow starts.

Chimaphila umbellata—This is the primary medicine for *urinary retention* from prostatic hypertrophy; the patient must press a long time before the flow starts. *Chimaphila umbellata* can be given solely on this indication. In extreme cases, the patient is only able to urinate while standing bent forward with his legs apart. On sitting down the patient may feel as if there is a bullet lodged in the perineum.

Conium maculatum—*Stony hardness* of the prostate, with heaviness and needle-like pain can be treated with *Conium maculatum*. There is intermittent flow of urine from prostatic hypertrophy; urine flows better when standing up. There is involuntary dribbling of urine with nocturia. *Conium* affects the sexual sphere; there may be incomplete erections, or involuntary ejaculation while thinking about sex, being near one he is attracted to, or having a bowel movement. Historically, illnesses were thought to arise from adult men and women abstaining from sex for prolonged periods of time (e.g., monastics and widowers). *Conium* was the chief medicine for these illnesses. The patient as a whole is made ill from alcoholic drinks, is very thirsty, and likes salty food. There may be vertigo on turning the head, or profuse perspiration on going to sleep.

Digitalis purpurea—*Digitalis purpurea* is used to treat prostatic hypertrophy in patients with heart disease involving *bradycardia* or tachycardia with slow conduction (Morrison, 1993); congestive heart failure; or angina that extends to the left arm with numbness and weakness in the limb that is aggravated by coition, excitement, or exertion. The patient experiences nightly seminal emission and great weakness of the genitals after intercourse. He describes the sensation that the heart will stop beating; this sensation is aggravated by exertion. There is involuntary dribbling of urine, as well as a slow, weak, and delayed flow.

Ferrum picricum—There is frequent nocturia, and a full, *pressing* feeling in the rectum. The patient describes smarting at the neck of the bladder and penis. The patient retains urine (compare with *Chimaphila umbellata*), and dribbles urine. Symptoms may be accompanied by buzzing in the ears, deafness, or gout.

Iodium—*Iodium* is used to treat involuntary urination in older men with enlarged prostates. They may be *hurried*, nervous, restless, and *hot*. The patient may be hyperthyroid.

Lycopodium clavatum—Urination is retarded; the patient must *wait* for flow to start. There is dribbling in the afternoon at 4:00 p.m., nocturia, and frequent urination during perspiration. Urination is incomplete, intermittent, or involuntary. There are *emissions* of prostatic fluid without erections. The patient desires *sweets* and *warm* drinks.

Sabal serrulata—*Sabal serrulata* is indicated for prostatic hypertrophy with retarded urination and dribbling. The patient must press and *wait* a long time for flow to start. He has nocturia, delayed flow of urine, and heaviness in the perineum. Involuntary urine dribbling is intermittent. Compare with *Lycopodium clavatum*.

Selenium metallicum—*Selenium metallicum* is prescribed for exhausted older men who have a strong sexual desire, but are impotent. There is emission of prostatic fluid without erections. The prostate is indurated. The erections are slow and insufficient. The patient describes the constant sensation at the end of the urethra as if a *drop of urine* were about to come out. The patient may have alopecia with loss of *body hair* and eyebrows. Concurrent conditions include impaired memory, forgetfulness, hepatomegaly, headaches with pain located over the left eye, and/or oily skin with comedones.

Staphysagria—There is frequent urination, and burning in the urethra when *not* urinating. Hemorrhoids may accompany the enlarged prostate. This medicine is usually indicated for passive men with a *high libido*, who frequently masturbate. Urination is dribbling, slow to start, or incomplete.

Thuja occidentalis—*Thuja occidentalis* has the most urinary symptoms of any medicine for prostatic hypertrophy. The patient must wait for urine to start, especially when there are others in the men's room. The strream is *forked* and thin. *Thuja occidentalis* is the main medicine for *involuntary urination in older men* (compare with *Selenium metallicum*, above). The patient has nocturia with incontinence in bed. Urination is frequent during perspiration and involuntary if the desire is resisted. At the end of urination, it feels incomplete. Urine dribbles after urination. The prostate is indurated.

Elevated PSA

Dr. Ramakrishnan of India claims success in reducing elevated prostate-specific antigen by alternating single doses of *Conium maculatum*, 200C and *Sabal serrulata*, 200C every other week. This prescription could easily be studied scientifically.

URINARY TRACT

The following differentials of homeopathic medicines for urinary tract symptoms is inclusive of men, women, and children.

Urinary Lithiasis

The following are medicines for pain from urinary stones. These are reputed to be helpful in palliating the pain, and occasionally help the patient to successfully pass the stone. Urine should be macroscopically examined in a clear container for gross abnormalities of its appearance. In cases with severe pain, the clinician should give the medicine in the 30C potency every 15 min. If the pain has not abated in 1 hr, the clinician should try another medicine. When improvement is noted, the patient can repeat the same medicine as needed when pain recurs. The quality of the pain can be important (see Exhibit 24–1).

Apis mellifica—Stones that become lodged in the ureter because of *swelling* from traumatic inflammation should be treated with *Apis mellifica*. Urine is loaded with casts.

Exhibit 24–1 Quality and Location of Pain in Urinary Lithiasis and the Associated Medicines

> **Bruised**—*Arnica montana*
> **Cramping**—*Dioscorea villosa*
> **Doubling up**—*Colocynthis*
> **Agnozing**—*Ocinum canum*
> **Radiating**—*Berberis vulgaris*
> **Stinging**—*Apis mellifica*
> **Left**—*Hedeoma pulegioides*
> **Right**—*Lithium carbonicum, Lycopodium clavatum,* and *Sarsparilla*
> **Extending down thighs**—*Pariera brava*

Arnica montana—There is hematuria and *bruised* feeling from calculi.

Berberis vulgaris—There is *radiating* renal pain, outward or downward; pain is exacerbated during the urge to urinate. There is burning, soreness, or bubbling in the kidney region. The pain radiates from the ureters to the testes, urethra, or thigh. The urine is turbid, thick, yellow, red, or slimy with mealy or sandy sediment.

Benzoicum acidum—The urine is very strong-smelling, like *horse urine;* it is concentrated and brownish with sediment.

Calcarea carbonica—This medicine is for kidney stones when there are *not* clear and distinct symptoms of another medicine present. Urine may be dark, brown, sour, milky, foul, or strong-smelling, and contain white sediment. There may be hematuria.

Colocynthis—The pain makes the patient *double up.*

Dioscorea villosa—Writhing with cramping pains, the patient is compelled to move around. This cramping pain is aggravated by *bending forward.*

Hedeoma pulegioides—There is burning irritation at the neck of the bladder that causes frequent intense desire to urinate and inability to retain urine for more than a few minutes. It is alleviated by urinating. There is pain along the *left ureter,* and dull, burning pain over the *left kidney.* The patient describes frequent urging and cutting pains. There is dragging pain from the kidney to the bladder.

Lithium carbonicum—The patient presents with urinary lithiasis with soreness of the bladder; there is pain in the *right kidney and ureter.* Scant, dark, turbid, and acrid urine contains mucus and sediment.

Lycopodium clavatum—*Right-sided* kidney stones with red sediment in the urine can be treated with *Lycopodium clavatum*. The patient may have the general characteristics associated with this medicine, such as desire for warm drinks and sweets, flatulence, and symptoms' being aggravated in the late afternoon and early evening.

Ocinum canum—There is *agonizing* pain that causes nausea and vomiting. The patient twists, *screams,* and groans. There is pain in the *ureters*, with cramps in the kidneys, predominately on the *right* side. There is turbid, thick, purulent, and bloody urine with uric acid crystals, and brick dust red or yellow sediment. The urine smells musky.

Pariera brava—The patient strains greatly to urinate with pain extending *down the thighs*. It is said the patient needing this medicine can emit urine only when he kneels, pressing head firmly against the floor. The clinician should not wait to hear that symptom to prescibe this medicine. There may be dribbling after urination.

Sarsaparilla—*Right-sided* renal stones, especially when red and accompanied with *burning and hematuria* are indicative of *Sarsaparilla*. The patients may also have skin symptoms and cracking of the hands and the soles of the feet (compare with *Lycopodium clavatum*).

Urinary Tract Infection

Some clinicians find it surprising that homeopathic clinicians rarely fall back on antibiotics for the urinary tract infection. Because it is a bacterial condition, these nonhomeopaths assume that bacterial infection can only be cured by killing bacteria. Yet, it has been shown in childhood diarrheas that the presence of bacteria is not an obstacle to homeopathic treatment (Jacobs, Jiminez, Gloyd, Gale, & Crothers, 1994).

There are a few common medicines for this condition; each has distinctive symptomatology. If the patient is not at the end of his or her patience with the pain, relief will be felt within a few hours of the first dose of the correct medicine. It is advisable to treat the patient who cannot wait that long with antibiotics and Pyridium. If Pyridium is given concurrently with homeopathic treatment, the main symptom used to evaluate the effectiveness of the medicine (pain) is masked, thereby, making it possible to mistakenly continue the patient on an ineffective medicine.

More detailed data will need to be gathered from the patient than is needed in conventional medicine. The common symptoms of urgency, frequency, and pain are of no help in distinguishing which medicines will be needed for this particular infection. If frequent sex is linked to the onset of urinary symptoms, that should be noted. The quality, exact location, extension, and timing of the pain is very important. For example, there is an important distinction between pain before, at the beginning of, during, at the close of, and after urination. The urine should be examined *macroscopically* as well as microscopically. When blood in the urine is mentioned in a homeopathic context, it refers to gross blood, not microscopic hematuria.

The usual instruction to push fluids should be given, and cranberry juice in tablet or liquid form can be advised. Cranberry juice does not interfere with homeopathy and has been shown to be clinically effective. A 30C potency can be given every 3 hr for three doses. If it is effective, it may be given three times a day until symptoms have resolved completely.

Most Commonly Indicated Medicines

Cantharis—Extremely *painful* frequent or constant *urging* with tenesmus is treated with *Cantharis*. The patient has strangury; the urine is released one drop at a time. There are violent episodes of knife-like or burning pain of the whole urinary tract. There may be involuntary dribbling. The urine is jelly-like and contains shreds or scales of tissue looking like wheat bran in the water, or gross hematuria. The patient may have pyelonephritis; the kidney region is very sensitive.

Pulsatilla—There is cramping or pressure in the bladder *after* urination. The patient has the urge to urinate when supine. The patient may have the usual general symptoms associated with *Pulsatilla* such as crying, desire for consolation, discomfort in stuffy rooms, and decreased thirst. (See Chapter 14, *Pulsatilla*.)

Sarsaparilla—The *close* of urination is so painful that the patient screams. There is jerking along the urethra. Some patients can only pass urine when standing during the day, but at night urine flows freely in bed. It can also dribble while sitting. The patient passes drops of blood or white acrid material at the close of urination. Air passes from bladder during urination. There may be urinary sediment. The pain in the urethra extends back to the abdomen. There may be pus in the urine.

Staphysagria—This is the preeminent medicine for postcoital ("*honeymoon*") cystitis. There is a large study that confirms its routine use for this condition. Ustianowski (1974) found *Staphysagria*, 30C highly effective in a double-blind, placebo-controlled study (*n* = 200), which had poor internal validity (Linde et al., 1997). This study should be replicated with improved methodology. The specific symptoms are frequency, and the urine's passing in a thin stream one drop at a time. There is burning in the urethra when *not* urinating. The patient may have a sensation as if a drop of urine is rolling continuously along the urethra; this symptom is aggravated after jiggling motions such walking or riding a horse, and is alleviated by urinating. Ineffectual urge to urinate is present after *frequent intercourse* or during pregnancy. There is urging after urination, as if the bladder had not emptied.

Less Commonly Indicated Medicines

Belladonna—Bladder pain may be accompanied by *fever, red face*, decreased thirst, and pulsating pains, and be aggravated by being jiggled or *jarred*. There is involuntary urination, on lying down or standing, or when sleepy. There may be frequent and profuse urination and idiopathic hematuria. The patient may have a sensation in the bladder as if a worm were turning inside. (See Chapter 4, *Belladonna*.)

Cannabis sativa—The clinical trials of marijuana as a homeopathic medicine revealed physical symptoms as well as the well-known cognitive and emotional symptoms of the drug. *Cannabis sativa* has specific symptoms that point to its use in urinary tract infection, regardless of the patient's marijuana use, but this symptom complex is most commonly found in marijuana smokers. Patients should be advised to discontinue its use for a period of time and see if that alone alleviates their discomfort. The patient must *strain* to urinate and has to pause before the urine flows. Urine dribbles after flow ceases. Scant urine passes one drop at a time, with *burning* pain extending to the bladder from the *urethra*, especially the meatus, during or at the end of urination. There is pain in the kidney while laughing.

Copaiva officinalis—This is a rarely used medicine for urinary tract infection in men with pulsation in the penis. The urethra feels wide open. The urine is acrid, scant, and bloody, and has a *flowery* odor. There is dysuria and mucous discharge from the bladder.

Mercurius corrosivus—The patient has intense burning and bleeding of the urethra. He or she describes stabbing pain extending up the urethra into the bladder. The urine is hot and passes one drop at a time. Urination is scant, bloody, and frequent. Dribbling is aggravated by sitting. There is bladder urging accompanied by *tenesmus of the rectum*. The patient perspires after urinating. The patient may have pyelonephritis.

Petrosilinum sativum—There is very painful urination causing the patient to shiver and *dance* around the room in agony. The patient experiences a sudden, irresistible urging to urinate with drawing, tingling, crawling, and itching from the perineum throughout the urethra. There is also urinary tract infection with signs of pain and shivering during urination in infants.

Sepia—The patient describes cutting pain in the bladder *before* urination. Urination is feeble and slow. Urine is thick, offensive, white, gritty, bloody, milky, or sticky. It can have red, sandy sediment. Urging is followed by *shuddering* when urination is delayed. The patient in general may be *irritable and apathetic*. This type of urinary tract infection is more common in women who are in menopause, are pregnant, or are lactating. The patient may have a sudden craving for *vinegar,* pickles, or dark chocolate, or an aversion to the fat on meat.

Terebinthina—The patient has urethritis, strangury, and hematuria. Inflamed kidneys and ureters with burning pain may have arisen following any acute disease. The pains alternate between navel and bladder, and are alleviated by walking. The urine is smoky colored with "coffee grounds," or thick, yellow, slimy, and muddy sediment. The urine may have a flowery odor.

Uva ursi—*Uva ursi* is indicated for frequent urging, with severe *spasms* of the bladder and burning and tearing pain. The pain follows the discharge of purulent, mucus-filled, and bloody urine. The patient can have involuntary urination, and reportedly greenish urine. The patient may have pyelonephritis.

CHAPTER 25

Infectious Disease

This chapter will cover infectious diseases that are common in North America, but have not been addressed elsewhere in the text. The medicines common to the inflammatory process will appear repeatedly when treating infectious disease. *Aconitum napellus* and *Belladonna* are both indicated for the sudden beginning of an inflammatory or febrile process. *Hepar sulphuris calcareum* and *Mercurius* are indicated for the stage of pus formation; *Arsenicum album* and *Mercurius* (again) often come in when the patient's defenses have decompensated to some degree, and they are generally ill. *Gelsemium sempervirens* and *Bryonia alba* are commonly used for viral illnesses that come on gradually and send the patient to bed with myalgia and fatigue. It is, therefore, much more efficient to know the key symptoms of each of these medicines, so that they can be recognized no matter where the seat of infection is.

COXSACKIEVIRUS INFECTIONS

Simple coxsackie fever would be expected to respond to the medicines in the discussion of uncomplicated fevers below. Hand, foot, and mouth syndrome is likely to benefit from treatment with one of the medicines that follow. Prescribing can be done according to the general guidelines in Chapter 1, unless the child is in intense distress from painful oral lesions. If this is the case, examination of the oropharynx can be difficult, if not impossible. If the child is screaming angrily, refuses to be examined, or strikes out, and is alleviated only by being carried by the parent, treatment may begin by giving a single dose of *Chamomilla*, 30C or a higher potency. The child can then be left in the exam room with the parent for 10–15 min with toys to play with, while he or she calms. If the child is intensely frightened, *Aconitum napellus* should be given in the same way. Then, the child may be examined properly, which will help with selection of the medicine for the illness itself. Once the appropriate medicine is selected for the illness, the 30C potency should be prescribed every half hour for three doses. There should be increased comfort at that point if the medicine is correct. Parents should obtain the second-choice medicine as well as the prescribed one, if the initial selection of medicine is not very clear. This second choice can be started if the child has not improved after 2 hr on the first medicine. Improvement is measured in increased comfort and calm. After a medicine has been shown to be effective, it can be repeated by the parents as needed for discomfort.

Arsenicum album—The patient presents with ulcers on the tongue, and vesicles on the hands and feet. The tongue is reddened in general, reddened only at the edges, or is bluish white. It is either dry or coated white or yellow. The teeth leave an imprint on the tongue. There is burning pain in the tongue and swelling around the root. Other symptoms include halitosis and bloody saliva. The patient has the usual symptoms of *anxiety*, restlessness, chilliness, and thirst for frequent sips, associated with *Arsenicum album* (see Chapter 3).

Lachesis mutus—There are burning, raw ulcers on the tongue and vesicles on the hands and feet that are worse on the *left* side. These ulcers and vesicles are aggravated by hot food and drink. The tongue is swollen; may *tremble when protruding;* catch on the teeth; and may appear red, dry, and cracked at tip. The patient has thick, difficult speech, and cannot open the mouth wide. He or she has halitosis as well as profuse, thick, and pasty saliva. The patient is sensitive to heat. Emotionally, the patient may be excessively *talkative*, and appears suspicious of the clinician and of the medicines prescribed. The patient is intolerant of being touched on the neck.

Mercurius vivus or Mercurius solubilis—There are ulcers on the tongue, inside the cheek, and vesicles on the hands. The patient has extreme *halitosis*. The gums are painful, ragged, swollen, and bleeding. There is increased salivation, and the patient drools during sleep. Saliva may be yellow, bloody, metallic-tasting, and offensive. The tongue is swollen, spongy, and yellow, and shows *indentations* of teeth. There may be a sensation of needles' pricking the tip. There are ulcers behind the tongue. The patient in general is moist, has an offensive odor, and has a narrow range of comfort with the ambient temperature. (See Chapter 11, *Mercurius vivus or Mercurius solubilis.*)

Herpangina, a Coxsackievirus infection of the throat, causes red-ringed blisters and ulcers on the tonsils and soft palate, the fleshy back portion of the roof of the mouth. *Arsenicum album, Lachesis mutus,* and *Mercurius* (as above) have all been reported to cure such symptoms. In addition, the clinician should consider *Kali bichromicum* if the child has a thick, *stringy,* green, or yellow nasal discharge accompanying the illness, and *Nitricum acidum* if the child's palate is sore, with sharp *splinter-like* pain. There may be a moist, fissured, or mapped tongue and halitosis.

Sulphur—*Sulphur* is indicated for ulcers on the tongue and vesicles on the hands and feet. The oral cavity is very *erythematous.* The patient in general is intolerant of heat, especially in bed. (See Chapter 16, *Sulphur.*)

FEVER OF UNKNOWN ORIGIN, ROSEOLA, FIFTH DISEASE, AND SIMPLE COXSACKIE FEVER

A nondescript fever is regarded as easy to prescribe for in homeopathy, and if treated early, is believed to shorten the illness and prevent sequelae (such as convulsions). Knowing five symptoms of each medicine will allow you to prescribe for most uncomplicated fevers.

Low to moderate fevers (approximately 102.5°F or lower in children, 101°F or lower in adults) may be prescribed the 30C potency every 4–6 hr for three doses, then evaluated and be given as needed for return of symptoms if effective. High fevers generally require frequent repetition of the dose of the appropriate homeopathic medicine. A 30C potency may be given every hour for three doses, evaluated, and then be given as needed for return of symptoms if effective. If a clinician deals with fevers frequently, it would be appropriate to obtain a 200C potency, and a 1M potency of *Belladonna, Ferrum phosphoricum,* and *Aconitum napellus* for the office. (These higher potencies are available through the mail from the manufacturing pharmacy.) If a 200C potency is available, use it only for the higher fevers, every 2 hr for three doses, and then as necessary as above. If the 1M is available, prescribe it every 3 hr for three doses for higher fevers only, and then as necessary as above.

Improvement from the medicine should be seen in the first 2 hr, usually within minutes. The fever may not immediately subside, or may even spike higher briefly, but there is a striking improvement in comfort following the correct medicine. The patient will typically go to sleep and wake up afebrile. There is no need to wake him or her to administer further doses if this occurs; the medicine may be repeated symptomatically if and when the fever and discomfort return.

As might be expected, fevers are not considered to be a bad thing by homeopathic clinicians, but a part of the person's self-healing process. Acetaminophen and sponge baths are rarely if ever recommended in a homeopathic practice, except in patients with seizure disorders or prior febrile seizures. The usual instructions encouraging fluids and rest should be given. If a fever is related to influenza, refer to the section on that illness.

Aconitum napellus—A fever appears suddenly, perhaps after being out in a cold wind. It may spike to high levels quickly. The patient is restless and anxious as though facing death. The patient has increased thirst for water, usually cold.

Belladonna—The patient has sudden fevers that are usually high. The pupils are dilated and the eyes are glistening. The patient may be photophobic. The patient may have a faraway look in the eyes, or be experiencing outright hallucinations. There is pulsating pain (e.g., a throbbing headache). The face is hot and red, and there are bright red exanthems (roseola, fifth disease, and scarlet fever).

Chamomilla—The child is in an ugly, cross mood. The fever may arise during teething. The child screams and cries if not carried. Symptoms are generally aggravated from warmth and at night. The child has one hot and red cheek and one pale and cool cheek.

Ferrum phosphoricum—The patient presents with a moderate fever. The face is red or pale. The infection is nondescript, and has no apparent seat. The patient is thirsty.

HEPATITIS

The body of knowledge of the homeopathic treatment of hepatitis developed long before it was distinguished by type. These medicines are prescribed for acute alcoholic hepatitis and types A and B. Since all of these medicines have been known to cause/cure jaundice and hepatomegaly, these common symptoms are not helpful in distinguishing between them. Dr. Francisco Eizayaga, a senior homeopathic physician from Argentina who is experienced with treating hepatitis A, named the top medicines in treating that illness during his lectures in the United States. These observations are included below (Eizayaga, 1986). The primary medicines for alcoholic hepatitis are *Arsenicum album, Carduus marianus, Lachesis mutus, Nux vomica,* and *Sulphur.*

The clinician should prescribe the 30C potency three times a day for 5 days. If there is no improvement, he or she should select another medicine. The clinician should advise the patient to stop drinking coffee and alcohol. If the patient's subjective symptoms have improved (not necessarily the lab work or hepatomegaly) the medicine should be continued twice a day for 5 more days, and then once a day for 5 days beyond that. There can be a great deal of flexibility in this treatment plan, depending on how quickly the patient is responding. The goal is to avoid creating proving symptoms by continuing a patient on a medicine that is not clearly of benefit.

Most Commonly Indicated Medicines

Chelidonium majus—The patient presents with an enlarged and tender liver with pain referred to *inferior angle of the right scapula*, shooting posteriorly, or shooting in all directions. The epigastric region may be tender as well, and the patient may have the sensation as if there were an animal wriggling there. This medicine should be considered especially for hepatitis with jaundice in pregnancy, infants, and neonates (type A), and jaundice concurrent with pulmonary disease. There is a *bitter taste* in the mouth; the tongue is discolored yellow; teeth leave an imprint on the tongue; and the breath is offensive. There is constriction across the abdomen, like a string. The stools are pasty, pale, bright yellow, clayey, or hard balls. The patient alternates between diarrhea and constipation. This is no urticaria. There is profuse, foaming, and yellow urine that is like beer. It stains the diaper dark yellow. There is ascites with yellow palms. The symptoms are right-sided in general. Slight exertion fatigues the patient. Emotionally, the patient presents as depressed, despairing, guilt-ridden, fearful of going insane, and as crying for no reason. If *Lycopodium clavatum* seems indicated, but fails to alleviate symptoms, *Chelidonium* should be considered. Symptoms are aggravated by motion and being touched; they worsen at 4:00 a.m. and 4:00 p.m. Symptoms are alleviated by hot food, milk, pressure, a hot bath, bending backward, and lying on the abdomen.

Hepar sulphuris calcareum—The patient feels *needle-like* pains in the hepatic region that are aggravated by any sort of jiggling (e.g., from walking, coughing, breathing, or being touched). Stools are soft, but expelled with difficulty. They can be white or clay-colored with a sour odor. The abdomen is distended and tense. There may be a hepatic abscess. The patient may have urticaria. The patient is very *chilly* as a whole, and exceedingly sensitive to cool drafts. Hence, he or she wants to be completely *covered up*. The patient may be touchy, dissatisfied, argumentative, dejected, or normal in affect. Infants and children tend to be cross. *Hepar sulphuris calcareum* is reportedly one of the common medicines for Hepatitis A. Symptoms are aggravated by cold, dry air; drafts, touch; noise, exertion; and lying on the painful liver. They worsen at night. Symptoms are alleviated by wrapping up warmly and moist heat. (See Chapter 9, *Hepar sulphuris calcareum.*)

Mercurius vivus or Mercurius solubilis—The patient presents with an enlarged, sore, and indurated liver with jaundice. He or she is restless and has much offensive *perspiration*. There is generalized *adenitis*. There is a metallic taste in the mouth. A spongy tongue shows the imprint of teeth. The patient is thirsty, becomes too hot or too cold, and may have slimy, green diarrhea or a clay-colored or ashen white stool. On the emotional level, the patient may desire to travel or feel apathetic. The patient may be indifferent about eating, is slow in answering questions, and moans and groans. *Mercurius* is used to treat Hepatitis A of newborns. Symptoms are aggravated by perspiration, lying on right side, heating up, and drafts. They worsen at night. The symptoms are alleviated by moderate temperatures, sexual intercourse, and rest. (See Chapter 11, *Mercurius vivus or Mercurius solubilis.*)

Natrum sulphuricum—The patient has hepatitis with jaundice and possibly vomiting of bile. The liver is sore with sharp, needle-like pains. The patient lies on the *right side* with the legs curled up. Symptoms are aggravated by lying on the left side. Like with *Lycopodium clavatum*, the patient cannot bear tight clothing around the waist. Flatulence and gas in the ascending colon is aggravated before breakfast. There are loose stools in the morning and involuntary stools when passing flatus. The stool is very large in general and often clay-colored. There is bile in the urine. The patient may appear serious and emotional closed, and have an aversion to talking or being spoken to. There may also be depression with a desire to commit suicide, especially with a gun, but the patient resists the impulse because of personal responsibilities. The patient may crave *yogurt* and ice-cold water. Symptoms are aggravated by damp weather and basements, lying on the left side, lifting, touch, pressure, wind, light, subdued light, music, vegetables, fruits, cold food and drinks, and lying too long in one position. They worsen in the late evening. Symptoms are alleviated by warm, dry open air, a change of position, breakfast, and lying in a supine position.

Phosphorus—Reputedly the most commonly prescribed medicine for hepatitis A in newborns, *Phosphorus* is a common medicine for any kind of hepatitis at any age, or during pregnancy. The patient is weak and describes an empty sensation in the abdomen. He or she rubs the abdomen for relief. The patient has exhausting diarrhea. The stools may be clay-colored, granular, slender, fetid, or tough. There is jaundice and large yellow spots on the abdomen. The patient is thirsty for *ice-cold* drinks, and craves chocolate, chocolate ice cream, and spicy food. He or she desires *company*, and has an anxious affect with poor concentration. Symptoms are aggravated by touch, warm food, physical or mental exertion, twilight, or ascending stairs. They are alleviated by darkness; sleep; cold food; cold, open air; and washing with cold water. Historically, *Phosphorus* has been used for acute yellow atrophy from fulminant hepatitis with massive hepatic necrosis. (See Chapter 13, *Phosphorus*.)

Less Commonly Indicated Medicines

Aconitum napellus—The patient presents with hepatitis of *sudden* onset with fever, anxiety, and increased thirst. The stools may be clay-colored. The patient may have urticaria. *Aconitum napellus* is indicated in the first few days of the illness only.

Arsenicum album—The liver is enlarged and painful. The patient is restless, chilly, weak, and *anxious*, and tosses around in bed, or moves from bed to bed. The patient is thirsty for *sips* frequently, especially of warm drinks. The patient may be frightened he or she will *die*; he or she wants company and is demanding of everyone, including the primary care provider. There is an excessive sensitivity to disorder in the environment. The stools may be clay-colored. He or she may be an alcoholic and may have urticaria. Symptoms are aggravated by cold, ice cream, cold food, vegetables, lying on the liver, and exertion. They are worse from 11:00 p.m. to 2:00 a.m. They are alleviated by a hot-water bottle, a heating pad, hot food and drinks, wrapping up warmly, motion, walking around, lying with the head elevated, sitting erect, company, perspiring, and open air. (See Chapter 3, *Arsenicum album*.)

Belladonna—*Belladonna* is indicated during the first few days of hepatitis. The patient has a fever, *red face*, and decreased thirst. Stools may be clay-colored. Pain in the liver is aggravated by *jarring* or jiggling, such as taking a false step. The abdomen is distended and hot. The patient may have urticaria. (See Chapter 4, *Belladonna*.)

Bryonia alba—*Bryonia alba* is indicated for hepatitis with gradual onset and low fever. The patient is irritable and wants to be left *alone*. The liver is heavy, sore, and swollen, and the pain is alleviated by lying on it. The abdominal wall is very tender. The patient has constipation, but the stool is not clay-colored. The patient is jaundiced and may have urticaria. The patient is thirsty for large quantities of liquid at long intervals. He or she feels generally worse from moving. (See Chapter 5, *Bryonia alba*.)

Carduus marianus—The patient presents with a liver that is swollen *laterally*. It is painful when pressed on. There are *needle-like* pains near the spleen, which are aggravated by inspiration and stooping; in the liver, which are aggravated lying on the left side; and in the sides of the chest while coughing. The abdomen is distended and rumbles. The patient passes hard, knotty, and clay-like stools that are difficult to pass. There may be concurrent asthma, but no urticaria.

Dolichos pruriens—The patient presents with generalized, unbearable *itching* of the skin during hepatitis with jaundice, but no rash. Symptoms worsen at night, and are accompanied by great despair, and even suicidal thoughts. Symptoms are alleviated by cold bathing. There is pale, white stool.

Lachesis mutus—Hepatitis, especially the alcoholic type, with a *throbbing* soreness deep in the liver is best treated with *Lachesis mutus*. The patient cannot bear anything (such as belts) around the waist. There may possibly be a hepatic abscess. The patient describes knife-like pain in the right side of the abdomen that causes fainting. The abdomen is hot, sensitive, and painfully stiff. The patient may pass clay-colored stool. The patient present as *talkative*, yet be suspicious. The patient is intolerant of heat, sun, and clothing around the neck. He or she desires sour foods. There is no urticaria.

Lycopodium clavatum—The patient's liver is sensitive and congested with a sensation of something *moving* up and down or rolling there when the patient turns to the right side. The patient describes the sensation of a *band about the waist,* and is intolerant of belts (like with *Lachesis mutus* and *Nux vomica*). *Lycopodium* would not be prescribed unless there were much *flatulence* that passes noisily. The patient may have ascites from liver disease. The stool is not clay-colored. There are brown spots on the abdomen. The patient may have urticaria. Symptoms are alleviated by warm drinks. They worsen 4:00–8:00 p.m.

Magnesia muriatica—The liver is sore and enlarged; the abdomen is bloated. The pain extends from the liver to the *spine or epigastrium.* There is pressure-like pain in the liver that is aggravated by lying on the right side. The tongue is yellow, and the stools are dry, *little balls,* like sheep dung; clayey; gray; or crumble at the anus. The patient does not want to pass stools. There is no urticaria. Symptoms are generally alleviated by hard pressure, lying bent, gentle motion, and cool, open air. *Magnesia muriatica* is more commonly indicated for anxious adult women with a history of uterine disease and indigestion, and has a fearful effect. Symptoms worsen at night, immediately after eating. They are aggravated by salt, milk, touch, and mental exertion. They are alleviated by open air, pressure, and motion.

Nux vomica—The patient presents with jaundice with an enlarged liver that is sore and has sticking pains. The abdominal wall feels bruised and sore. Like with *Lachesis mutus* and *Lycopodium clavatum,* the patient requiring *Nux vomica* has an aversion to the feeling of clothes around the waist. The general symptoms of *Nux vomica* (Chapter 12) point to the use of the medicine in hepatitis, especially alcoholic hepatitis. The patient is *irritable,* hard-driving, exacting, and impatient. He or she craves spicy food, coffee, alcohol, and cigarettes or drugs (especially stimulants). There may be constipation with straining at stool, but stools are not clay-colored. There is no urticaria. The patient is sensitive to noise, odors, and touch. Compare with *Hepar sulphuris calcareum.* Symptoms are aggravated in the early morning, and from cold, open air; drafts; uncovering; overindulgence; disturbed sleep; and belts. They are alleviated by napping, hot drinks, milk, fat, damp air, and a side-lying position.

Podophyllum peltatum—The liver and whole abdominal viscera are sore; they are alleviated by *rubbing.* The patient has hepatitis with profuse, sputtering, and yellow diarrhea, or clay-colored stool. There is no urticaria.

Sulphur—*Sulphur* is used to treat *relapsing* hepatitis or alcoholic hepatitis with jaundice. There are needle-like pains in the hepatic region. The abdomen is sore, very sensitive to pressure, and heavy like a *lump*. The patient desires sweets, salt, and high-fat foods, and becomes easily overheated. He or she uncovers one or both feet in bed at night to cool down. The stool is not clay-colored. The patient has concurrent, *itchy*, cutaneous lesions such as urticaria (compare with *Dolichos pruriens*). The patient may appear to be unconcerned with personal appearance and grooming, and indifferent to the fact that his or her home has become very *disorderly* during the illness. The patient perspires excessively and dozes off and on during the night. Symptoms are aggravated by bathing, becoming overheated, milk, standing, stooping, reaching high, and sweets. They are worse at 11:00 a.m. They are alleviated by open air, motion, perspiring, lying on the right side, walking, and dry heat. (See Chapter 16, *Sulphur*.)

INFLUENZA

Influenza accounts for more work days lost in the United States during the winter than any other acute illness. There is some evidence that homeopathy can shorten the course of the illness.

There have been several published randomized, placebo-controlled studies on homeopathic treatment of influenza (Casanova & Bilan, 1992; Ferley & Zmirou, 1989; Lecoq, 1985; Papp et al., 1998), and three on prevention (Ferley, Zmirou, D'Adhemar, & Balducci, 1987; Heilman, 1992; and Nollevaux, 1994). Four of the studies on treatment evaluated the effectiveness of *Oscillococcinum*, 200C, a propri-etary product of Boiron Laboratories in France. The Casanova study (*n* = 300) evaluated it in terms of how many subjects had fever on the third day. The results favored homeopathy over placebo. Internal validity of this study was evaluated by independent researchers as a 40 on the Jadad scale and a 57 on a more elaborate internal validity scale, both out of a possible 100 (Linde et al., 1997). Ferley et al. (1987) studied *Oscillococcinum*, 200C as well, and enrolled 1,270 subjects in their study, making it the largest scientifically based study in the history of homeopathy. The results were evaluated according to which patients were well after 48 hr; the results favored homeopathy, but not as strongly as in the Casanova study. This study was evaluated independently as having fairly good internal validity (60 on Jadad scale, 79 on the more elaborate scale).

More recently, researchers at the University of Erlangen-Nuremberg in Germany conducted two studies and found that recovery of 188 patients with influenza-like syndromes within 48 hr of treatment was 63% greater in terms of symptoms in the *Oscillococcinum* treatment group than among the control group given a placebo (Papp et al., 1998). Effectiveness was defined as a statistically significant greater decrease in symptoms or a shorter duration of symptoms. After 48 hr the symptoms of the patients in the treatment group were significantly milder ($P = 0.023$) than in the placebo group. The number of patients with no symptoms was significantly higher in the treatment group from the second day onwards (*Oscillococcinum*: 17.4%; placebo: 6.6%) until the end of the patients' recording (day 5 in the evening: *Oscillococcinum*: 73.7%, placebo: 67.7%). The biggest group difference was recorded for the time between the evening of the second day (10.6% more patients with no symptoms) and the morning of the fourth day (10.2% more patients with no symptoms). The researchers concluded that treatment of influenza-like syndromes with *Oscillococcinum* has a positive effect on the decline of symptoms and on the duration of the disease.

Lecoq (1985) used a complex medicine called L52 not sold in the United States in a study of 60 people with influenza (40 on Jadad, 50 on the more elaborate scale). The results, evaluated through a global assessment by the patient, were very favorable over placebo.

In France, *Oscillococcinum* is the top-selling, over-the-counter influenza medicine. The active ingredient—*Anas barbariae hepatis et cordis extractum,* 200C—has duck liver and heart as its base substance. Its effect was discovered in 1919 by Dr. Joseph Roy of France. *Anas barbariae hepatis et cordis extractum,* 200C is inexpensive and sold over the counter at health food stores and many drug stores in North America, under various trade names. A course of treatment consists of three doses of the 200C potency given over 18 hr at the start of the general symptoms of influenza: headache, myalgia, fever, chills, and malaise.

If treatment begins after the influenza has progressed, individualized treatment with homeopathic medicines should be favored over treatment with *Anas barbariae hepatis et cordis extractum* (see Exhibit 25–1). The 30C potency of the indicated medicine may be given three times a day for 24 hr then continued three times a day for 3 more days if effective.

If the illness starts primarily with a high fever, instead of myalgia and fatigue, *Aconitum napellus, Belladonna,* or *Ferrum phosphoricum* should be preferred (refer to the section above entitled "Fever of Unknown Origin, Roseola, Fifth Disease, and Simple Coxsackie Fever").

Exhibit 25-1 Prescribing Clues to the Common Influenza Medicines

> *Anas barbariae hepatitis et cordis extractum*, 200C (Trade names *Oscillococcinum* or Flue Solution)—as labeled, starting at the onset of symptoms
> *Arsenicum album*—Anxiety, restlessness, exactitude, and chills, and wanting sips
> *Bryonia alba*—Irritability, wanting to be alone, gulps, and myalgia aggravated by motion
> *Eupatorium perfoliatum*—Severe aching myalgia, and increased thirst
> *Gelsemium sempervirens*—Weakness, dullness, decreased thirst, and low fever
> *Mercurius*—Perspiring, alternating chills and warmth, thirsty, and metallic taste
> *Phosphorus*—Ice-cold drinks, vomiting, anxiety, desirous of company, well appearance despite high fever
> *Rhus toxicodendron*—Stiffness and myalgia, alleviated warmth, and red triangle at tongue tip

Most Commonly Indicated Medicines

Arsenicum album—The patient is *anxious*, restless, chilly, and thirsty for frequent sips of liquids, which are preferred warm. Symptoms generally aggravated between midnight and 2:00 a.m, especially the fever. Patient desires company, is sensitive to disorder in the environment, and is exacting about his or her needs. (See Chapter 3, *Arsenicum album*.)

Bryonia alba—The patient is *irritable* with low-to-moderate fever and wants to be left alone. He or she is thirsty for large volumes of water at long intervals. There is myalgia that is more painful on motion. The patient wants pressure and possibly cool compresses on the painful part. The patient prefers to lie alone very still in a darkened room, and is annoyed when disturbed. (See Chapter 5, *Bryonia alba*.)

Eupatorium perfoliatum—There is intense *soreness* in the back and possibly the extremities, stiffness, tremendous aching, and pain in the eyeballs. The patient has increased thirst for cold water.

Gelsemium sempervirens—Dizzy, droopy, drowsy, and dull, the patient who benefits from *Gelsemium sempervirens* is the stereotype of a summertime influenza patient. He or she lies *limply* in bed, with the head propped high on pillows, and *trembles* when it is time to rise and weakly shuffle to the bathroom. There may be chills up and down the spine and myalgia. There may be a headache that feels like a *band* around the head. Thirst is decreased. (See Chapter 8, *Gelsemium sempervirens*.)

Mercurius vivus or *Mercurius solubilis*—Offensive-smelling breath, increased salivation, body odor, and perhaps offensive stool accompany the influenza. The patient *perspires* freely and has a metallic taste in his or her mouth. There is adenopathy and increased thirst for water. The patient alternates feeling too chilly or too hot. (See Chapter 11, *Mercurius vivus or Mercurius solubilis*.)

Phosphorus—The patient may look well even though he or she has a high fever. The patient craves *ice-cold drinks*, which may be vomited after a few minutes to an hour, and chocolate ice cream. There is circumscribed redness of the cheeks and possibly epistaxis. The patient lacks concentration, is anxious, desires company, and is easily reassured by those around him or her. (See Chapter 13, *Phosphorus*.)

Rhus toxicodendron—The patient complains of *stiffness* and aching that is aggravated on first motion, then alleviated with continued motion. He or she is physically restless. He or she perspires while covered with bedclothes. There is a red triangle at the tip of the tongue. The patient thirsts for cold water or cold milk. Symptoms are alleviated by *warmth*. Occasionally, an eruption of oral herpes accompanies the influenza. (See Chapter 15, *Rhus toxicodendron*.)

Less Commonly Indicated Medicines

Arnica montana—The patient is weak, sleepy, and stiff. He or she feels *bruised*. The patient complains that the bed is too hard. The face is red and hot; the nose and body are cold. The patient has halitosis and increased thirst. He or she refuses assistance or a visit with a doctor. (See Chapter 2, *Arnica montana*.)

Arsenicum iodatum—The symptoms of the illness fit those requiring *Arsenicum album*, but there is even greater restlessness, and the patient is *warm* instead of chilly.

Baptisia tinctoria—The patient presents with low, long-lasting fever with *delirium* or mental confusion. Like with *Arnica montana*, the patient feels bruised in any position. He or she has halitosis and produces an offensive stool. There is tenderness in the right iliac fossa. The patient is very thirsty, but gags on solid food. There may be a delusion that the parts of the body are scattered over the bed.

Camphora—The patient is extremely *cold* and shivers, but is averse to covering. The patient has fevers with rapid alternation of heat and shaking chills, followed by prostration. The patient is very weak and has a pulsating headache. Symptoms are alleviated by perspiring and drinking cold water.

Nux vomica—The patient is irritable, hurried, *impatient*, chilly, and possibly constipated. (See Chapter 12, *Nux vomica*.)

Pyrogenium—The patient is cold with *chills that begin in the back*. His or her temperature spikes rapidly, with profuse hot perspiration, but perspiring does not cause a fall in temperature. On occasion, the pulse will not rise as expected with the temperature, or there will be tachycardia during the afebrile period. The patient is restless and anxious. The patient may have the delusion of being "crowded" with arms and legs (compare with *Baptisia*). The patient may have a bursting headache and aching through the whole body as if the bed were too hard.

Prevention

Influenzinum, 30C (made from an influenza virus) taken once a week in the influenza season is reputed to *prevent* influenza, and perhaps upper respiratory infections as well. There has been no good study conducted yet to test this hypothesis, but many patients who have been prone to winter illness have reported success with this regimen. Some pharmacies carry both a general *Influenzinum* and one prepared from the viruses anticipated to be active over the coming influenza season, like the annual vaccine. It is not known whether one is more effective than the other.

MONONUCLEOSIS

One of the major claims of homeopathy is that it can address viral illnesses that have no effective treatment in conventional medicine. Yet, the treatment of mononucleosis, cytomegalovirus, and human immunodeficiency virus are not yet well-documented in the homeopathic literature (Messer, 2000). All of the medicines in the differential for pharyngitis, most notably *Mercurius*, can be indicated for mononucleosis when the throat symptoms predominate (Chapter 20, Ear, Nose, and Throat). The clinician should prescribe the 30C potency three times a day for a week, then once a day for a week if it appears to have made a marked improvement in the patient's comfort and energy level. Additional doses may then be taken by the patient on an as-needed basis if the fatigue returns

The acute prescribing approach presented in this book is reputed to be insufficient to complete the cure of some of the more prolonged cases of mononucleosis. Homeopathic specialists follow the acute medicine with a medicine to address the factors that made the patient susceptible to a more prolonged illness from a virus that causes a mild illness in most people. This approach is beyond the scope of this book. When the pharyngitis is not the predominant symptom, the primary care prescribing approach varies depending on whether the patient has mild symptoms, hepatomegaly, or hepatomegaly and splenomegaly.

Mild Mononucleosis

Calcarea carbonica—The patient is weak and chilly, and has *cold hands and feet,* so he or she wears socks to bed. Adenopathy may include mesenteric glands. The patient desires sweets and eggs. His or her head may perspire during sleep. The mononucleosis may have come on during a period of *overwork* with heavy responsibility. The patient experiences some anxiety.

Gelsemium sempervirens—The patient has a low-grade fever during which he or she is thirstless. Other symptoms include headache, dizziness, drowsiness, apathy, mental dullness, and cervical adenitis. (See Chapter 8, *Gelsemium sempervirens.*)

Phosphorus—*Phosphorus* is for the open, sympathetic, and anxious patient who is thirsty for ice cold drinks. The patient desires salty food, spicy food, ice cream, and chocolate. He or she may have *circumscribed redness* of one or both cheeks when febrile. Vomiting or vertigo may accompany the illness. (See Chapter 13, *Phosphorus.*)

Mononucleosis with Hepatomegaly

Calcarea carbonica—Symptoms are as profiled above.

Conium maculatum—The patient has *indurated* adenopathy, which may include the mesenteric glands. The patient is weak and has vertigo and *night sweats,* which may begin as soon as the eyes are closed.

Ferrum metallicum—*Ferrum metallicum* is used to treat weak, *pale*, possibly anemic patients with pale lips, who nonetheless flush easily when excited. They are hypersensitive to *noise*. Symptoms are generally aggravated by eating eggs, and they worsen at night.

Phosphorus—Symptoms are as profiled above.

Silicea—Very *chilly* patients, with cold hands and feet (like with *Calcarea carbonica*) respond well to *Silicea*. There is generalized adenopathy and perspiration on the *neck and subocciput*. The patient is mild-mannered when ill. The patient is constipated; the stool recedes after partially emerging from the anus. The upper part of the body, the head and the neck, perspire profusely. The feet produce an offensive perspiration.

Sulphur—The patient becomes *overheated* easily since the start of the illness; he or she sticks one or both feet out of the covers to cool off. Adenopathy may include the mesenteric glands. He or she is indifferent to the fact that his or her home has become very messy, and has ceased to care much about personal hygiene. There is offensive perspiration. The patient craves sweets, spicy foods, and pizza. He or she stays up late and sleeps late. Symptoms are worse at night in bed and at 11:00 a.m. They are aggravated when standing and bathing. They are alleviated by lying down. (See Chapter 16, *Sulphur*.)

Mononucleosis with Hepatomegaly and Splenomegaly

Ferrum metallicum and *Phosphorus*, as discussed above, can have splenomegaly in addition to hepatomegaly. The following also come into consideration:

Ferrum arsenicium—Fever in thirstless, pale patients with *burning* sensation in the body are best treated with *Ferrum Arsenicicum*. Other symptoms include undigested stool; anemia; and dry skin, eczema, psoriasis, or impetigo.

Muriaticum acidum—This is a major medicine for great physical *prostration*; the patient may or may not be febrile. There is such weakness that she or he *slides down* in the bed. The patient has pharyngitis with a swollen uvula, pharyngeal ulcers, spasms, and choking on swallowing. The throat is edematous, dark, and raw. The tongue is pale, swollen, dry, and leathery; it may have deep ulcers or aphthae. Gums and glands are swollen. The patient has halitosis. These symptoms of the oropharynx resemble those indicative of

Ailanthus glandulosus, with which it should not be confused (Chapter 20, Ear, Nose, and Throat). The patient is irritable and sad. The patient may on the one hand prefer to suffer in silence; on the other hand he or she may prefer to moan loudly. Extremities feel heavy, painful, and weak. There may be a headache (feeling as if the brain were crushed) that accompanies the illness. There may be vertigo aggravated by lying on the left side. The patient has a strong appetite with aversion to meat and constant thirst.

Carbo vegetabilis—*Carbo vegetabilis* is used to treat *weak, cold, and bloated* patients with great flatulence. Although cold, the patient does not want to be covered up. Symptoms are alleviated by passing flatus or sitting in front of a fan. He or she wants to sit up, not lie flat. Apathy or irritability may accompany the illness.

Prolonged Mononucleosis

Cistus canadensis—The patient is *chilly* and sensitive to even slight drafts. The throat is sore, swollen, painful, and dry, and is aggravated by cold air. It is alleviated by drinking liquids or expectorating mucus. There may be lymphadenitis especially when there are chains of enlarged cervical nodes. The patient may crave *cheese.*

Persistent or Recurring Symptoms Following Acute Mononucleosis

Prominent British homeopathic authors (Foubister, 1989; Gibson, 1981) recommend three routine medicines for the treatment of persistent or recurring symptoms from Epstein-Barr virus. First, the clinician should prescribe *Carcinosinum*, 200C every 6 hr for three doses. If not improved in a week, the clinician should give *Ailanthus glandulosus*, 200C according to the same regimen. The clinician can also inquire at the homeopathic manufacturer about the availability of a medicine made from the Epstein-Barr virus, which English pharmaceutical manufacturers call Glandular Fever Nosode. The 200C can be prescribed according to the above regimen (Foubister).

VARICELLA

Some parents choose to confer lifelong natural immunity to the virus by exposing their child to another child with active chickenpox.

The process is sometimes difficult now because of decreasing incidence due to the vaccination. For those who are "successful," there is homeopathic treatment that can make the chickenpox slightly shorter and much more comfortable. The usual measures, such as trimming nails to prevent impetigo, should not be omitted. The initial fever will respond to the common fever medicines for children, such as *Belladonna*. The most commonly indicated medicine thereafter is *Rhus toxicodendron*.

Antimonium crudum—The patient has *sore* eruptions. He or she is irritable on being washed, touched, or observed.

Antimonium tartaricum—When the eruptions emerge slowly and include *large vesicles, Antimonium tartaricum* is indicated. The child may have bronchitis with a rattling cough concurrently.

Arsenicum album—The child has large, *burning* vesicles filled with pus, and is chilly, restless, and anxious. Symptoms are generally worse around midnight. (See Chapter 3, *Arsenicum album*.)

Mercurius vivus or Mercurius solubilis—The child has a sick smell, with clammy *perspiration and halitosis*. The purulent exudate from the vesicles can be profuse. The child is more uncomfortable at *night*. He or she feels too chilly or too warm. There is adenopathy and increased thirst. (See Chapter 11, *Mercurius vivus or Mercurius solubilis*.)

Pulsatilla—The child is *weepy*, clingy, and endearing, and wants company and consolation. He or she is thirstless and feels better with the windows open or outdoors. Symptoms are aggravated in a warm, stuffy room, or from being wrapped up warmly. (See Chapter 14, *Pulsatilla*.)

Rhus toxicodendron—There is intense pruritis that is worse at *night*, from scratching, and when at rest. The child is restless and sleepless. *Rhus toxicodendron* is reputedly the most commonly prescribed medicine for chickenpox. (See Chapter 15, *Rhus toxicodendron*.)

CHAPTER 26

Brain and Nervous System

HEADACHES

Homeopathic treatment is believed to diminish the pain during any kind of headache as well as shorten its duration. An integrative clinician can help the patient to be more comfortable during a headache without the potential for rebound headache or drug dependency. Chronic headaches are reported to respond well to treatment by homeopathic specialists, but the research outcomes have been mixed. Whitmarsh, Coleston-Shields, & Steiner (1997) studied 60 outpatients with migraine with or without aura with a 4-month, randomized, placebo-controlled, double-blind, parallel-groups trial of individualized homeopathic prophylaxis. The first month was baseline with all patients on placebo. Overall, there was no significant benefit over placebo for homeopathic treatment. The subjects in this study had migraine headaches for an average of 20 years. It is possible homeopathy cannot address headaches of such chronicity. On the other hand, it is possible a 3-month treatment period was insufficient to see improvement, given the severity of the illness.

Another randomized, double-blind controlled study of 60 cases of recurrent migraine treated by homeopathy had a different outcome (Brigo & Serpelloni, 1991). Each patient was given a single dose of the 30C potency at four separate times over 2-week intervals. The authors individualized one of the eight following medicines for each patient, with the option of associating any two: *Belladonna, Ignatia amara, Lachesis mutus, Silicea, Gelsemium sempervirens, Cyclamen europaeum, Natrum muriaticum,* and *Sulphur.* The homeopathically treated group had a significant reduction in the periodicity, frequency, and duration of migraines.

Even if not currently experiencing a headache, the patient should be asked to describe the specific quality and location of the pain during the headache, as well as the alleviating and aggravating factors. The clinician should ask whether mental and emotional changes occur during headache (e.g., irritability) or if there are any general changes in the body during an episode (e.g., chilliness), or accompanying symptoms (e.g., constipation). A medicine can be prescribed in the 30C potency once every 15 min or half hour if the symptoms are severe, or every 6 hr if symptoms are very mild. If the medicine is correct, improvement should be noted by the third dose. If improvement is noted, the medicine should be continued three times a day until symptoms are resolved. If no improvement has occurred, the medicine is viewed as an incorrect selection that should be discontinued, and another medicine started.

Ibuprofen, aspirin, and acetaminophen are not generally regarded as contraindicated during homeopathic treatment. It is difficult, however, to evaluate results when they are being used concurrently. The conventional medical treatment for migraine changes rapidly with advances in pharmacology. It has not been established whether migraine medicines interfere with homeopathic treatment.

There are a group of medicines that are broadly used in the treatment of headache, whatever the diagnosis. This is not surprising since many headaches are now regarded to have features of both muscle tension and migraine.

Cluster Headache

Each of the following medicines is useful for headaches that have the common symptoms of cluster headaches: pain in the eye area with painful throbbing in the temple that comes on at night and extends to one side of the head. Rhinorrhea that accompanies headache is also common to all the medicines below. Any of these medicines could treat cluster headaches that are triggered by alcohol consumption. This list covers most, but not all kinds of cluster headaches.

Belladonna—The patient presents with a red face, dilated pupils, and predominantly *right-sided* symptoms. There is lacrimation during the headache. Pain may extend upward from the eye. Affected eyelid may droop, and the conjunctiva may become red. The headache is aggravated from being jiggled and jarred, and from light. The general symptoms of *Belladonna* may be present as well. (See Chapter 4, *Belladonna*.)

Chelidonium majus—*Chelidonium majus* is most commonly indicated when the patient has concurrent liver disease. The pain is over the *right eye, right cheek bone, and right ear;* there is excessive lacrimation especially when trying to focus the eye. The headache extends backwards. The occiput feels very heavy, and icy coldness extends there from the nape of the neck. The cranium feels too small. Sclera have a dirty yellow hue. Soreness in the eyes is aggravated by looking upwards. There may be a dazzling spot before the eyes. The patient may not be able to open the eyes from the pain. Symptoms are aggravated by motion, touch, change of weather, a northeast wind, and looking upwards. They are worse at 4:00 a.m. and 4:00 p.m. Symptoms are alleviated by hot food, eating, dinner, milk, pressure, a hot bath, bending backward, and lying on the abdomen.

Glonoinum—*Glonoinum* treats severe headaches that are accompanied by unusual sensations in the head and a unique kind of cognitive impairment. The sensations include violent pulsating as if blood were rushing upwards into the head, waves of severe *bursting* pounding pain, the feeling as though one were standing on the head, an expanding and contracting feeling, and a sensation as though the skull were too small for the brain. In some patients, there may be a feeling as if blood were surging back and forth in the head, alternating between the temples. The temporal vessels are swollen. The patient holds the head tightly. Clothing seems constrictive. The conjunctiva or lids are red. There is a wild look in the eyes, which appear to be protruding. The face is hot and flushed. The cognitive impairment is such that the person becomes confused about where he or she is and becomes *lost* in well-known localities. Symptoms are aggravated by heat of the sun on the head, hot weather, bright snow, motion, jarring, shaking, extending the neck, eating fruit (especially peaches), weight of a hat, cutting hair, and fright. They are alleviated by open air, elevating the head, and cold compresses.

Lachesis mutus—The patient describes a heavy, bursting sensation in the head; the right side feels "cut off," and there is pressure and burning on the vertex. Waves of pain are worse after motion. The patient does not want the *hair touched.* Other symptoms include visual flickering, dim vision, and very pale face. The eyes feel small as if drawn together by cords that were tied in a knot at the root of the nose, and there may be reddened conjunctiva on the affected side and lacrimation with the pain. The patients who need *Lachesis mutus* may be surprisingly *talkative* considering they have a headache. Symptoms are aggravated by sleep, sun, slight touch or pressure, standing or stopping, motion, and closing the eyes. They are alleviated by open air, hard pressure, cold drinks, eating (especially fruits), and warm compresses.

Spigelia anthelmia—The conjunctiva of the affected side are red with lacrimation from that side during the headache. The pain runs from the left occiput to *over the left eye*. It is aggravated by stooping, making a false step, and opening the mouth. There may be severe pain in and around the eyes extending deep into the sockets. Pains are violent; burning, like hot needles or wires; jerking; tearing; or radiating. The head and eyes feel too large. The patient has difficulty in raising the eyelids with painful sensation of stiffness or involuntary winking. Symptoms are aggravated by touch, motion, tobacco, coition, thinking about pain, stooping, and blowing the nose. They worsen after eating. They are alleviated by lying on the right side with the head high, steady pressure, and eating.

Sulphur—The patient presents with a *hot head*, red face, and cold feet. The pupils are dilated. There is a heaviness, fullness, and pressure in the temples. This beating headache is aggravated by stooping, and is sometimes accompanied by vertigo. There may be a bursting pain in the eyeballs. The eyes tremble, the eyelids quiver. The conjunctiva of the affected side are red with lacrimation during the headache (compare with *Belladonna*). The patient may have the general symptoms indicative of *Sulphur*. The symptoms are aggravated by becoming heated from exercise or from becoming too warm, covers on the bed, talking, stooping, sweets, and looking down. They are alleviated by open air; motion; perspiration; dry, warm weather; lying on right side; walking; and dry heat. (See Chapter 16, *Sulphur*.)

Migraine Headache

As in conventional medicine, migraines respond better to homeopathy when the medicine is given early in the headache, or in the prodromal period when the patient has signs that one is about to begin. Prescribing for this condition is generally not difficult because the symptoms are often distinctive. Vomiting during headache is a common indicative symptom of all of the following medicines except *Chamomilla*. Visual aura can precede or accompany the migraines treated by *Belladonna*, *Cyclamen europaeum*, *Gelsemium sempervirens*, *Iris versicolor*, *Lac defloratum*, *Lachesis mutus*, and *Natrum muriaticum*. Although a medicine may be more likely to be known for treating unilateral headaches on a particular side, most of these medicines could also treat a headache of the contralateral side if the general symptoms are clearly present. There are varying degrees of photophobia in the symptomatology of all these medicines.

In addition to the usual format of homeopathic data gathering, the clinician should anticipate that any factor that *alleviates* the headache is of high importance in arriving at the correct prescription. See Table 26–1 (data from van Zandvoort, 1997). Patients accustomed to taking

Table 26–1 Medicines Indicated for Migraine Headaches and Their Associated Alleviating Factors

	Vomiting alleviates pain	Hard pressure alleviates pain	Cold compresses alleviate pain	Warm compresses alleviate pain	Profuse urination alleviates pain	Darkness alleviates pain	Open air alleviates pain	Closing eyes alleviates pain	Lying down alleviates pain	Wrapping up head alleviates pain	Pain alleviated after eating
Belladonna		✓	✓			✓	✓	✓	✓	✓	
Bryonia alba		✓	✓	✓		✓		✓	✓	✓	
Chamomilla		✓									
Cinchona officinalis		✓		✓				✓	✓	✓	
Cocculus indicus								✓	✓		
Colocynthis				✓			✓				
Coffea cruda							✓	✓			
Gelsemium sempervirens	✓			✓	✓				✓	✓	✓
Ipecacuanha								✓			
Iris versicolor				✓							
Lac defloratum	✓	✓	✓			✓	✓		✓	✓	
Lachesis mutus	✓			✓	✓		✓		✓	✓	
Melilotus officinalis						✓				✓	
Nux vomica							✓	✓	✓	✓	
Sanguinaria canadensis	✓	✓				✓	✓	✓	✓	✓	
Stannum metallicum	✓						✓				

analgesics may have a difficult time identifying anything that improves the pain, while they can usually easily enumerate a long list of aggravating factors. The clinician should press on with open-ended questioning about alleviating factors. If that line of inquiry brings no responses, the clinician should offer the patient a generous laundry list of things that could help head pain. Temporary relief and mild (but definite) alleviation are significant for the homeopathic prescription.

Acute Migraine

The clinician should prescribe the 30C potency every 2 hr for up to three doses, and change the prescription if substantial improvement has not occurred by the third dose. *Belladonna, Ignatia amara*, and *Gelsemium sempervirens*, which are on the recurring migraine list that follows, are equally commonly indicated for acute headaches.

Bryonia alba—The patient has a pressing headache that is aggravated from the slightest *motion*, stooping, or opening the eyes. The patient describes the pain as if the head would burst, thereby forcing the contents out, or as if the head were hit by a hammer from within. The headache often begins in the area of the left eye or forehead, and then becomes seated in the occiput. Other symptoms include vertigo, nausea, faintness on rising, and great thirst for large quantities at long intervals. The patient is *irritable* and wants to be alone. Symptoms are aggravated by motion, motion of the eyes, stooping, coughing, morning, constipation, ironing, and being jarred. They are alleviated by closed eyes and pressure. (See Chapter 5, *Bryonia alba*.)

Chamomilla—The patient presents with a paroxysmal, throbbing, unilateral headache, with a desire to extend the neck. The pain is intolerable, and brings on anger accompanied by demands of instant relief. The distinctive emotional state is usually what guides one to *Chamomilla*. The patient is very *irritable*, snappish, and abrupt. Nothing others do for the patient pleases him or her. The patient is averse to being touched, spoken to, or observed. The patient may state that he or she would rather die than continue in pain. The patient may thrash around with the pains. *Chamomilla* is particularly suited to the headaches of children and women, especially when exhausted or pregnant. *Chamomilla* is often overlooked in adult treatment (and *Nux vomica* incorrectly prescribed) because of its reputation for children's illnesses. This migraine may have followed coffee drinking or intoxication from alcohol or narcotics. Symptoms are aggravated by anger;

night; cold air; damp air; wind; lying in bed; music; warm food; touch, being looked at; and abuse of coffee, narcotics, and alcohol (compare *Nux vomica*). Symptoms worsen in the morning and at 9:00 p.m. They are alleviated by perspiration and cold applications. The pain lessens when the mind is engaged. (See Chapter 6, *Chamomilla*.)

Cinchona officinalis—The patient presents with bursting, throbbing pain in the head with throbbing of the carotids. Needle-like pains extend from temple to temple. The scalp is sore and sensitive to touch or combing the hair. The patient may have a sensation as if the brain were painfully swashing back and forth, thereby causing a bruised pain, which is worst at the temples. The patient is stubborn, irritable, and disobedient with contempt for everything. This migraine may be triggered by a fluid volume deficit following loss of blood, diarrhea, excessive perspiration, or vomiting. The symptoms are aggravated by touch, jarring, noise, cold, winds, open air, eating, fruits, milk, tea, mental exertion, smoking, and sun. They are alleviated by hard pressure and flexing and extending the neck.

Cocculus indicus—There is unilateral headache or pain in the occiput and nape of the neck that is aggravated by *lying* on it and alleviated by extending the head backwards. There may be an "opening-and-shutting" sensation in the head especially at the occiput. The patient may be talkative, witty, and joking, yet very sad, and easily upset. He or she is very anxious about the health of others. The senses are acute. Compare with *Ignatia amara*. This migraine may be caused by loss of sleep, nursing a loved one, mental and physical overstrain, anger, fright, grief, anxiety, and disappointment. Symptoms are aggravated by motion; touch; noise; being jarred; stooping; menses; eating; cold, open air; coffee; traveling; sun; tea; and lying on the back. The symptoms are alleviated by sitting, a side-lying position, or extending the neck.

Coffea cruda—It feels to the patient as if the brain were torn to pieces, shattered or crushed, or as if a nail were driven into the head (like with *Ignatia amara*). The head feels tight or too small. The temples throb, and the eyes burn. *Coffea cruda* is indicated for migraines that follow a surprising event that led to a state of *overstimulation* and hypersensitivity. Usually such a state is created by good news and excessive laughing, but less frequently some individuals respond this way to fright, disappointment in love, overfatigue, and long journeys. The state of coffee stimulation is so familiar, it hardly needs to be described: great activity of mind and body, many ideas, nervous agitation, insomnia, restlessness, and alternation between happiness and sadness. Pain, touch, noise, and odors become intolerable to the patient. Symptoms are aggravated by noise; touch; odors; cold, windy air; overeating; alcohol; and narcotics. They are worse at night. Symptoms are alleviated by lying down, sleep, and warmth.

Colocynthis—The patient describes the sensation as if the head is being encircled with an *iron band* or a clamp that is being screwed up tightly (compare with *Gelsemium sempervirens*). The pain is pinching, knife-like, gnawing, or boring, and is accompanied by nausea and vomiting. Pains are followed by numbness. The roots of hair are painful (compare with *Belladonna* and *Cinchona officinalis*). The head is hot. *Colocynthis* is more commonly used in women when a migraine comes on after a strong feeling of anger with *indignation*. The patient is easily offended by everything (compare with *Ignatia amara*) and impatient. He or she wants to walk around and may scream with pain or be silent. Symptoms are aggravated by lying on the painless side, being in bed, drafts, stooping, lying on the back, and moving the eyelids. They worsen at night. They are alleviated by hard pressure, heat, rest, and gentle motion.

Ipecacuanha—The patient experiences continuous nausea and *vomiting* during the migraine. The pain in the occiput is as if the occiput were bruised or crushed and extends to the root of the tongue. There is cold sweat on the forehead and nausea from looking at moving objects. This migraine comes from physical injuries or disguised annoyance at not getting one's way. Other etiologies include adverse reactions to quinine, opiates, indigestible food, or loss of blood. Symptoms are aggravated by warmth, damp room, overeating, ice-cold desserts, pork, veal, mixed or rich foods, candy, fruit, raisins, salads, lemon peel, berries, vomiting, motion, and lying down. They are alleviated by open air, rest, pressure, closing eyes, and cold drinks.

Iris versicolor—*Iris versicolor* is the leading medicine for treating vomiting during migraine (compare with *Bryonia alba, Ipecacuanha, Lac defloratum,* and *Sanguinaria canadensis*). The migraine begins with a *blur* in the visual field, often after relaxing from a mental strain. The pain then comes in the frontal region and is accompanied by nausea. The scalp feels constricted, and the right temple is especially affected. Symptoms are aggravated by rest and worse during the evening and at night. Symptoms are alleviated by continuous motion.

Lac defloratum—This migraine may be triggered by anemia or by dairy intake by a lactose-intolerant patient. The patient experiences a *blindness* followed by a throbbing frontal headache, with copius pale urination. There is the sensation as if the eyes were full of little stones. The migraine *ceases at sunset*. The patient is exhausted. Emotionally, the patient may feel despondent, does not care about living, and has no fear of death. The patient believes that death is approaching. He or she is severely photophobic; even candle light is unbearable. Symptoms are aggravated by noise, light, motion, menses, cold, drafts, being wet, hands in cold water, and loss of sleep. They are alleviated by rest, conversation, and bandaging the head.

Melilotus officinalis—Rushes of blood to the head result in a sensation of *fullness* with violent throbbing. Debility accompanies the headache. The patient wants to run away and hide. These are migraines of people in the *mania* stage of bipolar disorder, or of patients with paranoia, with delusions that everyone is looking them, and who may whisper out of fear of talking loudly. The patient fears danger and being arrested. He or she may have suicidal urges and make homicidal threats. Symptoms are aggravated by walking and changeable, stormy, and rainy weather. Symptoms are alleviated by profuse urination epistaxis, menstruation, or from the application of vinegar to the head.

Nux vomica—Vertigo may accompany the migraine, but mood and etiology are the prime indicators that *Nux vomica* should be prescribed for a headache. The patient is made angry and *impatient* by the pain (compare with *Chamomilla, Cinchona officinalis, Colocynthis,* and *Bryonia alba*). This migraine resembles the headache of a "hangover," with hypersensitivity to noise, odors, and light; it is accompanied by nausea. In fact, the medicine is useful for those who have abused alcohol, drugs, caffeine, and/or cigarettes, or are overworked because of a deadline. The brain feels bruised; the head seems larger than the body. The migraine may be a frontal headache; the patient looks for release by pressing on his or her head. The patient may also be constipated (with urging). The symptoms are aggravated by sunshine, excitement, digestive troubles, shaking the head, cold air, footsteps, and wind. They are alleviated by wrapping the head. The pain feels better while in bed in the evening. (See Chapter 12, *Nux vomica*.)

Sanguinaria canadensis—The pain is over the *right eye*; it begins in the occiput and radiates to the right eye. The hemicrania is right-sided, and the intensity increases and decreases with the sun. The veins in the temples are distended. The pain in the occiput is like a flash of lightning. The mood is a grumbling kind of morose irritability. Symptoms are aggravated by fasting, odors, light, sweets, motion, looking up, touch, and raising the arms. They are worse at night, especially at 3:00 a.m. Symptoms are alleviated by sleep, vomiting, being supine, lying on the left side, cool air, and copious urination.

Spigelia anthelmia—*Spigelia anthelmia* is indicated for sharp headaches with pain above or through the left eye; pain may have radiated from the occiput. Symptoms are aggravated by walking in open air, touch, motion, jarring, staring, stooping, noise, smoke, and opening the mouth. They are worse in the morning. They are alleviated by closing the eyes, cold compresses, and pressure.

Stannum metallicum—The distinguishing characteristic of this headache is that the *pains increase gradually, and then gradually subside.* There is severe constrictive pain in the forehead and temples, a sensation of pressure, or violent pains like the head is being beaten. Cooking odors cause nausea and vomiting. The patient is anxious and depressed and may cry. This migraine is caused by emotions, especially fright. The symptoms are aggravated by cold, lying on the right side, gentle motion, warm drinks, during stool, going up or down stairs, touch, and jarring. They are worst at 10:00 a.m. The symptoms are alleviated by vomiting (compare with *Sanguinaria canadensis*).

Recurring Migraines

The word *recurring* is here used to designate patients that have had multiple migraine headaches, which began less that 2 years previously. Some difficult cases of chronic headache over many years may benefit from long-term treatment by a homeopathic specialist, but this has not been substantiated by research (Whitmarsh, Coleston-Shields, & Steiner, 1997).

If the patient has a headache during the office visit, and has the typical characteristics of one of the medicines that follow, the 30C potency can be given in the office and continued twice a week for 6 weeks, and then evaluated for effectiveness as a prophylactic. The migraines will gradually decrease in frequency and severity if the medicine is correct. There are many other medicines that may be indicated in the treatment of chronic migraine, but since the Brigo and Serpelloni (1991) study had a positive outcome it seems likely that most of the medicines called for fall in the following group. Patients who do not fit these descriptions should be referred to a homeopathic specialist.

Belladonna—These are *pulsating* head pains, often on the *right* side. The face is red and the pupils are dilated. Pain is aggravated from being jarred and from light. The patient is thirstless. (See Chapter 4, *Belladonna*.)

Cyclamen europaeum—The patient's head aches in the morning with flickering of various colors in the visual field, or with vertigo. The headaches are unilateral. Head pain may be aggravated in the open air, on stooping, in the morning, or from missing a menstrual period. More commonly indicated for weak, anemic women who have a serious affect and cry easily.

Gelsemium sempervirens—*Gelsemium*-indicated migraines are distinguished by the general symptoms of *fatigue, heaviness, and weakness*. The patient wants to lie down quietly, half reclined. Dizziness and cognitive dullness may accompany the headache. There is often a sensation as though there is a *band around the head*, or as though a tight cap is on the head. The patient may have pain in the temples extending into the ear, wing of nose, and chin. The scalp is sore. The patient describes the sensation of blood rushing from the occiput to the forehead. His or her head is hot, but the extremities are cold, like when *Belladonna* is indicated. The eyelids are heavy and drooping. A visual aura precedes the migraine. It may be blurring, dimness, diplopia when looking sideways, complete loss of vision, or an illusion of gauze in the visual field. Eye pains extend to the occiput. The migraine may start routinely at 2:00 or 3:00 a.m., or after a fright, or as a result of depression, an angry episode, or an unpleasant surprise. Symptoms are aggravated by motion, heat of the sun, summer, and tobacco use. They are alleviated by profuse urination, alcoholic drinks, mental efforts, bending forward, continued motion, or reclining with the head elevated. The patient feels better in the afternoon. (See Chapter 8, *Gelsemium sempervirens*.)

Ignatia amara—The patient presents with a migraine that appeared after a loss. The patient has difficulty expressing grief and develops somatic symptoms. He or she is easily offended and indignant. The patient describes the sensation of a nail being driven into the head. The patient may also have the sensation of a lump in the throat. Cigarette smoke offends the person or aggravates the headache. Symptoms are aggravated by fright, grief, stooping, morning, cold wind, touch, light, looking up, staring, mental exertion, odors, talking, and smoking. The symptoms are alleviated by closing the eyes, pressure, and profuse urination. (See Chapter 10, *Ignatia amara*.)

Lachesis mutus—*Lachesis mutus* is useful in migraine as well as cluster headache. The headache comes on *during sleep*, with pain through the head on waking. This medicine is used to treat premenstrual migraines that resolve when the *menses begin*. The head feels heavy, with waves of bursting pain that extend down to the root of the nose; the right side feels cut off. The pain extends from head to neck and shoulders. There is weight, pressure, or burning of the vertex. The headaches may be brought on by the sun. Other symptoms include flickering or dim vision, pale face, numbness, and crawling (left). The patient does not want his or her hair touched. Lacrimation results from pain. The patient may be talkative. Symptoms are aggravated by sleep, heat of sun, alcohol, hot drinks, motion, closing the eyes, light, and touch. They are alleviated by open air, cold drinks, hard pressure, eating, warm applications, and menstruation.

Natrum muriaticum—*Natrum muriaticum* is used to treat headaches from grief or from head injury in any kind of person, but especially schoolgirls (e.g., parents divorcing or battling). The headache may be felt in any location, but more often on the right side with partial numbness or disturbed vision (e.g., blurred vision, wavering vision, hemiopia, sparks, black spots, and/or fiery zigzags). Bursting (on coughing), hammering, or a heavy sensation is felt in the head. *Natrum muriaticum* is generally viewed as a prophylactic medicine, rather than one that will swiftly resolve an acute headache. It works best for reserved patients who are averse to being consoled, like to be alone, are thirsty, and have a desire for or aversion to salt. *Bryonia alba* may be the medicine for the acute headache for these same patients. Once the acute headache subsides, *Natrum muriaticum*, 30C can be started twice a week as a preventive medicine. Symptoms are worse at 10:00 a.m.; from 10:00 a.m. to 3:00 p.m.; on awakening; from sunrise to sunset; and/or during, before, or after menses. They are aggravated by motion (even of eyes), frowning, reading, light, sun, and noise. The symptoms are alleviated by sleep; pressure on the eyes; lying with the head high; sitting still; lying in a dark, quiet room; perspiration; and a cold compress.

Sanguinaria canadensis—The pain is over the *right eye*; it may begin in the occiput and radiate to the right eye. The hemicrania is right-sided, and increases and decreases with the sun. The veins in the temples are distended. The pain in the occiput is like a flash of lightning. The patient's mood is a grumbling kind of morose irritability. Symptoms are aggravated by fasting, odors, light, sweets, motion, looking up, touch, and raising the arms. They are worse at night, especially at 3:00 a.m. They are alleviated by sleep, vomiting, being supine, lying on the left side, cool air, and copious urination.

Silicea—*Silicea* is indicated for headache that arises from fasting or skipping meals. The pain begins at the occiput; spreads over head; and settles over the eyes, forehead, or the right side of the head. The pain is alleviated by pressure. There may be throbbing pain at the vertex. Chronic headaches having these characteristics may have begun after a serious illness, and then returned at regular intervals. Symptoms are aggravated by cold and drafts, mental exertion, menses, and uncovering the head. They are alleviated by lying with eyes closed, being in the dark, warming or wrapping up the head, and pressure.

Sulphur—*Sulphur* is used to treat migraines that occur on the weekend or at other regular intervals in people with the general characteristics indicative of *Sulphur*. This medicine can treat headaches with various qualities and locations of pain. Especially characteristic are burning pain of the vertex, a band-about-the-head sensation (like *Gelsemium sempervirens* and *Colocynthis*), a beating feeling, heaviness and fullness, and pressure in the temples. Vertigo may accompany the headache. Symptoms are aggravated by winter, the weekend, stooping, and odors. They are alleviated by cold compresses. (See Chapter 16, *Sulphur*.)

Tension Headache

The local symptoms of muscle tension headache are less distinctive than migraine; therefore the prescription is even more strongly based on the general symptoms of the person as well as the emotional state that accompanies the pain. *Arsenicum album, Belladonna, Bryonia alba, Ignatia amara*, and *Nux vomica* treat most tension headaches (see Part II). *Sanguinaria canadensis* is usually the prescription for right-sided headaches that do not have the pulsating pain associated with *Belladonna*, or the irritability and striking aggravation from motion indicative of *Bryonia alba*. *Spigelia anthelmia*, likewise, is the indicated medicine for sharp pains in or around the left eye and frontal region in a patient who lacks the general symptoms of another medicine.

NERVOUS SYSTEM

Bell's Palsy

Although there has been no research on homeopathic treatment of this condition, there are three medicines mentioned frequently in the literature for it. The 30C potency of the indicated medicine may be prescribed twice a day for 5 days, less if the paralysis resolves more quickly.

Aconitum napellus—*Sudden* facial paralysis with tingling and numbness from being out in a cold wind is best treated with *Aconitum napellus*. The paralysis is usually left-sided and often accompanied by great fear and restlessness.

Cadmium sulphuratum—The patient presents with facial paralysis, more often *left*-sided, caused from being exposed to cold or wind. It often involves the mouth and causes some dysphasia.

Causticum—*Causticum* is the medicine mentioned most frequently in the homeopathic literature for Bell's palsy. The paralysis is on the *right* side from exposure to cold, cold wind, or after getting wet.

Herpes Zoster

Homeopathy is reputed to bring relief to the immense suffering of herpes zoster patients, especially from the pain of postherpetic neuralgia. There is no research to support or refute this.

Data collection should follow the usual homeopathic lines. The physical exam is very important because the location and characteristics of the eruptions can be important in homeopathic prescribing. If the pain is moderate, treatment should begin with a 30C potency administered three times a day for 5 days. The patient may return to the office at this time. If improvement is noted, a patient may control the frequency of repetition of the medicine, taking a dose when pain recurs, and ceasing when the neuralgia has completely resolved. If no improvement is noted, another medicine should be selected. If the medicine palliates the pain but does not cure it, treatment by a homeopathic specialist for the underlying immunocompromised state may be indicated.

For patients with severe pain, five pellets of the medicine should be dissolved in warm water. (The pellets do not need to completely dissolve.) The patient should sip this solution every 15 min for 2 hr, then reduce the frequency to every 2 hr. After 6 hr, the patient should be evaluated. If even slight improvement is seen, a patient may control the frequency of repetition of the medicine, as above until the neuralgia has completely resolved. If no improvement is noted, another medicine should be selected.

Immunocompromised patients may respond more slowly. Patients receiving chemotherapy, antiretrovirals, and radiation treatment may not respond to homeopathic treatment. On the other hand, no reports of adverse reactions to concurrent treatment with these medicines have been reported in the homeopathic literature.

Herpes Zoster on the Abdomen

Arsenicum album—Itching, *burning* eruptions that are aggravated by cold and scratching, and alleviated by warmth are best treated with *Arsenicum album*. The neuralgic pains are outlined in the section entitled, "Neuralgia in General." The vesicles or bullae can break open and become ulcers with an offensive discharge, or become gangrenous. (See Chapter 3, *Arsenicum album*.)

Graphites—The rash begins with *vesicles* that may itch. There are moist, crusty eruptions and ulcers with thin, yellow, and adhesive-like exudate that are accompanied by swelling and induration of glands. Symptoms are aggravated by warmth, and worse at night. A cognitive *dullness* and general chilliness often accompany the rash.

Iris versicolor—*Nausea* and even bitter and sour vomiting accompany the pain. Herpes zoster eruptions are found on the right side of the abdomen. There are violent supraorbital pains.

Mercurius vivus or Mercurius solubilis—The patient presents with *moist,* crusty eruptions. Ulcers are irregular, spreading, and shallow. *Mercurius* is one of the few medicines for hemorrhagic eruptions (compare with *Lachesis mutus*). The patient itches at night in bed, and has glandular swelling. He or she may have the general symptoms indicative of *Mercurius,* such as sensitivity to ambient temperature, foul *perspiration* and breath, and thirstiness. (See Chapter 11, *Mercurius vivus or Mercurius solubilis*.)

Rhus toxicodendron—The eruptions resemble contact dermatitis from the *Rhus toxicodendron* botanical genus; there is pruritis from vesicular eruption. The vesicles contain *yellow* exudate. The person has the general symptoms outlined in Chapter 15: restlessness, achiness, stiffness, aggravation from first motion, and alleviation from continued motion. The patient thirsts for cold milk. The tip of tongue is red.

Sulphur—The eruptions itch severely then *burn* when scratched. The eruptive phase lingers; lesions are slow to heal. Symptoms are aggravated at *night in bed*, from bathing, and from exposure to air. The person has the general symptoms of *Sulphur*. (See Chapter 16, *Sulphur*.)

Thuja occidentalis—The eruptions itch or burn violently, and are aggravated by cold bathing. The ulcers are flat, with *bluish* bottoms. The discomfort is alleviated by rubbing and scratching.

Herpes Zoster on the Back

Arsenicum album, Mercurius, and *Rhus toxicodendron* are also indicated in this region.

Cistus canadensis—The patient has the general symptoms of extreme *chilliness*, glandular enlargement and induration, and desire for cheese.

Lachesis mutus—The eruptions are *purple or black*, and may progress to gangrene. It is more likely a left-sided dermatome. The patient is generally physically warm and very talkative—jumping from one subject to another. He or she may be suspicious and fear the medicine is toxic. The pains are aggravated by sleep and heat, and alleviated by hard pressure and bathing the affected part. They are worse in the morning.

Herpes Zoster on the Chest

Graphites, Lachesis mutus, Mercurius, and *Rhus toxicodendron,* as profiled above, may also be needed for shingles on the chest. In addition, the following medicines may be indicated.

Mezereum—*Mezereum* is used to treat an *intercostal* neuralgia that is aggravated by touch or motion and the heat of bed. It improves from exposure to radiated heat. There are violent, burning, and darting pains in the muscles. The pains are sudden and followed by chilliness, numbness, and soreness, and possibly a sensation of a cool breeze blowing on the part. The patient is excessively sensitive to air, even a fan. The patient may identify this pain as being in the nerves, on the skin, in the muscles, or in the bones. There is violent itching. There are two kinds of eruptions: (1) itching, *burning vesicles* that contain a thick white to yellow liquid, and (2) thick, hard, and whitish crusts, which when detached, release a white or yellowish, acrid, and gluey exudate from an underlying ulcer. These ulcers can be deep or small, hard, and painful. The patient feels apprehension in the stomach and is argumentative.

Ranunculus bulbosus—The patient presents with bluish vesicles that contain a *bloody* liquid. This is an *intercostal* neuralgia that is usually left-sided. The rash is burning and intensely itching, and aggravated by touch. There are flat burning and *stinging ulcers*. The neuralgia is *paroxysmal,* severe, sharp, knife-like, or needle-like. The patient weeps from the pain and cannot rest in any position. This medicine is more commonly indicated in alcoholics and argumentative, depressed patients. The symptoms are aggravated by change of position, alcohol, motion of arms, breathing, and touch. They are alleviated by standing or sitting bent forward.

Ranunculus sceleratus—When this medicine is indicated, the eruptions are more *acrid and irritating* than those needing treatment with *Ranunculus bulbosus*. The vesicles are yellow, and the *bullae* have acrid contents. The neuralgia consists of raw, burning, smarting, gnawing, or boring pains. The pains cause fainting or shortness of breath. The patient feels sore all over. There are *needle-like* pains in the chest muscles; the chest and sternum are sensitive to touch. The patient may describe the sensation of a plug's being forced between the ribs, which is aggravated by deep breathing. There is some burning behind the sternum. Pain is aggravated by motion, deep breathing, and touch, and is worse in the evening. The pains are alleviated after midnight.

Trigeminal and Ciliary Herpes Zoster

Most of the medicines for ciliary and trigeminal herpes zoster are profiled elsewhere in this section. *Agaricus muscarius, Arsenicum album, Cinchona officinalis, Mezereum, Phosphorus, Prunus spinosa*, and *Spigelia anthelmia* are described later under "Neuralgia in General." *Graphites, Iris versicolor, Rhus toxicodendron*, and *Sulphur* are discussed under sections that discuss other regions of the body. The following medicines may also be used in facial neuralgias from shingles.

Causticum—*Right-sided* facial neuralgia aggravated by cold wind is best treated with *Causticum*. There is a sensation of burning as if the skin were raw. Pain is aggravated by dry, cold air and is worse about 3:00 a.m. It is alleviated by rainy, humid, and hot weather. (Compare with *Arsenicum album* and *Magnesia phosphorica*.)

Plantago major—There is neuralgia of the *ears*, teeth, and face. The pains are sharp and shifting; they extend between the ears and teeth. They are worse at night and in a warm room. They are alleviated by sleep and eating. Periodical prosopalgia is worse from 7:00 a.m. to 2:00 p.m. Other symptoms include *lacrimation*, photophobia, and pain radiating to temples and lower jaw. The skin itches and burns.

Miscellaneous Medicines for Any Area of the Body

Apis mellifica—The eruptions are *puffy and red* with stinging pains. The pain, which is worse on the right side, is aggravated from warm compresses, and touch. Cool compresses alleviate the pain.

Cantharis—There are *burning* and itching vesicles. The patient is restless. The affected area appears burnt.

Rhus venenata—There are *numerous* small, severely itching vesicles; the discomfort is relieved by contact with hot water. The person suffers from a gloomy depression with no desire to live.

Postherpetic Neuralgia

The pain may respond to one of the medicines under "Neuralgia in General," *Causticum*, or to one of the medicines that follow. If a definite good fit cannot not be found, the patient may require treatment by a homeopathic specialist.

Dolichos pruriens—The patient suffers from intense itching, usually on the right side, long *after eruptions* have resolved. The eruptions are worse at night and are aggravated by scratching.

Variolinum—*Variolinum* is indicated for *long-lasting* neuralgia following herpes zoster, with no distinctive characteristics to lead the clinician to prescribe another medicine.

Neuralgia in General

The 30C potency of the indicated medicine may be prescribed twice a day for 5 days, less if the pain resolves more quickly.

Agaricus muscarius—Facial neuralgia with severe stabbing pains and *tics* is treated with *Agaricus muscarius*. Pains are exacerbated by the lightest touch. There is always some twitching of the muscles, followed by a sensation of *coldness and stiffness* of the area.

Arsenicum album—There are *burning* pains along the course of a nerve that are aggravated by cold, and are worse at night. They are alleviated by warmth. The left supraorbital area and the right sciatic nerve are most often affected. The patient may exhibit the characteristic *chilliness, restlessness, and anxiety* of Arsenicum album. (See Chapter 3, *Arsenicum album*.)

Bryonia alba—The patient has neuralgia of the *right ulnar nerve*. The pain begins above the elbow (with a sensitive spot exterior to the olecranon) and extends to the shoulder joint. As with all conditions requiring *Bryonia alba*, it is aggravated by *motion*. (See Chapter 5, *Bryonia alba*.)

Chamomilla—*Chamomilla* is used to treat neuralgias and hypersensitivity in patients *withdrawing* from narcotics, cocaine, or coffee. These patients are demanding, angry, and irritable, and the pain seems unendurable. (See Chapter 6, *Chamomilla*.)

Cinchona officinalis—The infraorbital pain and pain generated by the superior maxillary branches of the *fifth cranial nerve* are aggravated by the slightest touch or breeze. The pain is alleviated by firm *pressure*. This neuralgia may have arisen during a fluid volume deficit or electrolyte imbalance.

Hypericum perforatum—This medicine is especially useful for treating *shooting* pain as well as tingling, burning, and numbness following nerve injury from accidents or surgery. The pains shoot *proximally* along the nerve. This medicine is also good for shooting pains that travel up or down the sides of the trunk with crawling and numbness, and pains of the head, chest, epigastric area, thoracic spine, and finger tips. Neuralgic pain of the sacrum and hips with severe headache following forceps delivery is best treated with this medicine. *Hypericum perforatum* is also indicated for coccydynia with pain radiating up the spine and down the limbs, especially after a fall on the coccyx. Aching in the sciatic nerve after prolonged sitting can also be treated with this medicine.

Kalmia latifolia—*Kalmia latifolia* is indicated for *right-sided* neuralgias, with tingling, numbness and trembling or paralytic weakness. The pains shift rapidly and shoot outward along the nerves. They are accompanied by nausea and bradycardia. The patient describes an aching, bruised, and stiff feeling. This medicine is also suited for neuralgia after the disappearance of herpetic eruptions. The pains shoot from the nape to the vertex and the face. There is *supraorbital* pain (especially on the right). There are pains over a large part of an extremity. Other symptoms include weakness, *numbness*, pricking, and a sense of coldness in the extremities. The left arm may tingle and be numb. The pain travels from the neck down the arm (*brachialgia*). There may be pains along the ulnar nerve into the third or fourth finger. Pain is aggravated by motion, lying on the left side, bending forward, becoming cold, and the sun. It is alleviated by eating, cloudy weather, continued motion, and a recumbent position.

Magnesia phosphorica—Most neuralgias (often right-sided) that are markedly alleviated from *warmth* (e.g., a heating pad) and aggravated by cold in any form, respond to *Magnesia phosphorica* (compare with *Arsenicum album*). The pain is sharp, shooting, lightning-like, radiating, boring, and constricting. It may suddenly change places. The patient cries out from pain, is restless and weak, and twitches. There may be supraorbital pains. The toothache is alleviated by *heat and hot liquids*. There may be painful contraction of the temporomandibular joint with backward jerking that is alleviated by *warm compresses*. The patient is thirsty for very cold drinks, despite the general improvement from warmth. Symptoms are aggravated by cold air, cold food, cold water, drafts, uncovering, water, lying on the right side, touch, milk, and exhaustion. Symptoms are worse at night. They are alleviated by warmth, pressure, and rubbing.

Mezereum—*Mezereum* is used to treat ciliary neuralgia or prosopalgia with *numbness* following herpes of the lips, eye surgery, or dental cavities. The patient's cheek muscles may twitch. The symptoms are aggravated from motion or touch, and are worse at night.

Phosphorus—The patient presents with *prosopalgia* with burning, tearing, and drawing pains that are aggravated by *motion* of the facial muscles. Vertigo may accompany the attacks. (See Chapter 13, *Phosphorus*.)

Prunus spinosa—The skull feels as if it were being pressed apart. There is a lightning-like, shooting sensation from the right frontal region or eyeball through the brain to the occiput. There is *ciliary neuralgia* with pain in the right eyeball, and a sensation as if the *eyeball would burst*. The left eye, too, may feel as though it might burst; this sensation is alleviated by lacrimation.

Spigelia anthelmia—Neuralgia in the vicinity of the *left eye* and left brachial plexus that is aggravated by motion is best treated with this medicine. Discomfort may be alleviated by constant pressure.

Verbascum thapsus—*Verbascum thapsus* is indicated for neuralgia affecting the zygoma, the inferior maxillary branch of the *fifth cranial nerves*, temporomaxillary joint, and the ear, particularly on the *left* side. The patient describes the sensation as if the area were being crushed with tongs. There are pains like flashes, often occurring at the same hour in the morning and the afternoon each day. The pain is aggravated by a change of temperature, talking, the least movement, sneezing, and biting hard (inferior dental nerve). The pain is worse from 9:00 a.m. to 4:00 p.m.

CHAPTER 27

Gynecology and Primary Care for Pregnancy and Childbirth

Well-woman care in pregnancy and childbirth is a vast topic that has been thoroughly addressed by other homeopathic authors and lecturers (Castro, 1992; Moscowitz, 1992; Perko, 1997; Zaren, 1985). Nausea and vomiting during pregnancy as well as mastitis bring many women to homeopathy because they are concerned about the effects that medicines might have on their babies. General gynecology has been less frequently addressed by modern authors. One reason for this is that common conditions such as uterine myoma, ovarian cysts, infertility, premenstrual syndrome, and chronically irregular menses are complex health issues that require more in-depth training in homeopathy, and cannot be adequately addressed by simple clinical differentials between medicines.

VULVOVAGINITIS

Many fewer women present with acute vaginitis to their primary care providers than used to before over-the-counter yeast medicines were available. To the homeopath, frequent candidal yeast infections represent an underlying imbalance in the person (usually more subtle than diabetes and AIDS). Some women with chronic vaginitis have nutritional issues, psychosexual issues, or generally depressed immunity. Patient education about reducing or eliminating concentrated sugars from the diet, increasing protein, wearing cotton underwear, cooking underwear (after it has been washed and dried) in the microwave oven to ensure they are completely yeast-free, and practicing proper personal hygiene practices, should be conducted.

Most patients with candida will want a topical treatment as well as an orally administered medicine. A tampon coated in plain unscented aloe vera gel, sprinkled with some *Acidophilus* powder (available at the health food store), and inserted during the night for each night for 5–7 days has been reported to alleviate symptoms. The patient can take *Acidophilus* capsules orally as well; a typical prescription is two capsules three times a day with meals for 2–4 weeks. Herbal douches and home remedies for vaginitis abound, but because the risk of pelvic inflammatory disease and metritis are reportedly greater in women who douche frequently, the clinician should study the professional herbal and naturopathic literature before making recommendations.

The homeopathic treatment of vaginitis requires careful data gathering, including date of last menstrual period (to assess at what stage of the cycle the symptoms occurred), aggravating and alleviating factors, concurrent changes in the person's health as a whole, and a careful exam. The clinician accustomed to doing wet preps should remember to observe the color and texture of the discharge *macroscopically* as well because the appearance may help the selection of the homeopathic medicine. It goes without saying that sexually active women should be screened for gonorrhea and *Chlamydia*. Gonorrhea, *Chlamydia*, and *Trichomonas* should be given the standard medical treatment.

Candidal Vulvovaginitis

The appropriate medicine may be prescribed in the 30C potency twice each day in the midday and evening for 1 week. *Candida albicans*, 30C may also be prescribed once a day on first waking in the morning for the same period of time. There has been a double-blind, placebo-controlled study of 40 women with vaginal discharge, using *Candida albicans*, 30C as a routine treatment (Carey, 1986). The results significantly favored homeopathy over placebo. The internal validity of this study was evaluated as a 40 on the Jadad scale and 57 on a more elaborate internal validity scale by independent reviewers (Linde et al., 1997). This pathogen-specific treatment approach is called isopathy. Some strictly classical homeopathic clinicians frown on isopathy, and the alternation of medicines in a treatment plan, while at the same time acknowledge the difficulty of treating vaginitis exclusively with the classical medicine.

Most Commonly Indicated Medicines

Calcarea carbonica—The patient presents with copious itching and burning vaginal discharge, that is *milky* in color and consistency. The discharge does not have much odor or affect the woman's sex drive. It is aggravated before the menses, and from urination and exercise. The discharge is accompanied with headache, chilliness, cramping, and perspiration of the genitals. *Calcarea carbonica* is a common medicine for yeast infection of girls and infants with cold hands and feet and perspiring heads.

Kreosotum—The vaginitis that requires this medicine *always* has violent pruritus and sometimes severe *burning* as well. The vaginitis is often concurrent with a urinary tract infection (UTI), or symptoms that mimic UTI. The discharge may have an offensive odor. Urine burns the vulva, and the itching is aggravated when the patient urinates. There is an intense desire to scratch, with sexual stimulation when she does. Itching and discharge are aggravated before the menstrual period.

Pulsatilla—*Pulsatilla* is indicated for vaginitis with *thick*, creamy white discharge that may be acrid or bland. There is no intense burning. The discharge is aggravated before and after the menses. The patient displays a mood that is changeable and has easy weeping. *Pulsatilla* is one of the most common medicines for vaginitis, including when needed during pregnancy. Also, it is used for vaginitis in girls. There may be low thirst, desire for open air, and other general symptoms of *Pulsatilla*. (See Chapter 14, *Pulsatilla*.)

Less Commonly Indicated Medicines

Borax—The patient has vaginal discharge that is like the white of an *egg*, and is *hot or pasty*, with the sensation as if warm water were flowing down the legs. The patient has pruritus of the vulva. The clitoris feels distended, and the patient is indifferent to sex. The patient, in general, may have concurrent headaches and/or aphthous lesions of the mouth.

Graphites—*Graphites* is used to treat the most copious of all the discharges; it may *run down the leg*. It is gushing, nonodorous, milky, acrid, and especially irritating to the outer labia. Because of the discharge, there is aversion to sex. The patient usually appears dull and heavy and has an aversion to sweets.

Helonias dioica—Itching candidal vulvovaginitis with *uterine prolapse* is best treated with *Helonias dioica*. The patient is aware of the uterus moving when she changes position. There is a dragging feeling in the sacrum from prolapse. The nipples are tender.

Hydrastis canadensis—The discharge *sticks to the walls* of the vagina; the clinician has to pull it out of the vagina to get a sample. The discharge may be acrid, white, or greenish yellow. It is aggravated after menses.

Mercurius vivus or Mercurius solubilis—Occasionally used for the thick, white discharge of yeast, the characteristic symptoms of *Mercurius*-indicated vaginitis are outlined under *"Bacterial Vaginosis,"* below. (See Chapter 11, *Mercurius vivus or Mercurius solubilis*.)

Sepia—Occasionally *Sepia* will be called for to treat a yeast vaginitis (white discharge); the characteristic symptoms are discussed below under "Bacterial Vaginosis."

Bacterial Vaginosis

Arsenicum album—There is a clear, acrid, and watery discharge, or a thick and yellow one with no itch at all. The vulva is red, and it *burns*. The patient is restless and anxious; symptoms are aggravated around midnight. (See Chapter 3, *Arsenicum album*.)

Kali bichromicum—The discharge is thick, *sticky* (like when *Hydrastis canadensis* is indicated), and yellow. The patient has pruritus. Symptoms are aggravated in hot weather.

Kreosotum—*Kreosotum* is used as profiled above for yeast infection, but also indicated for bacterial vaginosis with yellow discharge and offensive odor.

Mercurius vivus or Mercurius solubilis—The patient presents with a yellow or green-yellow discharge that has a *rotten or putrid* odor. The vulva itches and is sore, raw, and burning. It is aggravated at night and before the menstrual period, and is alleviated by washing in cold water. The patient may have increased thirst, perspiration, and a metallic taste in the mouth. (See Chapter 11, *Mercurius vivus or Mercurius solubilis*.)

Nitricum acidum—The vulva burns and itches and has *brown*, flesh-colored, or watery discharge. The patient may have *fissures* at the introitus or on the vulva. The patient may be irritable in the morning, and disproportionately anxious about her health matters.

Sepia—There is copious yellow or green discharge, yet the vagina feels very dry, causing painful intercourse. The patient has a low libido. The discharge *increases after sex*. There is burning, itching, and the sensation of heat on the vulva or inside the vagina. Symptoms are worse from ovulation to immediately before the menses. The patient may become irritable and want to be left alone. *Sepia* is used to treat vaginal infection in girls.

PREGNANCY

Constipation in Pregnancy

The customary dietary advice should be given to control constipation, including adding bran and psyllium husks to the diet for bulk and soft stool. If the constipation does not resolve from these measures, one of the following medicines may be prescribed three times a day for 3 days in the 30C potency.

Nux vomica—The patient is frustrated by a constant desire to pass stool, with unsuccessful *straining*. The constipation may be related to a lack of exercise or nicotine withdrawal. It may alternate with diarrhea. There may be large and hard stools, or an unfinished feeling after passing small stools. The most characteristic symptom is that the patient becomes *irritable*, impatient, and exacting. She is sensitive to noise, odors, and light. (See Chapter 12, *Nux vomica*.)

Pulsatilla—*Pulsatilla* is indicated for intermittent constipation; the stool is changeable. There may be varicosities of the feet and groin. There are swift mood changes including easy *crying*. The usual thirstlessness indicative of *Pulsatilla* may not be present during pregnancy. The patient feels generally alleviated by going for slow walks in the open air. Like when *Sulphur* is indicated, she uncovers one or both feet in bed at night. The patient may have a new aversion to the fat on meat, and desire for creamy foods such as cream-filled pastries. (See Chapter 14, *Pulsatilla*.)

Sepia—*Sepia* is reputed to be the most commonly indicated medicine for constipation in pregnancy, especially in cases where there was no history of constipation prior to pregnancy. Usually *Sepia* is indicated for multiparous women with poor muscle tone who feel worn out from motherhood, but that is by no means always the case. The patient cannot pass the *large, hard, and dry* stool. She may have distended and engorged varicose veins. Usually, there is some level of diminished feeling of love and tenderness for her family and partner, coupled with a general *apathy*, that gives the impression of being purely a result of the hormonal changes of pregnancy. The patient is generally relieved by vigorous exercise or dance.

Sulphur—The patient is unsuccessful in passing stool despite frequent urging. There is pain in the rectum from burning and itching hemorrhoids when she passes stool. The stool has a very offensive odor, and the anus is *red*. The patient in general is quite overheated in pregnancy, sticking the feet out of the covers at night to cool off (like with *Pulsatilla*), and searching for cool spots in the sheets. There is easy flushing of the face, and a desire for spicy, salty, and fatty foods. (See Chapter 16, *Sulphur*.)

Nausea and Vomiting of Pregnancy

Women frequently seek homeopathic care for nausea of pregnancy because homeopathic medicines are assumed not to be teratogenic. The correct homeopathic medicine will ease the nausea considerably, but usually not eliminate it. The medicine will need to be repeated or changed during the first trimester more often than is usual in homeopathy. Because the medicine will need to be taken frequently, it is advisable to start the patient on the 12C potency three times a day. If the patient's symptoms indicate that the medicine is wearing off between doses, she can be prescribed the 30C potency once or twice a day, thereby reducing the frequency of doses when the nausea is manageable. All the common medicines for nausea of pregnancy can be used to treat vomiting as well.

Most Commonly Indicated Medicines

Arsenicum album—The patient vomits all through the pregnancy. She vomits every time she eats and drinks. She is weak, *anxious, and restless*. Her mouth is dry, and small sips of warm liquid temporarily alleviate her nausea. Usually, chilliness is a key symptom of *Arsenicum*, but this is not true in pregnancy. (See Chapter 3, *Arsenicum album*.)

Colchicum autumnale—The patient's nausea is greatly aggravated by *odors*, particularly from food. Eggs or fish cooking are intolerable. The patient feels nauseous even looking at, or *thinking* about food. She is carsick, and vomits from swallowing saliva.

Ipecacuanha—*Ipecacuanha* stands out for treating continuous nausea that is not alleviated by vomiting. The nausea is aggravated by the odor of food and eating rich food. This morning sickness is not at its worst in the morning, but rather at other times of the day. The tongue has *no coating* even when the patient is very ill.

Kreosotum—The patient vomits *undigested food* after eating, which does not relieve the nausea. The vomiting may be concurrent with terribly itchy vaginitis. The patient has a bitter taste in the mouth after swallowing water and can tolerate warm food better than cold food.

Nux vomica—Impatience, restlessness, criticalness, and *irritability* accompany the nausea. The nausea is distinctly aggravated in the morning or after rising. The patient is usually constipated. She is sensitive to noise, odors, and light. (See Chapter 12, *Nux vomica*.)

Pulsatilla—This medicine is probably the second most commonly indicated medicine for nausea of pregnancy after *Sepia*. The patient is weepy, and desires company, reassurance, and consolation. The nausea is changeable and is aggravated by *rich food, heat, and from not eating*. Fresh air may alleviate the nausea. A whitish yellow coating is on the tongue. (See Chapter 14, *Pulsatilla*.)

Sepia—*Sepia* is reputedly the most common medicine for nausea of pregnancy. The nausea is aggravated by odors, particularly the odor of food. The *thought* of food, or of the nausea itself, makes her feel worse. The nausea is worse in the morning, and aggravated by not eating. This is the main medicine for the famous symptom, "craves pickles in pregnancy" and other *sour foods* such as lemonade or vinegar. Patient becomes apathetic, even toward loved ones, as well as irritable and complaining. She vomits a milky substance and has dry heaves. Symptoms are worse 3:00–5:00 p.m. There are eructations on rising in the morning.

Symphoricarpus racemosus—This medicine can be given when *no distinctive picture* of another medicine is present. The patient has no appetite. The nausea increases from the smell or thought of food, motion, rising, or lying on the back. There may be incessant vomiting and waterbrash.

Less Commonly Indicated Medicines

Anacardium orientale—There is tremendous alleviation of nausea from *eating*. The patient has a loss of appetite, alternating with violent hunger.

Cocculus indicus—This medicine is used to treat motion sickness that is milder than that indicative of *Tabacum*. The patient becomes nauseous from the smell or thought of food.

Ignatia amara—*Ignatia amara* is used for nausea of pregnancy, with strange contradictory symptoms that follow a *loss*. The patient is sighing, and generally aggravated from cigarette smoke. (See Chapter 10, *Ignatia amara*.)

Phosphorus—*Phosphorus* is used to treat nausea with intense thirst for *ice-cold* drinks that are vomited after becoming warm in the stomach. Patient is "spaced out," anxious, and wants company. She experiences sudden nausea on rising in the morning. (See Chapter 13, *Phosphorus*.)

Sulphur—The patient has sudden vomiting in the morning that is aggravated by looking at food. The patient becomes *overheated* and sticks the feet out of the covers at night to cool off. (See Chapter 16, *Sulphur*.)

Tabacum—*Tabacum* is used to treat severe *carsickness* with vomiting during pregnancy. The patient is pale and covered in perspiration. Symptoms are alleviated outdoors.

Pyrosis of Pregnancy

The 30C potency may be prescribed once a day for 5 days, then as needed for heartburn if it seems to have helped.

Capsicum annuum—The patient has eructations of material that taste like *hot peppers*.

Mercurius vivus or Mercurius solubilis—There is a *metallic* taste in the mouth, halitosis, and drooling during sleep. (Refer to Chapter 11, *Mercurius vivus or Mercurius solubilis*.)

Muriaticum acidum—Great *weakness* and fatigue accompany the heartburn; the patient slides down in bed from weakness.

Natrum muriaticum—There is a burning sensation in the chest, and a *salty* taste in the mouth. The patient desires salt and has an increased thirst.

Robinia pseudoacacia—The patient has hyperacidity. Dyspepsia interferes with sleep because it is aggravated by *lying down at night*.

Threatened Spontaneous Abortion

Homeopathy is reputed to have prevented many spontaneous abortions when the fetus is viable and the pregnant woman has begun to hemorrhage. The key symptoms on which to prescribe for this condition are clear and distinct. They should not be difficult for a new prescriber who carefully gathers data from the patient about the characteristics of the bleeding or pain, and any concurrent changes in the state of the patient as a whole. A 30C potency can be prescribed once every 3 hr for three doses. If the symptoms abate during this time, the patient can cease taking the medicine and carry the medicine with her, taking a single dose as needed if symptoms return. There has been no formal research conducted on threatened miscarriage and homeopathy.

If the homeopathic medicine most appropriate for the problems associated with spontaneous abortion while it is occurring cannot be found in this section, it may be found in the sections entitled, "Prolonged Dysfunctional Labor" and uterine hemorrhage (see Chapter 17, Injuries and Emergencies).

More Commonly Indicated Medicines

Aconitum napellus—Hemorrhage threatening abortion that follows cystitis or a *fright* is best treated with *Aconitum napellus*. The patient has intense fear of her own or the fetus' death, or of more bleeding and cramping. The patient refuses to turn in bed or move from her great fear. She is restless and thirsty for cold water.

Apis mellifica—Copious and dark hemorrhage that threatens abortion in the second or third month should be treated with *Apis mellifica*. There are uterine contractions that extend to the thighs, and the sensation of *pinpricks* on the cervix, like stinging. The patient yawns when not sleepy. The patient may be physically awkward, jealous, or irritable.

Arnica montana—*Arnica montana* is used to treat threatened or actual miscarriage from a *fall, shock, or contusion*. There is a painless hemorrhage of blood that appears red, coagulated, and clotted. The patient feels as though the fetus is sideways. She feels bruised all over, and has pain on motion; even the bed feels too hard. The patient guards her injury and does not want to be examined, claiming she is fine. (See Chapter 2, *Arnica montana*.)

Belladonna—There is intermittent, bright red hemorrhage consistency of *hot*, coagulated blood with bright red clots. The face is flushed, and the eyes glisten. There are violent aching pains all through the body. A downward pressure is felt in the pelvis as though something is being forced out. (See Chapter 4, *Belladonna*.)

Bryonia alba—There is dark red hemorrhage. The patient wants to be left *alone*. She may be constipated and have dry lips and mouth. There is a burning pain in the uterus. (See Chapter 5, *Bryonia alba*.)

Cantharis—There is *burning* pain in the uterus with dark hemorrhage. The patient constantly desires to urinate, but only a few drops come out.

Chamomilla—The patient is *hypersensitive* to pain. She is irritable, snappish, and whiny. She asks for things and then rejects them when they are offered. There is a painful discharge of dark blood during urination. The urine may be colorless. (See Chapter 6, *Chamomilla*.)

Cinchona officinalis—The patient is *bloated* and distended with flatus. There is a bright red hemorrhage that threatens abortion. This medicine can be used to treat retained membranes with continuous hemorrhage after spontaneous abortion. There may be anemia from blood loss.

Cimicifuga racemosa—Pains fly across the abdomen from *right to left*; the patient doubles up in pain. Miscarriages in the third month, in women with a history of miscarriages and/or arthritis are best treated with *Cimicifuga racemosa*.

Ipecacuanha—There is constant *nausea* without relief. Hyperemesis gravidarum accompanies hemorrhage of bright red blood with no clots. Pains start near the umbilicus and extend from left to right.

Kali carbonicum—Hemorrhage in the second and third month can be treated with *Kali carbonicum*. All the pain is in the *back*; it extends down to the thighs. The patient feels better when lying down. She may have concurrent anxiety or irritability.

Lilium tigrinum—The pain starts at the ovaries and extends down the inside of the patient's thighs. She hemorrhages only when she *moves*. The patient feels constant pressure in the rectum; she feels subjectively as though everything is going to fall out. Other symptoms include aimless motion, *hurried* affect, and irritability with complaining.

Pulsatilla—There is intermittent discharge of very dark blood during miscarriage. Pains *alternate* with the hemorrhaging. The patient may be *weepy,* may not be able to tolerate a closed room, has reduced thirst, and desires open air. (See Chapter 14, *Pulsatilla*.)

Rhus toxicodendron—The patient presents with threatened miscarriage from injury, especially wrenching injury. She is very *restless* and has cramps in her legs. Hemorrhage is intermittent and bright red. There is *stiffness and achiness* that is alleviated on continued motion. (See Chapter 15, *Rhus toxicodendron*.)

Sabina—*Sabina* is indicated for spontaneous abortion in the third month. The pain starts at the *small of the back* and travels to the *pubes*. There is hemorrhage of bright red and clotted blood, aggravated by movement.

Secale cornutum—Threatened or incomplete abortion in the third month in older multiparas is commonly treated with *Secale cornutum*. There is slow hemorrhage of *black blood*, which may have an offensive odor. There is tingling all over the body; the patient desires to have the legs or thighs massaged. Her fingers spread apart during the pain. The patient feels easily overheated.

Viburnum opulus—The patient presents with cramping pain on either side of the pelvic abdomen that shoots *down the legs*. *Viburnum opulus* is perhaps the most commonly indicated medicine for threatened abortion. It is usually indicated in the early weeks of pregnancy. She bleeds only in gushes; there is no blood between gushes. There may be cognitive or emotional symptoms such as poor concentration, irritability, wanting to be alone, and an aversion to being touched. The miscarriage may be preceded by leg cramps, and followed by both leg and abdominal cramps.

Less Commonly Indicated Medicines

Aletris farinosa—There is hemorrhage of dark blood with contractions. The patient is *anemic* and so weak that she cannot lift her head. She may have a previous history of spontaneous abortion.

Sepia—*Sepia* is indicated for spontaneous abortion in the third to seventh month; fetal movements are feeble. The patient is usually, but not always, an older multiparous woman. She feels flushes of heat and the sensation as though the fetus and her organs will *fall from the vagina*. She is apathetic about everything, especially about her loved ones. She may weep while telling her symptoms to the clinician. She desires sour foods, and is averse to the fat on meat.

Sulphur—The patient experiences flushes of *heat* with cold feet during the threatened miscarriage. There is vulval pruritis, and the top of the head is hot. (See Chapter 16, *Sulphur*.)

Ustilago maidis—The patient presents with a slow hemorrhage of *huge clots* followed by bleeding of red or dark blood, and then more clots. The patient may be depressed and crying.

LABOR

Prolonged/Dysfunctional Labor

For dysfunctional labor, the 30C potency may be administered once. The labor would be expected to pick up within a few seconds or minutes after administration of the first dose; the contractions becoming longer and more efficient. If this is the case, the clinician can administer the medicine again only if it is needed. *Arnica montana* is needed in most labors for intense soreness, and helps prevent bruising of the neonate's head. The patient needing *Arnica montana* will complain that the bed is too *hard*.

Caulophyllum thalictroides has been used in several studies related to pregnancy and labor. British veterinary researchers conducted trials showing that *Caulophyllum thalictroides*, 30C could lower the rate of stillbirths in pigs (Day, 1984). Pigs given a placebo had 103 births and 27 stillbirths (20.8%), while those given *Caulophyllum*, 30C had 104 births and 12 stillbirths (10.3%). Dorfman, Lasserre, and Tetau (1987) conducted double-blind, placebo-controlled study ($n = 93$) in which women were given a complex medicine containing the 5C potency of the following remedies: *Arnica montana*, *Caulophyllum thalictroides*, *Cimicifuga racemosa*, *Gelsemium sempervirens*, and *Pulsatilla* twice a day during the ninth month of pregnancy. The women given the homeopathic medicines experienced a 40% shorter labor than those given a placebo. The women in the placebo group had four times as many complications of labor as those given the homeopathic medicines.

When the study was independently reviewed, the internal validity of the study was ranked as a 60 on the Jadad scale, and a 71 on a more elaborate internal validity scale (Linde et al., 1997).

In a more recent study, *Caulophyllum thalictroides*, 7C alone was administered during the active phase of labor (one dose/hr repeated for a maximum of 4 hr) to 22 healthy primiparas. The time of labor for those women given the homeopathic medicine was 38% shorter than for women given a placebo (Eid, Felisi, & Sideri, 1993). This trial was single-blind; the researchers later completed a double-blind trial and confirmed their earlier results (Eid, Felisi, & Sideri, 1994).

Coudert (1981) is reported to have conducted a double-blind, placebo-controlled trial ($n = 34$) of *Caulophyllum thalictroides*, 5C, which also had a highly positive result in shortening labor, but unfortunately it is reported only in a French language unpublished thesis (Linde et al., 1997).

Classical homeopaths are concerned that, while *Caulophyllum* is a very commonly needed medicine in pregnancy, these studies may overstate its role. What follows are the indicated medicines when labor is judged to actually be delayed.

Aconitum napellus—The patient has intense *fear* that something bad will happen. The baby is posterior; the contractions are ineffectual. The patient is thirsty; has an accelerated heart rate; may have violent, frightful labor pains; and has warm perspiration.

Belladonna—*Belladonna* is indicated for *sudden* onset and cessation of pains, which fly in every direction. There is a bearing down sensation as if the contents of the uterus would fall out. There is a subjective sensation of mild pressure on the sacrum. The cervix does *not dilate* when membranes rupture, despite the normal contractions. Some patients who are prescribed *Belladonna* may be quiet and appear normal and robust, often athletic. Others may have an animalistic affect during labor: wild eyes, reddened face, and boring of the head into the pillow. Other symptoms include headache, intolerance of being jarred (e.g., someone sitting on her bed), and cramps in her legs. (See Chapter 4, *Belladonna*.)

Carbo vegetabilis—The pains are *weak* or have ceased completely from hypovolemia. There are weak fetal heart tones. There may be varicosities of the vulva, flatulence, and eructations. The skin is cool to touch. The mother has tachycardia and a weak pulse.

Caulophyllum thalictroides—There is failure to progress from ineffectual uterine contractions centered on the lower pelvis, including the bladder, groin, and lower extremities, or exclusively in the fundus. The uterus *relaxes* to its normal length after each contraction. The labor pains are sharp, spasmodic, brief, unstable, and flitting here and there. There is prickling on the cervix. The patient *fails to dilate*; the cervix remains thick, rigid, and closed. There is a mucusy discharge from the vagina. The patient is exhausted, chilly, trembling, shivering, and filled with nervous excitement. *Pulsatilla* is often incorrectly prescribed when *Caulophyllum* is indicated, perhaps because rapid changes in mood are within the sphere of both medicines.

Chamomilla—The patient shows extreme *sensitivity* to labor pains, which extend down the inner side of the legs. The contractions are weak; the urine is *colorless*. The patient is very irritable and refuses what is offered. The baby may be posterior. There may be back pain. (See Chapter 6, *Chamomilla*.)

Cimicifuga racemosa—The contraction begins normally and *diffuses*, or becomes a neuralgic pain. The patient may scream and grasp the hips during the contraction. When the woman becomes distracted, the labor ceases. Labor pain is felt primarily in the lower uterine segment and cervix, which is rigidly closed and fails to dilate, or the pain may travel from left to right, or dart from one side to the other. Pain may dart down to the hips and thighs. The patient may display shivering in the first stage. The patient is generally alleviated by massage. Her affect is negative, gloomy, sighing, and dejected; there is a feeling that a *black cloud* surrounds her. There may be strange fears of going *insane* or dying. She has disconnected thoughts and displays coarse and jerky movements (e.g., chorea, athetosis, and grimacing).

Gelsemium sempervirens—There are counterproductive contractions that make the baby *ascend*. Labor begins normally, and then the contractions start getting shorter. The os is rigid. Labor pains may travel from the posterior to the superior part of the uterus. The patient has chills, is *drowsy*, yawns, naps, has slurred speech, and displays mental dullness. Her muscles seem not to obey the will. She may have diplopia. Compare with *Caulophyllum*. (See Chapter 8, *Gelsemium sempervirens*.)

Gossypium herbaceum—The patient fails to progress. The labor has been long and *almost painless* with an extremely rigid, *hard*, thick os. There are intermittent pains in the ovarian region and irregular contractions. This medicine is more commonly indicated in primiparas women, and is the most common medicine for placenta accreta.

Ignatia amara—The labor is dysfunctional from *grief*, whether related to another event in the patient's life, or from grieving the end of the pregnancy. The patient stretches her extremities and sighs, sobs, or twitches. She may have a wild expression and tear the hair (like when *Belladonna* is indicated). She may be irritable and hostile, and alternate laughter and weeping. Symptoms are similar to those indicative of *Cimicifuga racemosa*. (See Chapter 10, *Ignatia amara*.)

Kali carbonicum—The patient has *back labor*, or needle-like labor pains that are alleviated by hard pressure or rubbing. She experiences diffuse anxiety.

Pulsatilla—The contractions are sluggish and irregular. The first stage is prolonged. The patient depends on her partner for support and confidence, and *does not want to exert* herself during labor. Labor pains may travel from the sacrum to the epigastrium; she desires firm pressure on the sacrum. The os dilates normally. The patient wants many people to attend the birth. (See Chapter 14, *Pulsatilla*.)

In any pregnancy with *breech* or *transverse* presentation, when no clear indication for another medicine is present, *Pulsatilla* 30C may be administered as a routine medicine three times a day for three days followed by a *Pulsatilla*, 200C single dose 1 week later if necessary to turn the baby. The clinician should wait until weeks 26–35 to do this, so that the baby will be less apt to turn back (Moscowitz, 1992). (See Chapter 14, *Pulsatilla*.)

Secale cornutum—*Secale cornutum* is used to treat the older multiparous woman with *poor muscle tone* and poor nutrition. She has excessive, yet ineffective, labor pains. There is a bearing-down feeling as though something will fall out. There are *burning* pains and involuntary spreading of fingers. She wants to have her legs rubbed, to be uncovered, and to be exposed to the open air.

Sepia—The contractions have a spasmodic quality. Dilatation ceases at 4–5 cm. There may be an *anterior lip* that does not dilate. Labor pains are felt above the pubic bones. There may be a subjective feeling that the baby is going to drop out. Pressure in the rectum gives the erroneous impression that it is time to push. There may be a needle-like pain in the cervix extending upward. She has hot body and cold feet and wants her socks on. Back pain is alleviated by hard pressure. Fetal movements are feeble. There is constipation during labor.

POSTPARTUM CARE AND CARE OF THE NEONATE

Postpartum hemorrhage and asphyxia neonatorum are addressed in Chapter 17, Injuries and Emergencies.

Afterpains

A few doses of a 30C potency of one of the medicines below is reputed to relieve severe afterpains.

Arnica montana—The patient feels *bruised* and sore or has violent afterpains, and does not want to be *touched*. *Arnica montana* helps expel retained tissue and clots, and stop dribbling of urine after birth. The pain is aggravated by motion and lying on the left side, and is alleviated when the head lies low. (See Chapter 2, *Arnica montana*.)

Chamomilla—The patient is very *irritable* and hypersensitive to pain. The afterpains continue longer than would be expected and are aggravated by nursing. (See Chapter 6, *Chamomilla*.)

Cuprum metallicum—This medicine is indicated for multiparous women with afterpains accompanied by *cramping* pains in the legs.

Hypericum perforatum—*Hypericum perforatum* is used to treat pains in the *coccyx* and hips after instrumented delivery.

Kali carbonicum—The afterpains are needle-like and centered in the *lower back*; they shoot down to the gluteal region or hips.

Pulsatilla—The patient in general is weepy and dependent, and needs reassurance and consolation. The afterpains are changeable. (See Chapter 14, *Pulsatilla*.)

Rhus toxicodendron—The patient is *restless* because moving and changing position alleviates the pains. (See Chapter 15, *Rhus toxicodendron*.)

Sabina—Afterpains extend from the *sacrum to the pubis*.

Secale cornutum—*Secale cornutum* is indicated for older mothers with prolonged *labor-like* afterpains. The blood is dark and offensive.

Viburnum opulus—There are violent, spasmodic pains that radiate down the *thighs*. There is cramping pain in the cervix.

Xanthoxylum fraxineum—This medicine is for the multiparous woman with severe afterpains and distress that are aggravated by nursing. There may be *hot prickling* in the right ovary that extends to the back, hips, and thighs. She gasps from the pains. There is profuse lochea. Sometimes, there is a peppery taste in the mouth.

Perineal Tears, Lacerations, and Episiotomy

A *Calendula officinalis* tincture diluted 20 to 1 or more with water, or an herbal infusion (strong tea) of *Calendula* may be sprayed on the perineum, or put in a sitz bath, to help tears and surgical incisions. *Calendula officinalis*, 30C or *Staphysagria*, 30C may be given three times a day for 2 days if the wound is not healing well; professional opinion is split on which medicine is superior. *Arnica montana*, 6X was studied for its possible effectiveness as a routine prescription for perineal pain in a double-blind, placebo-controlled study of 122 women (with impeccable methodology); it was found to have no effect (Hofmeyr, Piccioni, & Blauhof, 1990).

For bruising of the pelvic organs, *Bellis perennis*, 30C may be prescribed three times a day for 1–2 days. It is reputed to be more effective than *Arnica montana*, unless the specific symptoms of *Arnica* are present.

Infected Umbilicus

Mild infections of the neonatal umbilicus will respond to being irrigated with a dilute solution of a *Calendula officinalis* tincture in water, and then dressed with a *Calendula* ointment. More severe infections respond to one of two medicines. *Abrotanum*, 30C three times a day for 3 days, then as needed for symptoms, is prescribed for odorless oozing of mucus, blood, and pus from the umbilicus in emaciated infants with poor nutrition or failure to thrive. *Mercurius vivus*, 30C is prescribed in the same fashion for discharge of pus with offensive odor.

Neonatal Jaundice

The clinician should prescribe the 30C potency of the indicated medicine for the infant every 3 hr for three doses. Improvement should be noted within 12 hr. The medicine my be given again if symptoms reappear. Phototherapy does not interfere with homeopathic treatment or vice versa. Clinicians report that the great majority of cases respond to one of the following medicines. One or two pellets may be dissolved in a little water and administered by mouth if there is concern about giving a sucrose or lactose pellet in the mouth. However, there have been no reports in the homeopathic literature of infants choking on homeopathic sugar pellets.

Aconitum napellus—There is a *sudden* onset of symptoms with restlessness. This medicine may be prescribed in addition to conventional treatment for hemolytic jaundice from Rh or ABO incompatibility.

Arnica montana—*Arnica montana* is prescribed for physiological jaundice with excessive *bruising*. (See Chapter 2, *Arnica montana*.)

Ceanothus americanus—Jaundice with *splenomegaly* is treated with *Ceanothus americanus*.

Chelidonium majus—Jaundice discolors the upper part of the body more than the lower part. The baby is averse to being moved. He or she is generally worse 4–8 p.m.

Cinchona officinalis—This medicine is used to treat the *weak* and lethargic baby suffering from flatulence and jaundice.

Natrum sulphuricum—*Natrum sulphuricum* is used as a routine prescription for physiologic jaundice when there are no symptoms that indicate another medicine.

Thrush

The indicated medicine can be prescribed in the 30C potency twice a day for 3 days.

Borax—*Borax* is by far the most common medicine for thrush (Jonas & Jacobs, 1996). There are adherent white patches in the mouth; the gums are inflamed and tender with friable ulcers. The child cries while nursing, and, hence, avoids nursing. A well-known symptom, that need not be present to prescribe this medicine, is an aversion to downward motion, such as going downstairs or being laid down.

Mercurius vivus or Mercurius solubilis—Symptoms include bleeding gums, a thickly coated tongue, ulcers inside the mouth, *halitosis,* and excessive drooling. These are the hallmarks of *Mercurius.* The baby is more uncomfortable at night. (See Chapter 11, *Mercurius vivus or Mercurius solubilis.*)

Sulphur—The infant seems to be intolerant of *heat,* and attempts to kick off the wraps. The tongue has a white coating down the center, with red tip and sides. The lips and gums are very *inflamed,* and markedly erythematous. (See Chapter 16, *Sulphur.*)

Mastitis and Lactation

Mastitis is believed to respond well to homeopathy. The 30C potency can be prescribed every 4 hr, for three doses, and then three times a day if there has been an improvement in pain; for up to 5 days if symptoms persist. If the patient's symptoms change, a new medicine can be prescribed according to that constellation of symptoms. The clinician will be able to treat the majority of cases of mastitis with *Belladonna* or *Bryonia alba,* but the key symptoms of the other medicines that follow should be kept in mind for the minority (Moscowitz, 1992).

Belladonna—*Belladonna* is the most commonly indicated medicine for mastitis. There is a sudden high fever, and violent *throbbing* or bursting pains in the breast. The breast is swollen, *bright red,* even shiny, and has red streaks radiating from the center. This is usually a right-sided mastitis. It is tender, and sensitive to the slightest jar. The mastitis may be accompanied by a throbbing or bursting headache, and the usual general symptoms of *Belladonna* such as sensitivity to light and noise. (See Chapter 4, *Belladonna.*)

Bryonia alba—The second most common medicine for mastitis is *Bryonia alba.* Pain and inflammation of the breast comes on slowly and begins with chills. The breasts feel *heavy and hard,* and the pains are sharp. The patient lies on the painful side, aggravated from the slightest motion. The patient will usually display some of the general symptoms of *Bryonia alba,* such as irritability, desire to be alone, thirst for large amounts of water at long intervals, and desire to be still. (See Chapter 5, *Bryonia alba.*)

Phytolacca—There is pain in the nipple that radiates to the whole body on nursing. The breast is *lumpy, congested,* and tender on palpation in spots. It is more likely to be indicated for mastitis of the left breast. The axillary glands are enlarged. This medicine may follow

Belladonna or *Bryonia alba* after the acute inflammation has been quelled.

Silicea—There is pain from the *nipple to the uterus* on nursing, with indurated *lumps* in the breast signifying abscesses, galactoceles, or draining sinuses after mastitis. Other symptoms include itching breasts, caseous discharge, and chilliness. This medicine is more often indicated for mastitis of the right breast.

Less Commonly Indicated Medicines

Croton tiglium—There is pain from the *nipple to the back* with each suck of the baby. There are nodules in the breast, with pain from the nipple to the scapula. The breast is indurated and swollen. The nipples are very sore to touch.

Hepar sulphuris calcareum—The breasts are swollen; nipples appear small, and the pain is alleviated by *heat*. In general, the patient is irritable and sensitive. (See Chapter 9, *Hepar sulphuris calcareum*.)

Lac caninum—The patient gets mastitis first on *one side*, then on the *other*. Milk is scant. Pain is aggravated by the least jar, like when *Belladonna* is indicated.

Phellandrium aquaticum—There is pain in the milk ducts when *not* nursing; the nipples themselves may be painful during nursing. Ductile pain may radiate to abdomen or back.

Pulsatilla—The patient weeps every time the child is put to the breast. There is a disproportionate amount of discomfort from the pressure of milk letdown while nursing. The usual general symptoms indicative of *Pulsatilla* are present. (See Chapter 14, *Pulsatilla*.)

DYSMENORRHEA

The following are homeopathic medicines used for the *palliation* of dysmenorrhea. Since the advent of nonsteroidal, anti-inflammatory medicines, patients are much less likely to request homeopathic treatment for pain control than they once were. Homeopathic specialists claim success with *prevention* of menstrual cramps, but a long visit with an advanced clinician is required. The following medicines for palliation can be prescribed in the 30C potency every 2 hr for three

doses, then again if pain persists. The earlier in the episode the
medicine is begun, the more effective it will be.

Most Commonly Indicated Medicines

Belladonna—The patient presents with labor-like pain and pressure in the pelvis. The pain is sharp, knife-like, or *throbbing*, and often
worse on the *right* side. There is profuse, hot menstrual blood. The
pain is somewhat alleviated by pressure and doubling up. It is aggravated by being *jarred* or from motion. (See Chapter 4, *Belladonna*.)

Chamomilla—The patient is tremendously irritable. She asks for
things that are then rejected when offered. The patient must *double up*
with the menstrual pain, yet the position does not alleviate it. There
may be diarrhea and back pain. (See Chapter 6, *Chamomilla*.)

Colocynthis—*Colocynthis* is used to treat severe dysmenorrhea
that is primarily alleviated by *pressure* and *bending double*. To a lesser
degree the pain may be alleviated by warmth. The patient is angry
with the pain, and may have diarrhea concurrently.

Magnesia phosphorica—*Magnesia phosphorica* is the general medicine for menstrual pains that are best alleviated by *warmth* and to a
lesser degree by pressure or doubling up. The blood can contain shreds
of membrane. Diarrhea may also occur during menstruation.

Pulsatilla—There are variable pains that can *wander* from place to
place. The patient moans and cries and wants to be with someone.
The pain is alleviated by bending double, warmth, and sympathy.
There may also be nausea, diarrhea, and/or back pain. (See Chapter 14,
Pulsatilla.)

Less Commonly Indicated Medicines

Caulophyllum thalictroides—This medicine is used to treat
labor-like pains that fly to remote parts of the body including the
breast. There are spasms from emotions during this kind of dysmenorrhea. The pain may be violent, intermittent, and cramping and may
extend down the legs.

Cimicafuga racemosa—The menstrual pain is proportionate with
the flow. Menstrual blood is profuse, dark, coagulated, or scanty and
may be accompanied with backache. The patient has spasms due to

emotions during the menstrual period. The *affect* is *strange*; the patient fears going insane.

Nux vomica—*Nux vomica* is used to treat irritability with *impatience*. The dysmenorrhea is accompanied with constipation with straining at the stool, or alternating diarrhea and constipation. Symptoms are alleviated by doubling up and by warmth. The patient may have back pain during menstruation. (See Chapter 12, *Nux vomica*.)

Veratrum album—Dysmenorrhea is accompanied by faintness, menorrhagia, nausea, vomiting, and/or diarrhea. There is *cold perspiration* and general coldness of the body.

Viburnum opulis—The pain extends to the upper *inner thighs*. There is an aching in the sacrum and pubic area. Blood may be scanty, delayed, and offensive. There may also be diarrhea.

MENOPAUSE

Most of the ailments women experience in the perimenopausal and menopausal time of life are constitutional issues impractical to address homeopathically in the primary care office. Mild hot flashes are a normal part of menopause for most women; more severe vasomotor instability can sometimes be addressed with a quick prescription from the list below. The medicine can be given in the 30C potency twice a week, for 6 weeks, then reduced in frequency as symptoms subside. If symptoms do not improve, referral to a homeopathic specialist has a higher likelihood of success. There are many other health issues that arise surrounding menopause that are addressed in the popular homeopathic literature (Ikenze, 1998).

Most Commonly Indicated Medicines

Amyl nitrosum—Hot flashes are centered in the face and head and followed by profuse perspiration. A red, hot face and head are triggered by heat and stuffy rooms, and may be accompanied by *headache or palpitations*, as well as a desire for fresh air. There is a choking feeling in the throat, and the collar itself feels constricting. There may be hiccup and yawning with stretching.

Lachesis mutus—The patient presents with intense hot flashes of the head and neck; she is intolerant of scarves or collars, and belts around the waist. There is no perspiration with the hot flashes. The patient may be extremely *talkative* and suspicious, and jump from one subject to the next.

Calcarea carbonica—The patient feels subjectively hot, but the skin is objectively *cold and clammy*. There is perspiration on the head and neck. There is profuse perspiration on the slightest activity. The hands and feet are cold. The patient wears socks to bed. She desires soft-boiled eggs, milk, cookies, nuts, olives, and bread. The patient may express generalized anxiety and a sense of being overwhelmed with responsibilities. She gains weight easily and may have uterine fibroids.

Ignatia amara—*Ignatia amara* is used to treat hot flashes brought on or exacerbated by *grief*. There is perspiration on the face. (See Chapter 10, *Ignatia amara*.)

Pilocarpus—*Pilocarpus* is indicated for hot flashes, *salivation*, nausea, and profuse perspiration in trembling anxious women. The patient's chest becomes suddenly hot and red. There are concurrent *visual disturbances* of many kinds, such as white spots or vitreous opacities in the visual field.

Sanguinaria canadensis—The patient describes *burning* hot flashes. There is circumscribed redness of the cheeks, abdomen, or tongue, with a sensation of congested blood in the head, chest, or abdomen. There are general pulsations, and the breasts are sore and enlarged.

Sepia—The patient is chilly during the day, and warm at night. Hot flashes are better in the morning. The patient may experience *drenching perspiration* followed by chilliness and insomnia from hot flashes. Patient is usually apathetic and irritable and desires sour foods. Symptoms are alleviated by vigorous exercise, such as running or dancing.

Sulphur—Since these patients are already warm, the excess heat of the menopausal period may be intolerable for them. There is excessive, strong-smelling perspiration. The patient is *itchy and hot* in bed at night, and hence, sticks one or both feet out of the covers at night to cool off. There is a tendency to develop rashes and skin conditions that are aggravated by heat. (See Chapter 16, *Sulphur*.)

Ustilago maidis—This medicine is used to treat troublesome hot flashes in women with menses (or a history of menses) that consisted of strings of dark clots held together with mucus in watery fluid blood; the flow was *half liquid, half clotted*. There may be concurrent uterine hypertrophy or myomas. The flashes may feel like boiling water flowing along the back, or be nondescript. The patient may have general accompanying symptoms, such as depression, weeping, loss of hair and nails, general aggravation from motion, and cramping of the lower extremities.

CHAPTER 28

Postsurgical Care

Surgery might be the last place one would expect to find homeopathy useful. After all, surgery and emergency treatment are the arenas in which contemporary western medicine unquestionably excels above all other systems of healing. Yet, if there could be a role for homeopathic medicines in calming the patient before surgery, or reducing pain, infection, or other negative sequelae, the patient should have access to the best of both worlds.

Before surgery, some homeopathic physicians recommend prescribing *Arnica montana*, 30C or 200C. One dose should be given the evening before surgery and one in the morning before surgery, and one immediately before being anesthetized to prevent bruising and shock (Foubister, 1989). Others recommend *Phosphorus*, 9C the night before and the morning of surgery to prevent hemorrhage (Jouanny, 1980). Homeopathic medicines can be administered in a single drop of liquid or on a tiny single lactose or sucrose pellet given sublingually, thus the risk of aspiration during surgery is not increased. Some homeopathic physicians omit presurgical preventive treatment presumably because they question the validity of giving a medicine before the symptom exists that it is supposed to treat (Jonas & Jacobs, 1996).

ANXIETY BEFORE SURGERY

Adults

The following medicines have been mentioned in the homeopathic literature for adults with preoperative anxiety. A dose of the indicated medicine may be offered in the 30C potency the evening before surgery.

Chamomilla—*Chamomilla* is indicated for patients who are *irritable* and argumentative from tooth pain before dental surgery. (See Chapter 6, *Chamomilla*.)

Ignatia amara—*Ignatia amara* is indicated for patients who are sighing and crying from grief about the potential loss of a body part, change in appearance, or a poor prognosis. It is also very useful in very young children who believe they will be permanently abandoned by the parents in the hospital. (See Chapter 10, *Ignatia amara*.)

Gelsemium sempervirens—The patient trembles from worry. The patient's mental state is dull, and he or she is weak and frequently urinates. (See Chapter 8, *Gelsemium sempervirens*.)

Coffea cruda—Fearful anticipation of the pain creates *insomnia*.

Children

Phosphorus—*Phosphorus* is the most common medicine for preoperative anxiety in children. The child's eyes follow every movement of the doctor or nurse; a desire for cold drinks may be present. The child fears being left alone by the parents. He or she shrinks from the doctor saying, "What are you going to do to me?" (Foubister, 1989). (See Chapter 13, *Phosphorus*.)

Pulsatilla—The child cries sweetly, and is clingy and dependent. Thirst is diminished. (See Chapter 14, *Pulsatilla*.)

SURGICAL DRESSINGS

Calendula officinalis—During the nineteenth century, the first half of the twentieth century, and the First World War, there were a number of British and American surgeons who were also homeopathic physicians. There were numerous homeopathic hospitals in the United States in the nineteenth century, and the Royal London Homeopathic Hospital is still in existence in England. The preferred wound dressing for the classically trained homeopathic surgeon was a botanical tincture made from the single-stemmed pot marigold, *Calendula officinalis*. The historical homeopathic medical literature was replete with numerous reports of the superiority of *Calendula officinalis* to the iodine-based dressings of the time (Carlton, 1996; Shadman, 1958).

Typically, the wound was covered with cotton, and an alcohol-based botanical tincture of *Calendula officinalis* (usually diluted 20:1 with water) was poured over the bandage. The bandage was left in place, and more of this solution was applied when it dried.

The reputation of this treatment was that it was bacteriostatic, stopped bleeding quickly, and speeded wound healing. The only negative report was that incised or lacerated wounds could rapidly heal on the surface, thereby leaving pockets of pus deep inside. *Calendula* preparations are still widely available in health food stores and from homeopathic pharmacies, and remain candidates for scientific study in comparison with contemporary dressings. The ratio of alcohol to water can be adjusted to minimize stinging. Normal saline can be used as a diluent instead of water.

POSTSURGICAL HOMEOPATHIC PROTOCOLS

Several decades ago the National Health Council of the National Health Service of Great Britain approved the following protocol (see Exhibit 28–1) for postsurgical, preventive medical treatment, which was used by the Royal London Homeopathic Hospital. It uses the 30C potency exclusively. In North America, it is the custom to give a 200C potency according to the same schedule, or a 1M potency with less frequent dosing.

Arnica montana—A few studies have been conducted to date on the routine postsurgical prescription of *Arnica montana* as a sole medical treatment after surgery, particularly oral and facial surgery, to prevent bruising, swelling, pain, and infection. The results thus far have not been impressive (Ernst & Pittler, 1998). For example, one study showed *Arnica montana*, 200C less effective than metronidazole in reducing postsurgical complications (Kizaro, 1984). It is too early to conclude that *Arnica montana* is ineffective; yet at this time, there is no scientific evidence to support using *Arnica montana* alone for oral or facial surgery. A randomized, controlled, two-period, crossover clinical trial on the effects of *Arnica montana* on blood coagulation (Baillargeon, Drouin, Desjardins, Leroux, & Audet, 1993) did *not* show that this homeopathic medicine had a significant impact on various parameters of blood coagulation in healthy volunteers in the period immediately following administration. One unpublished study with very poor internal validity reportedly showed *Apis mellifica*, 7C and

Exhibit 28–1 Postsurgical, Preventive Medical Treatment

- **Hysterectomy:** *Causticum*, 30C three times a day (t.i.d.) for 3 days
- **Dilation and curettage:** *Belladonna*, 30C q 6 hr
- **Mastectomy:** *Hamamelis virginiana*, 30C q 4 hr
- **Varicose veins:** *Ledum palustre*, 30C t.i.d. for 3 days
- **Appendectomy:** *Rhus toxicodendron*, 30C t.i.d. for 3 days
- **Partial gastrectomy:** *Raphanus sativus*, 30C t.i.d. for 3 days, and when necessary (p.r.n.) for flatulence
- **Cholecystectomy:** *Lycopodium clavatum*, 30C t.i.d. for 3 days
- **Eye operations:** *Ledum palustre*, 30C q 4 hr
- **Tonsillectomy and adenoidectomy:** *Rhus toxicodendron*, 30C q 4 hr and p.r.n. for pain
- **Orthopedic surgery:** *Arnica montana*, 30C t.i.d. for 3 days
  —Involving cartilage and periosteum: *Ruta graveolens*, 30C q 4 hr
  —Including the spine: *Hypericum perforatum*, 30C q 4 hr
- **Mastoidectomy:** *Arnica montana*, 30C
- **Hemorrhoids:** *Staphysagria* or *Aesculus hippocastanum*, 30C q 4 hr for 2–3 days
- **Circumcision:** *Staphysagria*, 30C and *Arnica montana*, 30C q 4 hr

The following prescriptions have been suggested by physicians elsewhere in the homeopathic literature for these additional situations:

- **Plastic surgery:** *Arnica montana*, 200C or 1M q 12 hr for three doses
  —Face: *Apis mellifica*, 9C, *Arnica montana*, 9C, and *Histaminum hydrochloricum*, 9C every half hour in alternation (Jouanny, 1980); others might use the 200C q 4–6 hr for three to six doses
- **Uterine/ovarian surgery:** *Bellis perennis*, 200C q 12 hr for six doses
- **Episiotomy:** *Calendula officinalis*, 200C t.i.d. for six doses
- Large wounds with loss of flesh and poorly healing wounds: *Calendula officinalis*, 200C t.i.d. for three days
- **Hypersensitivity to pain and clean-cut wound:** *Staphysagria*, 200C q 4 hr then p.r.n. for pain
- **Dental work:** *Apis mellifica*, 7C and *Arnica montana*, 15C in alternation q 2 hr

Arnica montana, 15C given together to be more effective than placebo for preventing edema after tooth extraction (Michaud, 1981). This finding suggests further research needs to be conducted to determine whether *Apis mellifica* alone might help prevent edema after oral surgery or tooth extraction. (See Chapter 2, *Arnica montana*.)

COMPLICATIONS AFTER SURGERY

Agitation in Infants

Alibeu and Jobert (1990) conducted a double-blind placebo-controlled study of 50 infants with postoperative pain and intense anxiety using *Aconitum napellus*, 4C (*n* = 50). The results were highly favorable for homeopathy over placebo. Internal validity was evaluated as a 40 on the Jadad scale, and 57 on a more elaborate scale (of 100) by independent researchers (Linde et al., 1997). Most homeopathic clinicians in North America would predict that a higher potency medicine, such as 30C, would be even more effective.

Anesthesia Reactions

The medicine can be prescribed in the 30C potency every half hour for three doses. If there is concern about aspiration of the pellets, the medicine can be diluted in a little pure water and a drop placed on the tongue. If these classical homeopathic medicines for difficult recovery do not prove effective with contemporary problems, the actual anesthesias used in surgery could be made into homeopathic medicines, and, as an experiment, given when needed postoperatively.

Opium—The patient has difficulty recovering from anesthesia. He or she is semicomatose, and has a red face and stertorous respiration.

Phosphorus—Post anesthesia nausea or vomiting is experienced.

Flatulent Distension

Carbo vegetabilis—The clinician should prescribe the 30C or 200C, six doses, every half hour if the patient is alleviated by *eructations*.

Phytolacca decandra or Pulsatilla—If the patient is *not* relieved by eructations or passing flatus, the clinician should prescribe one or the other of these for six doses every half hour (Foubister, 1989).

Ileus

There have been six studies on the treatment of ileus with *Raphanus sativus, Arnica montana, Cinchona officinalis, Opium,* and *Pyrogenium* in low potencies, in various combinations and alone; the results were very mixed. Some could speculate that the lackluster results could be ascribed to the exclusive use of low, less-effective potencies. The studies that included *Arnica montana* and *Raphanus sativus* in the 7C or lower potencies had no effect on the resolution of ileus, while a study of a complex that included *Raphanus sativus* and *Arnica montana*, 9C showed a positive effect. This promising study of 200 patients showed *Opium*, 9C; *Raphanus sativus*, 9C; and *Arnica montana*, 9C in combination to be significantly more effective than placebo according to global assessment by the patient (Aulagnier, 1985). Independent reviewers rated this study as having moderately good internal validity (Linde, et al., 1997). *Opium* by itself has not been consistently effective in any potency in these trials. The clinician could prescribe *Arnica montana* and *Raphanus sativus* hourly in the 9C potency, or opt for a more effective potency and alternate the 30C of these two medicines every 2 hr while the patient is awake, until the first stool is passed.

Nerve Pain

Hypericum perforatum—The 200C potency can be given two to three times a day, then as needed for *shooting*, needle-like, or jolting pains from nerve damage or regeneration.

Ocular Surgery, Sequelae

The 30C potency of the indicated medicine may be prescribed three times a day for 3 days.

Arnica montana—*Arnica montana* is prescribed for diplopia, muscular paralysis, and retinal hemorrhage.

Asarum europium—This medicine is indicated for darting pains in the eyes.

Bryonia alba—Pressing, crushing, and aching pain in the eye can be treated with *Bryonia alba*. The patient has soreness from touch and motion of the eye.

Crocus sativa—The patient experiences electric sparks in the visual field. He or she must wipe the eyes as if mucus or water were in them. The patient has a sensation in the eyes as though she or he had been crying violently, as if cold air were rushing through them, or as if there were smoke in them. The pupils are dilated and slow to react. The lids are heavy. There may be ciliary neuralgia, extreme photophobia, or an embolism of the central retinal artery.

Ignatia amara—*Ignatia amara* is used to treat spasms of the lids and neuralgic pain around the eyes. There are flickering zigzags in the visual field.

Ledum palustre—There are contused wounds with aching in the eyes. There is extravasation of blood in the lids, conjunctivae, or vitreous body.

Rhus toxicodendron—The orbits are swollen, red, and edematous. The patient is photophobic. The eyes exude a profuse flow of yellow pus. The lids are edematous and inflamed; they stick together when closed. There is a circumscribed corneal injection. The cornea is ulcerated. The eye is painful to turn, or press on. There is profuse lacrimation; hot, scalding tears gush out when the lids are open.

Zincum metallicum—The patient sees luminous bodies in the visual field or experiences intense burning after eye surgery.

Phantom Limb Pain

There has been no research done on the homeopathic treatment of phantom limb pain, but the following medicines are mentioned in homeopathic reference materials (Boericke, 1983; Phatak, 1977; van Zandvoort, 1997). The clinician may prescribe the 200C two times a day for three doses, then again as needed if it proves helpful for the pain.

Allium cepa—Neuralgic pains feel like fine threads.

Hypericum perforatum—There is sharp pain that feels as though it is shooting up the amputated limb.

Symphytum officinale—If the above regimes are ineffective, *Symphytum officinale* may be prescribed.

Scar Tissue

The following medicines have been reported to be helpful for problems with stenosis or keloids following surgery; there has been no relevant research conducted. The 12C potency could be given a trial twice a day for several months.

Thiosinaminum—*Thiosinaminum* is the routine medicine for problems related to scar tissue, especially when scar tissue causes stenosis of the intestines or fallopian tubes. There are anecdotal reports of female infertility being corrected by this medicine when the cause was scar tissue obstructing the tubes. The clinician should prescribe the 30C potency once a day for a week. If it appears to be effective, it may be continued until it is no longer needed or effective.

Carcinosinum—*Carcinosinum* is reportedly helpful for keloid scars from plastic surgery.

Graphites—*Graphites* is used to treat keloids in patients with generally rough, hard, and dry skin, and thickened and discolored nails. Some cognitive dullness is usually reported by the patient regardless of their level of intelligence. This medicine is typically useful in chilly, solidly built, and heavyset patients.

Iris tenax—*Iris tenax* is used for scar tissue of the right iliac fossa.

Silicea—*Silicea* is indicated for keloids and scars that suddenly become painful. Foreign bodies in the body, splinters, and pieces of metal are reputedly expelled through the skin when this medicine is taken internally. The patients are chilly and mild-mannered.

Sepsis

Pyrogenium, 200C may be given three times a day concurrently with antibiotics. It is especially indicated when the fever spikes with minimal or no acceleration of pulse and then the pulse accelerates when the fever reduces. *Arsenicum album* is the medicine to use when the patient is restless, chilly, anxious, irritable, and thirsty for sips of fluids.

Weakness

The medicine should be prescribed in the 30C potency twice a day for a few days.

Cinchona officinalis—*Cinchona officinalis* is used for postsurgical weakness, abdominal distension, and hyperesthesia to contact.

Wound Infection

The medicines for infected surgical wounds are the same as those for infection following injury. See Chapter 17, Injuries and Emergencies.

PART IV

Homeopathic Medicine: The Big Picture

Part IV is a resource for those who want to go beyond basic practical prescribing information. To understand the matrix from which modern homeopathy evolved, it is necessary to obtain an overview of its rich professional and philosophical history. The field of homeopathy is replete with resources for those who want to explore the possibilities of further education, a specialty practice in homeopathy, or research. The appendixes provide an up-to-date guide to all the official homeopathic medicines (and the source material from which they were prepared); a directory of accredited educational programs; contact information for professional support, information, and modes of access to the homeopathic literature; patient education materials; and a guide to well-established homeopathic pharmacies.

CHAPTER 29

History and Conceptual Framework of Homeopathic Medicine

ORIGINS OF HOMEOPATHIC MEDICINE

In 1784 a physician named Samuel Hahnemann was dissatisfied with the results he was having practicing the conventional medicine of the time, as the town doctor for Gommern, Germany (Bradford, 1894). The medical use of strong mercury compounds, leeches, and bloodletting was common in that period. Hahnemann felt he could not ethically continue practicing medicine even though he had eliminated the most dangerous treatments from his practice. He did not feel it was proper to prescribe drugs that were unreliable. He had a growing family to support, and the loss of employment caused them great hardship. After he closed his practice, he made his living translating medical books from French, English, and Italian into German, and conducting research in chemistry.

In 1790 Hahnemann translated *Cullen's Materia Medica*, a botanical medicine text, from English to German. In this *materia medica*, the therapeutic uses of drugs were noted, juxtaposed with the toxic effects produced by them. The book included a monograph on *Cinchona*, a Peruvian bark from which quinine is derived, which was used then as now to treat malaria. Malaria is characterized by periodic attacks of chills, fever, malaise, myalgia, and headache, and has a chronic, relapsing nature. A healthy patient who has received a toxic dose of *Cinchona* will experience periodic attacks of chills, fever, malaise, myalgia, and headache. Hahnemann thought this was noteworthy and postulated, based on his experience working with botanical and mineral medicines, that there was a universal law of nature that "like cures like." From this theory, the name *homeopathy* was derived. *Homeos* means similar in Latin, and *pathos* means disease or pathology.

In 1810 Hahnemann's (1982, reprint) *Organon of Medicine*, the first homeopathy textbook, was published. It presented his conceptual framework for the practice of homeopathy, as well as practical instruction for how to accurately and effectively gather data from patients about their subjective symptoms, how to make homeopathic "potencies" from the base substance, and how to prescribe them. It also presented detailed instruction about diet and lifestyle. The book was the fruition of 20 years of testing his new theory in clinical practice.

In *Organon of Medicine*, Hahnemann expressed hostility toward the medical profession and criticized mainstream medical practices mercilessly. He vehemently decried therapies that did not boost the patient's health, but instead treated single symptoms or sets of symptoms. He based his critiques on his experience of practicing according to his holistic, vitalistic theory of health and healing, compared to the conventional style of medicine he had practiced and observed as a young physician. He believed that treating the symptom as the disease, instead of rooting out the cause was not only ineffective in the long term, but had the potential to cause a variety of more serious chronic diseases.

Hostile though he was to conventional medicine, he and the majority of his students were educated as physicians. Hahnemann called homeopathy the practice of *medicine*. Thus, its practice has been viewed as such in most of the countries where it has taken root, not a form of energetic or spiritual healing that happens to involve little sugary pellets.

The practice of homeopathy subsequently rapidly rose in popularity in Europe in the nineteenth century because death rates of patients treated in epidemic diseases such as scarlet fever, cholera, diptheria, and measles were lower for patients treated by homeopathic physicians and later at homeopathic hospitals, than by conventional ones (Bradford, 1894). In a well-documented episode in 1854, a cholera epidemic in England had a death rate of over 60% when treated by standard medicine, while a death rate under 30% was achieved by homeopathic doctors. It might be supposed that homeopathic hospitals had significantly better oral rehydration programs, less severe cases, or other factors that would account for the difference. However, this appears not to be true, according to one medical historian (Leary, 1987, 1994).

HOMEOPATHY IN NORTH AMERICA

Hans Burch Gram was the first homeopathic physician to practice in the United States. He was born in Boston, went to Copenhagen for his medical education, and finally settled in New York City to practice in 1825. The second was John Grey, who presented Dr. Gram with three patients who had been unresponsive to conventional treatment, who were then cured by homeopathy. Many of the homeopathic physicians in U.S. medical history were converts to homeopathic medicine (Coulter, 1973; Winston, 1995). They developed a zeal for homeopathy as converts that was rarely equaled by later graduates of homeopathic medical schools.

The first physicians began practicing homeopathy in Canada in the mid-1840s. Drs. J. O. Rosenstein and Arthur Fisher, MD of Montréal, Quebec, and Dr. Joseph J. Lancaster (1813–1884) of Norwich, Ontario, were among the earliest. The first national professional society, the Homeopathic Medical Society of Canada, was founded in 1854 (Ania, 1995). Only a few homeopathic hospitals opened in Canada.

The first homeopathic medical college was founded in 1833 in Allentown, Pa., called the North American Academy of the Homeopathic Healing Art, or simply the Allentown Academy (Winston, 1995). Classes were taught primarily to German immigrants. Virtually all of the great homeopathic physicians of the mid-nineteenth century were trained or taught there. Homeopathy was most popular in Pennsylvania and New York at this time primarily because of the large numbers of German immigrants there.

The New England Female Homeopathic Medical College was founded in Boston in 1843—the first women's medical college in the United States. It later merged with Boston University, which continued teaching homeopathic medicine into the twentieth century. There were similar homeopathic medical schools subsumed into larger institutions at the University of Minnesota, the University of Michigan, MCP Hahnemann University in Philadelphia, and elsewhere (Coulter, 1973).

The American Institute of Homeopathy, the first national medical organization in the United States, was founded in 1844. The American Medical Association (AMA) was formed by the conventional medical doctors (then termed the "regulars") in 1847, partly in response to the threat of organized homeopathic medicine. Homeopathy had already been stigmatized as quackery by the regulars by the 1840s (Coulter, 1973, p.181). The original charter of the AMA prohibited consultation by any of their members with physicians "whose practice is based on an exclusive dogma to the rejection of the accumulated experience of the profession" at the risk of expulsion. While there were legitimate reasons for rejecting homeopathy as no more than placebo medicine (because the doses used by most homeopathic doctors were believed to be too low to be effective), this stigmatization of homeopathic physicians by the AMA may have had less altruistic motives as well. There is some evidence that the homeopathic physicians of the time made more money on average from their practices than did conventional medical doctors (Coulter, 1973). Also, consultations with homeopaths by regular physicians had resulted in conversions to the practice of homeopathy. In 1903 the AMA finally invited homeopathic physicians to join, yet when homeopathic doctors did join that organization, their papers were invariably rejected for presentation or publication because they were "unscientific."

In Canada a series of regulatory acts was passed allowing the practice of homeopathic medicine. The first was passed on May 4, 1859, "An Act Respecting Homeopathy," which established the Homeopathic Medical Board of Upper Canada (Ania, 1995). In a unique legislative move in 1869, the province of Ontario began to regulate homeopathic and eclectic doctors with the conventional medical doctors as part of the same provincial body—The College of Physicians and Surgeons of Ontario. Dr. Charles Ernest Bond was the last homeopathic representative on the Council of the College serving until his death on April 1, 1960.

In the 1850s, homeopathic pharmacies began selling what were called homeopathic domestic kits, which were collections of the most commonly used homeopathic medicines—including all the medicines featured in Part II of this book, for self-care by families isolated from medical care. These kits became the only medical care available for white settlers in remote areas, and initiated widespread use of homeopathy as a form of self-care, which has continued to this day.

In 1892, at the peak of homeopathy's popularity, there were approximately 110 homeopathic hospitals in the United States. In addition, there were 145 homeopathic dispensaries (free clinics), 62 homeopathic orphan asylums and rest homes for the elderly, 30 homeopathic nursing homes and sanitaria, and 16 homeopathic insane asylums (Coulter, 1973, p. 304). These were often supported by public funds or community fund-raising.

By 1900 there were over 1,000 homeopathic pharmacies and 15,000 homeopathic physicians in the United States, of which 2,500 were members of the American Institute of Homeopathy. Between 1895 and 1900, it is estimated that 12–20% of all physicians were homeopathic (Coulter, 1973; Starr, 1982). These figures can be misleading because many of these physicians mixed homeopathic and conventional medical approaches, thereby creating the kind of integrative medical approach that has been discussed in this book. Of these physicians, less than 150 doctors were purely homeopathic in their approach. These homeopathic specialists joined a rival homeopathic professional association with more strict inclusion criteria.

Homeopathy never reached the level of popularity in Canada that it did in the United States. At the profession's peak in 1884, there were 80 homeopathic doctors practicing in Canada (Ania, 1995).

Enrollment in homeopathic medical schools began to drop between 1900 and 1909. In 1910 the famous Flexner Report was issued; it evaluated the quality of all the medical schools in the United States. It was extremely critical of the 22 American homeopathic medical colleges, both of their facilities and their clinical instruction. As a result of this report, graduates of these schools were not allowed to sit for their state medical boards, and funding was lost from major donors. The legitimacy of the poor ratings is debated within the homeopathic medical community to this day. Most feel that the criteria used to evaluate the schools showed an inherent bias, not surprising since the AMA was involved in creating them. Yet, in those times, funding was already limited for the homeopathic medical schools because of falling enrollment, and this funding deficiency could be a partial explanation for the inadequate basic science instruction, facilities, and equipment. Given limited resources, funds were prioritized for the teaching of therapeutics and theory. A much larger amount of detail about the therapeutic uses of medicines is undeniably required for homeopathic practice than for conventional medical practice.

By 1918 there were only seven remaining homeopathic medical schools in the United States. In the 1930s the homeopathic hospitals were phased out. By 1959 Hahnemann College in Philadelphia dropped the last homeopathic course, an elective, taught at a medical school in the United States. It was not until the 1990s that homeopathy reemerged as part of a course in medical schools. Today it is usually addressed in a single lecture as a part of an elective survey course in complementary and alternative medicine at many medical schools.

In 1938, before homeopathy's virtual extinction as a medical specialty in the United States, the Food and Drug Act was passed by Congress. Homeopathic medicines were included with the help of Senator Royal Copeland, who had himself been trained as a homeopathic physician (and later practiced primarily conventional medicine) before being elected to the U.S. Senate. The Homeopathic Pharmacopoeia of the United States was recognized in the act as the formulary for homeopathic medicines, thus ensuring that they would be regulated as drugs and protected from becoming outlawed in the medically conservative times that followed.

The longest surviving homeopathic hospital in Canada was located in Montréal. The Homeopathic Hospital was founded in 1894, and later changed its name to the Homeopathic Hospital of Montréal. In 1951 the word *homeopathic* was finally dropped from its name. It became the Queen Elizabeth Hospital (Ania, 1995).

Without the continuing interest and support of a loyal group of consumers who persisted in practicing homeopathic self-care in the 1940s, '50s, and '60s, homeopathy—including the homeopathic manufacturing pharmacies—would have most certainly become extinct in North America.

The other development that helped sustain homeopathy in North America was the emergence of the naturopathic medical profession. In 1956 the National College of Naturopathic Medicine was founded as the first accredited school of naturopathic medicine in North America. Naturopathic medicine is a distinct system of primary health care; it is the art, science, philosophy, and practice of diagnosis, treatment, and prevention of illness. The techniques of naturopathic medicine include modern, traditional, scientific, and empirical methods. Naturopathic practice includes the following diagnostic and therapeutic modalities: nutritional medicine; botanical medicine; naturopathic physical medicine, including naturopathic manipulative therapy and hydrotherapy; public health measures and hygiene; counseling; minor surgery; homeopathy; acupuncture; naturopathic midwifery (natural childbirth); and appropriate methods of laboratory and clinical diagnosis. Graduates of naturopathic medical schools are licensed to practice in some states and provinces in the United States and Canada. They can specialize in homeopathy if they wish, and many of these specialists are highly regarded in the homeopathic field.

Today there are five North American naturopathic medical schools, two of which, the National College of Naturopathic Medicine in Portland, Ore., and Bastyr University in Seattle, Wash., are fully accredited by the Council on Naturopathic Medical Education. The Southwest College of Natural Health Sciences in Scottsdale, Ariz., and the Canadian College of Naturopathic Medicine in Toronto, Ontario, have been accepted as candidates for accreditation. The College of

Naturopathic Education at the University of Bridgeport is the newest start-up, licensed by the state of Connecticut Department of Education since 1996. Recently, two of the U.S. Naturopathic medical schools and the Canadian College of Naturopathic Medicine in Toronto moved to considerably larger campuses in order to meet their growing student bodies. In 1999, Bastyr University alone had over 1,000 students enrolled in its various degree-granting programs.

Beginning in the 1970s, homeopathy began a general resurgence in the United States, thanks to increased interest in natural and holistic therapies. Doctors and consumers interested in learning about homeopathy invited expert homeopaths from countries where homeopathy had never fallen to the low ebb that it did in North America to teach here. Among the first was George Vithoulkes of Greece, who is not a doctor of any kind, yet had so impressed many doctors in his homeland that he supervised them and ran a homeopathic educational program primarily for physicians in Athens. Virtually all of the North American clinicians who later became influential teachers in their own right were his early students. Later, Dr. Francisco Eizayaga of Argentina, who also greatly influenced homeopathy in the United States, and many teachers from India and England began to lead seminars in the United States. The students of these international educators started most of the formal American and Canadian homeopathic educational programs established in the 1980s. A complete list of accredited schools is in Appendix B.

In Canada, a series of legislative acts has allowed homeopaths to practice under the supervision of a duly registered homeopathic practitioner since 1970 (Ania, 1995). Homeopathic clinicians are attempting to amend the act again to reflect the opening of homeopathic educational programs in Ontario and the greatly increased demand for homeopathic care. A professional association called the Ontario Homeopathic Association was formed. An instructional program, the International Academy of Homeopathy, was begun in 1991, and in 1996, they inaugurated the first full-time, 3-year homeopathic educational program in North America.

HISTORY AND STATUS OF HOMEOPATHIC MEDICINE OVERSEAS

While in 1895, homeopathy was more popular in America than anywhere else in the world, the tide changed early in the twentieth century. Homeopathy became considerably more popular abroad, especially in Europe, South America, and South Asia, than it was in the United States.

At least six French medical schools offer courses leading to a degree in homeopathy, and homeopathy is taught in all pharmacy schools and in four veterinary schools. The most popular over-the-counter cold and influenza medicine in that country is *Oscillococcinum*, a proprietary name for *Anas barbariae hepatis et cordis extractum*, 200C.

In Great Britain, physician-rendered homeopathic treatment is provided in the National Health Service, and the Royal London Homeopathic Hospital carries on a 150-year legacy of hospital-based homeopathic treatment. The London Homeopathic Hospital was founded in 1849 by Dr. Quin, England's first homeopathic physician, for the free treatment of the poor.

Some of the most popular over-the-counter medicines in Germany are homeopathic, and significant inroads are being made by the homeopathic medical profession as well. The German Public Insurance Plans (IKK) and the German Association of Homeopathic Doctors launched a large field study in 1997. The goal of this project is for public insurances to cover homeopathic treatment by a physician. Early results indicated that over 80% of the treated patients showed significant improvement of their health problems, and no adverse reactions were reported from homeopathic treatment. After 1 year of observation, potential savings were documented, and patients' work-related disability claims were smaller. Only MDs with title "Homöopathischer Arzt," meaning 3 years of homeopathic education and regular participation in required homeopathic continuing medical education are allowed to participate in that study. Homeopathy is also popular throughout the rest of Europe, although less so in Russia.

In India there are over 100,000 homeopathic doctors and over 100 homeopathic medical colleges. In 1987 the government established homeopathic drug detoxification clinics in six different police stations in New Delhi. In addition to their support of homeopathic drug detoxification clinics, the Indian government supports five major homeopathic research centers, and dozens of affiliated clinics that collect data on the results of homeopathic treatment (Jonas & Jacobs, 1996). Mother Teresa offered homeopathic care at her missions; she opened her first charitable homeopathic dispensary in Calcutta in 1950 (Ullman, 1996).

Homeopathy is also relatively popular in Mexico and South America. In Brazil, the homeopathic medicine specialty started with the arrival in 1840 of Benoit Jules Mure, a French doctor. Homeopathic medical doctors have practiced freely in Brazil since that time. In 1980 the

Federal Council of Medicine recognized homeopathy as a medical specialty. Homeopathy is also widely used in Argentina, and in Mexico, there are five homeopathic medical colleges, including two in Mexico City (Ullman, 1996).

It is important to note that not all homeopathic clinicians have been physicians. In India and the United Kingdom, there are professional homeopaths who trained in freestanding homeopathic colleges, who can practice legally. There is a large group of nonmedical people who attend advanced courses in homeopathy in the United States. There are also systems of certification and registration emerging. These programs will ultimately lead to a legal structure for a separate homeopathic profession in America. Nurses, nurse practitioners, and physician assistants have also become educated as expert homeopathic clinicians. Some dentists, chiropractors, and veterinarians have also incorporated homeopathy into their practices.

HAHNEMANN'S GRAND THEORY

Homeopathy, Health, and Illness

Hahnemann (1982, reprint) presented a unique model of health and disease in his *Organon of Medicine*. He believed that the human body had what might now be called an energetic field that pervaded and animated it. This vital force is what distinguishes the living human being from a corpse, and prevents decay of the body into the chemicals of which it is composed. "The body is the material instrument of this life force" (Hahnemann, 1982, reprint, para. 10).

This vitalist view of life is antithetical to the predominant mechanist view of the twentieth century. A modern physiologist summarized, "The mechanist view of life holds that all phenomena, no matter how complex, are ultimately describable in terms of physical and chemical laws and that no 'vital force' distinct from matter and energy is required to explain life. The human being is a machine—an enormously complex machine, but a machine nevertheless" (Vander, Sherman, & Luciano, 1985, p. 1)

Interestingly, the only significant group of mainstream health care professionals who openly hold to a vitalist view of health and disease today are holistic nurses, who often call themselves nurse-healers. They are the progeny of three influential maverick nurses: the Nurse Theorists Martha Rogers and her protégé Margaret Newman, and the Formulator of Therapeutic Touch (a kind of healing that is believed to work with energy fields), Dolores Krieger (Krieger, 1981).

Rogers proposed in her theory, the Science of Unitary Human Beings, that a person is more than the sum of parts; he or she possesses an energy field that is the fundamental unit of the living. The energy field is infinite and dynamic and in continuous exchange with the environment (Rogers, Malinski, & Manhart-Barrett, 1994). This energy field has a pattern and organization that identifies the person.

Among Newman's main thrusts is that health is not a state of absence of disease, but instead encompasses illness and pathology. She believes, as Hahnemann did, that the pattern that eventually manifests itself as pathology is primary, and exists prior to structural and functional changes. The removal of the pathology will not change the pattern of the individual (Marriner, 1986). Like Hahnemann, she stated that pathological conditions are manifestations of the total pattern of the individual.

Hahnemann believed that when a person is healthy "the spirit-like vital force animating the material human organism reigns in supreme sovereignty" (Hahnemann, 1982, reprint, para. 9). Without a preexisting untunement of this energetic field, he hypothesized, there would be little susceptibility to disease agents and stressors. If a person's invisible vital force is weak or in disorder, disease agents are more apt to cause further disorder in the field. Illness is simply a disordered vital force. In a patient with a curable disease, there will always be symptoms present—the expression of this energetic disorder. Illness does not exist as a separate entity from the person who has symptoms. When the disease agent or stressor has been removed from the patient's life or environment, and there are no more symptoms and signs, then the illness has been cured (Hahnemann, para. 8). Hahnemann made two exceptions to his statement that the illness is gone when the symptoms are gone: (1) purely surgical cases and (2) incurable cases (Hahnemann, paras. 14, 29).

Hahnemann did not claim any specific knowledge of *how* disease agents and stressors create disorders in the field of the patient. His hypothesis for how homeopathic medicines affected the person was that the process of serially diluting and vigorously shaking the medicines as they are being prepared (succussion) released their dynamic powers. Each substance has spirit-like characteristics inherent within it, which are made more potent by the manufacturing process. This force he specifically compared to a magnetic field—a force of nature, which is invisible and yet powerful.

A person taking any medicine experienced a temporary alteration in his or her energetic field, Hahnemann believed, and that alteration had a specific pattern. If the force of the medicine was strong enough, this alteration inevitably created symptoms in a certain pattern specific to the medicine (which he called an *artificial disease*). In conventional medicine, this pattern of symptoms would be called the adverse reactions to the drug. The specific symptom set of a "potentized" homeopathic medicine is called the "proving" symptoms. In conventional medicine, this pattern of symptoms of the drug usually bears no relationship to its therapeutic uses (although therapeutics that fit the homeopathic principle of "like cures like" are not unknown). Hahnemann (1982, reprint, para. 22) named the heterogeneous approach to prescribing *allopathic medicine*.

The *Organon of Medicine* also was critical of traditional botanical medical practitioners who used medicines that created the opposite group of symptoms in the patient than the symptoms of the disease (e.g., prescribing chilling herbs to a patient with a fever). He felt this led to temporary relief and rebound illness. He also felt polypharmacy was too muddled to be truly scientific.

Hahnemann proposed that only a medicine whose symptom pattern most closely resembled the symptom pattern of the disease it is supposed to treat should be prescribed. Then, by using the medicine in an energetically potent form (a homeopathic potency), the energetic pattern of the medicine extinguishes the energetic pattern of the illness, which is inherently weaker (Hahnemann, 1982, reprint, para. 26). The effect of the homeopathic medicine naturally wanes, and the disease does not return, thereby leaving the patient as healthy as before becoming ill.

Hahnemann waited many years after developing this series of hypotheses about health and healing before publicizing them. During this time, he was very active in clinical practice, reported great success in the treatment of acute disease, and won fame for achieving a very low death rate for his patients during a cholera epidemic.

Chronic Illness

Chronic disease proved more unresponsive to treatment according to this basic homeopathic approach. Certain patients seemed to respond and be free of symptoms, and then relapse or develop another malady. He came to believe that chronic disease is related to an underlying diathesis he called a *miasm*. Hahnemann began elucidating this theory in the *Organon of Medicine* and continued, decades later, in a book on the subject called *The Chronic Diseases* (Hahnemann, 1835).

He felt that all the chronic diseases of his day fell into three metadiseases, or diatheses, that were the underlying cause of many diseases called by different names. The least common diathesis he called *sycosis* (not psychosis), which was evidenced by genital warts, gonorrhea, and contraction of the muscles of the flexor tendons, especially the fingers. The second most common was *syphilis*. Hahnemann's most controversial theory was that the most common cause of chronic disease in his patients was a diathesis he called *psora*. This almost ubiquitous disease was evidenced by a tendency for itchy vesicular eruptions, such as that caused by a bacterial suprainfection over itchy skin diseases such as scabies, lichen planus, pediculosis, urticaria, or bullous pemphigoid. Some medical historians link Hahnemann's references to psora as an ancient disease as connoting a relationship to Hansen's disease (leprosy).

Hahnemann decried the use of local measures to eliminate external symptoms found at the start of these three metadiseases. It is easy for a modern clinician to understand the negative ramifications of cauterizing a syphilitic chancre, and of eliminating a urethral discharge of gonorrhea with no further evaluation or treatment, although this sort of approach was apparently not uncommon in Europe in Hahnemann's day. The underlying diseases of syphilis and gonorrhea progress despite palliation of the symptoms.

Harder to believe for the contemporary clinician is the idea that most cutaneous eruptions are part of a healing process that externalizes a deeper disorder, and in doing so protects the vital functions of the physiological systems of the body. This concept, later elaborated by other homeopathic theorists (Vithoulkes, 1980) is that when the person's energetic field becomes disordered, the initial pattern of representative symptoms that results will usually be superficial, often eruptions of the integument or membranes. If these symptoms are eliminated through local medical or surgical means, the underlying disease not only persists, but the energetic field becomes more seriously and deeply disordered and more serious illnesses—that may appear to be unrelated—can develop as a result.

In modern society, people are often stigmatized if they have a skin disease or rash, and viewed as unhealthy. According to Hahnemann, people with skin conditions (while not in perfect health) are usually more healthy than people with other chronic health complaints.

Constantine Hering, a prominent nineteenth-century physician and professor, put together some guidelines for evaluating a patient's response to homeopathic treatment. These are commonly referred to as Hering's Laws, which organized his observations and those of his colleagues in the homeopathic treatment of chronic disease. When a truly curative treatment is administered to a sick person, the symptoms are said to resolve:

1. From above downward
2. From the center to the periphery
3. From the most essential to the least essential organs
4. In the reverse order of their original occurrence

All of which may be summarized as predicting a general course of a recovery in which the deeper, more serious, symptoms of the person are replaced by less serious and more superficial ones. The process of recovery may even retrace the patient's previous pattern of decline.

If, for example, an asthma patient had a chronic rash that was suppressed with cortisone cream immediately preceding the onset of the asthma, the rash would be expected to return when homeopathic medicine successfully treated the asthma. The rash, or rather the whole imbalance of the person, would then be treated with homeopathy and eventually resolve as well.

Hahnemann believed that there were special antisycotic, antisyphilitic, and antipsoric medicines that had the ability to cure the chronic diseases of his day. If they were also used in the treatment of acute illnesses, these medicines are called *polycrests*, a term that indicated their versatility in a wide variety of medical situations.

Many of Hahnemann's colleagues, and respected homeopaths since then, disagree with Hahnemann's thesis about miasms, or feel it is not relevant today. Some feel that any of the over 1,000 homeopathic medicines now extant might be useful for chronic disease; some of them (Hahnemann's antimiasmatic medicines) just happen to be more commonly indicated. Some homeopathic specialists believe that a specific nosode—a medicine made from a disease product—may be necessary during the treatment of a patient with a chronic disease. This sort of prescription is often made in a situation where a person's decline in health was preceded by a disease that was suppressed with drugs.

To a homeopath the removal of a pathogen, such as the treatment of a bacterial illness with antibiotics, is not necessarily truly curative of the person as a whole. For example, the treatment of *gonococcus* or *Helicobacter pylori* with antibiotics, while effective in the acute condition, might trigger the decline of a person's health in general. Therefore, a nosode made from a (killed) gonorrheal, urethral discharge (one of Hahnemann's original antisycotic medicines) or from *H. pylori* might be used during the treatment of a patient with a chronic disease that started after the infection was conventionally treated.

All classically trained homeopathic clinicians, however, treat patients with chronic illnesses primarily with a single medicine indicated by all of their patient's symptoms according to the Law of Similars. The need for meticulous and exhaustive data gathering was stressed by Hahnemann, who specifically instructed his students to learn about the constitution, emotional and intellectual character, activities, way of life, social position, family relations, stage of life, and sexual health of the patient in addition to all his or her cognitive, emotional, and physical symptoms. Doing so necessitates a long interview and appropriate physical examination for new patients, typically 1–2 hr in length.

CONTEMPORARY APPROACHES TO HOMEOPATHIC THEORY

Hahnemann's grand theory is too abstract to be scientifically testable. However, there are several contemporary explanatory and predictive theories that emerge from it that can be translated into testable hypotheses.

1. A "vital force" exists. Since Hahnemann used the analogy of magnetism to describe the effect of a well-selected homeopathic potency on a human being, Hahnemannian theory could be reframed in terms of the emerging scientific field of bioelectromagnetics (BEM) and human health. There is hope that BEM may offer an explanation of why many different alternative medical practices work (e.g., homeopathy, acupuncture, and energy healing). Like the vital force elucidated by Hahnemann, electrical currents exist in the body that produce electrical fields that extend beyond the epidermis. The interactions of oscillating nonionizing EM fields in an extremely low-frequency (ELF) range with the human magnetic field have been observed to have positive and vigorous biological effects (Becker & Marino, 1982; Brighton & Pollack, 1991). The biological effects of low-level energy fields are being investigated by researchers from various fields (see "Suggested Readings on Bioelectromagnetics and Human Health"). New generations of magnetometers and electrometers, which are more sensitive than electroencephalography and electrocardiography technologies, have made the investigations of nonionizing BEM fields possible.

The question remains: What is the role of water in relation to BEM fields? Could the process of serial dilution and agitation of a substance in water stimulate the formation of a electrodynamic polarization field unique to the substance that was diluted? This has not yet been studied. If it is possible for water to carry this kind of information, some theorists hypothesize that the healing effect of homeopathic medicines could be related to the organizing effect of such a field on other molecules (like light organizes the molecules it contacts) or a coherent excitation effect in which molecules vibrating at one frequency induce other molecules to vibrate at the same frequency (Jonas & Jacobs, 1996, p. 87).

2.a. The dynamic power of a substance is released through the process of serially diluted agitated preparations of homeopathic medicines.

Several outdated studies used early nuclear magnetic resonance spectroscopy to examine homeopathic medicines; some suggested a difference between homeopathic potencies and placebo. Replication could be attempted with current technology.

2b. The homeopathic manufacturing process of potentization (the dilution and agitation process) makes higher potency medicines more clinically effective than lower potencies of the same medicine.

In a recent meta-analysis of all the available double-blind, placebo-controlled homeopathic clinical research thus far, Linde et al. (1997) found a pooled odds ratio of 2·66 in favor of homeopathy in the subset of 31 studies that used high potencies exclusively. There have not been studies replicated with significantly different potencies using the same protocols.

3. The therapeutic efficacy of the individualization of a single homeopathic medicine should be based on the totality of the person's symptoms.

Although not statistically significant, the meta-analysis of Linde et al. (1997) of the extant homeopathic clinical research suggests that an *isopathic* approach to acute illness may equal or exceed in effectiveness the individualized approach to homeopathic prescribing.

Isopathy is the routine prescribing of a medicine manufactured from the chemical, drug, or diseased tissue for illnesses they have caused (e.g., candida in potency for a yeast infection, the measles–mumps–rubella vaccine for someone who has never been well since they had the MMR shot). Other forms of homeopathic prescribing have not yet shown the efficacy of the isopathic or classical homeopathic approaches.

There is a substantial body of scientific research, much of it from outside the homeopathic field, that has shown a biological effect from ultradilute, aqueous solutions (see "Suggested Readings on Research on Ultradilute Solutions"). Some explanatory theories for why these unexpected effects might occur include the organization of water molecules in cage-like clusters (clathrates) that vary according to the chemical that was dissolved, and isotopic self-organization effects of oxygen isotopes (Jonas & Jacobs, 1996, p. 87).

There have been a few book-length attempts to organize a contemporary, science-based, grand theory about how homeopathy works from explanatory theories discussed in this chapter and elsewhere (Bastide, 1997; Bellavite & Signorini, 1995; Conte, Lasne, Berliocchi, & Vernot, 1996). However, for the average primary care clinician, who is neither a physicist nor a biochemist, it is difficult to assess the fundamental soundness of the highly technical, interdisciplinary material presented by these theorists/scientists. This much is certain: if these theories prove to be reliably predictive of experimental outcomes, they will revolutionize not only medicine, but biology and chemistry as well. And, if no scientific explanation is ultimately found as the basis of homeopathy, no number of positive clinical studies will convince skeptics of its effectiveness.

SUGGESTED READINGS ON BIOELECTROMAGNETICS AND HUMAN HEALTH

Adair, R.K. (1991). Constraints on biological effects of weak extremely low-frequency electromagnetic fields. *Physical Review, 43,* 1039–1048.

Adey, W.R. (1992). Collective properties of cell membranes. In B. Norden and C. Ramel (Eds.), *Interaction mechanisms of low-level electromagnetic fields in living systems* (pp. 47–77). Symposium, Royal Swedish Academy of Sciences, Stockholm. New York: Oxford University Press.

Becker, R.O. (1990). A technique for producing regenerative healing in humans. *Frontier Perspectives, 1*(2), 1–2.

Becker, R.O. (1992). Effect of anodally generated silver ions on fibrosarcoma cells. *Electro- and Magnetobiology, 11,* 57–65.

Becker, R.O., & Marino, A.A. (1982). *Electromagnetism and life.* Albany, NY: State University of New York Press.

Blank, M., &. Findl, E. (Eds.). (1987). *Mechanistic approaches to interactions of electric and electromagnetic fields with living systems.* New York: Plenum Publishing.

Brighton, C.T., & Pollack, S.R. (Eds.). (1991). *Electromagnetics in medicine and biology.* San Francisco: San Francisco Press, Inc.

Frohlich, H. (1984). General theory of coherent excitations in biological systems. In A.R. Adey & A.F. Lawrence (Eds.), *Nonlinear electrodynamics in biological systems* (pp. 491–496). New York: Plenum Publishing.

Grundler, W. (1985). Frequency-dependent biological effects of low intensity microwaves. In A. Chiabrara, C. Nicolini, & H.P. Schwan (Eds.), *Interactions between electromagnetic fields and cells* (pp. 459–482). New York: Plenum Publishing.

Liboff, A.R. (1985). Cyclotron resonance in membrane transport. In A. Chiaberra, C. Nicolini, & H.P. Schwan (Eds.), *Intersection between electromagnetic fields and cells* (pp. 281–296). New York: Plenum Publishing.

Marino, A.A. (Ed.). (1988). *Modern bioelectricity.* New York: Marcel Dekker, Inc.

Michaelson, S.M. (1985). Subtle effects of radiofrequency energy absorption and their physiological implications. In A. Chiaberra, C. Nicolini, & H.P. Schwan (Eds.), *Intersection between electromagnetic fields and cells* (pp. 281–296). New York: Plenum Publishing.

O'Connor, M.E., Bentall, R.H.C., & Monahan, J.C. (Eds.). (1990). *Emerging electromagnetic medicine conference proceedings.* New York: Springer-Verlag New York.

O'Connor, M.E., & Lovely, R.H. (Eds.). (1988). *Electromagnetic fields and neurobehavioral Function.* New York: Alan R. Liss, Inc.

Popp, F.A., Warnke, U., Konig, H.L., & Peschka, W. (1989). *Electromagnetic bio-information.* Baltimore: Urban & Schwarzenberg.

Ramel, C., & Norden, B. (Eds.). (1991). *Interaction mechanisms of low-level electromagnetic fields with living systems.* London: Oxford University Press.

SUGGESTED READINGS ON RESEARCH ON ULTRADILUTE SOLUTIONS

Aguejoue, O., Belougne-Malfatti, E., Doutremepuich, F., Belon, P., & Doutremepuich, C. (1998a). Thromboembolic complications several days after a single-dose administration of aspirin. *Thrombosis Research, 89,* 123–127.

Aguejoue O., Belougne-Malfattim E., Doutremepuich, F., Belon, P., & Doutremepuich, C. (1998b). Combination of two doses of acetyl salicylic acid: Experimental study of arterial thrombosis. *Thrombosis Research, 90,* 215–221.

Bastide, M. (1997). *Signal and images.* Dordrecht, The Netherlands: Kluwer Academic Publishers.

Bastide, M., Daurat, V., Doucet-Jeboeuf, M., Pelegrin, A., & Dorfman, P. (1987). Immunomodulator activity of very low doses of *Thymulin* in mice. *International Journal of Immunotherapy, 3*(3), 191–200.

Bastide, M., Doucet-Jebocuf, M., & Daurat, V. (1985). Activity and chronopharmacology of very low doses of physiological immune inducers. *Immunology Today, 6*(8), 234–235.

Bastide, M., & Lagache, A. (1992). *The paradigm of signifiers.* Paris: Alpha Bleue Publishers.

Belon P., Cumps J., Ennis M., Mannaioni, P.F., Sainte-Laudy, J., Roberfroid, M., & Weigant, F.A.C. (1999). Inhibition of human basophil degranulation by successive histamine dilutions: Results of a European multi-centre trial. *Inflammation-Research, Res 48* (Suppl. 1), S17–S18.

Bonavida, B., Safrit, J., Morimoto, H., Mizutani, Y., Uslu, R. Borsellino, N., Frost, P., Berek, J., Belldegrun, A., Zighelboim, J., Chuen-pei, Ng, C., & Mori, S. (1997). Cross-resistance of tumor cells to chemotherapy and immunotherapy: Approaches to reverse resistance and implications in gene therapy (review). *Oncology Reports, 4,* 201–205.

Cazin, J.C., Cazin, M., & Boiron, J. (1987). A study of the effect of decimal and centessimal dilutions of arsenic on the retention and mobilization of arsenic in rats. *Human Toxicology, 135*(6), 315–320.

Demidem, A., Lam, T., Alas, S., Hariharan, K., Hanna, N., & Bonavida, B. (1997). Chimeric anti-CD20 (IDEC- C2B8): Monoclonal antibody sensitizes a B-Cell lymphoma cell line to cell killing by cytotoxic drugs. *Cancer Biotherapy & Radiopharmaceuticals, 12*(3), 177–186.

Doucet-Jaboeuf, M., Pélegrin, A., Cot, M.C., Guillemain, J., & Bastide, M. (1984). Seasonal variations in the humoral immune response in mice following administration of thymic hormones. *Annual Review Chronopharmacology, 1,* 231–234.

Doutremepuich, C. (Ed.). (1991). *Ultra low doses.* London: Taylor & Francis Publishers.

Doutremepuich, C., Aguejoue, M.S., & Belon, P. (1996). Effects of ultra-low dose aspirin on embolization in a model of laser-induced thrombosus formation. *Seminars in Thrombosis and Hemostasis, 22* (Suppl. 1).

Doutremepuich, C., Aguejoute, O., Pintigny, D., Sertillanges, M.N., & De Seze, O. (1994). Thrombogenic properties of ultra low dose of acetylsalicylic acid in a vessel model of laser-induced thrombus formation. *Thrombosis Research, 76*(2), 225–229.

Doutremepuich, C., De Seze, O., Le roy, D., Lalanne, M.C., & Anne, M.C. (1990). Aspirin at very ultra low dosage in healthy volunteers: Effects on bleeding time, platelet aggregation and coagulation. *Haemostasis, 20,* 99–105.

Doutremepuich, C., De Seze, O., Anne, M.C., Hariveau, E., & Quilichini, R. (1987). Platelet aggregation on whole blood after administration of ultra low dosage acetylsalicylic acid in healthy volunteers. *Thrombosis Research, 47,* 373–377.

Doutremepuich, C., Pailley, D., Anne, M.C., De Seze, O., Paccalin, J., & Quilichini, R. (1987). Template bleeding time after ingestion of ultra low dosages of acetylsalicylic acid in healthy subjects: Preliminary study. *Thrombosis Research, 48,* 501–504.

Endler, P.C., Pongrantz, W., Kastberger, G., Wiegant, F.A.C., & Schulte, J. (1994). The effect of highly diluted thyroxine on the climbing activity of frogs. *Veterinary and Human Toxicology, 36*(1), 56–59.

Endler, P.C., Pongratz, W., Smith, C.W., & Schulte, J. (1995). Non-molecular information transfer from thyroxine to frogs with regards to homeopathic toxicology. *Veterinary and Human Toxicology 37,* 259–260.

Frost, P., Peing, C., Belldegrun, A., & Bonavida, B. (1997). Immunosensitization of prostate carcinoma cell lines for lymphocytes. (CTL, TIL, LAK)-mediated apoptosis via the Fas-Fas ligand pathway of cytotoxicity. *Cellular Immunology, 180,* 70–83.

Lalanne, M.C., De Seze, O., Doutremepuich, C., & Belon, P. (1991). Could proteolytic enzyme modulate the interaction platelets/vessel wall in the presence of ASA at ultra low doses? *Thrombosis Research, 63,* 419–426.

Lalanne, M.C., Doutremepuich, C., De Seze, O., & Belon, P. (1990). What is the effect of acetylsalicylic acid at ultra low dose on the interaction platelets/vessel wall? *Thrombosis Research, 60,* 231–236.

Lalanne, M.C., Ramboer, I., De Seze, O., & Doutremepuich, C. (1992). In-vitro platelets/endothelial cells interactions in presence of acetylsalicylic acid at various dosages. *Thrombosis Research, 65,* 33–43.

Lee, M., Cryer, B., & Feldman, M. (1994). Dose effects of aspirin on gastric prostaglandins and stomach mucosal injury. *Annals of Internal Medicine, 120,* 184–189.

Markovac, J., & Goldstein, G.W. (1988). Picomolar concentrations of lead stimulate brain protein kinase C. *Nature, 334,* 71–73.

Marotta, P., & Taddel-Ferretli. (Eds.). (1998). *High dilution effects on cells and integrated systems.* London: World Scientific Publications.

Mizutani, Y., & Bonavida, B. (1993). Overcoming TNFalpha and CDDP resistance of a human ovarian cancer cell line (C30) by treatment with buthionine sulfoximine in combination with TNFalpha and/or CDDP. *International Journal of Oncology, 3,* 229–235.

Mizutani, Y., & Bonavida, B. (1994). Pentoxifylline enhances sensitivity of human ovarian cancer cell line (OVC-8) to TNFalpha. *Biotherapy, 7,* 109–114.

Mizutani, Y., Bonavida, B., & Yoshida, O. (1994a). Cytotoxic effect of diphtheria toxin used alone or in combination with other agents on human renal cell carcinoma cell lines. *Urological Research, 22,* 261–266.

Mizutani, Y., Bonavida, B., & Yoshida, O. (1994b). Enhancement of sensitivity of urinary bladder tumor cells to CDDP by c-myc antisense olignonucleotides. *Cancer, 74*(9), 2546–2554.

Mizutani, Y., Bonavida B., Koishihara, Y., Ohsugi Y., & Yoshida, O. (1995). Sensitization of human renal cell carcinoma cells to cis-diammi-nedichloroplatinum (II) by treatment with anti-IL-6 or anti-IL-6 receptor monoclonal antibody. *Cancer Research, 55,* 590–596.

Mizutani, Y., Bonavida, B., Niu, Y., & Yoshida, O. (1994). Overcoming TNFalpha and drug resistance of human renal cell carcinoma cells by treatment with pentoxifylline in combination with TNFalpha or drugs. The role of TNFalpha mRNA downregulation in tumor cells. *Journal of Urology, 151*(6), 1697–1702.

Mizutani, Y., Yoshida, O., & Bonavida, B. (1997). Bacillus Calmette-Guerin (BCG) in the treatment of superficial bladder cancer: Development of resistance to BCG and strategies for overcoming resistance to BCG (review). *International Journal of Oncology, 11,* 0–00.

Sainte-Laudy, J. (1987). Standardization of basophil degranulation for pharmaceutical studies. *Journal of Immunological Methods, 98,* 279–282.

Sainte-Laudy, J., & Belon, P. (1993). Inhibition of human basophil activation by high dilutions of histamine. *Agents Actions, 38,* C245–C247.

Sainte-Laudy, J., & Belon, P. (1996). Analysis of immunosuppressive activity of serial dilutions of histamine on human basophil activation by flow cytometry. *Inflammation Research, Res. 45* (Suppl. 1), S33–S34.

Sainte-Laudy, J., & Belon, P. (1997). Application of flow cytometry to the analysis of the immunosuppressive effect of histamine dilutions on human basophil activation: Effect of cimetidine. *Inflammation Research, Res 46* (Suppl. 1), S37–S38.

Schultz, J., & Endler, P.C. (1998). *Fundamental research in ultra high dilution and homeopathy.* Dordrecht, The Netherlands: Kluwer Academic Publishers.

Uslu, R., Jewet, A., & Bonavida, B. (1996). Sensitization of human ovarian tumor cells by subtoxic CDDP to anti-Fas antibody-mediated cytotoxicity and apoptosis. *Gynecologic Oncology, 62,* 282–291.

Vesvres, M.H., Doutremepuich, F., Lalanne, M.C.L., & Doutremepuich, C.H. (1993). Effects of aspirin on embolization in an arterial model of laser-induced thrombus formation. *Haemostasis, 23,* 8–12.

Youbicier-Simo, B.J., Boudard, F., Mekaouche, M., Bastide, M., & Bayl, J.D. (1993). Effects of embryonic bursectomy and in-ovo administration of highly diluted bursin on adrenocorticotropic and immune response of chickens. *International Journal of Immunotherapy, 9,* 169–180.

Youbicier-Simo, B.J., Boudard, F., Mekaouche, M., Baylé, J.D., & Bastide, M. (1996a). A role for bursa fabricii and bursin in the ontogeny of the pineal biosynthetic activity in the chicken. *Journal of Pineal Research, 21,* 35–43.

Youbicier-Simo, B.J., Boudard, F., Mekaouche, M., Baylé, J.D., & Bastide, M. (1996b). Specific abolition reversal of pituitary-adrenal activity and control of the humoral immunity in bursectomized chickens through highly dilute bursin. *International Journal of Immunopathological Pharmacology, 9,* 43–51.

Yu, W.K., Morimoto, H., & Bonavida, B. (1995). Regulation of tamoxifen-mediated antitumor cytotoxicity by protein phosphatases and their role in synergy with combination of tamoxifen and TNFalpha. *Cellular Pharmacology, 2,* 15–22.

CHAPTER 30

Taking It Further

After the material in this book has been mastered, the reader can pursue homeopathy further in three general arenas. The first is to keep current through continuing education offerings, through the professional literature, and by joining a professional organization. The second option is to train as a specialist in homeopathy. The third is to conduct or collaborate in research on homeopathy.

PROFESSIONAL DEVELOPMENT FOR THE INTEGRATIVE CLINICIAN

Each health care profession has its own homeopathic organization; some providing board certification options. A person with a serious interest in homeopathy should join a professional organization. A list of such organizations is provided in Appendix C. These groups can provide information about legal and reimbursement issues facing the various professions and connect interested persons with colleagues in their states or provinces. In a few U.S. states, physicians can be licensed under a homeopathic medical board. Information about this can be obtained through the American Institute of Homeopathy.

There are a number of homeopathic professional journals available of which the *British Homeopathic Journal*, the *Journal of the American Institute of Homeopathy, and Biomedical Therapy* are most likely to publish research results. The *New England Journal of Homeopathy* and *Simillimum* have a readership of homeopathic specialists, and are largely composed of case studies of chronic diseases with analyses. There are catalogs that specialize in homeopathic literature and software. The central calendar for continuing education programs for professionals in the United States is in *Homeopathy Today*, the newsletter for members of the National Center for Homeopathy. Subscription information for all of these publications is provided in Appendix C.

ADVANCED HOMEOPATHIC EDUCATION

Advanced acute prescribing and the homeopathic treatment of chronic disease require a formal course of study. The Council on Homeopathic Education reviews the curricula of homeopathic medical courses for acceptable content based on generally acceptable criteria. Appendix B contains a list of all currently accredited professional courses. These schools usually offer a certificate of completion for the program. Most are designed for the working adult. A certificate has no legal standing and does not guarantee one's legal standing with regard to practicing.

Some courses offer a broad overview of various styles of practice and approaches to prescribing homeopathic medicines; others emphasize the preferred approach of the faculty members. Some programs are taught by teams of several instructors, and others have one main teacher (often a maverick international lecturer and author). Prospective students would benefit from reading the work of faculty members to ensure a good fit with their educational needs. It is also advisable to thoroughly investigate all available programs during the selection process. Student financial aid for health professionals is unlikely.

Video presentations of actual patients are generally accepted to be indispensable to learning through case studies. Before the age of video, patients were routinely interviewed in front of classes, which presented ethical concerns for some.

Some questions to ask the admissions staff of homeopathic educational programs:

- What are your admissions criteria?
- Would some of my classmates have no medical background?
- What percentage of applicants are rejected for admission?
- Is the school a for-profit business or a nonprofit organization?
- If it is a business, who owns it?
- Who are the faculty, and what are their credentials?
- How many years have they practiced homeopathy, and are they still practicing?

- Do they teach a variety of prescribing styles?
- Is there any literature that reflects the school's approach to the practice of homeopathy, or the educational process?
- What percentage of the learning process is formatted as faculty lecture, small group work, homework, and independent study?
- Are patient videos used as part of the educational process?
- Is written permission obtained from patients whose "cases" are presented?
- Is clinical supervision part of the course of study?
- How are students evaluated?
- Are graduates of your school being followed to see how many are actually using homeopathy in practice? If so, what is the percentage?
- Can you provide me with the names of some graduates I can talk to about their experiences as students here?
- Is there any research being conducted at your institution?
- Is any community service being provided by your institution, and is there any requirement for public service by faculty or students?
- Are credits transferable to any other institution?
- Are there any homeopathic specialty boards that have accepted course work at your institution toward their course requirements?

THE ROLE OF THE HOMEOPATHIC SPECIALIST

In the 1990s, the term *homeopathic specialist* came into use to describe clinicians who practice primarily homeopathy and have some mastery over not only the kind of acute prescribing addressed in this book, which can be called integrative primary care homeopathy, but also the treatment of chronic and recurring disease. This model was first used by physicians in Scotland as a basis for developing continuing education curricula and certification in homeopathy for conventionally trained physicians. Some homeopathic doctors who are family practitioners protest that this terminology does not describe them well.

Today, some homeopathic specialists in North America maintain a small office functioning strictly as consultants for chronic illness. Others run larger, fully staffed (more high-profile) offices, and combine the function of expert consultant for clients unresponsive to other treatments for their lingering illnesses with a primary care family or pediatric practice that fulfills all the function of that role. Some MDs and DOs maintain hospital privileges. Nurse practitioners and physician assistants who specialize in homeopathy work in the practices of homeopathic physicians or in private practices. Some physicians, particularly in large metropolitan areas where demand exceeds supply, can meet income expectations for their practices. Other physicians, physician assistants, and nurse practitioners voluntarily live on much lower incomes than their conventional cohorts because of the nonmonetary rewards of this kind of practice. They also may supplement their incomes with work in conventional health care settings. The development of HMOs has had a negative effect on private practices of all kinds, including homeopathic ones.

Legal Issues for the Homeopathic Specialist

In the United States, the licensure of health care professionals is a function of the state. Therefore, the appropriate professional licensing board should be consulted about practice issues.

Medical doctors should be aware that the American Medical Association, with its long history of opposition to homeopathy, does not yet recognize homeopathy as a medical specialty. Unfortunately, that fact has a profound effect on reimbursement from third-party payers. For example, a family practice doctor can currently only be reimbursed as a family practice doctor even if he or she has years of specialized coursework, clinical experience, and board certification in homeopathy.

Nurse practitioners and physician assistants should be aware that in some states all prescribing is viewed as a delegated medical function. For those in such states, homeopathic medicines must be included in the joint practice agreements, protocols, or standardized procedures between the nurse and the collaborating physician. While most homeopathic medicines are regulated as over-the-counter drugs, some commonly used for the homeopathic treatment of chronic disease are technically prescription-only items.

THE RESEARCH ROLE

Integrative clinicians who have become fascinated by the results they have had with homeopathic medicines can take part in homeopathic research. A network of researchers into homeopathy has organized internationally, and there are many studies underway, some of which the clinician might be able to collaborate with. This informal group can be contacted through the American Institute of Homeopathy or the Center for Alternative Medicine Research of Beth Israel Deaconess Medical Center (contact information in Appendix C). The consensus of the network of clinical researchers is that studies must continue to be conducted that prove homeopathy's effectiveness, and research should also be conducted that adds invaluable data to the homeopathic knowledge base (Jacobs, 2000). Large-scale studies in cost-effectiveness and safety issues are underway. Studies need to be replicated and conducted by researchers at more than one location. Both placebo-controlled research and studies comparing homeopathic versus conventional treatment need to be conducted. Large-scale research into cost and safety issues have also been undertaken.

Researchers are beginning to be interested in studies about homeopathy's effectiveness in low-tech primary care, run by clinicians who are not experts, but instead work with protocols (like the medicine differentials in this book), or alternatively with complex homeopathic medicines. It should be clear to anyone who has applied the material in this book in practice that some differentials are exceedingly simple, and could easily and inexpensively be subjected to a placebo-controlled, double-blind study by an investigator with access to a large pool of potential subjects. Many of the studies that have been conducted so far could be replicated with better methodology by working with university-based researchers, the Integrative Medicine Institute, or (in the United States) the Extramural Affairs Program of the National Center for Complementary and Alternative Medicine of the National Institutes of Health (contact information in Appendix C). The Integrative Medicine Institute is an organization based in New Mexico that focuses on practice-based research using innovative research methods across disciplinary boundaries, and links health care providers and research institutes around the world.

Examples of simple studies that need to be conducted follow.

1. In the oral surgeon's office: *Apis mellifica*, 30C or 200C versus a placebo could be evaluated for the prevention of edema after oral surgery or tooth extraction. One unpublished study with very poor internal validity reportedly showed *Apis mellifica*, 7C and *Arnica montana*, 15C given together were more effective than a placebo for preventing edema after tooth extraction (Michaud, 1981). *Arnica montana* has not been shown to be effective in other studies. The higher potencies are reputed to be more effective than the lower ones are.

2. In the urologist's office: A pilot study could evaluate the practice of alternating single doses of *Conium maculatum*, 200C and *Sabal serrulata*, 200C every other week versus placebo in patients with elevated prostate-specific antigen.
3. In the obstetrician's office: *Pulsatilla* may be studied as a routine medicine for breech presentation. The 30C potency could be given to pregnant women three times a day for 3 days during weeks 26–35, followed by *Pulsatilla*, 200C single dose 1 week later (Moscowitz, 1992). Some very old studies purported to show an effect.
4. In the family practitioner's office: *Staphysagria* versus a placebo could be studied as a treatment for postcoital *"honeymoon"* cystitis. There is a large study with poor internal validity confirming its traditional use in this condition. Ustianowski (1974) found *Staphysagria*, 30C highly effective in a double-blind, placebo-controlled study (*n* = 200). *Nitricum acidum* versus a placebo could be investigated in the treatment of anorectal fissures. Bignamini, Saruggia, and Sansonetti (1991) had a highly favorable result with the 9C potency in a previous double-blind, placebo-controlled trial. This potency or higher could be studied.
5. In a community women's health clinic: *Candida albicans*, 30C versus a placebo could be tested in treatment of candidal vulvovaginitis. There has been a double-blind, placebo-controlled study of 40 women with vaginal discharge, using *Candida albicans*, 30C as a routine treatment (Carey, 1986). The results significantly favored homeopathy over placebo.
6. In an occupational health setting: The simple differential between *Actaea spicata, Causticum, Ferrum phosphoricum, Guaiacum, Ruta graveolens*, and *Viola odorata* could be tested against a placebo or conventional treatment of repetitive stress injury. Alternatively, these medicines could be combined into a low-potency complex medicine and compared in effectiveness to a placebo.
7. On the in-patient surgical unit: *Arnica montana*, 30C and *Raphanus sativus*, 30C could be tested versus placebos for speed of resolution of paralytic ileus. Several studies have been done on this condition; they have shown that very low potency medicines (7C and below) have no effect. One promising study of 200 patients showed *Opium*, 9C; *Raphanus*, 9C; and *Arnica montana*, 9C in combination to be significantly more effective than placebos according to global assessment by the patient (Aulagnier, 1985). *Opium* by itself has not been shown to have an effect on the resolution of ileus.

8. In the emergency room: Pilot studies could be done on *Agaricus muscarius* versus a placebo for frostbite or *Cantharis* versus a placebo for second-degree burns.

CONCLUSION

The integration of homeopathic medicines into a primary care practice is a managable undertaking for a busy clinician, as long as he or she does not overreach by attempting to treat chronic disease or serious acute illnesses that fall outside his or her comfort threshold and competence. The aspiration of the author in writing this book was to systematize a body of material appropriate for clinicians who are new to homeopathy, so that they could then safely and incrementally increase the scope and effectiveness of their homeopathic prescribing. Those who want to go further, either as homeopathic specialists or as researchers, should see Appendix C for a listing of the ample resources available to help them in their quests.

REFERENCES

Alibeu, J.P., & Jobert, J. (1990). Aconit en dilution homeopathique et agitation post-operatoire de l'enfant. *Pediatrie, 45,* 465–66.

Allen, T.F. (1875). *Encyclopedia of pure materia medica.* Philadelphia: Boericke and Tafel.

American Association of Naturopathic Physicians. (1999). History of naturopathic medicine. http:// www.Bastyr.edu/about/natmed.asp. Accessed May 2, 2000.

Andrade, L., Ferraz, M.B., Atra, E., Castro, A., & Silva, M.S.M. (1991). A randomized controlled trial to evaluate the effectiveness of homoeopathy in rheumatoid arthritis. *Scandinavian Journal of Rheumatology, 20,* 204–208.

Ania, F. (1995). *Homeopathy in Canada: A synopsis.* Paper presented at the Eighth International Conference of Traditional Medicine and Folklore, St. John's, Newfoundland.

Astin, J.A., Marie, A., Pellatier, K.R., Hansen, E., & Haskell, W.L. (1998). A review of incorporation of complementary and alternative medicine by mainstream physicians. *Archives of Internal Medicine, 158*(21), 2303–2310.

Aulagnier, G. (1985). Action d'un traitement homéopathique sur la reprise du transit post-opératoire. *Homéopathie, 1,* 47.

Baillargeon, L., Drouin J., Desjardins, L., Leroux, D., & Audet, D. (1993). The effects of *Arnica montana* on blood coagulation: Randomized controlled trial (published erratum appears in *Canadian Family Physician, 40,* 225), *Canadian Family Physician, 39,* 2362–2367.

Bakshi, J.P.S. (1990). Homeopathy—a new approach to detoxification. *Proceedings of the National Congress on Homeopathy and Drug Abuse,* pp. 20–28. New Delhi, India.

Bastide, M. (Ed). (1997). *Signal and images.* Dordrecht, the Netherlands: Kluwer Academic Publisher.

Becker, R.D., & Murino, A.A. (1982). *Electromagnetism and life.* Albany, NY: State University of New York Press.

Bell, J.B. (no date, nineteenth-century reprint). *The homeopathic therapeutics of diarrhea.* Calcutta, India: Haren and Brother.

Bellavite, P., & Signorini, A. (1995). *Homeopathy: A frontier in medical science.* Berkeley, CA: North Atlantic.

Berman, B.M. (1998). A primary physicians and complementary and alternative medicine: training, attitudes and practice patterns. *Journal of the American Board of Family Practice, 124,* 879–885.

Berman, B.M., Singh, B.K., Lao, L., Singh, B.B., Ferentz, K.S., & Hartnoll, S.M. (1995). Physicians' attitudes toward complementary or alternative medicine: A regional survey. *Journal of the American Board Family Practice, 8,* 361–366.

Bignamini, M., Saruggia, M., & Sansonetti, G. (1991). Homoeopathic treatment of anal fissures using *Nitricum acidum. Berlin Journal of Research in Homeopathy, 1,* 286–287.

Boericke, W., & Dewey, W.A. (1914, reprinted 1972). *The twelve tissue remedies of Schussler.* New Delhi, India: B. Jain Publishers.

Boericke, W. (1983). *Pocket manual of homeopathic materia media.* New Delhi, India: B. Jain Publishers.

Borland, D. (1982). *Homeopathy in practice.* Beaconsfield, England: Beaconsfield Publishers.

Bourgois, J.C. (1984). Protection du capital veineux chez les perfusées au long cours dans la cancer du sein: Essai clinique en double aveugle. Unpublished thesis, Université Paris Nord, Paris, Villetaneuse, France.

Boucher, T.A., & Lenz, S.K. (1998). An organizational survey of physicians' attitudes about and practice of complementary and alternative medicine. *Alternative Therapies, 4*(6), 59–65.

Bradford, T.L. (1894). *Life and letters of Hahnemann.* Philadelphia: Boericke and Tafel.

Bradford, T.L. (1900). *The logic of figures or comparative results of homeopathic and other treatments.* Philadelphia: Boericke and Tafel.

Brighton, C.T., & Pollack, S.R. (Eds.). (1991). *Electromagnetics in medicine and biology.* San Francisco: San Francisco Press.

Brigo, B., & Serpelloni, G. (1991). Homeopathic treatment of migraines: A randomized double-blind study of sixty cases (homeopathic remedy versus placebo). *Berlin Journal of Research in Homeopathy, 1*(2), 286–287.

Bruning, N., & Weinstein, C. (1996). *Healing homeopathic remedies* (p. 158). New York: Dell.

Calabrese, E.J., & Baldwin, L.A. (1998). Hormesis as a biological hypothesis. *Environmental Health Perspectives, 106*(Suppl. 1), 357–362.

Casanova, P., & Bilan, G.R. (1992). Bilan de 3 annees d'etudes randomisées multicentriques *Oscillococcinum*/placebo. *Oscillococcinum*—rassegna della letterature internationale (pp. 11–16). Milan: Laboratiores Boiron.

Carey, H. (1986). Double-blind clinical trial of borax and candida in the treatment of vaginal discharge. *British Homeopathic Research Group Comm., 15,* 12–14.

Carlton, E. (1996, reprint). *Homeopathy in medicine and surgery.* New Delhi, India: B. Jain Publishers.

Castro, M. (1992). *Homeopathy for pregnancy, birth, and the first year.* New York: St. Martin's Press.

Chapman, E.H., Angelica, J., Spitalny, G., & Strauss, M. (1994). Results of a study of the homeopathic treatment of PMS. *Journal of the American Institute of Homeopathy, 87,* 14–21.

Chapman, E.H., Weintraub, R.J., Milburn, M.A., Pirozzi, T.O., & Woo, E. (1999). Homeopathic treatment of mild traumatic brain injury: A randomized, double-blind, placebo-controlled clinical trial. *Journal of Head Trauma Rehabilitation, 14*(6), 521–542.

Clarke, J.H. (1982). *Dictionary of* Materia Medica (Vols. 1–3). Essex, England: Health Science Press.

Conte, R.R., Lasne, Y., Berliocchi, H., & Vernot, G. (1996). *Theory of high dilutions and experimental aspects.* Paris, France: Polytechnica.

Coudert, M. (1981). *Etude expérimentale de l'action du Caulophyllum dans le faux travail et de la dystocie de démarrage.* Unpublished thesis, Université de Limoges, Limoge, France.

Coulter, H.L. (1973). *Divided legacy: The conflict between homeopathy and the American Medical Association.* Berkeley, CA: North Atlantic Books.

Cummings, S., & Ullman, D. (1984). *Everybody's guide to homeopathic medicines.* Los Angeles: Jeremy P. Tarcher.

Davidson, J.R., Morrison, R.M., Shore, J., Davidson R.T., & Bedayn, G. (1997). Homeopathic treatment of depression and anxiety. *Alternative Therapies in Health and Medicine, 3*(1), 46–49.

Davies, A.E. (1971). Clinical investigations into the action of potencies. *British Homeopathy Journal, 60,* 36–41.

Day, C. (1984). Control of stillbirths in pigs using homoeopathy. *Veterinary Record, 114*(9), 216. Also in *Journal of the American Institute of Homeopathy,* December 1986, *779*(4), 146–147.

de Lange de Klerk, E., Blommers, J, Kuik, D.J., Bezemer, P.D., & Feenstra, L. (1994). Effects of homeopathic medicines on daily burden of symptoms in children with recurrent upper respiratory tract infections. *BMJ, 309,* 1329–1332.

Dorfman, P., Amodeo, C., Ricciotti, F., Tétau, M., & Véroux, G. (1991). Evaluation de l'activité d'arnica 5 CH sur les troubles veineux après perfusion prolongée. *Cahiers Biothérapie, 98* (Suppl.), 77–82.

Dorfman, P., Lasserre, M.N., & Tétau, M. (1987). Preparation a l'accouchement par homeopathie-experimentation en double insu versus placebo. *Cahiers Biothérapie, 94,* 77–81.

Eid, P., Felisi, E., & Sideri, M. (1993). Applicability of homoeopathic caulophyllum thalictroides during labour. *British Homoeopathic Journal, 82*(4), 245–248.

Eid, P. Felisi, E., & Sideri, M. (1994). Super-placebo ou action Pharmacologique? Une etude en double aveugle, randomisée avec un remedé homéopathique (*Caulophyllum thalictroides*) dans le travail de l'accouchement. *Proceedings of the 5th Congress of the Organization for Homeopathic Medicine,* Paris, France.

Eisenberg, D.M., Kessler, R.C., Foster, C., Norlock, F.E., Colkins D.R., & Delbanco, T.L. (1993). Unconventional medicine in the United States: Prevalence, costs, and patterns of use. *New England Journal of Medicine, 328*(4), 246–252.

Eisenberg, D.M., Davis, R.B., Ettner, S.L., Appel, S., Wilkey, S., Van Rompay, M., & Kessler, R.C. (1998). Trends in alternative medicine in the United States 1990–1997: Results of a follow-up national survey. *Journal of the American Medical Association, 280*(18), 1569–1575.

Eizayaga, F. (1986). *Disease algorithms, V. 5.0* (software), San Rafael, CA: Kent Homeopathic Associates.

Elder, N.C., Gillcrist, A., & Minz, R. (1997). Use of alternative health care by family practice patients. *Archives of Family Medicine 6,* 181–184.

Endler, P.C., Pongratz, W., & Smith, C.W. (1995). Non-molecular information transfer from thyroxine to frogs with regard to homeopathic toxicology. *Vet Hom Toxicol 37,* 259–260.

Epstein, W. (1998). Poison ivy, poison oak, and poison sumac dermatitis: Answers to questions your patients often ask. *Consultant, 38*(7), 1689–1701.

Ernst, E., & Pittler, M.H. (1998). Efficacy of homeopathic *Arnica*: A systemic review of placebo-controlled clinical trials. *Archives of Surgery, 133*(11), 1187–1190.

Ernst, E., Resch, K.L., & White, A.R. (1995). Complementary medicine: What physicians think of it: A meta-analysis. *Archives of Internal Medicine, 155*, 2405–2408.

Ferley J.P., & Zmirou, D. (1989). A controlled evaluation of a homoeopathic preparation in the treatment of influenza-like syndromes. *British Journal of Pharmacology, 27*, 329–335.

Ferley, J.P., Zmirou, D., D'Adhemar, D., & Balducci, F. (1987). Evaluation en médicine ambulatoire de l'activité d'un complexe homéopathiques dans la prévention de la grippe et des symptomes grippaux. *Immunologic Medicine, 20*, 22–28.

Fontanarosa, P.B., & Lundberg, G.D. (1997). Complementary, alternative, unconventional, and integrative medicine. Call for papers for the annual coordinated theme issues of the A.M.A. journals. *Journal of the American Medical Association, 278*(23), 2111–2112.

Foubister, D. (1989). *Tutorials on homeopathy.* Beaconsfield, England: Beaconsfield Publishers.

Friese, K.H., Kruse, S., & Moeller, H. (1997). Acute otitis media in children: A comparison of conventional and homeopathic treatment. *Biomedical Therapy, 60*(4), 113–116. (Originally published in German in Hals-Nasen-Ohren. [1996]. *Head, Nose, and Otolaryngology, August*, 462–466.)

Frietas, L., Goldenstein, E., & Sanna, O.M. (1995). A relaçao médico-paceinte indereta e o tratamento homeopático na asma infantil. *Rev Homeopathia, 60*, 26–31.

Gibson, D.M. (1981). *First aid homeopathy in accidents and ailments.* London: British Homeopathic Association.

Gibson, R.G., Gibson, S., MacNeill, A.D., & Watson, W.B. (1980). Homeopathic therapy in rheumatoid arthritis: Evaluation by double-blind, placebo therapeutical trial. *British Journal of Clinical Phamacology, 9*, 453–459.

Gupta, R., Bhardwaj, O.P., & Manchanda, R.K. (1991). Homoeopathy in the treatment of warts. *British Homeopathic Journal, 80*(2), 108–111.

Hahnemann, S. (1982, reprint). *Organon of medicine.* Los Angeles: JP Tarcher, Inc.

Hahnemann, S. (1835, undated reprint). *The chronic diseases.* New Delhi, India: Jain Publishing Company.

Heilmann, A. (1992). Ein injizierbares kombinationspräparat (Engystol N) als prophylaktikum des grippalen infektes. *Biolog Med., 21*, 225–229.

Hofmeyr, G.J., Piccioni, V., & Blauhof, P. (1990). Postpartum homoeopathic *Arnica montana*: A potency-finding pilot study. *British Journal of Clinical Practice, 44*, 619–621.

Houghton, H.C. (1885). *Lectures on clinical otology.* Boston: Otis Clapp & Son.

Ikenze, I. (1998). *Menopause and homeopathy.* Berkeley, CA: North Atlantic Books.

Jacobs, J. (2000). Effectiveness research in homeopathy: Report from the London conference. *Homeopathy Today, 20*(2), 12–15.

Jacobs, J.J. (1995). Building bridges between two worlds: The NIH's Office of Alternative Medicine. *Academic Medicine, 70*, 40–41.

Jacobs, J., Chapman, E.H., & Crothers, D. (1998). Patient characteristics and practice patterns of physicians using homeopathy. *Archives of Family Medicine, 7*(6), 537–540.

Jacobs, J., Jiminez, L.M., Gloyd, S.S., Gale J.L., & Crothers, D. (1994). Treatment of childhood diarrhea with homeopathic medicines: A randomized clinical trial in Nicaragua. *Pediatrics, 93,* 719–725.

Jonas, W.B. (1997). Researching alternative medicine. *Nature Medicine, 3,* 824–827.

Jonas, W.B., & Jacobs, J. (1996). *Healing with homeopathy: The doctors' guide.* New York: Warner Books.

Jouanny, J. (1980). *The essentials of homeopathic therapeutics* (p. 90). Lyon, France: Laboratoires Boiron. (Foreword).

Jouanny, J. (1984). *The essentials of homeopathic materia medica.* Lyon, France: Laboratoires Boiron.

Kaziro, G.S. (1984). Metronidazole (Flagyl) and *Arnica montana* in the prevention of post-surgical complications: A comparative placebo-controlled clinical trial. *British Journal of Oral and Maxillofacial Surgery, 22,* 42–49.

Kennedy, C.O. (1971). A controlled trial. *British Homeopathy Journal, 60,* 120–127.

Kleijnen, J., Knipschild, P., & ter Riet, G. (1991). Clinical trials of homeopathy. *BMJ, 302,* 316–323.

Kohler, T. (1991). Wirksamkeitnachweis eines homoopathikums bei niedergelassenen artzen. *Der Kassenarst, 13,* 48–52.

Krieger, D. (1981). *Foundations for holistic nursing practices: The renaissance nurse.* Philadelphia: J.B. Lippincott Co.

Labrecque, M., Audet, D., Latulippe, L.G., & Drouin, J. (1992). Homeopathic treatment of plantar warts. *Canadian Medical Association Journal, 146*(10), 1749–1753.

Lecoq, P.L. (1985). Les volies thérapeutiques des syndrome grippaux. *Cahiers Biothérapie, 87,* 65–73.

Leary, B. (1987). Cholera and homeopathy in the nineteenth century. *British Homeopathic Journal, 76,* 290–294.

Leary, B. (1994). Cholera 1854: Update. *British Homeopathic Journal, 83,* 117–121.

Lepaisant, C. (1994). *Essais thérapeutiques du syndrome prémenstruel.* Unpublished thesis, Université de Caen, Caen, France.

Linde, K., Clausius, N., Ramirez, G., Melchart, D., Eitel, F., Hedges, L.V., & Jonas, W.B. (1997). Are the clinical effects of homeopathy placebo effects? A meta-analysis of placebo-controlled trials. *Lancet, 350,* 834–843.

Lokken, P., Straumsheim, P.A., Tveiten, D., Skelbred, P., & Borchgrevink, C.F. (1995). Effect of homeopathy and other events after acute trauma: Placebo-controlled trial with bilateral oral surgery. *BMJ, 310,* 1439–1442.

Marriner, A. (1986). *Nursing theorists and their world.* St. Louis, MO: The CV Mosby Company.

Master, F.J. (1987). Scope of homeopathic drugs in the treatment of Broca's aphasia. *Proceedings of the 42nd Congress LMHI,* Arlington, VA, 330–334.

Messer, S.A. (2000). Infectious mononucleosis. *Homeopathy Today, 20*(2), 4–6.

Michaud, J. (1981). Action d'apis mellifica et d' *Arnica montana* dans la prévention des oedèmes post-opératoires en chirurgie maxillo-faciale â propos d'une expérimentation clinique sur 60. Unpublished thesis, Université de Nantes, Nantes, France.

Morawiec-Bajda, A., Lukomski, M., & Latkowski, B. (1993). The clinical efficacy of Vertigoheel in the treatment of vertigo of various etiology. *Panminerva Med., 35*(2), 101–104.

Morrison, R. (1993). *Desktop guide to keynotes and confirmatory symptoms*. Berkeley, CA: Hahnemann Clinic Publishing.

Moscowitz, R. (1992). *Homeopathic medicines for pregnancy and childbirth*. Berkeley, CA: North Atlantic Books.

Mossinger, P. (1980). Zur therapeutischen wirksamkeit von hepar sulphuris calcareum D4 bei pyodermien and furunkein. *Allg-homöopath Ztg., 225*, 22–28.

Mossinger, P. (1984). *Homöopathie und naturwissenschaftliche medizin—zur überwindung der gagensätze*. Stuttgart: Hippokrates, 165–169.

National Council Against Health Fraud. (1994). *NCAHF position paper on homeopathy*. Allentown, PA: National Council Against Health Fraud.

Nollevaux, M. (1994). Unpublished paper in German on *Mucococcinum* 200C vs. placebo for prevention of upper respiratory infection, reported in Linde et al., above.

Papp, R., Schuback, G., Beck, E., Burkard, O., Bengel, J., Siergfried, L., & Belon, P. (1998). *Oscillococcinum* in patients with influenza-like syndromes: A placebo-controlled, double-blind evaluation. *British Homoeopathic Journal 87*, 69–76.

Perko, S. (1997). *Homeopathy for the modern pregnant woman and her infant*. San Antonio, TX: Benchmark Homeopathic Publications.

Phatak, S.R. (1977). *Materia medica of homeopathic medicines*. New Delhi, India: Indian Books and Periodicals Syndicate.

Pitkaranta, A., Jero, J., Arruda, E., Virolainen, A., & Hayden, F.G. (1998). Polymerase chain reaction-based detection of minovirus, respiratory syncytial virus and coronavirus infection in otitis media with effusion. *Journal of Pediatrics, 133*(3), 390–394.

Reilly, D.T., & Taylor, M.A. (1985). Potent placebo or potency? A proposed study model with initial findings using homoeopathically prepared pollens in hayfever. *British Homoeopathy Journal 74*(2), 65–75.

Reilly, D., Taylor, M., Beattie, N.G., Campbell, J.H., McSharry, C., Aitchison, T.C., Carter, R., & Stevenson, R.D. (1994). Is evidence for homeopathy reproducible? *Lancet, 344*, 8937.

Reilly, D.T., Taylor, M., McSharry, C., & Aitchison, T. (1986). Is homeopathy a placebo response? *The Lancet, 2*(8512), 881–886.

Rogers, M., Malinski, V.M., & Manhart-Barrett, E.A. (1994). *Martha Rogers, her life and her work*. Philadelphia: F.A. Davis.

Royal, G.R. (1923, reprinted 1982). *Text-book of homeopathic theory and practice of medicine*. New Delhi, India: Jain Publishing Co.

Sankaran, R. (1991). *The spirit of homeopathy*. Bombay, India: Homeopathic Medical Publishers.

Schmitt, B.D. (1992). *Instructions for pediatric patients*. Philadelphia: W.B. Saunders Company.

Schroyens, F. (1998). *Synthesis—repertorium homeopathicum syntheticum*. Greifenberg, Belgium: Hahnemann Institut für homöopathische Dokumentation.

Shadman, A.J. (1958). *Who is your doctor and why?* Boston: House of Edinboro.

Shepherd, D. (1982). *Homeopathy for the first aider*. Essex, England: Health Science Press.

Sherr, J. (1994). *The dynamics and methodology of homeopathic provings*. West Malvern, England: Dynamis Books.

Sherr, J. (Undated). *The homeopathic proving of hydrogen*. Malvern Worcs: Self-Published.

Shore, J. (1994). How I treat seasonal allergies. *British Homeopathic Journal, 83*, 68–74.

Sikand, A., & Laken, M. (1998). Pediatricians' experience with and attitudes toward complementary/alternative medicine. *Archives of Pediatric and Adolescent Medicine, 152,* 1059–1064.

Smolle, J., Prause, G., & Kerl, H. (1998). A double-blind, controlled clinical trial of homeopathy and an analysis of lunar phases and postoperative outcome (children with warts). *Archives of Dermatology, 134*(11), 1368–1370.

Stapleton, S. (1997). New journal examines alternative medicine claims. *American Medical News, 14,* 14.

Starr, P. (1982). *The social transformation of American medicine.* New York: Basic Books.

Studdert, D.M., Eisenberg, D.M., Miller, F.H., Curto, D.A., Kaptchuk, T.J., & Brenan, T.A. (1998). Medical malpractice implications of alternative medicine. *Journal of the American Medical Association, 280*(18), 1610–1615.

Tyler, M. (1980). *Homeopathic drug pictures.* New Delhi, India: Jain Publishing Co.

Ullman, D. (1996). *The consumer's guide to homeopathy.* New York: Jeremy Tarcher/Putnam.

Ullman, D. (1999). Homeopathy in managed care: Manageable or unmanageable? *Journal of Alternative and Complementary Medicine, 5*(1), 66–73.

Ustianowski, P.A. (1974). A clinical trial of *Staphysagria* in post-coital cystitis. *British Homeopathy Journal 63,* 276–277.

Vander, A.J., Sherman, J.H., & Luciano, D.S. (1985). *Human physiology: The mechanism of body function* (4th ed.). New York: McGraw-Hill.

van Zandvoort, R. (1997). *Complete repertory* (Vols. 1–3). Leidshendam, The Netherlands: Institute for Research in Homeopathic Information and Symptomatology.

Vermeulen, F. (1997). *Concordant materia medica.* Haarlem, The Netherlands: Emryss bv.

Vickers, A.J., Fisher, P., Smith, C., Wylie, S.E., & Rees, R. (1998). Homeopathic *Arnica* 30X is ineffective for muscle soreness after running: A randomized, double-blind, placebo-controlled trial. *Clinical Journal of Pain, 14*(3), 227–231.

Vithoulkes, G. (1980). *The science of homeopathy.* New York: Grove Press, Inc.

Voegeli, A. (1981). *Homeopathic prescribing.* Wellingborough, England: Thorsons Publishers Limited.

Wadman, M. (1997). Row over alternative medicine's status at NIH. *Nature, 389,* 652.

Weinstein, C. (1996). *Healing homeopathic remedies.* New York: Dell Publishing.

Weiser, M., & Clasen, B. (1994). Klinische studie zur untersuchung der wirksam keit und verträglichkeit von *Euphorbium compoitum*-masentropfen S bei chroninscher sinusitis. *Forsch Komlementärmed, 1,* 251–259.

Weiser, M., Gegenheimer, L.H., & Klein, P. (1999). A randomized equivalence trial comparing the efficacy and safety of Luffa comp.-Heel nasal spray with cromolyn sodium spray in the treatment of seasonal allergic rhinitis. *Forsch Komplementärmed, 6*(3), 142–148.

Weiser, M., Strosser, W., & Klein, P. (1998). Homeopathic versus conventional treatment of vertigo: A randomized double-blind controlled clinical study. *Archives Otolaryngology—Head and Neck Surgery, 124,* 879–885.

Wetzel, M.S., Eisenberg, D.M., & Kaptchuk, T.J. (1998). Courses involving complementary and alternative medicine at U.S. medical schools. *Journal of the American Medical Association, 280*(9), 784–787.

Whitmarsh, T.E., Coleston-Shields, D.M., & Steiner, T.J. (1997). Double-blind, randomized, placebo-controlled study of homeopathic prophylaxis of migraine. *Cephalalgia, 17*(5), 600–604.

Wiesenauer, M., & Gaus, W. (1991). Wirksamkeitnachweis eines homöopathikums bei chronischer polyarthritis. Eine renaodmisierte doppelblindstudie bei neidergellasenen Arzten. *Akrt. Rheumatol. 16,* 1–9.

Wiesenauer, M., & Ludtke, R. (1996). A meta-analysis of the homeopathic treatment of pollinosis with *Galphimea glauca* (A review of 11 annual studies). *Forsch Komplementarmed, 3,* 230–234.

Winston, J. (1995). *The Faces of homeopathy* (Video). Available from National Center for Homeopathy, Alexandria, VA.

Zaren, A. (circa 1985). *Women's health: A homeopathic approach.* [An audio-taped course.] (No longer available.)

Zicari, D., Ricciotti, F., Vingolo, E., & Zicari, N. (1992). Valutazione dell'azione angioprotettiva di preparati di *Arnica* nel trattamento della retinopatia diabetica. *Bolletino de Oculistica, 71*(5), 841–848.

Medicines in the Homeopathic Pharmacopoeia of the United States, 1999

Official Name	Contemporary Name
α-ketoglutaricum acidum	α-ketoglutaric acid
α-lipoicum acidum	α-lipoic acid
Abelmoschus	Abelmosk *(Hibiscus abelmoschus)*
Abies canadensis	Hemlock spruce
Abies nigra	Black spruce
Abrotanum	Southernwood
Absinthium	Common wormwood
Acacia arabica	Gum arabic
Acalypha indica	Indian nettle
Acetaldehyde	Acetaldehyde
Acetanilidum	Antifebrinum
Aceticum acidum	Acetic acid
Acetylsalicylicum acidum	Acetylsalicylic acid
Achyranthes calea	*Achyranthes calea*
Aconitinum	Indian aconite
Aconitum ferox	*Aconitum ferox*
Aconitum lycoctonum	Great yellow wolfsbane
Aconitum napellus	Monkshood
Aconitum, radix	Monkshood root
Actaea spicata	Baneberry
Adamas	Diamond
Adelheidsquelle	Mineral spring at Heilbrunn, Germany
Adenosinum cyclophosphoricum	Cyclic AMP
Adeps suillus	Lard

Official Name	*Contemporary Name*
Adonis vernalis	Pheasant's eye
Adrenalinum	Epinephrine
Adrenocorticotrophin	ACTH
Aesculinum	Esculin, a glucoside of *Aesculus*
Aesculus carnea, flos	Hayne/red horse chestnut *(Aesulus carnea)*
Aesculus glabra	Ohio buckeye
Aesculus hippocastanum	Horse chestnut
Aesculus hippocastanum, flos	Horse chestnut flower
Aethiops antimonialis	Antimony and quicksilver
Aethiops mercurialis-mineralis	Black sulphide mercury
Aethusa cynapium	Fool's parsley
Agaricinum	Agaric acid
Agaricus campanulatus	*Panaeolus sphinctrinus*
Agaricus campestris	*Psalliota campestris quélet*
Agaricus citrinus	*Amanita citrina roques*
Agaricus emeticus	Emetic mushroom *(Russula emetica)*
Agaricus muscarius	Bug agaric *(Amanita muscana)*
Agaricus pantherinus	Panther fungus *(Amanita pantherina)*
Agaricus phalloides	*Agaricus bulbosus*
Agaricus procerus	Parasol mushroom *(Leucoagarucus procerus)*
Agaricus semiglobatus	*Stropharia semiglobata*
Agaricus stercorarius	*Agaricus stercorarius*
Agave americana	Century plant
Agave tequilana	Weber blue agave
Agnus castus	The chaste tree
Agraphis nutans	Bluebell
Agrimonia eupatoria	Sticklewort
Agrimonia eupatoria, flos	Sticklewort flower
Agrimonia odorata, flos	Agrimony flower
Agrostemma githago	Corn cockle seed *(Lychnis githago)*
Ailanthus glandulosus	Chinese sumach
Aletris farinosa	Stargrass
Alfalfa	Alfalfa
Alisma plantago	American water plantain *(Alisma subcordatum)*
Allium cepa	Red onion
Allium sativum	Garlic

Official Name	*Contemporary Name*
Alloxanum	Alloxan
Alnus glutinosa	Common elder of Europe
Alnus serrulata	Smooth alder
Aloe socotrina	*Socotrine aloes*
Alstonia constricta	Bitter bark
Alstonia scholaris	Dita bark
Althaea officinalis	Althea
Alumen	Common potassium alum
Alumina	Oxide of alumina
Alumina silicata	Andalusite rock
Aluminium metallicum	Aluminum
Aluminium muriaticum	Aluminum chloride
Ambra grisea	Ambergris
Ambrosia artemisiaefolia	Ragweed
Ammi visnaga	Khella
Ammoniacum gummi	Ammoniac (gum resin)
Ammonium aceticum	Ammonium acetate
Ammonium benzoicum	Ammonium benzoate
Ammonium bromatum	Ammonium bromide
Ammonium carbonicum	Ammonium carbonate
Ammonium causticum	Ammonium hydroxide
Ammonium citricum	Ammonium citrate, dibasic
Ammonium iodatum	Ammonia iodide
Ammonium muriaticum	Ammonium chloride
Ammonium nitricum	Ammonium nitrate
Ammonium phosphoricum	Ammonium phosphate
Ammonium picricum	Ammonium picrate
Ammonium tartaricum	Ammonium tartrate
Ammonium valerianicum	Ammonium valerate
Ammonium vanadium	Ammonium vanadate
Amorphophallus rivieri	Chinese umbel
Ampelopsis quinquefolia	Virginia creeper
Amygdala amara	Bitter almond
Amygdalae amarae aqua	Distilled bitter almond
Amygdalae amarae oleum	Oil of bitter almond
Amygdalus persica	Peach tree
Amyl nitrosum	Amyl nitrate
Anacardium occidentale	Cashew nut
Anacardium orientale	Marking nut
Anagallis arvensis	Scarlet pimpernel

Official Name	Contemporary Name
Ananassa	Pineapple
Anas barbariae, hepatis et cordis extractum	Duck liver and heart
Anatherum muricatum	Cuscus grass
Anchusa officinalis	Bugloss
Anemone nemorosa	European wood anenome
Anemopsis californica	Yerba mansa
Anethum graveolens	Dill
Angelica archangelica	European angelica
Angelica atropurpurea	American angelica
Angelica sinensis, radix	Chinese angelica
Angophora lanceolata	Red gum, dried sap
Angustura vera	*Galipea cusparia* bark
Anhalonium lewinii	Mescal button/peyote
Anilinum	Amidobenzene
Anilinum sulphuricum	Aniline hemisulfate
Anisum	Same as *Illicum anisatum*
Anthemis nobilis	Roman chamomile
Anthemis pyrethrum	Pellitory
Anthoxanthum odoratum	Sweet vernal grass
Anthracinum	Anthrax
Antimonium arsenicicum	Antimony arsenite
Antimonium crudum	Black sulfide of antimony
Antimonium iodatum	Antimony teriodide
Antimonium muriaticum	Antimony chloride
Antimonium oxydatum	Antimony trioxide
Antimonium sulphuratum aureum	Antimony pentasuphide
Antimonium tartaricum	Tartar emetic
Antipyrinum	Phenazon
Apiolum	Active principal in parsley
Apis mellifica	Honeybee
Apis venenum purum	Pure honeybee venom
Apium graveolens	Common celery
Apocynum androsaemifolium	Dogbane
Apocynum cannabinum	Indian hemp
Apomorphinum	Apomorphine
Apomorphinum muriaticum	Apomorphine hydrochloride
Aqua marina	Sea water
Aquilegia vulgaris	Columbine
Aralia hispida	Bristly sarsaparilla

Official Name	*Contemporary Name*
Aralia quinquefolia	Wild ginseng
Aralia racemosa	American spikenard
Aranea diadema	Papal cross spider
Arbutinum	4-hydroxyphenyl-β-glucopyanoside
Arbutus andrachne	Strawberry tree
Areca catechu	Betel nut
Argemone mexicana	Prickly poppy
Argentum cyanatum	Silver cyanide
Argentum iodatum	Silver iodide
Argentum metallicum	Silver
Argentum muriaticum	Silver chloride
Argentum nitricum	Silver nitrate
Argentum oxydatum	Silver oxide
Argentum phosphoricum	Silver phosphate
Aristolochia clematitis	European snakeroot, birthwort
Aristolochia milhomens	Brazilian snakeroot
Aristolochia serpentaria	Virginia snakeroot
Arnica montana	Leopard's bane
Arnica montana, radix	Leopard's bane root
Arsenicum album	Arsenic trioxide
Arsenicum bromatum	Arsenic bromide
Arsenicum iodatum	Arsenic iodide
Arsenicum metallicum	Metallic arsenic
Arsenicum sulphuratum flavum	Arsenic sulfide-yellow
Arsenicum sulphuratum rubrum	Arsenic sulfide-red
Artemisia vulgaris	Mugwort
Arum dracontium	Green dragon
Arum italicum	*Arum italicum*
Arum maculatum	Cockoo-pint
Arum triphyllum	Jack-in-the-pulpit
Arundo mauritanica	Reed
Asafoetida	Gum of the stinkasand
Asarum canadense	Wild ginger
Asarum europaeum	European snakeroot
Asclepias curassavica	Blood flower
Asclepias incarnata	Swamp milkweed
Asclepias syriaca	Silkweed
Asclepias tuberosa	Pleurisy root

Official Name	*Contemporary Name*
Asclepias vincetoxicum	Black smallwort (*Cynanchum vincetoxicum*)
Asclepias vincetoxicum, folia	Black smallwort (*Cynanchum vincetoxicum*) leaves
Asimina triloba	American papaw
Asparagus officinalis	Asparagus
Asperula odorata	Woodruff
Astacus fluviatilis	Crawfish
Asterias rubens	Starfish
Astragalus menziesii	*Astragalus menziesii*
Atropinum	Atropine
Atropinum sulphuricum	Atropine sulfate
Aurum bromatum	Gold bromide
Aurum iodatum	Gold iodide
Aurum metallicum	Gold
Aurum muriaticum	Gold chloride
Aurum muriaticum kalinatum	Double chloride of potassium and gold
Aurum muriaticum natronatum	Sodium chloroaurate
Aurum sulphuratum	Gold sulfide
Avena sativa	Common oat
Azadirachta indica	Margosa bark
Bacillinum pulmo	Tubercular lung
Badiaga	Freshwater sponge
Baja	East Indian drug
Balsamum peruvianum	Peruvian balsam
Baptisia tinctoria	Wild indigo
Barosma	Buchu
Baryta acetica	Barium acetate
Baryta carbonica	Barium carbonate
Baryta iodata	Barium iodide
Baryta muriatica	Barium chloride
BCG	BCG vaccine
Belladonna	Deadly nightshade
Belladonna, radix	Deadly nightshade root
Bellis perennis	English daisy
Benzinum	Benzene
Benzinum dinitricum	Dinitrobenzene
Benzoicum acidum	Benzoic acid
Benzoin odoriferum	Spice bush

Official Name	Contemporary Name
Benzoinum	Gum benzoin
Berberinum	Berberine chloride
Berberis aquifolium	Mountain grape/mahonia
Berberis vulgaris	Barberry
Berberis vulgaris, fructus	Barberry fruit
Beryllium metallicum	Beryllium
Beta vulgaris	Beet root
Betainum muriaticum	Salt obtained from beet root
Betula pendula, cortex	European birch
Betula pendula, folia	European birch leaf
Bismuthum metallicum	Bismuth
Bismuthum oxydatum	Bismuth oxydate
Bismuthum subnitricum	Bismuth subnitrate
Bixa orellana	Annato
Blatta americana	Cockroach
Blatta orientalis	Indian cockroach
Boldo	*Pneumus boldus, molina*
Boletus luridus	*Boletus nigrescens*
Boletus satanus	*Boletus satanus*
Bombyx processionea	Procession moth
Borago officinalis	Borage
Borax	Sodium borate
Boricum acidum	Boric acid
Bovista	Puff ball
Brassica napus	Rape seed
Bromium	Bromine
Bromus ramosus, flos	Wild oat/hairy brome grass, flower
Brucinum	Bark of poison nut (*Nux vomica*) tree
Bryonia alba	Wild hops
Bufo rana	Toad poison
Bunias orientalis	Hill mustard (*Bunias orientalis*)
Buthus australis	Buthus, Prionuris
Butyricum acidum	Butyric acid
Buxus sempervirens	Boxwood
Cacao	Theobroma cacao/cocoa
Cactus grandiflorus	Night-blooming cereus
Cadmium bromatum	Cadmium bromide
Cadmium iodatum	Cadmium iodide

Official Name	Contemporary Name
Cadmium metallicum	Cadmium
Cadmium muriaticum	Cadmium chloride
Cadmium sulphuratum	Cadmium sulfide
Cadmium sulphuricum	Cadmium sulfate
Caffeinum	Caffeine
Cahinca	Chiococca
Cajuputum	Cajuput oil
Caladium seguinum	American arum
Calcarea acetica	Calcium acetate
Calcarea arsenicica	Calcium arsenite
Calcarea carbonica	Calcium carbonate
Calcarea caustica	Calcium hydroxide
Calcarea fluorica	Calcium flouride
Calcarea flourophosphorica naturale	Apatite
Calcarea hypochlorata	Calcium hypoclorite
Calcarea hypophosphorosa	Calcium hypophosphate
Calcarea iodata	Calcium iodide
Calcarea lactica	Calcium lactate
Calcarea muriatica	Calcium chloride
Calcarea oxalica	Calcium oxalate
Calcarea phosphorica	Calcium phosphate
Calcarea picrata	Calcium picrate
Calcarea silicata	Calcium silicate
Calcarea sulphurica	Calcium sulfate/plaster of Paris
Calendula officinalis	Single-stemmed pot marigold
Calluna vulgaris, flos	Heather
Calotropis gigantea	Mader bark
Caltha palustris	Cowslip
Camphora	Camphor
Camphora monobromata	Camphor bromide
Camphoricum acidum	Camphoric acid
Canchalagua	Centaury
Candida albicans	Yeast (Candida albicans)
Candida parapsilosis	Yeast (Candida parapsilosis)
Canna angustifolia	Indian shot
Cannabis indica	Hashish
Cannabis sativa	Marijuana
Cantharidinum	Glomerular nephritis
Cantharis	Spanish fly
Capsicum annuum	Capsicum

Official Name	*Contemporary Name*
Carbo animalis	Animal charcoal
Carbo vegetabilis	Vegetable charcoal
Carbolicum acidum	Carbolic acid
Carboneum	Lamp black
Carboneum chloratum	Carbon tetrachloride
Carboneum hydrogenisatum	Methane
Carboneum oxygenisatum	Carbinous oxide
Carboneum sulphuratum	Carbon disulfide
Cardiospermum	Balloon vine (*Cardiospermum halicacabum*)
Carduus benedictus	Blessed thistle (*Cnicus benedictus*)
Carduus marianus	St. Mary's thistle
Carpinus betulus, flos	European hornbeam flower
Cartilago	Porcine cartilage
Carum carvi	Caraway
Cascarilla	Sweet bark (*Croton eleuteria*)
Cassada	Yuca, tapioca, manioc (*Manihot esculenta, crantz*)
Castanea sativa, flos	European chestnut flower
Castanea vesca	Chestnut leaves
Castor equi	Rudimentary thumbnail of the horse
Castoreum	Beaver
Catalpa bignonioides	Catalpa
Caulophyllum thalictroides	Blue cohosh
Causticum	Potassium hydrate
Ceanothus americanus	New Jersey tea
Cedron	Rattlesnake bean (*Simaba cedrom*)
Celtis occidentalis	Hackberry
Cenchris contortrix	Copperhead snake
Centaurea tagana	*Centaurea tagana*
Centaurium umbellatum, flos	European centaury
Cephalanthus occidentalis	Button bush
Cerasus virginiana	Chokecherry (*Prunus virginiana*)
Ceratostigma willmottianum, flos	Cerato
Cereus bonplandii	Night-blooming cereus
Cereus serpentinus	*Cereus serpentinus*
Cerium oxalicum	Cerium oxalate
Cetraria islandica	Iceland moss
Chamomilla	German chamomile

Official Name	Contemporary Name
Cheiranthus cheiri	Common wallflower
Chelidonium majus	Celandine
Chelidonium majus, radix	Celandine root
Chelone glabra	Snake head
Chenopodii glauci aphis	Aphids from Chenopodium
Chenopodium anthelminticum	Jerusalem oak
Chenopodium vulvaria	Stinkender
Chimaphila maculata	Spotted wintergreen
Chimaphila umbellata	Pipsissewa
Chininum arsenicicum	Quinine arsenate
Chininum arsenicosum	Quinine arsenite
Chininum muriaticum	Quinine muriate
Chininum purum	Quinine
Chininum salicylicum	Quinine salicylate
Chininum sulphuricum	Quinine sulfite
Chionanthus virginica	Fringe tree
Chloralum	Chloral hydrate
Chloramphenicolum	Chloramphenicol
Chlorinum	Chlorine
Chloroformum	Chloroform
Chlorpromazinum	Chlorpromazine
Cholesterinum	Cholesterine
Cholinum	Choline
Chromicum acidum	Chromic acid
Chromium kali sulphuricum	Potassium chromium sulfate
Chromium oxydatum	Chromic oxide
Chromium sulphuricum	Chromium (III) sulfate
Chrysanthemum leucanthemum	Chrysanthemum leucanthemum
Chrysarobinum	Araroba
Cicer arietinum	Garbanzo bean
Cichorium intybus	Chicory
Cichorium intybus, flos	Chickory flower
Cicuta maculata	Water hemlock
Cicuta virosa	Water hemlock
Cimex lectularius	Bedbug
Cimicifuga racemosa	Black snakeroot
Cina	Wormseed
Cinchona officinalis	Peruvian bark
Cinchoninum sulphuricum	Cinchonin sulfate
Cineraria maritima	Dusty miller

Official Name	Contemporary Name
Cineraria maritima, succus	Dusty miller juice
Cinnamomum	Cinnamon
Cistus canadensis	Rock rose
Citricum acidum	Citric acid
Citrus decumana	Osbeck, shaddock (*Citrus grandis*)
Citrus limonum	Lemon
Citrus vulgaris	Bitter orange
Clematis erecta	Virgin's bower
Clematis virginiana	Virgin's bower
Clematis vitalba, flos	Traveler's joy flower
Clematis vitalba, folia	Traveler's joy leaves
Cobaltum metallicum	Cobalt
Cobaltum muriaticum	Cobaltous chloride
Cobaltum nitricum	Cobaltous nitrate
Cocainum	Cocaine
Cocainum muriaticum	Cocaine hydrochloride
Coccinella septempunctata	Ladybug
Cocculus indicus	Indian cockle
Coccus cacti	Cochineal
Cochlearia armoracia	Horseradish
Cochlearia officinalis	Scurvy grass
Codeinum	Codeine
Coenzyme a	Coenzyme A
Coffea cruda	Unroasted coffee
Coffea tosta	Roasted coffee
Colchicinum	Colchicine
Colchicum autumnale	Meadow saffron
Colibacillinum cum natrum muriaticum	*Escherichia coli* with sodium chloride
Collinsonia canadensis	Stoneroot
Colocynthinum	Colocynthin
Colocynthis	Bitter cucumber
Colostrum	Colostrum
Comocladia dentata	Guao
Conchiolinum	Mother of pearl
Condurango	Condor plant
Coniinum	Conicine
Coniinum bromatum	Bromohydrate of conicine
Conium maculatum	Poison hemlock
Convallaria majalis	Lily of the valley

Official Name	Contemporary Name
Convolvulus arvensis	Bindweed
Copaiva officinalis	Balsam of copaiva
Corallium rubrum	Red coral
Corallorhiza odontorhiza	Crawley root
Coriaria ruscifolia	Toot-berry
Cornus alternifolia	Swamp walnut
Cornus circinata	Round-leaved dogwood
Cornus florida	Dogwood
Cortisone aceticum	Cortisone
Corydalis canadensis	Turkey pea
Cotyledon umbilicus	Pennywort
Coumarinum	Coumarin
Crataegus oxyacantha	Hawthorn berries
Cresolum	Cresol
Crocus sativus	Saffron (*Crocus sativa*)
Crotalus cascavella	A Brazilian rattlesnake
Crotalus horridus	Rattlesnake
Croton tiglium	Croton-oil (*Croton tiglium*)
Crotonchloralum	Butyl chloralhydrate
Cubeba officinalis	Cubebs
Cucurbita citrullus	Watermelon seed
Cucurbita pepo, flos	Pumpkin flower
Cucurbita pepo, semen	Pumpkin seed
Culex musca	Mosquito
Cuphea petiolata	Fluxweed
Cupressus australis	Cypress (*Cupressus australis*)
Cupressus lawsoniana	Cypress (*Cupressus lawsonia*)
Cuprum aceticum	Copper acetate
Cuprum ammonio-sulphuricum	Copper tetraammine sulfate
Cuprum arsenicosum	Copper arsenite
Cuprum carbonicum	Basic cupric carbonate
Cuprum metallicum	Copper
Cuprum muriaticum	Cupric chloride
Cuprum nitricum	Cupric nitrate
Cuprum oxydatum nigrum	Cupric oxide
Cuprum sulphuricum	Copper sulfate
Curare	Curare
Cyclamen europaeum	Sowbread
Cydonia vulgaris	Quince
Cynara scolymus	Artichoke

Official Name	Contemporary Name
Cynodon dactylon	Doorba
Cypripedium pubescens	Yellow ladyslipper
Cysteinum	Cysteine
Cytisus scoparius	Wild laburnum
Damiana	Damiana (*Turnera diffusa*)
Daphne indica	Spurge laurel
Datura arborea	*Brugmansia suaveolens*
Datura metel	Indian datura
DDT	DDT
Delphininum	Delphinium
Derris pinnata	Derris plant
Dichapetalum	*Dichapetalum thunbergh*
Dictamnus albus	Fraxinella
Digitalinum	Active glycoside of digitalis
Digitalis purpurea	Foxglove
Digitoxinum	Digitoxin
Dioscorea villosa	Wild yam
Dioscoreinum	Dioscorea
Diphtherinum	Diptheria
Dirca palustris	Leatherwood
DNA	DNA
Dolichos pruriens	Cowhage
Doryphora decemlineata	Colorado potato bug
Draba verna	Whitlow grasse
Drosera rotundifolia	Sundew
Duboisia myoporoides	Corkwood elm
Dulcamara	Bittersweet
Dulcamara, flos	Bittersweet flower
Echinacea angustifolia	Coneflower
Echinacea purpurea	Purple coneflower
Elaeis guineensis	Aouara/avoira
Elaps corallinus	Coral snake
Elaterium	Squirting cucumber
Embryo	Porcine embryo
Emetinum	Emetine, an alkaloid of ipecac
Eosinum natrum	Sodium eosin
Ephedra vulgaris	Teamster's tea
Epigaea repens	Trailing arbutus
Epilobium palustre	Willow herb
Epiphegus virginiana	Beechdrop

Official Name	Contemporary Name
Equisetum arvense	Shave grass
Equisetum hyemale	Scouring rush
Eranthis hyemalis	Winter aconite
Erechtites hieracifolia	Fireweed
Erigeron canadensis	Fleabane
Eriodictyon californicum	Yerba santa
Erodium	Hemlock stork's bill
Eryngium aquaticum	Button snakeroot
Eryngium maritimum	Sea holly
Erythraea centaurium	European centaury
Erythroxylon coca	Coca shrub
Eschscholtzia californica	California poppy
Eserinum	Physostigmine
Etherum	Ethyl oxide
Ethylicum	Ethanol
Ethylum nitricum	Nitric ether
Eucalyptol	Eucalyptol
Eucalyptus globulus	Blue gum tree
Eugenia caryophyllata	Clove tree
Eugenia jambosa	Rose apple
Euonymus atropurpureus	Wahoo, burning bush
Euonymus europaeus	Spindle tree
Eupatorium aromaticum	Poolroot
Eupatorium cannabinum	Hemp agrimony
Eupatorium perfoliatum	Thoroughwort
Eupatorium purpureum	Queen of the meadow
Euphorbia amygdaloides	Wood spurge
Euphorbia corollata	Large flowering spurge
Euphorbia cyparissias	Cypress spurge
Euphorbia hypericifolia	Large spotted spurge
Euphorbia lathyris	Gopher plant
Euphorbia pilulifera	Pill-bearing spurge (*Euphorbia pilulifera*)
Euphorbium officinarum	Juice of *Euphorbia resinifera*
Euphrasia officinalis	Eyebright
Eupion	Wood-tar distillation
Fagopyrum esculentum	Buckwheat
Fagus sylvatica	Beech
Fagus sylvatica, flos	Beech flower
Fel tauri	Ox gall

Official Name	Contemporary Name
Ferrum aceticum	Basic ferric acetate
Ferrum arsenicicum	Iron arsenate
Ferrum bromatum	Iron bromide
Ferrum carbonicum	Ferrous carbonate (saccharated)
Ferrum citricum	Ferric citrate
Ferrum cyanatum	Ferric ferrocyanide
Ferrum iodatum	Iron iodide
Ferrum lacticum	Ferrous lactate
Ferrum metallicum	Iron
Ferrum muriaticum	Iron chloride
Ferrum pernitricum	Iron pernitrate
Ferrum phosphoricum	Iron phosphate
Ferrum picricum	Iron picrate
Ferrum sulphuricum	Iron sulfate
Ferrum tartaricum	Iron tartrate
Ferula glauca	*Ferula neapolitana*
Ficus religiosa	Ashwathya
Filix mas	Male fern
Foeniculum vulgare	Fennel
Folliculinum	Folliculin
Formalinum	Aqueous solution of formaldehyde gas
Formica rufa	Crushed live ants
Formicum acidum	Formic acid
Fragaria vesca	Wood strawberry
Franciscea uniflora	Manaca
Fraxinus americana	White ash
Fraxinus excelsior	Bird's tongue
Fuchsinum	Magenta, wine coloring
Fucus vesiculosus	Sea kelp
Fumaria officinalis	Fumitory/earth smoke
Fumaricum acidum	Fumeric acid
Funiculus umbilicalis	*Funiculus umbilicalis suis*
Galanthus nivalis	Snowdrop
Galega officinalis	Goat's rue
Galium aparine	Goose grass
Gallicum acidum	Gallic acid
Galphimia glauca	Thryallis, shower of gold (*Galphimia glauca*)
Gambogia	Gummi gutti

Official Name	Contemporary Name
Gaultheria procumbens	Wintergreen
Gelsemium sempervirens	Yellow jasmine
Genista tinctoria	Dyer's broom
Gentiana cruciata	Cross-leaved gentian
Gentiana lutea	Yellow gentian
Gentiana quinqueflora	Five-flowered gentian
Gentianella amarella, flos	Felwort
Geranium maculatum	Crane's bill
Geranium robertianum	Herb Robert
Geum rivale	Water avens
Geum urbanum	Bennet
Ginkgo biloba	Ginko biloba
Glandula suprarenalis suis	Suprarenal gland extract
Glechoma hederacea	Ground ivy
Glonoinum	Nitroglycerine
Glycerinum	Glycerine
Glycogenum	Glycogen
Glycyrrhiza glabra	Licorice
Gnaphalium leontopodium	Edelweiss
Gnaphalium polycephalum	Sweet-scented everlasting flower
Gnaphalium uliginosum	Low cudweed
Gossypium herbaceum	Cotton plant
Granatum	Pomegranate
Graphites	Graphite
Gratiola officinalis	Hedge hyssop
Grindelia	Rosin wood
Guaco	Mikania
Guaiacum	Resin of ligna vitae
Guarea trichilioides	Ballwood
Guatteria gaumeria	Bark of Guatteria gaumeria
Gunpowder	Carbon-sulfur-potassium-nitricum
Gymnocladus canadensis	American coffee tree
Haematoxylon campechianum	Logwood
Hamamelis virginiana	Witch hazel
Haronga madagascariensis	Haronga tree
Hedeoma pulegioides	Pennyroyal
Hedera helix	Ivy
Hekla lava	Lava from Mount Hecla
Helianthemum nummularium, flos	Rock rose flower

Official Name	*Contemporary Name*
Helianthus annuus	Sunflower
Heliotropium peruvianum	Heliotrope
Helix tosta	Toasted snail
Helleborus foetidus	Bear's foot
Helleborus niger	Snow rose
Helleborus viridis	Green hellebore
Heloderma	Gila monster
Helonias dioica	Unicorn root
Hepar suis	Porcine liver
Hepar sulphuris calcareum	Calcium sulfide
Hepar sulphuris kalinum	Potassium sulphide
Hepatica triloba	Liverwort
Heracleum sphondylium	Hogweed
Hippozaeninum	Gladerine-mallein
Hippuricum acidum	Hippuric acid
Hirudinum	Liquid residue of leech's head
Histaminum hydrochloricum	Histamine bichlorhydrate
Hoang-nan	*Strychnos gaultheriana*
Hoitzia coccinea	Colibri flower
Holarrhena antidysenterica	Kurchi
Homarus	Digestive fluid of live lobster
Hottonia palustris, flos	Water violet
Humulus lupulus	Hops
Hura brasiliensis	Assacu
Hura crepitans	Hura, possum wood (*Hura crepitans*)
Hydrangea arborescens	Hydrangea
Hydrastininum muriaticum	Alkaloid of hydrastis
Hydrastis canadensis	Goldenseal
Hydrocotyle asiatica	Indian pennywort
Hydrocyanicum acidum	Prussic acid
Hydrofluoricum acidum	Hydroflouric acid
Hydrophis cyanocinctus	Venom of *Hydrophis cyanocinctus*
Hydrophyllum virginianum	Virginia waterleaf
Hyoscyaminum	Alkaloid of hyoscyamus
Hyoscyaminum hydrobromatum	Hyoscyamine hydrobromide
Hyoscyamus niger	Henbane
Hypericum perforatum	St. John's wort
Hypothalamus	Extract of hypothalamus

Official Name	Contemporary Name
Iberis amara	Bitter candytuft
Ichthyolum	A fossil product of fish deposits
Ignatia amara	St. Ignatius bean
Ilex aquifolium	American holly
Ilex aquifolium, flos	Holly flower
Ilex paraguariensis	Yerbe maté
Illicium anisatum	Anise
Impatiens glandulifera, flos	Policeman's helmet
Imperatoria ostruthium	Hogfennel (*Peucedanum ostruthium*)
Indigo	Indigo
Indium metallicum	Indium
Indolum	Indol
Influenzinum	Influenza
Inula helenium	Scabwort
Iodium	Iodine
Iodoformum	Iodoform
Ipecacuanha	Ipecac root
Ipomoea stans	Quiebra plato
Iridium metallicum	Iridium
Iris florentina	Orris root
Iris foetidissima	Coral iris root (*Iris foetidissima*)
Iris germanica	Blue garden iris
Iris tenax	Iris minor
Iris versicolor	Blue flag
Jacaranda caroba	Brazilian caroba tree
Jalapa	Jalap
Jasminum officinale	White jessamine
Jasper	Jasper
Jatropha curcas	Purging nut
Jatropha urens	Sponge nettle
Jequirity	Crab's eye vine
Jonesia asoca	Bark of an Indian tree
Juglans cinerea	Butternut
Juglans regia	Walnut
Juglans regia, flos	Walnut flower
Juncus effusus	Soft rush
Juniperus communis	Juniper berries
Juniperus virginiana	Red cedar
Justicia adhatoda	Singhee, an Indian shrub
Kali aceticum	Potassium acetate

Official Name	Contemporary Name
Kali arsenicosum	Fowler's solution
Kali bichromicum	Potassium bichromate
Kali bromatum	Potassium bromide
Kali carbonicum	Potassium carbonate
Kali causticum	Potassium hydroxide
Kali chloricum	Potassium chlorate
Kali chromicum	Potassium chromate
Kali cyanatum	Potassium cyanide
Kali ferrocyanatum	Prussian blue
Kali iodatum	Potassium iodide
Kali muriaticum	Potassium chloride
Kali nitricum	Potassium nitrate, saltpeter
Kali oxalicum	Potassium binoxalate
Kali permanganicum	Potassium permanganate
Kali phosphoricum	Potassium phosphate
Kali picricum	Potassium picrate
Kali silicatum	Potassium silicate
Kali sulphuricum	Potassium sulfate
Kali tartaricum	Potassium tartrate
Kali telluricum	Potassium tellurate
Kalmia latifolia	Mountain laurel
Kamala	*Croton coccineus*
Karaka	*Corynocarpus laevigatus*
Karwinskia humboldtiana	*Karwinskia humboldtiana*
Kino australiensis	Astringent plant gum
Kousso	Kuso (*Hagenia abyssinica*)
Kreosotum	Beechwood creosote
Laburnum anagyroides	*Cystisus laburnum*
Lac caninum	Dog's milk
Lac defloratum	Skim milk
Lac felinum	Cat's milk
Lac vaccinum	Cow's milk
Lacerta agilis	Green lizard
Lachesis mutus	Surucucu snake
Lachnanthes tinctoria	Spiritweed
Lacticum acidum	Lactic acid
Lactuca virosa	Acrid lettuce
Lamium album	White nettle
Lapis albus	Silico-flouride of calcium
Lappa major	Burdock

Official Name	Contemporary Name
Larix decidua, flos	European larch
Lathyrus cicera	Lesser chickpea
Lathyrus sativus	Chickpea
Latrodectus katipo	*Lactrodectus katipo* spider
Latrodectus mactans	Black widow spider
Laurocerasus	Cherry laurel
Lecithin	Lecithin
Ledum palustre	Marsh tea
Lemna minor	Duckweed
Leonurus cardiaca	Motherwort
Lepidium bonariense	Brazilian cress
Leptandra virginica	Culver's root
Lespedeza capitata	Round-headed bush clover
Levico	Spring water of South Tyrol
Levisticum officinale	Lovage
Levomepromazinum	Levomepromazine
Liatris spicata	Colic root
Lilium tigrinum	Tiger lily
Limulus	King crab
Linaria vulgaris	Toad flax
Linum catharticum	Purging flax
Linum usitatissimum	Common flax
Lithium benzoicum	Lithium benzoate
Lithium bromatum	Lithium bromide
Lithium carbonicum	Lithium carbonate
Lithium muriaticum	Muriatic acid and lithium carbonate
Lobelia cardinalis	Cardinal flower
Lobelia erinus	*Lobelia erinus*
Lobelia inflata	Indian tobacco
Lobelia purpurescens	Purple lobelia
Lobelia syphilitica	Great blue lobelia
Lobelinum	Lobeline
Lolium temulentum	Bearded darnel
Lonicera caprifolium, flos	Honeysuckle
Lonicera periclymenum	Honeysuckle, woodbine
Lonicera xylosteum	European fly honeysuckle
Lophophytum leandri	Flor de Piedra
Luffa operculata	Esponjilla (*Luffa operculata*)
Lupulinum	Lupulin

Official Name	*Contemporary Name*
Lycopersicum esculentum	Tomato
Lycopodium clavatum	Club moss spore
Lycopus virginicus	Bugle weed
Lysimachia nummularia	Moneywort
Lyssin	Saliva of a rabid dog
Macrotinum	Resin of *Actea racemosa*
Magnesia carbonica	Magnesium carbonate
Magnesia muriatica	Magnesium chloride
Magnesia oxydata	Magnesium oxide
Magnesia phosphorica	Magnesium phosphate
Magnesia sulphurica	Magnesium sulfate/Epsom salts
Magnesium metallicum	Magnesium
Magnolia glauca	Sweet magnolia, sweet bay
Magnolia grandiflora	Magnolia
Malus pumila, flos	Crab apple flower
Mancinella	Mangeneel apple
Mandragora officinarum	Mandrake (*Mandragora officinarum*)
Manganum aceticum	Manganese acetate
Manganum carbonicum	Manganese carbonate
Manganum metallicum	Manganese dioxide
Manganum muriaticum	Manganese chloride
Manganum oxydatum nativum	Native black oxide of manganese, pyrolusite
Manganum oxydatum nigrum	Manganese dioxide
Manganum phosphoricum	Manganese phosphate dibasic
Manganum sulphuricum	Manganese sulfate
Mangifera indica	Mango bark
Marrubium vulgare	Horehound
Matico	*Piper angusti* leaf
Matthiola graeca	Stock gilliflower
Medorrhinum	Gonorrhea
Medulla ossis suis	Porcine bone marrow
Medusa	Jellyfish
Melastoma ackermani	*Melastoma ackermani*
Melilotus alba	Sweet clover-white
Melilotus officinalis	Sweet clover-yellow
Melissa officinalis	Lemon balm
Menispermum canadense	Moonseed
Mentha piperita	Peppermint

Official Name	Contemporary Name
Mentha pulegium	Pennyroyal
Mentha viridis	Spearmint
Mentholum	Menthol
Menyanthes trifoliata	Buckbean
Mephitis mephitica	Skunk
Mercurialis perennis	Dog's mercury
Mercurius aceticus	Mercurous acetate
Mercurius auratus	Mercury and gold amalgam
Mercurius bromatus	Mercurous bromide
Mercurius corrosivus	Mercuric chloride
Mercurius cum kali iodatus	Potassium tetraiodomercurate (II)
Mercurius cyanatus	Mercuric cyanide
Mercurius dulcis	Mercurous chloride
Mercurius iodatus flavus	Mercurous iodide
Mercurius iodatus ruber	Mercuric iodide
Mercurius methylenus	Dimethyl mercury
Mercurius nitricus	Mercuric nitrate
Mercurius praecipitatus albus	Mercurammonium chloride
Mercurius praecipitatus ruber	Mercuric oxide
Mercurius solubilis	Hahnemann's soluble mercury
Mercurius sulphocyanatus	Mercury sulfocyanide
Mercurius sulphuratus ruber	Mercuric sulfide
Mercurius sulphuricus	Mercuric sulphate-yellow
Mercurius vivus	Quicksilver, mercury
Methylene blue	Methylene blue
Mezereum	Spurge olive
Millefolium	Yarrow
Mimosa pudica	Sensitive plan
Mimulus guttatus, flos	Mimulus
Mitchella repens	Partridgeberry
Momordica balsamina	Balsam apple
Monotropa uniflora	Indian pipe
Morbillinum	Measles
Morphinum	Morphine
Morphinum muriaticum	Morphine hydrochlorate
Moschus	Musk
Mucosa nasalis	Mucus
Murex purpurea	Purple fish
Muriaticum acidum	Hydrochloric acid

Official Name	*Contemporary Name*
Musa sapientum	Banana
Mygale	Black Cuban spider
Myosotis arvensis	Forget-me-not
Myrica cerifera	Bayberry
Myristica sebifera	Brazilian ucuba
Myrrha	Myrrh
Myrtus communis	Myrtle
Nabalus serpentarius	White lettuce, rattlesnake root
Nadidum	Nadide
Naja tripudians	Cobra venom
Naphthalinum	Napthalene
Narceinum	Narceine
Narcissus pseudo-narcissus	Daffodil
Narcotinum	An opium alkaloid
Nasturtium aquaticum	Watercress
Natrum arsenicicum	Sodium arsenate
Natrum bicarbonicum	Sodium bicarbonate
Natrum bromatum	Sodium bromide
Natrum carbonicum	Sodium carbonate
Natrum fluoratum	Sodium flouride
Natrum hypochlorosum	Sodium hypochlorite
Natrum lacticum	Sodium lactate
Natrum muriaticum	Sodium chloride
Natrum nitricum	Sodium nitrate
Natrum nitrosum	Sodium nitrite
Natrum oxalaceticum	Sodium oxalate
Natrum phosphoricum	Sodium phosphate
Natrum pyruvicum	Sodium pyruvate
Natrum salicylicum	Sodium salicylate
Natrum silicofluoricum	Salufer
Natrum sulphuratum	Sodium sulfide
Natrum sulphuricum	Sodium sulfate
Natrum sulphurosum	Sodium sulfite
Negundo	Box elder
Nepenthes	*Nepenthes distillatoria*
Nepeta cataria	Catnip
Niccolum carbonicum	Nickel carbonate
Niccolum metallicum	Nickel
Niccolum sulphuricum	Nickel sulfate
Nicotinamidum	Nicotinamide

Official Name	Contemporary Name
Nicotinum	Nicotine
Nitri spiritus dulcis	Sweet spirit of nitre
Nitricum acidum	Nitric acid
Nitrogenum oxygenatum	Nitrous oxide
Nitromuriaticum acidum	Nitromuriatic acid
Nuphar luteum	Yellow pond lily
Nux moschata	Nutmeg
Nux vomica	Poison nut
Nymphaea odorata	Sweet water lily
Ocimum basilicum	Basil
Ocimum canum	Brazilian alfavaca
Ocimum sanctum	Monk's basil
Oenanthe crocata	Water dropwort
Oenothera biennis	Large evening primrose
Olea europaea, flos	Olive
Oleander	Oleander
Oleum animale	Dipple's animal bone oil (a distillation of stag's horns)
Oleum carvi	Caraway oil
Oleum morrhuae	Cod liver oil
Oleum ricini	Castor oil (Ricinus communis)
Oleum santali	Sandlewood oil
Olibanum	Frankincense
Oniscus	Wood louse
Ononis spinosa	Rest harrow
Onopordum	Common thistle, Scotch thistle
Onosmodium virginianum	False gromwell
Oophorinum	Ovarian extract (sheep, cow, or pig)
Opium	Opium
Opuntia vulgaris	Prickly pear
Orchitinum	Testicular extract
Oreodaphne californica	California laurel
Origanum majorana	Sweet marjoram
Ornithogalum umbellatum	Star of Bethlehem
Ornithogalum umbellatum, flos	Star of Bethlehem flower
Oroticum acidum	Orotic acid
Osmium metallicum	Osmium
Ostrya	Ironwood
Ova tosta	Roasted eggshells

Official Name	Contemporary Name
Ovi gallinae pellicula	Membrane of the eggshell
Oxalicum acidum	Oxalic acid
Oxalis acetosella	Wood sorrel
Oxydendrum arboreum	Sorrel tree
Oxytropis lambertii	Locoweed
Paeonia officinalis	Peony
Palladium metallicum	Palladium
Paloondo	Paloondo
Pancreas suis	Pancreas extract
Pancreatinum	Ox or sheep pancreatic and salivary glands
Papaver rhoeas	Corn poppy
Papaverinum	Papaverine
Paraffinum	Paraffin
Parathormonum	Parathyroid hormone
Pareira brava	Virgin vine
Parietaria officinalis	Pellitory of the wall
Paris quadrifolia	Oneberry
Paronichia illecebrum	Sanguinaria of Cuba
Parthenium	Bitterbroom
Passiflora incarnata	Passion flower
Pastinaca sativa	Parsnip
Paullinia pinnata	*Paullinia pinnata*
Paullinia sorbilis	*Paullinia sorbilis*
Pecten	Scallop
Pediculus capitis	Head louse
Penicillinum	Penicillin G
Penthorum sedoides	Virginia stonecrop
Pepsinum	Pepsin
Perhexilinum	*Perhexiline maleate* (generic angina drug)
Persea americana	Avocado
Pertussinum	Coqueluchin
Petiveria tetrandra	*Petiveria tetranda*
Petroleum	Coal oil
Petroselinum sativum	Parsley
Phallus impudicus	Stinkhorn
Phaseolus	Dwarf bean
Phellandrium aquaticum	Water dropwort
Phenacetinum	Phenacetin

Official Name	Contemporary Name
Phenobarbitalum	Phenoethylmalonylurea
Phloridzinum	Phlorizin
Phosphoricum acidum	Phosphoric acid
Phosphorus	Phosphorus
Physalis alkekengi	Winter cherry
Physostigma venenosum	Calabar bean
Phytolacca decandra	Pokeroot
Pichi	Pichi (Fabiana imbricata)
Picricum acidum	Picric acid
Picrotoxinum	Alkaloid of Cocculus indicus
Pilocarpinum	Pilocarpine
Pilocarpinum muriaticum	Pilocarpine hydrochlorate
Pilocarpinum nitricum	Pilocarpine nitrate
Pilocarpus	Jaborandi
Pimenta officinalis	Allspice
Pimpinella saxifraga	Burnet saxifrage
Pinus lambertiana	Sugar pine
Pinus sylvestris	Pinus sylvestris
Pinus sylvestris, flos	Scotch fir
Piper methysticum	Kava kava
Piper nigrum	Black pepper
Piperazinum	Ethyleneimine
Piscidia erythrina	Jamaica dogwood
Pituitarum posterium	Posterior pituitary extract
Pix liquida	Pine tar
Placenta totalis	Placenta
Plantago major	Plantain
Platanus	Sycamore
Platinum metallicum	Platinum
Platinum muriaticum	Platinum chloride
Plectranthus fruticosus	Plectranthus fruticosus (Austrian plant)
Plumbago littoralis	Star daisy (Melampodium paludosum)
Plumbum aceticum	Lead acetate
Plumbum carbonicum	Lead carbonate
Plumbum chromicum	Lead chromate
Plumbum iodatum	Lead iodide
Plumbum metallicum	Lead
Podophyllinum	Podophyllum resin

Official Name	Contemporary Name
Podophyllum peltatum	May apple
Polygonum punctatum	Smartweed
Polygonum sagittatum	Arrow-leaved tearthumb
Polyporus officinalis	White agaric
Polyporus pinicola	Pine agaric
Populus candicans	Balm of Gilead
Populus tremula, flos	European aspen
Populus tremuloides	American quaking aspen
Potentilla anserina	Silverweed
Pothos foetidus	Skunk cabbage
Primula obconica	Primrose
Primula veris	Cowslip
Primula vulgaris	Primrose
Proteus	Proteus
Prunus cerasifera, flos	Cherry plum
Prunus padus	Bird cherry
Prunus spinosa	Blackthorn
Prunus virginiana	Chokecherry
Psorinum	Scabies vesicle
Ptelea trifoliata	Wafer ash
Pulex irritans	Common flea
Pulsatilla	Wind flower
Pulsatilla nuttalliana	American pasque flower
Pyrethrum parthenium	Feverfew
Pyridoxinum hydrochloricum	Vitamin B6
Pyrogenium	Decomposed lean beef
Pyrus americana	Mountain ash
Quassia amara	Quassia wood
Quebracho	White quebracho
Quercus glandium spiritus	Distilled tincture of acorns
Quercus robur	English oak acorn
Quercus robur, flos	English oak flower
Quillaja saponaria	Chile soapbark
Radium bromatum	Radium bromide
Ranunculus acris	Meadow buttercup
Ranunculus bulbosus	Bulbous buttercup
Ranunculus ficaria	Lesser celandine, pilewort
Ranunculus glacialis	Glacier crowfoot (*Ranunculus glacialis*)
Ranunculus repens	Creeping buttercup

Official Name	Contemporary Name
Ranunculus sceleratus	Marsh buttercup
Raphanus sativus	Raphanus
Ratanhia	Ratanhia
Rauwolfia serpentina	*Rauwolfia*
Reserpinum	Reserpine
Resina laricis	Venice turpentine
Resorcinum	Resorcin
Rhamnus californica	California coffee tree
Rhamnus cathartica	Buckthorn
Rhamnus frangula	Alder buckthorn
Rhamnus purshiana	Sacred bark (*Cascara sagrada*)
Rheum officinale	Rhubarb
Rhodium metallicum	Rhodium
Rhododendron chrysanthum	Snow rose
Rhus aromatica	Fragrant sumac
Rhus diversiloba	California poison oak
Rhus glabra	Smooth sumac
Rhus toxicodendron	Poison ivy
Rhus venenata	Poison elder
Riboflavinum	Riboflavin
Ricinus communis	Castor oil
RNA	RNA
Robinia pseudoacacia	Robinia
Rock water	Springwater (Sotwell, Wallinford, England)
Rosa canina	Dog rose
Rosa canina, flos	Dog rose flower
Rosa damascena	Damask rose
Rosmarinus officinalis	Rosemary
Rubia tinctorum	Madder
Rumex acetosa	Sorrel
Rumex crispus	Yellow dock
Rumex obtusifolius	Common dock
Russula foetens	*Russula foetens* mushroom
Ruta graveolens	Rue
Sabadilla	Cevadilla seed
Sabal serrulata	Saw palmetto
Sabina	Savine
Saccharinum	Sugar
Saccharum lactis	Milk sugar

Official Name	Contemporary Name
Saccharum officinale	Cane sugar
Salicinum	Salicin
Salicylicum acidum	Salicylic acid
Salix alba	White willow
Salix nigra	Back willow
Salix purpurea	Red or purple willow
Salix vitellina, flos	Yellow willow
Salol	Salicylate of phenol
Salvia officinalis	Sage
Samarskite	Samarskite (mineral)
Sambucus canadensis	Elderbush
Sambucus nigra	Elder
Sanguinaria canadensis	Blood root
Sanguinarinum nitricum	Sanguinaria nitrate
Sanicula	Sanicula spring water, Ottawa, IL
Santoninum	Santonin
Saponaria officinalis	Soap root
Saponinum	Saponin, glucoside of *Saponaria officinalis*
Sarcolacticum acidum	Sarcolactic acid
Sarracenia purpurea	Pitcher plant
Sarsaparilla	Smilax rhizome
Sassafras officinale	Soapwort
Scammonium	Convulvus scammonia root
Schinus molle	Pepper tree (*Schinus molle*)
Scilla maritima	Sea onion
Scleranthus annuus, flos	Knawel flower
Scolopendra	Centipede
Scolopendrium vulgare	Hart's tongue
Scopolaminum hydrobromidum	Scopolamine hydrobromide
Scrophularia nodosa	Knotted figwort
Scutellaria lateriflora	Skullcap
Secale cornutum	Ergot
Sedum acre	Sedum acre
Selenium metallicum	Selenium
Sempervivum tectorum	Houseleek
Senecio aureus	Golden ragwort
Senecio jacobaea	St. James wort, staggerwort
Senega officinalis	Snakewort
Senna	Alexandrian senna (*Cassia acutifolia*)

Official Name	Contemporary Name
Sepia	Cuttlefish ink
Serum anguillae	Eel serum
Silica marina	Sea sand
Silicea	Silica
Silphium laciniatum	Rosinweed
Sinapis alba	White mustard
Sinapis arvensis, flos	Charlock, wild mustard
Sinapis nigra	Black mustard
Sinusitisinum	Sinusitis nosode
Sium latifolium	Water parsnip
Skatolum	Skatole from human feces
Skookum chuck	Salts from spring water of a certain lake near Spokane, Washington
Slag	Silico-sulfo-calcite of alumina
Solaninum	An alkaloid from various solanums
Solanum arrebenta	Horse nettle (Arrebenta cevallos)
Solanum carolinense	Horse nettle berries
Solanum mammosum	Apple of sodom
Solanum nigrum	Black nightshade
Solanum oleraceum	Juquerioba
Solanum tuberosum	Potato
Solidago virgaurea	Goldenrod
Sparteinum sulphuricum	Broom
Spigelia anthelmia	Pinkroot
Spigelia marilandica	Pinkroot
Spilanthes oleracea	Paracress
Spinacia	Spinach
Spiraea ulmaria	Hardhack
Spiranthes autumnalis	Lady's tresses
Spongia tosta	Roasted sponge
Stachys betonica	Wood betony
Stannum iodatum	Tin iodide
Stannum metallicum	Tin
Staphylococcinum	Staphylococcus
Staphysagria	Stavesacre (Delphinium staphisagria)
Stellaria media	Chickweed
Sterculia acuminata	Kola nut

Official Name	Contemporary Name
Stibium metallicum	Metallic antimony
Sticta pulmonaria	Lungwort
Stigmata maidis	Corn silk
Stillingia sylvatica	Queen's root
Stramonium	Thorn apple
Streptococcinum	*Streptococcus* bacteria
Strontium bromatum	Strontium bromide
Strontium carbonicum	Strontium carbonate
Strontium nitricum	Strontium nitrate
Strophanthus hispidus	Kombe seed
Strophanthus sarmentosus	Seeds of *Strophanthus sarmentosus*
Strychninum	Strychnine
Strychninum arsenicicum	Strychnine arsenate
Strychninum nitricum	Strychnine nitrate
Strychninum phosphoricum	Strychnine phosphate
Strychninum sulphuricum	Strychnine sulfate
Succinicum acidum	Succinic acid from distilled amber
Succinum	Amber
Sulphanilamidum	Paraamino-phenylsulfamide
Sulphonalum	Coal tar product
Sulphur	Sulfur
Sulphur hydrogenisatum	Sulfuretted hydrogen
Sulphur iodatum	Sulfur iodide
Sulphuricum acidum	Sulfuric acid
Sulphurosum acidum	Sulfurous acid
Sumbul	Musk root
Symphoricarpus racemosus	Snowberry
Symphytum officinale	Comfrey
Syphilinum	Syphilis
Syzygium jambolanum	Jambol seeds
Tabacum	Tobacco
Tamus communis	Black bryony, ladies seal
Tanacetum vulgare	Tansy
Tanghinia venenifera	*Tanghinia venenifera* seed
Tannicum acidum	Tannin
Taraxacum officinale	Dandelion
Taraxacum officinale, radix	Dandelion root
Tarentula cubensis	Cuban spider
Tarentula hispana	Spanish tarantula
Tartaricum acidum	Tartaric acid

Official Name	Contemporary Name
Taxus baccata	Yew
Tellurium metallicum	Tellurium
Teplitz	Mineral water of Teplitz
Terebinthina	Turpentine
Tetradymite	Tetradymite rock
Teucrium marum	Cat thyme
Teucrium scorodonia	Wood germander, wood sage
Thallium metallicum	Thallium
Thaspium aureum	Meadow parsnip
Thea sinensis	Tea
Theobrominum	Theobromine
Theridion	Orange spider
Thiaminum hydrochloricum	Vitamin B1
Thioproperazinum	Majeptil
Thiosinaminum	Allyl sulfocarbimide from mustard seed
Thlaspi bursa-pastoris	Shepherd's purse
Thuja lobbi	Red cedar
Thuja occidentalis	Arbor vitae
Thymolum	Paraisopropyl-metacresol
Thymus serpyllum	Wild thyme
Thyroidinum	Sheep, ox, or calf thyroid
Tilia europaea	Linden
Titanium metallicum	Titanium
Tongo	Coumarouna seed
Tormentilla	Bloodwort
Torula cerevisiae	Saccharomyces
Toxicophis pugnax	Moccasin snake
Tradescantia diuretica	*Tradescantia diuretica*
Tribulus terrestris	Ikshugandha
Trifolium pratense	Red clover
Trifolium repens	White clover
Trillium pendulum	White bethroot
Trimethylaminum	Propylaminum
Triosteum perfoliatum	Feverwort
Triticum repens	Couch grass
Tropaeolum majus	Indian cress
Tuberculinum	Tubercular abscess
Tuberculinum bovinum	Bovine tuberculin
Tussilago farfara	Common coltsfoot

Official Name	Contemporary Name
Tussilago fragrans	Italian or fragrant tussilage
Tussilago petasites	Butter burr
Ulex europaeus, flos	Gorseflower, furze flower
Ulmus fulva	American slippery elm
Ulmus procera, flos	English elm flower
Upas tieuté	Upas tree
Uranium nitricum	*Uranyl nitrate*
Urea	Carbamide
Uricum acidum	Uric acid
Urtica crenulata	Devil nettle (*Leportea crenulata*)
Urtica dioica	Common nettle
Urtica urens	Small stinging nettle
Usnea barbata	Tree moss
Ustilago maidis	Corn smut
Uva-ursi	Bearberry
Vaccinium myrtillus	Bilberry
Vaccinotoxinum	Smallpox
Valeriana officinalis	Valerian
Vanadium metallicum	Vanadium
Venus mercenaria	American scallop
Veratrinum	Plant alkaloid
Veratrum album	White hellebore
Veratrum nigrum	Dark-flowered veratrum
Veratrum viride	White American hellebore
Verbascum thapsus	Mullein
Verbena hastata	Ironweed
Verbena officinalis	Blue vervain
Verbena officinalis, flos	Blue vervain flower
Veronica beccabunga	Brooklime
Veronica officinalis	Speedwell
Vesicaria	*Vesicaria communis*
Vespa crabro	Live wasp
Viburnum opulus	High cranberry
Viburnum prunifolium	Black haw
Vinca minor	Lesser periwinkle
Viola odorata	Violet
Viola tricolor	Pansy
Vipera berus	Viper
Viscum album	Mistletoe
Vitis vinifera, flos	Grape flower

Official Name	Contemporary Name
Wiesbaden	Spring water from Wiesbaden
Wyethia helenioides	Poisonweed
X-ray	Alcohol exposed to X-rays
Xanthoxylum fraxineum	Prickly ash
Xerophyllum asphodeloides	Tamalpais lily
Yohimbinum	Coryanthe yohimbe
Yucca filamentosa	Bear grass
Zincum aceticum	Zinc acetate
Zincum bromatum	Zinc bromide
Zincum carbonicum	Zinc carbonate, basic
Zincum cyanatum	Zinc cyanide
Zincum gluconicum	Zinc gluconate
Zincum iodatum	Zinc iodide
Zincum metallicum	Zinc
Zincum muriaticum	Zinc chloride
Zincum oxydatum	Zinc oxide
Zincum phosphoratum	Zinc phosphide
Zincum picricum	Zinc picrate
Zincum sulphuricum	Zinc sulfate
Zincum valerianicum	Zinc valerianate
Zingiber officinale	Ginger

APPENDIX B

Homeopathic Educational Programs

SCHOOLS ACCREDITED OR IN THE PROCESS OF BECOMING ACCREDITED BY THE COUNCIL ON HOMEOPATHIC EDUCATION OF THE UNITED STATES

Canadian Academy of Homeopathy
(3-year program)
Suite 203, 3044 Bloor St., West
Toronto, ON M8X 1C4
Canada
(416) 503-4003
Fax: (416) 503-2799

Hahnemann College of Homeopathy
(4-year program)
80 Nicholl Ave.
Pt. Richmond, CA 94801
(510) 232-2079
Fax: (510) 512-9044
E-mail: hahnemann@igc.apc.org

Homeopathic College of Canada
(3-year program; part-time)
280 Eglinton Ave., East
Toronto, ON M4P 1L4
Canada
(416) 481-8816
Fax: (416) 481-4444
E-mail: info@homeopath.org

Homeopathy for the Primary Care Provider
(40-hour program)
Edward Chapman, MD
91 Cornell St.
Newton Lower Falls, MA 02162-1320
(617) 244-8780

International College of Homeopathy
(2-year program)
8306 Wilshire Blvd., #728
Beverly Hills, CA 90211
(310) 645-0443
Fax: (310) 645-1914

National Center for Homeopathy
(Summer School)
801 N. Fairfax St., Ste. 306
Alexandria, VA 22314-1757
(703) 548-7790
Fax: (703) 548-7792
E-mail: info@homeopathic.org

New England School of Homeopathy
(3-year program)
356 Middle St.
Amherst, MA 01002
(413) 256-5949
Fax: (413) 256-6223
E-mail: herscu@nesh.com

Teleosis School of Homeopathy
(2-year certificate program with additional 2 years of clinical
    training)
61 W. 62nd St.
New York, NY 10023
(212) 707-8481
E-mail: teleosis@igc.apc.org

GRADUATE COURSES; OPEN TO LICENSED AND UNLICENSED PERSONS

Bastyr University
(396 hours, part of Naturopathic Doctor [ND] program)
14500 Juanita Dr., N.E.
Bothell, WA 98011
(206) 823-1300
Web site: www.bastyr.edu

Caduceus Institute of Classical Homeopathy
(216 hours over 3 years)
516 Caledonia St.
Santa Cruz, CA 95062
(831) 466-3516
(800) 396-9778
E-mail: homeoUSA@aol.com
Web site: www.homeopathyhome.com/caduceus

Canadian College of Naturopathic Medicine
(205 hours, part of ND program)
P.O. Box 2431, 18th floor
Toronto, ON M4P 1E4
Canada
(416) 486-8584
Fax: (416) 484-6821
E-mail: info@ccnm.edu
Web site: www.ccnm.edu

Colorado Institute for Classical Homeopathy
(2-year program, clinical training in year 2)
2299 Pearl St., Ste. 401
Boulder, CO 80302
(303) 440-3717
Fax: (303) 442-6852
E-mail: bseideneck@aol.com

Curentur University
(675 classroom hours)
5519 South Centinela Ave.
Los Angeles, CA 90066
(310) 448-1700
Fax: (310) 448-1703
E-mail: dean@curentur.org

The Homeopathic College
(4-year program)
411 Andrews Rd.
University Office Park, Ste. 230
Durham, NC 27705
(919) 286-0500
(800) 218-7733

The Institute of Natural Health Sciences
(240 classroom hours plus 100 hours of independent study)
43000 Nine Mile Rd.
Novi, MI 48375
(248) 473-5458
Fax: (248) 473-8141

National Center for Homeopathy
(Summer school)
801 North Fairfax, Ste. 306
Alexandria, VA 22314
(703) 548-7790
Web site: www.homeopathic.org

National College of Naturopathic Medicine
(Lecture and clinical hours, part of ND program)
049 S.W. Porter St.
Portland, OR 97201
(503) 499-4343
Fax: (503) 499-0022

New England School of Homeopathy
(3-year program)
356 Middle St.
Amherst, MA 01002
(413) 256-5949
Fax: (413) 256-6223
E-mail: herscu@nesh.com

Northwestern Academy of Homeopathy
(3-year program, clinical in year 3)
10700 Old County Club Rd. 15,
Minneapolis, MN 55441
(612) 794-6445
Web site: www.homeopathicschool.org

Pacific Academy of Homeopathic Medicine
(2-year program with clinical, year 3 optional)
1199 Sanchez St.
San Francisco, CA 94114
(415) 458-8238
Fax: (415) 695-8220
E-mail: Pahm@slip.net

The School of Homeopathy, New York
(4-year program with clinical)
964 Third Ave., 8th Floor
New York, NY 10155-0003
(212) 570-2576
Fax: (212) 758-4079
E-mail: kathy@homeopathyschool.com

Toronto School of Homeopathic Medicine
(3-year program with clinical training)
17 Yorkville Ave., Ste. 200
Toronto, ON M4W 1L1
Canada
(800) 572-6001
Fax: (416) 966-1724
E-mail: Info@homeopathycanada.com
www.homeopathycanada.com

Vancouver Homeopathic Academy
(3-year program)
P.O. Box 34095
Vancouver, BC V6J 4M1
Canada
(604) 739-4633

CORRESPONDENCE COURSES: OPEN TO LICENSED AND UNLICENSED PERSONS

The British Institute of Homeopathy
520 Washington Blvd., Ste. 5109
Marina Del Rey, CA 90292
(310) 577-2235
Fax: (310) 577-0296

Canadian Academy of Homeopathy
1173 Blvd. du Mont Royal
Outremont, PQ H2V 2H6
Canada
(514) 279-6629
Fax: (514) 279-0111

Living Water School of Homeopathy
11802 Willow Valley Rd.
Nevada City, CA 95959
(530) 265-9464

The School of Homeopathy, Devon, England
United States address:
82 East Pearl St.
New Haven, CT 06513
(203) 624-8783 (phone/fax)
E-mail: Betsy@homeopathyschool.com
E-mail: schofhom@ctl.nai.net
Web site: www.homeopathyschool.com

Todd Rowe, MD
1118 E. Missouri, Suite A1
Phoenix, AZ 85014
(602) 439-1589

CURRENTLY ACCREDITED INSTITUTIONS PROVIDING EPISODIC SEMINARS

Althea Homeopathics
1217 West Howe
Seattle, WA 98119
(206) 284-5320

American Institute of Homeopathy
23200 Edmonds Way, Ste. A
Edmonds, WA 98026
(425) 542-5595

Dynamis School
c/o Josett Polzella, Administrator
40 Dancing Rock Rd.
Garrison, NY 10524
(914) 734-9347
Fax: (914) 762-8634
E-mail: Jpolzell@bestweb.net

Murray Feldman and Kim Boutilier
P.O. Box 34095, Stn. D
Vancouver, BC V6J 4M1
Canada
(604) 708-9387 (academy)
Web site: www.homeopathyvancouver.com

Homeopathic Academy of Naturopathic Physicians
12132 S.E. Foster Pl.
Portland, OR 97266
(503) 761-3298

National Center for Homeopathy
801 North Fairfax St., Ste. 306
Alexandria, VA 22314
(703) 438-7790
Web site: www.homeopathic.org

Naturally Divine, Inc.
1706 Hall Dr.
Tallahassee, FL 32303
(850) 386-6970

New England Homeopathic Academy
24 Minot Ave.
Acton, MA 12720
(508) 635-0605

New York Center for Homeopathy
964 Third Ave., 8th Floor
New York, NY 10015
(212) 570-1646

Ohio Homeopathic Medical Society
3531 Longwood Dr.
Medina, OH 44256
(330) 239-2762

Teleosis Homeopathic Educators
P.O. Box 7046
Berkeley, CA 94707
(510) 558-7285
and
333 W. 56th St., Apt. 1C
New York, NY 10019
(212) 977-8118

Texas Society of Homeopathy
1111 Highway 6, Ste. 150
Sugar Land, TX 77478
(281) 494-3460

APPENDIX C

Homeopathic Resources

RESEARCH RESOURCES

The Center for Alternative Medicine Research
Beth Israel Deaconess Medical Center
330 Brookline Ave.
Boston, MA 02215

Integrative Medicine Institute
P.O. Box 4310
Santa Fe, NM 87502
(505) 989-9018

National Center for Complementary and Alternative Medicine
Division of Extramural Research, Training and Review
National Institutes of Health
31 Center Dr., Room 5B-36
Bethesda, MD 20892-2182
(301) 402-2466

HOMEOPATHIC ORGANIZATIONS

National Center for Homeopathy
General organization for all supporters of homeopathy
801 North Fairfax St., Ste. 306
Alexandria, VA 22314
(703) 548-7790
Web site: www.homeopathic.org

Homeopathic Academy of Naturopathic Physicians
(ND)
12132 S.E. Foster Place
Portland, OR 97266
(503) 761-3298
Web site: www.healthy.net/pan/pa/homeopathic/hanp/index.html

American Institute of Homeopathy
(MD, DO, dentists and podiatrists, with associate memberships for
    physician assistants and nurse practitioners)
801 N. Fairfax, Ste. 306
Alexandria, VA 22314
(703) 246-9501

Homeopathic Nurses Association
(Registered nurses; intermittently active)
c/o Lia Bello, FNP
HC81 P.O. Box 6023
Questa, NM 87556

North American Society of Homeopaths (NASH)
1122 East Pike Street, Ste. 1122
Seattle, WA 98122
(206) 720-7000

International Homeopathy Medical League (LIGA)
an international organization of homeopathic physicians
c/o Dr. Charles Amengual Escoles
11-0713
Selva, Mallorca
Spain
Fax: (34) 71-515479

PROFESSIONAL JOURNALS

Biomedical Therapy
B.T. Menaco
P.O. Box 11280
Albuquerque, NM 87192

British Homeopathic Journal
Dept J, Stockton Press
345 Park Avenue South
New York, NY 10010-1707
(800) 747-3187

New England Journal of Homeopathy
Foundation for Homeopathic Education
115 Elm St., Ste. 210
Enfield, CT 06082
(860) 253-5041

Simillimum
The Journal of Homeopathic Academy of Naturopathic Physicians
12132 S.E. Foster Place
Portland, OR 97266
(503) 761-3298

Journal of the American Institute of Homeopathy
American Institute of Homeopathy
23200 Edmonds Way, #A
Edmonds, WA 98026

The American Homeopath
The Journal of the North American Society of Homeopaths
1122 E. Pike St., Ste. 1122
Seattle, WA 98122
(206) 720-7000

Alternative and Complementary Therapies
Mary Ann Liekert, Inc.
2 Madison Ave.
Lachmont, NY 10538
(914) 834-3100

Alternative Therapies in Health and Medicine
PMB #342, 369 Montezuma Ave.
Santa Fe, NM 87501-2626
(800) 345-8112
Web site: www.alternative-therapies.com

ACCESS TO HOMEOPATHIC LITERATURE:

Homeopathic Educational Services
2124 Kittredge St.
Berkeley, CA 94704
(510) 649-0294
Web site: www.homeopathic.com

Sandra Davies/Mary Gooch
Hom-Inform, British Homeopathic Library
Glasgow Homeopathic Hospital
1053 Great Western Rd.
Glasgow G12 0XQ
Scotland, UK
+44 (0)141 211 1617
Fax: +44 (0)141 211 1610
E-mail: hom-inform@dial.pipex.com
On-line searchable database: www.xcy76.dial.pipex.com/searchreq.html

Minimum Price Homeopathic Books
250 "H" St.
P.O. Box 2187
Blaine, WA 98231
(604) 597-4757
Web site: www.minimum.com

APPENDIX D

Patient Handouts

INTRODUCTION

The information under "Using the Instructions Form" will guide the clinician in the best way to use the form entitled, "Instructions for Taking Your Homeopathic Medicine."

The text under "What Are Homeopathic Medicines?" may be used on a handout to educate patients. It can be adapted to meet the needs of the population served.

USING THE INSTRUCTIONS FORM

Patient new to homeopathic medicine need explicit instructions about how to take their medicine. General information about how to determine the potency, frequency of doses, and duration of treatment for a given patient is elaborated in Chapter 1, An Introduction to Homeopathic Medicine. Guidelines about special considerations in developing treatment plans for patients with specific health problems are discussed in Part III under the relevant diagnosis. Failure to properly educate the patient may result in adverse reactions from overtreatment with an ineffective medicine, inadequate treatment, or improper follow-up. The use of clear written and verbal instructions also circumvents the need for most patients to call for information, an understandable phenomenon that can escalate to an unmanageable level.

The clinician should fill in the information about the name and potency of the medicine on the form, and circle the appropriate treatment plan. He or she should not abbreviate the name of the medicine because many homeopathic medicines have similar names.

What are Homeopathic Medicines?

Homeopathic medicines are made primarily from plants and minerals at specialized homeopathic pharmacies that are regulated in the United States by the Food and Drug Administration. Preparation of these medicines includes repeated dilution with water and vigorous shaking, which advocates believe makes those medicines capable of stimulating the healing process.

There have been a number of scientific studies that have shown homeopathic medicines can speed the healing of certain illnesses such as diarrhea, allergies, headaches, and asthma. While most of the studies done have shown homeopathic medicines to be effective, there are still people who believe that these medicines are too dilute to be effective. However, I am impressed with the 200-year track record of this healing art.

Many of my patients have shown a preference for a more natural approach to health care. For this reason, I use homeopathic medicines in my practice when I think they will help.

To prescribe a homeopathic medicine for you or your child, I need to ask questions about all of your symptoms, as well as how you or your child are feeling in general. You will play an active part in your health care by observing your own symptoms and accurately and honestly reporting them to me.

Instructions for Taking Your Homeopathic Medicine

You or your child have been prescribed a homeopathic medicine for an illness.

The name of the medicine is_____

Administer 4 pellets on or under the tongue, preferably at least 15 minutes before eating or brushing the teeth (or at least 15 minutes after) so that the mouth does not have a taste in it. Do not touch the medicine while administering it, but tip it into your mouth from the cap. Do not transfer the medicine to another container. Securely replace the cap between doses.

The medicine should be administered

1	2	3	4			times today
	then					
1	2	3	4			times a day
	for					
1	2	3	4	5	6	7 more days

As a general rule, you may modify this schedule by reducing the frequency of doses if you feel much better, or stopping the medicine if you feel completely better.

If you feel that there has been gradual improvement, there is no need to call us back. If there is no improvement in _____day(s), please call us.

It is ideal to abstain from coffee; marijuana; and skin products containing aromatic oils like camphor, eucalyptus, or tea tree oil during treatment.

Do not discontinue any other medicines that have been prescribed for you unless instructed to by your primary care provider.

APPENDIX E

Homeopathic Pharmaceutical Manufacturers in the United States and Canada

BHI–Biological Homeopathic Industries
11600 Cochiti, S.E.
Albuquerque, NM 87123
(800) 621-7644
Web site: www.heelbhi.com

Boericke and Tafel
2381 Circadian Way
Santa Rosa, CA 95407
(800) 876-9505

Boiron
6 Campus Blvd., Bldg. A
Newtown Square, PA 19073
(610) 325-7464
Web site: www.boiron.fr

Boiron
98C West Cochran St.
Simi Valley, CA 93065
(800) BLU-TUBE

Boiron Canada
816 Guimond Blvd.
Longeuil
Montréal, PQ J4G 1T5
Canada
(450) 442-4422
(800) 461-2066 (Canada only)

Dolisos
3014 Rigel Ave.
Las Vegas, NV 89102
(800) DOLISOS
Web site: www.dolisos.com

Hahnemann Laboratories, Inc.
1940 Fourth St.
San Rafael, CA 94901
888-4-ARNICA
Web site: www.hahnemannlabs.com

HomeoLab
3025 De L' Assomption
Montreal, PQ H1N 2H2
Canada
(800) 404-4666
Web site: www.homeolab.com

Luyties
4200 Laclede Ave.
St. Louis, MO 63108
(800) Homeopathy (466-3672)
Web site: www.1800homeopathy.com

Newton Laboratories, Inc.
Homeopathic Medicine
2360 Rockaway Industrial Blvd.
Conyers, GA 30012
(800) 448-7256

Standard Homeopathic Company
210 West 131st St.
P.O. Box 61067
Los Angeles, CA 90061
(800) 624-9659

Thompson's Homeopathic Supplies
844 Yonge St.
Toronto, ON M4W 2H1
Canada
(416) 922-2300
Web site: www.thompsonshomeopathic.com

Washington Homeopathic Products, Inc.
4914 Del Ray Ave.
Bethesda, MD 20814
(800) 336-1695
Web site: www.homeopathyworks.com

.

INDEX

neck pain, 58
pain aggravated by motion, 56
pneumonia, 57
typical symptoms, 60–61
viral infection, 57
Burn, 139–140
Business failure, 236–237

C

Calcium sulfide. *See Hepar sulphuris calcareum*
Candidal vulvovaginitis, 337–339
Carbuncle, 164–165
Carolina jasmine. *See Gelsemium sempervirens*
Case analysis, 17–18
Centessimal potency, 10–12
Cerebrovascular accident, 140
Cervical sprain, 153–154
Cervical strain, 153–154
Rhus toxicodendron, 114
Cervicobrachial neuralgia, *Nux vomica*, 91
Chamomilla, 62–66
abdominal pain, 63
asthma, 64
colic, 63
comparisons, 64
diarrhea, 63
dysmenorrhea, 63
epistaxis, 63
fever of unknown origin, 63
irritability, 63
key symptoms, 64
metrorrhagia, 63
otalgia, 62–63
otitis media, 62–63
premenstrual syndrome, 63
teething, 63
toothache, 64
typical symptoms, 65–66
whining, 63
Chest, herpes zoster, 330–331
Childbirth
Belladonna, 50–51
homeopathic medical research, 6
Children's illness

childhood diarrhea, homeopathic medical research, 7
Pulsatilla, 104
Cholecystopathy, 277–281
Chronic illness, homeopathic medical research, 7–9
Ciliary herpes zoster, 331–332
Clammy perspiration
Mercurius solubilis, 84–85
Mercurius vivus, 84–85
Clinginess, *Pulsatilla*, 104
Cluster headache, 316–318
Belladonna, 50
Coffee withdrawal, *Nux vomica*, 90
Cold
Mercurius solubilis, 84–85
Mercurius vivus, 84–85
Phosphorus, 96
Colic, 271–272
Chamomilla, 63
Nux vomica, 91
Common symptoms, 17
Complementary and alternative medicine
cost, xv
growth, xv
Journal of the American Medical Association, 5
liability, 27
physicians' attitudes toward, xvi
Complex homeopathic medicine, 19
Concentration, *Phosphorus*, 96
Concurrent symptoms, 18
Conjunctival inflammation, eye injury, 142
Conjunctivitis, 179–181
Belladonna, 50
Constipation, 257–259
Nux vomica, 91
pregnancy, 340–343
Contact dermatitis, 167–169
Contraindications, 25
Contusion, 140
Correspondence course, homeopathic educational program, 445–446
Cost, complementary and alternative medicine, xv
Cough, 232
Hepar sulphuris calcareum, 75
Phosphorus, 96

*Toxicodendron toxicarium. See Rhus
    toxicodendron*
Trauma
    Arnica montana, 35–37
    esophagitis, 248
Traumatic brain injury, homeopathic
    medical research, 8
Treatment plan, 18–24
Trigeminal herpes zoster, 331–332
Tuberculosis, *Phosphorus,* 97

U

Ultradilute solution, 384–386
Umbilicus infection, 352
Untidyness, *Sulphur,* 120
Upper respiratory infection, 200–212
    Gelsemium sempervirens, 71
    homeopathic medical research, 8
    Mercurius solubilis, 84, 85
    Mercurius vivus, 84, 85
    Nux vomica, 91
    Phosphorus, 97
    Pulsatilla, 105
Urinary lithiasis, 291–293
Urinary stone, 291–293
Urinary tract, 291–296
Urinary tract infection, 293–296
Urticaria, 173–174
Using the instructions form, patient
    handout, 453, 455
Uterine hemorrhage, 147–148

V

Vaginal discharge, *Pulsatilla,* 105
Varicella, *Pulsatilla,* 105

Varicocele, 283
Vertigo, 192–194
    elderly person, 193–194
    homeopathic medical research, 7
    Phosphorus, 97
Vibration, *Phosphorus,* 96
Viral gastroenteritis, 260–264
Viral group, 231–232
Viral illness
    Bryonia alba, 57
    Phosphorus, 97
Vital force, 384
Vithoulkes, George, 377
Vomiting, 255–256
    Phosphorus, 96, 97
Vulvovaginitis, 336–340

W

Wart, 174–176
Weeping, *Pulsatilla,* 104
Wen, 178
What are homeopathic medicines?,
    patient handout, 453, 454
Whining, *Chamomilla,* 63
White arsenic. *See Arsenicum album*
Wind flower. *See Pulsatilla*
Winter cough, 232
Woodbine. *See Gelsemium sempervirens*
Wound infection, 160–162
Wounded honor, 238–239

Y

Yellow jessamine. *See Gelsemium
    sempervirens*